S0-ASJ-424

THE LESSONS
OF THE
VIETNAM WAR

Edited by Jerold M. Starr
West Virginia University

CENTER FOR SOCIAL STUDIES EDUCATION
3857 Willow Avenue
Pittsburgh, Pennsylvania 15234

Copyrighted © 1996, 1994, 1991 by the Center for Social Studies Education

All rights reserved. No part of this book may be used or reproduced in any form or by any means, or stored in a database or retrieval system, without prior written permission of the publisher except in the case of brief quotations embodied in critical articles and reviews. Making copies of any part of this book for any purpose is a violation of the United States copyright law. For information, contact the Center for Social Studies Education, 3857 Willow Avenue, Pittsburgh, Pennsylvania 15234, (412) 341-1967.

ISBN 0-945919-15-8

Third Edition
Printed in the United States of America

INTRODUCTION

The U.S. war in Vietnam was the longest and second most costly in U.S. history. More than two million American boys were sent to fight. More than 58,000 were killed, more than 300,000 wounded, and almost 14,000 completely disabled. According to the U.S. Veteran's Administration, up to 800,000 Vietnam veterans have been diagnosed as having "significant" to "severe" problems of readjustment. The war cost U.S. taxpayers hundreds of billions of dollars and these costs will continue for decades in the form of veterans' benefits and interest on past loans.

In Vietnam today over two million dead are mourned. Four million were wounded and ten million displaced from their homes. More than five million acres of forest and croplands were laid waste by 18 million gallons of poisonous chemical herbicides. The present government has not been able to develop the economy to meet the needs of its people.

Public opinion polls over the years consistently show that two of three Americans judge the Vietnam War to have been a "mistake." Unfortunately, few claim to know what the U.S. should have done differently. Over half do not have "a clear idea" what the war was about; a third can't even remember which side we supported. The problem is even worse for American youth—future citizens and leaders—who have no experience of the war and little or no knowledge of it.

Many knowledgeable adults cannot talk to youth about the war. They served in Vietnam and memories of that experience still are too painful. A veteran from California confided to me that he cannot "read about Vietnam without the nightmares returning." Another from Texas shared, "My daughter asked me to speak to her high school class on the war. I could not do it for fear of losing my composure."

The schools, entrusted with passing on our heritage, have all but ignored Vietnam. Coverage in the standard textbooks ranges from a few paragraphs to a few pages. Perhaps the most common objection to teaching the war is that it is "controversial." We cannot allow educators to censor a subject for being controversial in a nation that has gone to war in the name of freedom. Moreover, such deliberate ignorance of America's longest war constitutes a grave disservice to the men and women who sacrificed there. We owe them and ourselves the whole truth about our national experience.

The Vietnam War was passionately debated precisely because it raised fundamental questions about what we as a nation stand for in the world. To censor such controversy is to tell our students that they will not learn in school what people care most about in life. To be sure, controversy can be fueled by extremist propaganda. In a democracy, however, the best defense is to give our youth the strength of mind and character to defend themselves. This curriculum shows teachers, parents and youth how to ask the important questions in ways that lead to deeper understanding rather than division.

Those of us who have been willing to teach about the Vietnam War have found it to be a most exciting and fulfilling experience. This is one subject for which student motivation is not a problem. Young people already are intensely interested in learning about the war. Movies, TV shows, paperback novels, magazines, and even comic books on the war have been enormously popular.

Many students have deep personal motives for searching out this history. They are the sons and daughters, nephews and nieces of those who served in Vietnam. I introduced a course on the war at West Virginia University in the fall of 1987. Half of the thirty students in the class had a close family member who was a Vietnam veteran. Eight of those fifteen relatives had refused to ever discuss it. One of my students told the school paper, "Both my dad and my uncles were glad that someone was teaching a class in the war because they didn't want to talk about their experience, but they wanted me to know." Two of my students later told me they used this textbook to open up discussion of the war with their fathers for the very first time.

The Vietnam War is important not only because of its prominent place in U.S. history, but because Vietnam is a clear case of the emerging pattern of modern warfare. Within weeks of the historic developments signalling the end of the Cold War, spokespersons for the U.S. Army and U.S. Air Force announced new missions to combat "instability" in Third World "trouble spots" though "low-intensity conflict" (eg, guerrilla warfare, counterinsurgency, pacification, etc.), rapid deployment forces (eg, the invasion of Panama), and surprise bombing raids (eg, Libya). Months later, half a million U.S. troops were preparing for battle in the Persian Gulf.

For several years, each new U.S. military intervention has been held up against the standard of Vietnam. In 1985, Secretary of State George Shultz said that Vietnam was an appropriate "analogy" for Reagan administration policy in Central America: "Our goals in Central America are like those we had in Vietnam: democracy, economic progress and security against aggression. Broken promises. Communist dictatorship. Refugees. Widened Soviet influence, this time near our very borders. Here is your parallel between Vietnam and Central America."

Many in Congress disagreed profoundly with Shultz's claims. That same month Texas high school senior Beth Bowels said to a Dallas *Times Herald* reporter: "I keep hearing people say Central America is just like Vietnam. How am I supposed to know if Nicaragua is like Vietnam if I don't know what Vietnam was like?" Throughout the months that President Bush built up U.S. forces in the Persian Gulf, he kept reassuring a worried public that the war against Iraq would "not be another Vietnam." Since all Americans, from the President down to the common people, agree that our nation cannot afford another Vietnam War, it clearly is time we examined that experience critically to learn what might be of value in making foreign policy decisions today.

In 1984, I established the Center for Social Studies Education in order to promote more and better teaching of the Vietnam War, its lessons and legacies. Over time almost 200 Vietnam

War scholars, teachers, and veterans rallied to the challenge. Participants varied greatly in social background and political orientation. However, we were agreed that ignorance was the enemy and that the best protection against another military disaster was an informed and active citizenry.

We set high standards for ourselves. All statements of fact had to be documented by official U.S. government sources or recognized works of scholarship in the field. We drew extensively on the Pentagon Papers study, commissioned in 1967 by U.S. Secretary of Defense Robert McNamara who was seeking an "encyclopedic and objective" history of U.S. involvement in Vietnam. Written over a year and a half by 36 experts from the Defense Department, State Department, and major institutes, the study totals 47 volumes of some 7,000 pages.

As for opinions, we strove for the broadest possible diversity. In these pages you will hear the voices of major political figures like Dean Rusk and William Fulbright, celebrity activists like Jane Fonda and Bob Hope, and many political and military experts. You also will hear from not-so-famous Vietnam veterans, ordinary Vietnamese and American citizens, whose views usually are left out of official accounts.

In addition to the many historical photographs, editorial cartoons, and instructional graphics, we also feature a variety of primary source materials—diary entries, letters home, GI poetry—whose purpose it is to humanize the war in ways that go beyond conventional narrative accounts. We are interested in what if felt like to be in the war.

While we consider the "grunt level" perspective important, our learning objectives are much broader. We seek in this curriculum to teach students how to think critically about conflict resolution in international relations, reason ethically about difficult moral choices and better understand people from other social backgrounds and cultures. The Vietnam War is a powerful vehicle for teaching those analytic skills youth need to become informed citizens. It is a vast, dramatic and complex event that pivots on numerous critical decisions based on mixed evidence and featuring very different points of view. Students are encouraged to examine conflicting points of view fairly and to reach their own conclusions. All materials have been reviewed and field tested extensively to ensure that they are factually correct, politically balanced, and appropriate for young people.

As you can see on the back cover, we are very proud of all the awards, endorsements, and adoptions this textbook has received. That is why we have taken the trouble to update it for 1994. This new edition includes extensive discussions of the Persian Gulf War, political events in post-war Cambodia, the ending of the U.S. trade embargo with Vietnam, economic reforms in Vietnam, scientific and legal developments on veterans' issues like Agent Orange and PTSD, as well as other matters.

We recognize that we still have a long way to go in our educational mission. Those now teaching the Vietnam War report that their students come in not even being able to find Vietnam on a world map. However, for those of us who would rather light a candle than curse the darkness, this mission is filled with hope.

Jerold M. Starr
West Virginia University

AUTHORS

LADY BORTON is the author of *Sensing the Enemy: an American Woman Among the Boat People of Vietnam* (Dial/Doubleday, 1984). She has produced radio segments from Vietnam for National Public Radio and set up and accompanied the "60 Minutes" staff for Morley Safer's double segment, "The Enemy." Lady recently opened an office for the American Friends Service Committee (AFSC) in Hanoi. She is the only foreigner whom the Vietnamese allow to live with families in the countryside. Those experiences, coupled with stories from her twenty years' work with Vietnam, form her new book, *After Sorrow*, due out in 1992.

MILLARD CLEMENTS is Professor of Curriculum and Instruction at New York University and Co-Director of the program in Environmental Conservation Education. He was educated at the University of California at Berkeley, San Francisco State College and Stanford University. He has written extensively on social studies education and problems of public education in the United States and Japan.

STEVE COHEN is a Program Associate at Facing History and Ourselves in Brookline, Massachusetts. He received his B.A. from Williams College and his Ph.D. in History from Brandeis University. He is the author of *Vietnam Anthology and Guide to a Television History* (1983). This book is used in schools across the country in conjunction with the PBS-TV series on the Vietnam War. He also is author of a similar sourcebook used with the PBS-TV series, *Eyes on the Prize.* He recently completed a curriculum on covert action called *Secrecy and Democracy,* published by Educators for Social Responsibility.

CHARLES DiBENEDETTI (deceased) was Professor of History at the University of Toledo. An authority on the history of the peace movement, his book, *The Peace Reform in American History* (1980), won wide critical acclaim. Dr. DiBenedetti was honored by the Society for Historians of American Foreign Relations with the Stuart Bernath Memorial Lectureship in 1982. His last book, *An American Ordeal: The Antiwar Movement of the Vietnam Era* (Syracuse University Press, 1990) was published posthumously through the efforts of Assisting Author, Charles Chatfield.

WILLIAM J. DUIKER is Professor of Asian History at The Pennsylvania State University. He received his Ph.D. from Georgetown University in 1968. An ex-foreign service officer, Duiker served with the U.S. Department of State in South Vietnam in the mid-1960s. He is the author of a number of books and articles about modern China and Vietnam, including *The Rise of Nationalism in Vietnam, The Communist Road to Power in Vietnam,* and *Cultures in Collision,* a popular history of the Boxer Rebellion. His most recent publications are *Vietnam Since the Fall of Saigon* and *China and Vietnam: The Roots of Conflict.*

JOE P. DUNN is Professor and Chair of the Department of History and Politics, Humanities Division Coordinator, and Director of Summer Programs at Converse College. He received his Ph.D. from the University of Missouri and did postdoctorate work at Duke University. Dunn served in combat in Vietnam in 1960-70, and taught for three years with the University of Maryland's program on military bases in Europe. He has conducted several summer institutes to prepare secondary teachers to teach the Middle East and the Vietnam War. Dunn has written *Teaching the Vietnam War: Resources and Assessments* (1990); edited *The Future South: A Historical Perspective for the Twenty-first Century* (1991); authored 40 articles and book chapters on Vietnam, conscription politics, the teaching of world affairs, and other topics; and published 300 book reviews appearing in more than 30 scholarly journals.

HOWARD A. ELTERMAN is an Adjunct Assistant Professor of Sociology at Baruch College, C.U.N.Y., and a teacher of Home Instruction for the New York City Board of Education. He received his Ph.D. from New York University and has served on the faculty of Tufts University, Drew University and Connecticut College. He has published articles and presented papers on mass communication, popular culture, the Vietnam War and the teaching of sociology.

MARY E. HAAS is Associate Professor of Curriculum and Instruction at West Virginia University and President of the West Virginia Council for the Social Studies. She has an Ed.D. from Indiana University with a specialization in Social Studies Education K-12. Haas has taught in universities in Mississippi and Arkansas and for ten years in the public schools of Indiana. She has published many lessons and units of instruction on a variety of social studies topics, including peace and war, in state and national journals.

GEORGE C. HERRING is Professor of History at the University of Kentucky. He received his Ph.D. from the University of Virginia and served on the faculty of Ohio University between 1965 and 1969. A specialist in the history of U.S. foreign relations, he edited the quarterly journal, *Diplomatic History,* from 1982 to 1986. He is the author of numerous books and articles on United States foreign policy since World War II. Among his major publications are *America's Longest War: The United States and Vietnam, 1950-1975* (rev. ed., 1985) and *The Secret Diplomacy of the Vietnam War: The 'Negotiating Volumes' of the Pentagon Papers* (1983).

KEVIN SIMON is a fellow at the Franklin and Eleanor Roosevelt Institute in Hyde Park, New York. He has been the Chair of the History Department of Sayre School, Lexington, Kentucky. Simon has a B.A. from Michigan State University, an M.A. in History from the University of Kentucky, and a post-graduate degree in History from Cambridge University. He has been recognized as "Outstanding Social Studies Teacher" for 1987-88 by the Kentucky Council for the Social Studies and "Outstanding History Teacher" for 1986-87 by the Kentucky Association of Teachers of History. Simon has served as an NEH Summer Fellow at Harvard University (1982) and Dartmouth College (1982), as well as a Curriculum Advisor for an NEH summer institute on the history of the Cold War, sponsored by the College of William and Mary (Virginia).

JEROLD M. STARR is Professor of Sociology at West Virginia University. He received his Ph.D. from Brandeis University and served on the faculty of the University of Pennsylvania from 1969 to 1976. Starr has been both a Fulbright and National Endowment for the Humanities Fellow. From 1983 to 1985, he represented the U.S., writing reports for the United Nations International Youth Year, 1985. Starr has authored many publications on youth, global education, and

peace and war, including a special issue on "Teaching the Vietnam War" (1988) for *Social Education,* the official journal of the National Council for the Social Studies.

FRED WILCOX is a professional writer and veterans advocate. He teaches full-time in the Writing Program at Ithaca College, and holds an M.F.A. degree with honors from Iowa's Writers Workshop, and a Doctor of Arts Degree from State University of New York at Albany. He is the author of *Waiting for an Army to Die: The Tragedy of Agent Orange* (Random House, 1983), which was chosen by the American Library Association as among its most notable books in two categories: Adult Nonfiction and Young Adult Nonfiction. Other works include *GRASS ROOTS: An Anti-Nuclear Source Book* (Crossing Press, 1981), and *Uncommon Martyrs: The Plowshare Movement and the Catholic Left* (Addison-Wesley, 1991).

CHRISTOPHER W. WILKINS is an instructor and counselor at Roxbury High School in Succasunna, New Jersey. He completed his undergraduate studies at the University of Maryland, has three Masters Degrees from Montclair State College and has recently begun doctoral studies at Rutgers University. Wilkins is a Vietnam veteran having served a tour of duty in Saigon as a military policeman during 1967/68. He has written many articles as well as developed a course of study on the history, background and issues of the Vietnam War.

Poetry Advisor - **W.D. EHRHART** enlisted in the U.S. Marines at age 17 in 1966, earning the Purple Heart Medal, two Presidential Unit Citations, the Vietnamese Cross of Gallantry, promotion to sergeant and an honorable discharge. He holds a B.A. from Swarthmore College and an M.A. from the University of Illinois at Chicago. Ehrhart is author of numerous collections of poetry including *To Those Who Have Gone Home Tired, The Outer Banks,* and *Just for Laughs,* as well as four nonfiction books, *Vietnam-Perkasie, Passing Time, Going Back,* and *In the Shadow of Vietnam.* He is editor of *Carrying the Darkness* and *Unaccustomed Mercy,* and co-editor of *Demilitarized Zones,* anthologies of Vietnam-related poetry.

CONTENTS

INTRODUCTION TO VIETNAM:
LAND, HISTORY AND CULTURE

*"Man is a shadow,
gone as soon as born
The trees,
so green in spring,
are bare in autumn
Greatness and decline,
why should we care?
The destiny
of men and empires
is like a dew-drop
on a grass leaf"*

Van Hanh 11th century

The Land

"Why are we in Vietnam?" had to be the most popular question of the era now called "the 60s." Few Americans even knew where Vietnam was, let alone why their sons were being sent there to fight. It wasn't apparent how that small country on the other side of the world could be so important to a great nation like the United States. Yet for thirty years, several American presidents had insisted that, if Vietnam were "lost to communism," the effects would be felt as far away as Japan and the Suez Canal; the entire American security position in the Pacific would be severely threatened.

What then is Vietnam, and why might it be important to the United States? It is, first of all, an oddly-shaped country (see map, page 3), stretching like a letter "S" along the coast of mainland Southeast Asia from the Chinese border to the Gulf of Thailand. Vietnam measures over 1,000 miles from north to south and often less than 100 miles from east to west. Its western border is a string of mountains known to the Vietnamese as the Truong Son (Central Mountains). Beyond the Truong Son lie Vietnam's immediate neighbors, Laos and Cambodia. Its eastern border is the South China Sea. The entire country lies roughly within the tropical zone. It is a region of dense jungles, swamps, and lush rice paddies. The temperature rarely falls below fifty degrees and usually averages in the eighties and low nineties.

The Vietnamese often compare the shape of their country to two baskets of rice suspended on a bamboo pole. The baskets represent the two major rice growing river deltas that support the majority of the population of the country—the Red River Valley in the north and the Mekong River Delta in the south. The bamboo pole is the narrow waistline of central Vietnam that connects the two river deltas. The delta areas of the Red River and the Mekong form the heartlands of modern Vietnam. About two-thirds of the country's sixty million people live here. These areas produce the bulk of the rice, the staple food in the typical Vietnamese diet.

Most of the people of Vietnam are ethnic Vietnamese. They are descended from people who inhabited the region of the Red River Delta in North Vietnam several centuries prior to the Christian era. In their physical characteristics, the Vietnamese are roughly similar to many neighboring peoples in Southeast Asia and China. However, Vietnam has been recognized as a distinct culture for over two thousand years. In fact, its language is a separate member of the world family of languages.

History and Culture

Throughout its history, perhaps the central fact of Vietnamese existence is the presence of its great neighbor China beyond the northern frontier. The importance of that presence was established early in Vietnamese history. During the first millennium B.C., Vietnam emerged as a small principality based on rice culture and local commerce in the lower Red River Delta. In the second century B.C., Vietnam was conquered and integrated into the expanding Chinese empire.

For one thousand years, Vietnam was part of China. Chinese officials administered the territory and attempted to assimilate the Vietnamese population into Chinese civilization, then one of the most advanced in the entire world. Chinese political and social institutions were introduced. Vietnamese education was based on the Confucian concept of the civil service examination system. Chinese styles also became dominant in literature and the arts. Educated Vietnamese conversed and wrote in Chinese, and the Chinese system of ideographic characters was adopted as the written form of the Vietnamese language. At the same time, much of the poetry, architecture and painting retained themes distinctive to Southeast Asia.

To the Chinese, the absorption of the Red River Delta represented the expansion of a superior civilization over people of primitive culture, a concept of "manifest destiny" not unlike the westward expansion of the United States in the nineteenth century. And there is no doubt that one thousand years of Chinese rule left

> *"Heaven entrusted us with a great responsibility.*
> *We had to surmount all obstacles."*
> Nguyen Trai 15th century

a lasting imprint on Vietnamese culture. But Chinese occupation did not extinguish the Vietnamese view of themselves as a separate and distinct people. On several occasions, popular uprisings broke out in an effort to evict the foreign intruder. Finally, in the mid-tenth century A.D., Vietnamese rebels took advantage of chaotic conditions in China, drove out the Chinese and restored Vietnamese independence.

The new state, which called itself Dai Viet (Greater Viet), soon became a major force in Southeast Asia. Although politically independent, Vietnam's new rulers found Chinese institutions and values useful in building a disciplined and powerful state. For several hundred years, Vietnamese political and social institutions continued to be based on Chinese models. Confucian philosophy and ethics emphasized the importance of the family and the community over the private interests of the individual. This concept reinforced the position of the monarch (who now called himself Emperor on the Chinese pattern) and the centralized power of the state.

But the power of the emperor was not absolute. While in many Southeast Asian societies the ruler was a god-king with unlimited powers, the Confucian system stressed that the behavior of the ruler was bound by a set of broad political principles (called in Chinese the Tao, or Way) that required compassion and concern for the needs of his people. Should he fail to live up to those

standards and oppress the people, then he would lose the "Mandate of Heaven" and could be deposed.

The Confucian system also was unique in its concern for the selection of talented and virtuous individuals to serve in the bureaucracy. Officials were not chosen exclusively from the landed aristocracy, as in much of the rest of the world, but through a series of civil service examinations that tested the candidate's knowledge of Confucian political, social and moral principles. The system was by no means totally egalitarian or democratic in the modern sense. Girls, for example, were not permitted to sit for the examinations because it was assumed that their place was in the home. But it did lay the foundation for an educated bureaucracy to administer the state and, thus restrict the power of the emperor and his court. And, most importantly, the system provided an opportunity for bright children from peasant households to escape the drudgery of rural life and rise to an influential position in Vietnamese society.

Spurred by its internal success, the Vietnamese state now began to expand southward. To a considerable degree, this southward expansion (known in Vietnamese history as "the March to the South") was a response to the growing need to locate additional cultivatable land for peasants living in the crowded Red River Delta.

The most available land was along the coast to the south, a region at that time controlled by an Indianized trading state known as Champa. Over the next several hundred years, rivalry with Champa led to an almost constant state of war between the two countries. The Vietnamese gradually pushed southward into areas controlled by Champa. Land-hungry peasants established settlements under the rule of the Vietnamese empire. By the eighteenth century, the state of Champa had entirely disappeared.

A similar process led to the Vietnamese seizure of the rich Mekong Delta from the declining state of Angkor in the sixteenth and seventeenth centuries. Founded in the seventh century, Angkor, later to become Cambodia, was for several hundred years the largest and most powerful state in mainland Southeast Asia. By the fifteenth century, however, Angkor was in decline. Taking advantage of the situation, both Vietnam and Thailand, Angkor's neighbor to the west, confiscated territories from the disintegrating state. By 1700, all of the Mekong River Delta was in Vietnamese hands. Two hundred years later, the remnants of the once-mighty Angkor empire had been transformed into a joint protectorate of Vietnam and Thailand.

FARMER'S SONG AT CAN THO

What is a man but a farmer,
bowels and a heart that sings,
who plants his rice in season
bowing then to the river,
I am a farmer and I know what I know.
This month's harvest is tall green rice.
Next month's harvest is hordes of hungry beetles.
How can peace come to a green country?

**FERRYMAN'S SONG
AT BINH MINH**

Vendors of green oranges
vendors of immaculate ducks
Children, lame musicians
begging with milky eyes
Ancients with their boys
they are moving altogether
Riding the back of the dragon
crossing the *Rach Can Tho*

—Herbert Krohn

The Peoples of Vietnam

Throughout this period, the life of the average Vietnamese peasant changed very little. Like most lowland peoples in Southeast Asia, the majority of the Vietnamese were rice farmers. Until the last years of the Vietnam War, more than eighty percent of the Vietnamese people lived on the land. The vast majority lived in thousands of villages and hamlets (surrounded by the lush green paddy fields that provided their livelihood) scattered throughout Vietnam.

For Vietnamese peasants, the village traditionally formed the horizon of their lives. It was there that they were born, lived and died, often in the home and on the land occupied by their forefathers. The village was their universe. All decisions relating to their lives were made, if not within the family, then by the council of elders composed of the more respected or wealthy landowners in the village.

The central government, represented by a magistrate and his staff in the district capital, seemed far away, an attitude exemplified by the famous saying, "The authority of the emperor stops at the village gate." For most villagers, the government meant two things: taxes and conscription for military service or community labor to work on the dikes or the irrigation system. All villages were expected to provide taxes and recruits to the state, but decisions on individual tax rates were normally made by the local council of elders on the basis of landholding and sent to the district magistrate for transmittal to the central government.

In such conditions, most Vietnamese did not develop a strong sense of participation in the political process. As was true in most traditional societies, major political decisions dealing with broad policy issues and national defense were made by the Emperor, assisted by his court and the imperial bureaucracy. In general, the Vietnamese respected strong government that would provide security, efficiency, and a measure of social justice for the population at large. They relied on the village council for their local needs, such as the resolution of civil disputes, the distribution of taxes and conscript labor, and the allocation of communal land.

Nor did the Vietnamese develop a strong sense of individualism and freedom of choice in the western sense. Because rice farming demanded a concentrated effort by all members of the family, individuals were expected to subordinate their needs to those of the group. Like China, Vietnam practiced the concept of the joint family system, with as many as three generations living under one roof. The family was patriarchal in nature, with the senior male playing—at least in theory—the dominant decision-making role in the family unit. According to Confucian ideology, women were expected to obey their husbands (although in practice they often played an influential role in family decisions). Children were admonished to obey their parents. Marriages usually were arranged, and sons were expected to remain on the ancestral land after

> "We have known both days of greatness and times of decline, but never have we lacked for heroes."
> Nguyen Trai 15th century

marriage to maintain the family plot and provide for the needs of their elders.

The demands of rice farming shaped the life of the average Vietnamese. Few had enough rice land to do more than eke out a bare existence for themselves and their families. Many had too little land or none at all. They were either forced to lease land from the wealthy, sometimes at exorbitant rents, or to sell themselves as hired labor. Most villages also reserved some common land to be distributed to the needy on a temporary basis. All too often, however, this land also was confiscated by the powerful for their own uses.

Even for those farmers with adequate land, life was hard. Although rice is one of the most prolific grain crops known to man, its cultivation demands a considerable amount of human labor for planting, weeding, maintaining the irrigation system, and bringing in the harvest. Farmers raised large families in the hopes of having male children to guarantee survival. This led to a growing population in the rich rice-growing areas. So long as the farmer was blessed with a bountiful harvest, large families were justified. All too often, however, natural disasters like floods, typhoons, or droughts damaged the crops and led to hunger and starvation. Even in good times, the farmer had to deal with high taxes, rents, and often heavy indebtedness. Once in debt, high rates of interest presented a heavy burden and often cost the farmer his land. For most Vietnamese, it was a hard life.

The ethnic Vietnamese make up approximately ninety percent of the total population of the country. The remaining ten percent are composed of a variety of peoples. These include: (1) various ethnic and cultural groups living in the mountainous areas of Vietnam (about three million); (2) the Cham (50,000) and the Khmer (400,000), who are descended from peoples

> "It is better to be a ghost in Vietnam than an emperor in China ."
> Tran Bing Trong 17th century

assimilated by the Vietnamese during their historic expansion to the south; and (3) three million descendants of Chinese settlers who migrated into Vietnam from south China during the past 300 years.

With so much of its population ethnic Vietnamese, Vietnam is one of the most homogeneous societies in Southeast Asia, a region noted for its ethnic and cultural diversity. This homogeneity has helped to promote Vietnam's exceptionally strong sense of national identity. As we shall see, the Vietnamese are a tough and resourceful people, fiercely dedicated to their independence and the pursuit of their national interests.

Yet there is another side to the Vietnamese character, one that helps to explain why the Vietnam War was much more than just an ideological struggle between communist and capitalist forces, but also a civil war among the Vietnamese people themselves. For although the ethnic Vietnamese are by far the dominant group in the country, they themselves have long been divided in important ways.

The major divisions among the Vietnamese are geographical and religious. The former is partly a product of Vietnamese expansion to the south. After the tenth century A.D., the Vietnamese began to expand southward from their crowded historical heartland into the vast and open reaches of the Mekong River Delta. In these new conditions, a "frontier village" atmosphere of freedom and individual choice developed. This way of life, comparable in some respects to the nineteenth century American West, was an extreme departure from traditional Vietnamese culture. During the colonial period in the late nineteenth and early twentieth centuries, the people of the south came under the influence of

French institutions and culture, further accentuating the regional differences. They were thus more receptive to the introduction of a system based on western capitalist practices and political democracy. These distinctive differences between North and South, as we shall see, contributed significantly to the course of the Vietnam War.

The second major division among the ethnic Vietnamese is religious. The majority of the population is at least nominally Buddhist, with an admixture of Confucian, Taoist, and animist beliefs. However, there are about three million Catholics, whose ancestors were converted by French missionaries between the seventeenth and the early twentieth centuries. The Catholics have been more educated in western ideas and thus more inclined than their Buddhist compatriots to favor a political system patterned after those of western Europe and the United States. They were among the

> "The truth is that over the last decade I have been victorious in both south and north. My success, I must admit was due to the unreserved support of my people ."
> Nguyen Hue 18th century

primary supporters of the Saigon regime in South Vietnam during the Vietnam War.

Finally, there are two major religious sects in Vietnam—the Cao Dai and the Hoa Hao—each composed of more than one million adherents. Both sects emerged in the Mekong Delta in response to the imposition of colonialism and the disintegration of the traditional Vietnamese state. The Hoa Hao religion is a form of reformed Buddhism, an attempt to put true Buddhist teaching into practice in "corrupt" everyday society. Cao Dai (meaning High Tower) is a religion that combines the tenets of several western and Asian creeds. Although both are considered religions, they also are highly political in orientation. Leaders of both religions have tried to create politically independent areas in the Mekong Delta, resisting the centralizing efforts of the Saigon regime and, more recently, the communist regime in Hanoi.

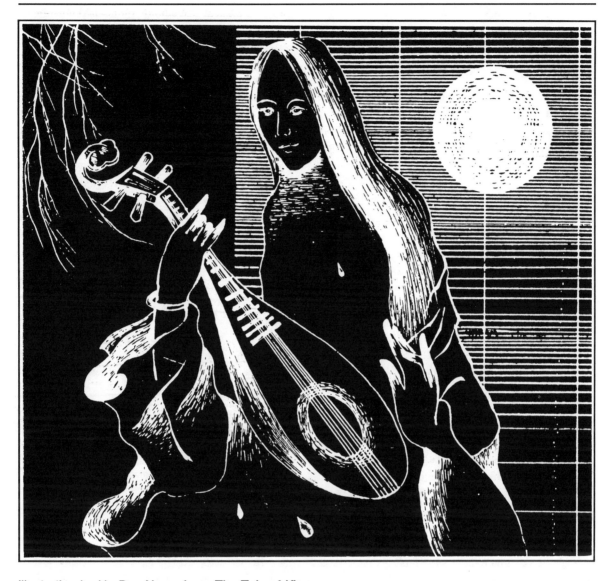

Illustration by Ho Dac Ngoc, from *The Tale of Kieu*

The Coming of the West

The expansion of the Vietnamese nation to the south after the tenth century had made Vietnam one of the most powerful states in the region. But it also brought problems. The "March to the South" had led to the creation of an unwieldy kingdom difficult to defend against its external enemies. The new lands in the Mekong Delta were inhabited by settlers with a frontier spirit unwilling to accept dictation from the imperial court at Hanoi in the north. By the seventeenth century, factionalism at court led to a civil war and the division of Vietnam into two competing regions. Each was controlled by a princely family (the Trinh in the north

---

"Blood is boiling in your heart
Countrymen! Draw forth your swords!
There is a heaven, earth and us.
That is what we call true unity!"
Phan Boi Chau 19th century

---

and the Nguyen in the south) who competed for dominance over the almost dead Le dynasty.

Unfortunately for the Vietnamese, the split in the state took place at a time of growing pressure on the entire region from a new source. In the early sixteenth century, European explorers, merchant adventurers and missionaries came in increasing numbers after the discovery of the route to the East. By 1600, Portugal, Spain, Holland, Great Britain, and France had begun to compete for territory, trade, and Christian converts in the area. At first, the Vietnamese permitted Europeans to trade and propagate Christianity but soon came to suspect their political motivation. By 1700, little was left of the European presence but a handful of missionaries, mainly French, who secretly served the several hundred thousand Vietnamese who had converted to Catholicism.

At the end of the eighteenth century, the civil war which had divided Vietnam for nearly two hundred years came to an end. In 1802, Nguyen Anh, a prince of the Nguyen house in South Vietnam, united the entire country under his rule. He was assisted in his rise to

power by French adventurers, who hoped that the new ruler would grant France commercial and religious privileges in the newly united empire, now called Vietnam (Southern Viet). But the new emperor and his successor were still suspicious of the French and tried to exterminate what remained of missionary influence. They persecuted Vietnamese Christians and executed French priests caught propagating their religion on Vietnamese territory.

But the effort to isolate Vietnam from western influence was unsuccessful. Spurred by the need for industrial raw materials and markets for their manufactured goods, nations like France, Great Britain, Germany and the United States sought to open Asian countries to western commerce. The British, from their base in India, seized Burma and the Malayan peninsula. The Dutch consolidated their hold over the oil-rich East Indies. Fearful of being left out of the scramble for territory in Asia, France decided to establish a "balcony on the Pacific" in Vietnam. In 1858, a French fleet landed at Da Nang harbor, near the new imperial capital at Hue, and attempted to force the Vietnamese court to accept a French protectorate. French troops were weakened by disease and local resistance; however, and the effort was soon abandoned. France now turned its attention further south and seized several provinces along the Mekong. In 1862, Vietnamese emperor Tu Duc signed a peace treaty ceding the southern provinces to the French. A year later the French added to their new possession, which they called Cochinchina, by establishing a protectorate over Cambodia.

Twenty years later, the French resumed their expansion in the area. On the pretext of protecting the

---

"When the enemy comes
Even the women must fight"
from the *Phu* 19th century

---

interests of French merchant adventurers operating in Hanoi, the French invaded the Red River Valley and in 1884 forced the Vietnamese emperor to accept a French protectorate over the remainder of the country. Within ten years, they added the tiny kingdom of Laos. To facilitate control, the entire region was organized into a single administrative unit called the Indochinese Union, directed by a French Governor-General appointed from Paris.

P. Dieulefils, Hanoi

French Colonial Rule

The French justified their conquest of Indochina on the grounds that they had a "mission civilisatrice" (civilizing mission) in the region, a French equivalent of the famous "White Man's Burden" which the British poet Rudyard Kipling had used to describe the obligation of the English speaking nations to bring civilization to the "backward" societies of Asia. Like all western countries, the French had come to the east primarily for political domination and economic profit. In nineteenth century Europe, national prestige and power were measured in terms of colonies held all over the globe. The United States joined the competition by seizing Cuba and the Philippines from Spain at the end of the century.

Admittedly, the French did provide a number of economic benefits to the Indochinese people under their charge. They drained the marshes of the Mekong Delta so the area could be cultivated and they built roads and railways. They also modernized Vietnamese political and social institutions and introduced the country to the expanding international economy. But France's primary interest was commercial profit. The export of rubber, rice, and other cash crops put money in the pockets of French merchants. Indochina also provided

an export market for French goods like wine, textiles and manufactured goods. Michelin made its tires from raw rubber originally exported from the plantations located along the Vietnamese-Cambodian border.

What were the political effects of French colonial rule on the peoples of Indochina? As with most colonial enterprises, the results were mixed. The French asserted that their goal in Indochina was to provide the native people with "a perceptible extension of their political rights" in order to give them "the instrument of liberation which will gradually lead you toward those superior spheres to which you aspire." The French administration did introduce the concept of the secret ballot and, over time, some of the institutions of representative government common to western societies.

But there was an inherent contradiction between carrying out such a civilizing mission while enjoying economic profit from their colonial possession. Certainly, the extension of political rights to the peoples of Indochina could only lead to a desire for national independence and the end of French colonial rule. Caught in this dilemma, French administrators said one thing and did another. They talked about native representation, but gave them few rights. Elected assemblies at the local level had only advisory powers and were based on a very restricted franchise that limited voting rights to French residents and a handful of wealthy natives.

Popular pressure led to a gradual expansion of representative institutions through the establishment of advisory assemblies at the provincial level. Yet even these new bodies were mainly "talking shops" which could voice complaints but not make policy. Openly opposing French rule or advocating independence was strictly prohibited and, when discovered, harshly punished.

The effects of French economic policy were equally harmful. The stated premise of French colonial rule was that western commercial and manufacturing practices would produce rapid economic growth. Eventually this was supposed to make Vietnam into a technologically advanced industrial society on the western model. In actuality, the primary objective of colonial policy was to provide cheap raw materials for French industry and a market for French manufactured goods. As a consequence, colonial policy actively discouraged the development of a manufacturing sector which would com-

> "A nation without the power to rule
> is like a child without a home ."
> Phan Boi Chau 19th century

pete with French imports. As one example, the Vietnamese were forbidden to produce local rice wine—often used for ritual purposes—which might compete with the import of French wines, made from grapes. Tariff policies favored the importation of cheap machine-made goods from France, a practice that starved out the traditional handicraft industry in Vietnamese villages.

It is true that the export of raw materials provided profits for some residents of Indochina. Yet even here, the benefits to the local population were limited. Rubber plantations were owned primarily by Europeans. Vietnamese laborers recruited to work on the plantations received starvation wages and frequently died from poor sanitation conditions. Another example was the case of rice exports. Spokesmen for the colonial regime pointed proudly to the increase in rice production that had followed the draining of the marshes in the Mekong Delta. During the 1930s, Indochina became one of the world's primary rice exporting regions. But most of the profit went to European or overseas Chinese exporters rather than to Vietnamese farmers.

In the Mekong Delta, the new lands were made available to the highest bidder, resulting in the concentration of land ownership in the hands of a small number of wealthy landlords. The poor were brought in as tenant farmers, but had to pay excessive rents to lease the land. Small private farmers were squeezed by high prices charged by Chinese rice millers and even higher interest rates to borrow money for the next year's harvest. The overall result was that while rice exports increased, per capita consumption stagnated and in some years even declined.

The Rise of Nationalism

How did the Vietnamese people react to French occupation? As we have seen, the imperial court had initially resisted French attacks at Da Nang and near the southern city of Saigon. But the ease of the French military conquest of the south made a strong impression on Emperor Tu Duc. Over the next two decades, the court at Hue attempted to conciliate the French in order to avoid further military conflict. After the French conquest of the north in 1884, some civilian and military officials attempted to rally support for guerrilla operations against French occupation forces. But without official support from the now powerless emperor in Hue, such operations had little success. By 1896, the first phase of anticolonial resistance had come to an end.

> "We are not fighting
> for freedom and independence.
> We are fighting because
> we are free and independent ."
> Student 20th century

With the opening of the new century, a new generation of Vietnamese began to take up the cause of Vietnamese independence. Unlike their predecessors, this new generation had no desire to return to the past. They were acquainted with the many benefits of western civilization through schooling or travel abroad. They aspired to restore Vietnamese independence while also creating a modern state built on the western or the Japanese model. At first, the leading members of

Cartoon drawn by Ho Chi Minh for the newspaper *Le Pariah* which he edited in Paris in the 1920s under the name of Nguyen Ai-Quoc.

Faster, Incognito! For God's sake, show a little loyalty!!!

this new nationalist movement were progressive members of the traditional Confucian scholar-official class. Soon, however, a sense of patriotism began to affect youth in the growing cities of Hanoi, Saigon, and Haiphong. While admiring the glitter of western science and democracy, many were intensely conscious of the humiliation of foreign rule. During the 1920s, this educated class of students, journalists, teachers, government workers, and small merchants began to form political organizations either to compel the French to grant political and social reforms or to drive the invaders from Vietnamese soil.

Parallel to this rising nationalism came a new awareness of the need to build a modern Vietnamese culture to replace the outmoded Sino-Vietnamese culture of the precolonial period. Spurred by French educational reforms, the traditional Confucian system was abandoned and replaced by one based on the western pattern. The old written language, based on the beautiful but cumbersome Chinese characters, gradually gave way to a new system based on the romanization of the spoken language (called quoc ngu, or national language). As a consequence of these

reforms, a new literature, art, and drama began to emerge. Western concepts such as the notion of individual freedom, political and economic equality, and women's rights began to win over increasing numbers of educated young Vietnamese.

By the mid-1920s, this new political activism began to shake the stability of French rule. Popular demonstrations, often led by disaffected students in large cities, provoked severe repression by the colonial regime. Secret political parties like the VNQDD (Vietnamese Nationalist Party) attempted to organize resistance to colonial rule. Unfortunately, many of these organizations were divided over tactics and unable to overcome regional differences between north and south. More important, most such organizations were composed primarily of urban middle class intellectuals who had little understanding of the problems and aspirations of factory workers, plantation laborers or peasants who made up the vast majority of the population. As a result, the program of such parties tended to concentrate on political issues such as freedom of speech and assembly and greater representation for natives in legislative councils. More basic concerns were ignored, including land reform, improving work conditions, and reducing the high rents and taxes that caused severe hardships for many Vietnamese farmers.

It was in this context that the young revolutionary Ho Chi Minh returned from Europe to south China. Ho Chi Minh had been born in Central Vietnam in 1890, the son of a Vietnamese official who had resigned from the imperial bureaucracy to protest the French conquest. Ho Chi Minh's father was a close friend of several of the early patriots who opposed French rule. From his childhood, the young Ho had absorbed tales of Vietnamese heroism against the nation's historical and modern enemies.

In 1911, after several years of schooling in the imperial capital at Hue, Ho accepted employment as a cook's helper on a French ocean liner. In his several years at sea, he visited ports all over the world. Thereafter, he worked briefly in the kitchen of a luxury hotel in London and then, at the end of World War I, he went to Paris. At that time the leaders of the victorious allied powers, including Great Britain, France and the United States were meeting at the Palace of Versailles to dictate

Ho Chi Minh

peace terms to the defeated Germans. Taking the pseudonym Nguyen Ai Quoc (Nguyen the Patriot), Ho Chi Minh submitted a petition to the allied leaders asking that the concept of self-determination, one of the key planks in President Woodrow Wilson's famous Fourteen Points, be applied to Indochina in order to free Vietnam from French rule. The petition was ignored, but it brought much attention to Ho Chi Minh in Vietnamese exile circles in France.

For the next few years, Ho Chi Minh became increasingly active in radical circles in Paris and, in 1920, was a founding member of the French Communist Party. As one of the most effective publicists and organizers in the Party, Ho soon came to the attention of leading members of the Communist International, an organization of communist parties directed by the Soviet Union. They invited Ho to Moscow to train as an agent. In 1924, after a year working and studying Marxist doctrine, he was sent to south China as a member of a mission to the government of Sun Yat-Sen. Although his assigned duty was to serve as an interpreter with the mission, Ho's real task was to help organize the first revolutionary movement in Indochina.

Ho immediately set to work attracting support from patriotic young Vietnamese living in exile in south China. First he formed a small organization called the Revolutionary Youth League, assigning recruits to training in communist doctrine and tactics in Canton, and then sending them back to Vietnam to find more recruits to organize a revolutionary movement. On the surface, the League sought to cooperate with other nationalist organizations. In actuality, Ho viewed the other parties as rivals and attempted to lure their members into his own organization.

By the end of 1929, the League had over 1,000 members and had become one of the most effective anticolonial parties in Indochina. One reason for its rapid success was Ho Chi Minh himself. Hard-working, self-sacrificing, gifted with an attractive personality, he earned the allegiance and devotion of many young patriotic Vietnamese who rushed to join his cause. Ho Chi Minh also appealed to the needs and aspirations of poor peasants and workers. In the late 1920s, the Vietnamese economy was severely hurt by the onset of the Great Depression. Unemployment rose and the price of rice fell drastically, causing a significant decline in the standard of living.

In February 1930, just as a major revolt broke out

These men in stocks were part of a 1908 plot to poison French officers of the Hanoi garrison and take control of the city.

among desperate peasants and workers in several provinces in central Vietnam, Ho transformed the League into a formal Indochinese Communist Party. Party activists supported the revolt, but the French reacted quickly and put down the uprising. Most of the leaders of the Communist Party were arrested, and many were executed. Ho Chi Minh himself was arrested and briefly imprisoned by the British in the colony of Hong Kong.

For the next few years, the Communist Party struggled to survive. Harassed by French agents, it established its headquarters in south China with new leaders trained in Moscow. Party members turned Vietnamese prisons into "schools of Bolshevism" as they taught other prisoners about Marxism and attempted to enlist them in the revolution.

The party began to revive in the late 1930s when the Soviet government, fearful of the rising threat of Imperial Japan and Nazi Germany, encouraged communist parties around the world to cooperate with all parties and governments that opposed world fascism. When the French Communist Party supported the government in Paris, the latter became more tolerant of communist and nationalist activities in Indochina and its other colonies. The Indochinese Communist Party took advantage of the situation by setting up various types of self-help organizations in villages, schools, and factories. This period of toleration came to an end in August 1939, when the Soviet Union signed a non-aggression pact with Nazi Germany. The French outlawed the Communist Party, and its leaders fled to the hills for survival.

The decisive event for the future of communism in Vietnam was the coming of the Second World War. In 1940, Japan demanded the right to station troops in French Indochina and use the area's natural resources. After a brief refusal, France agreed in return for Japanese recognition of continued French sovereignty over the area. But with Japanese occupation and the collapse of French resistance to Hitler in Europe, colonial authority in Indochina was severely weakened.

Under the cover of these events, the Communist Party began to organize a revolution to seize power at the end of the war. In 1940, Ho Chi Minh returned to south China after spending several years in the Soviet Union. In May 1941, a meeting of the top leadership of the Party launched a new movement to struggle for national independence. At the head of this movement was a new political organization called the Vietminh Front, or League of Independence of Vietnam. The Vietminh Front was set up by the Indochinese Communist Party, but its program emphasized issues such as national independence and moderate political and economic reform in order to broaden its appeal to all Vietnamese individuals and groups opposed to French colonial rule in Vietnam. As a result, it earned the support and participation of many Vietnamese who were motivated by patriotic aspirations rather than a desire to create a communist society.

During the next four years the Communist Party and its parallel organization, the Vietminh Front, attempted to organize a political network throughout the country while preparing guerrilla forces in the mountains of North Vietnam for an uprising planned for the end of the war. In March 1945, facing imminent defeat at the hands of the allied powers, Japan seized power in Indochina from the French, leaving the countryside almost wholly without colonial administration. This aided the Vietminh cause immensely. Vietnam also was struck by a disastrous famine that caused the death of over a million people. The Japanese forbade relief work and the French did nothing. However, the Vietminh confiscated rice stocks and helped the starving, further promoting their cause. The Vietminh had by now become widely recognized as the primary political force fighting for national independence and social justice in Vietnam.

The August Revolution

On August 14, soon after the dropping of two atomic bombs by the United States and a declaration of war by the Soviet Union, Japan surrendered. Ho Chi Minh took advantage of the sudden political vacuum and called for a general uprising to seize power from Japanese troops throughout Indochina. Guerrilla forces seized villages. They set up a revolutionary administration in the rural areas. Special units of workers and students took control of key installations from the Japanese authorities in the cities. In early September, in Hanoi, Ho Chi Minh proclaimed the formation of a new provisional Democratic Republic of Vietnam (DRV) with himself as president. The communists were the dominant force in the new government, but it was supported by many Vietnamese patriots and included members of several non-communist parties.

But the French were not ready to accept the loss of their most valuable possession in Asia. According to arrangements made by the victorious allies, occupation forces from Great Britain and the Republic of China were instructed to occupy the southern and northern

> *"Guns and bombs are not our way of life.*
> *We have never been friends of war.*
> *But here they are, fully armed.*
> *Shall we resign ourselves to slavery?"*
> Thanh Hai 20th century

halves of Indochina in order to accept the surrender of Japanese troops and maintain law and order until civil government could be restored. In the north, Ho Chi Minh's government was able to maintain a precarious authority by conciliating Chinese occupation forces and sharing power with non-communist parties. But in the south, the British commander agreed to assist the French in restoring colonial authority. Within two months, French troops had driven the Vietminh and other nationalist elements out of Saigon and restored control over the southern provinces of Vietnam.

By late fall of 1945, Vietnam was divided into two hostile regimes—the Vietminh in the north and the French in the south. In an effort to avoid conflict, the two sides opened negotiations. In early March 1946, Ho Chi Minh and the French representative in Vietnam, Jean Sainteny, reached a preliminary agreement according to which France recognized the DRV as a "free state" with its own parliament, army, and finances. In return, the economic, military, and cultural presence of the French was to be restored in the north. Because the two sides could not agree on the fate of the ex-French colony of Cochinchina, the decision was left to a popular referendum.

This agreement laid the basis for a possible comprise: autonomy for Vietnam and a continued French presence in the area. But the course of events was to lead in the opposite direction—a collapse of the agreement and, eventually, to war. In Paris, the new government that took over in the spring was not inclined to compromise with the Vietnamese. When formal negotiations got underway in June, the French refused to agree to a referendum in Cochinchina; and the peace talks broke

14

down. At the last minute, Ho Chi Minh negotiated a compromise calling for the resumption of negotiations early the following year.

Back in Vietnam, relations between the French and the DRV became increasingly tense, leading to bloody clashes between military forces on each side. Within the Vietnamese government in Hanoi, the delicate balance between communists and non-communists was upset; and in October Ho Chi Minh reconstituted the cabinet. The DRV was now totally under the domination of the Indochinese Communist Party. In November, a disagreement over the control of customs revenues led the French to bombard the port city of Haiphong, killing thousands of Vietnamese civilians. Convinced that war was inevitable, Ho Chi Minh instructed his Minister of Defense, Vo Nguyen Giap, to

prepare for armed conflict. On December 23, Vietminh forces launched a surprise attack on French installations in Hanoi while their main force units withdrew to prepared positions in the mountains north of the city. The first Indochina War had begun.

"At the center of Vietnamese history stood the peasant, grim and heroic defender of the land bequeathed by his ancestors against foreign aggressors, but also periodically rising up against the home rulers, in an endless revolt."
Nguyen Khac Vien
20th century

15

The First Indochina War (1945-1954)

Negotiations having failed, both sides now attempted to achieve their goals by force. The French, confident of their military superiority, hoped to suppress the rebellion quickly and restore French control over all of Indochina. The Vietminh armed forces were smaller in number and weaker in firepower. However, Ho Chi Minh sought to mobilize the mass of the population to wage a protracted guerrilla struggle, leading eventually to a major offensive to drive the French out of Vietnam.

The first two years of the war were inconclusive. The Vietminh built a base area in the mountainous region north of the Red River Valley, frustrating French efforts to win a quick victory. Gradually they began to build up their guerrilla forces. Poor peasants were attracted by the promise of land and urban middle class youth by the Vietminh program of national independence from foreign rule.

By 1948, growing Vietminh effectiveness clearly showed the French that more was needed than mere military pressure. The French lacked sufficient troops to suppress the revolt. They also lacked a symbol to unite the Vietnamese population against the "menace" of communism. For that symbol, Paris turned to the former emperor of Vietnam, Bao Dai. The last of the Nguyen emperors, Bao Dai, had come to the throne in 1925 while still an adolescent. In the 1930s, he was ruler in name but was given little power by the French.

After the August Revolution of 1945, Bao Dai was pressured by the Vietminh to abdicate the throne to assume another figurehead position as supreme political adviser in Ho's new republican government. Bao Dai soon sensed that he was being manipulated by the communists; however, and in the late summer of 1946, he settled in the British colony of Hong Kong.

The French then began a campaign to persuade Bao Dai to return to Vietnam to serve as Chief of State in a new "autonomous government" which would rally non-communist forces in Vietnam to join with the French against the Vietminh. Bao Dai was willing to return, but only on condition that the Vietnamese would be granted independence or at least substantial autonomy. The French, on the other hand, desperately needed some cooperation from the local population, but were unwilling to abandon their authority in Vietnam.

Ho Chi Minh and his high command planning the battle of Dienbienphu in their jungle headquarters.

French tanks departing Haiphong on May 11,1954, ending 100 years of French colonial rule in the port city.

October 9, 1954: Vietminh troops enjoy a "Parade of Victory" through the streets of Hanoi following the French withdrawal.

This fact became increasingly clear in 1949 when the Chinese Communist Party under the leadership of Chairman Mao Zedong seized control of China from the disintegrating Nationalist government under Generalissimo Chiang Kai-Shek.

By October, Chinese communist troops had arrived at the Vietnamese frontier and were in a position to provide assistance to the Vietminh. Under the pressure of this new threat, Bao Dai and the French agreed on the formation of an "Associated States of Vietnam" that would have some of the attributes of an independent state. However, the French would retain substantial authority in foreign and military affairs. Similar agreements were reached with Laos and Cambodia, both of which became "Associated States" under their monarchs.

The United States Enters the War

Under these conditions the United States first became actively involved in the Indochina conflict. Indochina had played a major role in bringing the United States into World War II. The United States had few interests in the region, except for its colony in the Philippines. The Roosevelt administration viewed Southeast Asia as a strategically important area with vast resources of tin, rubber and oil. In fact, the Japanese occupation of Indochina in 1940 had been a major factor in bringing Washington into a confrontation with Tokyo.

During World War II, U.S. intelligence sources watched Ho Chi Minh's Vietminh movement and even agreed to provide limited military assistance to it in return for information on Japanese troop movements in the area and Vietminh help in rescuing downed U.S. fliers. Ho Chi Minh attempted to use that relationship to obtain U.S. recognition of his movement as the legitimate representative of the Vietnamese people; but the United States was unwilling to antagonize the French, and ignored Ho's appeals. This decision is explored in depth in Chapter 2.

After the beginning of the Franco-Vietminh conflict, the French approached President Harry Truman for aid in fighting the communists. The Truman administra-

> *"Join strength, join hearts.*
> *The hardest job we'll finish."*
> Ho Chi Minh   20th century

tion was not happy about the communist complexion of the DRV but it also disapproved of French reluctance to grant independence to nationalist elements in Vietnam. At first, the United States refused to become involved. However, the victory of the communists in the Chinese Civil War convinced many U.S. officials that the Vietminh must be stopped in order to prevent the spread of communism throughout Southeast Asia. Several countries in the area had recently received their independence from colonial rule and Washington feared that the entire area could fall into the communist orbit if Ho Chi Minh were victorious in Indochina. In early 1950, the Truman administration agreed to provide military and economic assistance to the new "Associated States of Vietnam" under Chief of State Bao Dai, which it now recognized as the legitimate government of Vietnam. Although the new government did not possess full political or economic powers, the U.S. hoped that it would develop gradually into a viable state that could defeat the Vietminh and prevent the further spread of communism in the region.

The Road to Negotiations

For the Vietminh, the victory of communism in China presented a major opportunity to achieve a total victory in their struggle with the French. In early 1950, Ho Chi Minh visited Beijing. The Chinese agreed to provide assistance in the form of weapons and training for Vietminh forces in Indochina. Later in the year, the strengthened Vietminh forces launched a major offensive on the border to wipe out French posts and open up the area to the increased shipment of Chinese military equipment. In January 1951, Vo Nguyen Giap launched a major campaign designed to sweep French forces from the Red River Delta and achieve a total victory in the war. But French airpower proved too powerful, and the battered Vietminh were forced to regroup. At that point, the Vietminh returned to their guerrilla tactics. Vo Nguyen Giap's strategy featured surprise attacks on French installations and military posts all over the country so as to disperse enemy forces and wear down public support in France for the war.

During the next three years, the war dragged on inconclusively with no major breakthrough on either side. The level of U.S. aid increased gradually, and by 1953 the United States was paying almost 80 percent of French military expenditures for the war. The results, from Washington's point of view, were disappointing. The Vietminh situation improved steadily. In Laos and Cambodia, resistance forces under Vietminh direction posed an increasing threat to the new "Associated States" set up by the French. The French were losing the support of the Vietnamese people. Chief of State Bao Dai lacked leadership qualities and spent much of his time in France. His inexperienced government proved unable to meet the challenge of building popular support while the French retained ultimate control. In particular, the Bao Dai regime did little to end the inequality in landholdings that kept the majority of the rural population in conditions of abject poverty. In fact, at this time, a mere one-quarter of one percent of the population owned forty percent of the rice land in South Vietnam, 1,600 times their equal share. More importantly, two out of three peasants in the rice lands of the Mekong River Delta owned no land at all. These were the people for whom the Vietminh revolution had the most appeal.

By 1953, the French public was turning against the war, placing growing pressure on the government in Paris to seek a negotiated settlement. In October, for the first time, Premier Joseph Laniel mentioned the possibility of peace talks. A month later, Ho Chi Minh indicated that his government was willing to seek a cease-fire and a peace agreement. Early in 1954, arrangements were reached to hold a peace conference at Geneva in the spring.

News of the coming of peace talks, however, did not

'What's So Funny, Monsieur? I'm Only Trying to Find My Way'

slow down the war itself. In March, hoping that a significant battlefield victory would lead to success at the conference table, the Vietminh launched a major attack on the French outpost at Dienbienphu, in the mountains northwest of Hanoi.

The French government asked the United States to help by bombing Vietminh artillery emplacements near Dienbienphu. But President Eisenhower was reluctant to comply without the consent of Congress and without a larger U.S. role in making strategy. He proposed instead that the major western powers form a military alliance to ensure the defeat of the Vietminh. In early April, Secretary of State John Foster Dulles visited London and Paris to seek agreement on the formation of such an alliance. But the British were convinced that defeat in Indochina was inevitable and refused to join in such an agreement before the chances for a peace settlement had been explored at Geneva.

The French, too, were reluctant to expand the war and did not want to torpedo the conference. In the end, the proposal was temporarily shelved, and the U.S. reluctantly agreed to attend the proceedings at Geneva. This decision is analyzed in depth in Chapter 2. On May 7, 1954, delegations from the major world powers as well as the involved states in Indochina met at Geneva to discuss a settlement of the conflict. On the eve of the conference, the French military post at Dienbienphu fell to the Vietminh, leaving the French in a defeatist mood. In June, the Laniel government resigned. The new Prime Minister, Pierre Mendes-France, favored a French withdrawal and pledged to bring the war to an end by mid-summer. Similar pressure for a settlement was also imposed on the DRV by the Soviet Union and China. They both wanted an end to the conflict in order to promote peaceful coexistence with the West so they could concentrate on domestic concerns.

On July 21, an agreement to end the conflict was finally reached. There were in fact two agreements: a cease-fire between France and the DRV, and a political accord to achieve a lasting solution to the issues that had led to the war. The cease-fire was achieved by establishing two roughly equal regroupment zones, divided at the seventeenth parallel where a demilitarized zone (DMZ) was set up at the Ben Hai River. All Vietminh forces were to retreat north of the DMZ, while supporters of the Bao Dai government were to move to the south. On the insistence of both Vietnamese governments, these zones were not to be construed as sovereign political entities but as a temporary division to end the war until a political agreement could be reached (see Chapter 3 for a detailed discussion of the Geneva Agreement).

The process of achieving such an agreement was contained in the Political Accords, the second component of the Geneva Agreement. According to this arrangement, representatives of the two zones were to consult in July 1955 to agree on plans to hold reunification elections one year later. An International Control Commission was created to make sure the agreements were carried out. Related agreements brought an end to the conflicts in Laos and Cambodia. The "Associated States" created by the French were recognized as the legal government in both countries.

In Laos, the Vietminh-supported Pathet Lao move-

ment was granted two provinces in the mountainous northeast as a regroupment zone prior to negotiations with the royal government in Vientiane. The Khmer Rouge revolutionary forces in Cambodia received no such recognition. The government of Prince Norodom Sihanouk in Phnom Penh was recognized as the sole legal entity in the country, and all foreign troops—both French and Vietminh forces—were to withdraw. At the insistence of China, the entire area was declared neutral. None of the governments in Indochina were permitted to join military alliances, although they were allowed to seek military assistance if their security were threatened.

With the signing of the Geneva Agreements, the first Indochina war came to an end. But it ended on an ominous note. The United States, believing that reunification elections would lead to a victory for the widely popular Ho Chi Minh, refused to adhere to the political accords. In a written statement, it promised not to disturb them. But the Eisenhower administration also announced that it intended to build up what Secretary of State John Foster Dulles called "the truly independent states of Cambodia, Laos, and southern Vietnam." Finally, it served notice that it would seek to create an anti-communist alliance among its western allies and friendly states in Southeast Asia to resist further communist encroachment in the region. The stage was set for a new Cold War confrontation in Asia.

The Regime of Ngo Dinh Diem

After Geneva, two hostile governments faced each other across the DMZ. In North Vietnam, with its capital returned to Hanoi, President Ho Chi Minh's DRV attempted to build a socialist society with assistance from China and the Soviet Union. In the cities and towns, industry and commerce were nationalized. In the countryside, a massive program of land reform confiscated the property of wealthy farmers and redistributed it to the poor. According to contemporary estimates, about 60 percent of the peasants in North Vietnam received some land under the program. There

Ngo Dinh Diem with his two
brothers and influential
sister-in-law:
(left-right) Diem, Ngo Dinh Nhu,
Madame Nhu (center) and
Archbishop Thuc

was a violent side to the program, however. Many Vietnamese considered hostile to the revolution were arrested and some were executed. To placate critics, Ho Chi Minh fired the government minister in charge of the program and soon demoted the Party Secretary General, Truong Chinh.

In South Vietnam, the government of Bao Dai was replaced by a new regime under the veteran Vietnamese politician Ngo Dinh Diem. Diem was popular in Washington. Descended from a prominent Catholic family in central Vietnam, he disliked both the French and the communists. U.S. officials particularly liked the fact that he was Catholic, for many of the two million Vietnamese Catholics were among the best educated and most anti-communist elements in Vietnam. Diem's Catholicism assumed even greater importance when the Geneva agreement permitted all Vietnamese a grace period in order to settle in either zone depending on their political preference. Of the 900,000 refugees who fled to the South, two thirds, or 600,000, were Catholics. Most settled near the new capital of Saigon, where they became a major force in helping Diem to build a firm political base.

Under pressure from the United States, Bao Dai appointed Diem prime minister during the Geneva Conference. During the next few months, Diem moved rapidly to consolidate his position, removing pro-French elements from the Bao Dai administration, crushing opposition from the sects and attempting to eliminate those Vietminh elements the DRV had instructed to remain in South Vietnam after Geneva to represent its interests there. In October 1955, he organized a plebiscite between himself and Chief of State Bao Dai. In an election widely viewed as fraudulent, Diem received over 98 percent of the vote.

In July 1955, the Hanoi regime called for consultations on reunification elections as required by the Geneva Agreement. Diem refused on the grounds that the Bao Dai government, like the United States, had not ratified the accords. Conscious of the legal ambiguities in the situation, the Eisenhower administration recommended that Saigon agree to hold talks while placing stiff conditions on elections in the hope that Hanoi would refuse. But Diem refused even to hold consultations with North Vietnam and the United States publicly backed him.

Diem's refusal to agree to consultations on national elections was a severe blow to Hanoi. The DRV, needing time and resources to build an advanced socialist society in the north, undoubtedly hoped that national

21

elections would be held and a renewal of the war avoided. They also were confident that the popularity of Ho Chi Minh and the Vietminh mystique would guarantee an electoral victory over Ngo Dinh Diem. For the moment, however, Hanoi did nothing, hoping that the Diem regime would eventually collapse.

But in Washington, officials were optimistic for Ngo Dinh Diem appeared to be the answer to the U.S. "problem" in Vietnam. Backed by firm U.S. support, Diem established a presidential system based on the American model, with himself as President. On U.S. advice, Diem also launched a land reform program designed to reduce the inequality of land holding in the rice-rich Mekong Delta. With American aid, the Saigon

> *"South and North are washed by the same sea. In our hearts there can be no boundary ."*
>
> To Huu 20th century

regime built up its armed forces. Although the U.S. was prohibited from establishing a direct alliance with South Vietnam, it did set up a multinational Southeast Asia Treaty Organization (SEATO) to protect the states in the area from further communist encroachment. Although the Geneva Accords prohibited South Vietnam, Laos and Cambodia from becoming members of the alliance, the U.S. evaded that prohibition by including them in a so-called "umbrella clause" in the treaty (see Chapter 3 for more discussion).

By the late 1950s, unfortunately for the United States, the early promise of the Diem regime had begun to fade. Diem's autocratic tendencies alienated key groups within South Vietnam, including the sects, the tribal minorities, the overseas Chinese, and many intellectuals. Much of the criticism was directed at Diem's brother, the manipulative Ngo Dinh Nhu who, as Minister of the Interior, was the dominant figure in the Saigon regime. Diem responded to criticism with persecution and censorship.

The land reform program had only limited success because wealthy absentee landlords found it easy to evade the loose provisions of the limitations on land holding. Where the land reform program in North Vietnam had provided land to well over half the rural

population, in the south only about ten percent of those eligible to receive land actually did so. Finally, Diem's tendency to favor Catholics irritated many Buddhists, who represented the majority of the population.

The DRV, as we have seen, had left a small contingent of Party leaders in South Vietnam. During the late 1950s, they attempted to gain a following among the increasing number of discontented. Diem severely repressed all resistance to his regime, sending revolutionary tribunals from village to village to root out and eliminate suspected communist sympathizers. With their ranks severely depleted by Diem's campaign, and convinced that popular sentiment was turning in favor of the revolution, the DRV now decided to promote a new revolutionary uprising in South Vietnam. Several thousand southerners who had been sent north for training after Geneva were infiltrated back into the south to provide experienced leadership for the movement. Rebel forces began to attack isolated villages and South Vietnamese military posts, while special units assassinated village chiefs and other individuals identified with the Saigon regime.

By early 1961, when John F. Kennedy became President of the United States, the political situation in South Vietnam had become highly unstable. Sparked by Diem's repressive policies, many urban and rural Vietnamese responded to the appeal of the revolutionary movement. Some joined the People's Liberation Armed Forces, referred to by U.S. officials and the Diem regime as the Vietcong (Vietnamese communists). Thousands of others became members of a new political organization called the National Liberation Front for South Vietnam (NLF). Like its predecessor, the Vietminh, the NLF was created by party strategists in the DRV as a non-partisan alliance for all patriotic South Vietnamese opposed to the Diem regime and its American ally. Its program emphasized such popular issues as land reform, democratic freedoms, and social justice. It said little about communism and spoke only in vague terms about eventual reunification with the north.

Most major NLF strategy decisions apparently were made in Hanoi and many of the key officials in the Front also were members of the communist party. However, the NLF had its own organizational structure and included thousands of members who had joined for reasons of patriotism or the desire for political and social reform rather than because of a commitment to Marxist

The Vietnamese Buddhist monk 73-year-old Thich (venerable) Quang Duc immolates himself in front of a crowd of Buddhist monks and shocked onlookers.

doctrine. Even many of those who were aware of the close links with the north believed that, after the victory of the revolution, the south would be in a position to take its own road to national unity and socialism. Benefiting from Diem's mistakes as well as from the appeal of its own program, the NLF won wide support among many southerners who had grievances against the Diem regime, and who viewed the NLF as the legitimate representative of the South Vietnamese people.

Vietnam was not President Kennedy's only foreign policy problem. In its first few months, the new administration faced crises in Berlin, in Laos—where the Pathet Lao movement was becoming an increasing threat to the royal Lao government—and in Cuba, where the Bay of Pigs invasion had ended in an embarrassing fiasco. Convinced that only a firm stand on Vietnam would persuade Soviet leader Nikita Khrushchev of his willingness to defend U.S. interests,

Kennedy strengthened the U.S. commitment to the Diem regime. He increased the number of American advisers and made it clear that the United States intended to win in Vietnam. But Kennedy also was convinced that Diem could not succeed without improving his political performance and adopting a new strategy to counter the mounting guerrilla war in the South.

In late 1961, Kennedy approved an increase in U.S. military assistance, part of which called for increased training in counter-guerrilla warfare. But he rejected a proposal to send two divisions of American combat troops to South Vietnam as a symbol of U.S. determination. In fact, Kennedy warned Diem that, unless Saigon moved to reduce internal dissent to the regime, the United States might reevaluate its policy of providing firm support.

During the next two years, Diem, with U.S. support,

intensified his efforts to eliminate the insurgency movement in South Vietnam. The primary focus of his strategy was the construction of so-called "strategic hamlets" throughout much of the countryside. Strategic hamlets were villages that were fortified to isolate the rural population from the forces of the revolution. Sometimes, however, they were artificially created, and peasants were compelled to move from smaller and more vulnerable hamlets to larger units in order to facilitate the building of a defensive perimeter. Villagers were expected to bear the cost of fortifying the "strategic hamlet" and frequently resented official arrogance and insensitivity in carrying out the program. Moreover, contrary to U.S. advice, Diem hurriedly created large numbers of strategic hamlets in insecure areas, thus providing the NLF with the opportunity to destroy the hamlets and discredit the program.

Diem's failure to "win hearts and minds" in the countryside was repeated in the cities. After 1961, tension between the government and the Buddhist movement intensified. Many Buddhist monks and lay intellectuals not only resented Diem's tendency to favor Catholics, but they also opposed his policy of vigorously suppressing the revolutionary movement and refusing to hold peace talks with Hanoi. By 1963, popular feelings in the cities turned increasingly hostile to the Saigon regime, and particularly to Diem's brother, Nhu.

During the Spring of 1963, Buddhist protests against the regime accelerated. When some Buddhist monks participated in demonstrations, the police raided the temples and threw protestors in prison. To symbolize popular resistance to regime policies, one Buddhist monk, Thich Quang Duc, committed suicide by setting

Civilians pass a machine gun to helmeted rebel troops inside the gates of the Presidential Palace following the coup on November 3.

himself afire on a street in Saigon. That public gesture galvanized anti-Diem sentiment abroad. Even the Kennedy administration, exasperated at Diem's failure to follow U.S. advice, publicly disassociated itself from his actions.

Discontent within the South Vietnamese armed forces, which had originally surfaced in 1960, once more began to simmer. During the summer dissident officers secretly approached U.S. officials to ascertain Washington's reaction to a possible coup d'état to overthrow the Diem regime. At first, the Kennedy administration opposed a coup, fearing that it would lead to a collapse of anti-communist efforts in South Vietnam. But when Diem continued to refuse U.S. advice (including the suggestion that Ngo Dinh Nhu should be removed from the cabinet), Washington signalled its approval and agreed to provide communications assistance to the plotters.

The coup erupted on the night of November 1, 1963. Units commanded by dissident military officers took control of key installations and surrounded the Presidential Palace in Saigon. Diem phoned U.S. Ambassador Henry Cabot Lodge to request U.S. support. Lodge declined to provide assistance but offered the President asylum at the U.S. embassy. Diem refused and fled with his brother to a church in the nearby suburb of Cholon. The next morning they were apprehended by a rebel army officer who executed them in the back of the personnel carrier that was supposed to transport them back to Saigon.

President Kennedy was horrified at the murder of Ngo Dinh Diem but was resigned to the necessity of a change of government in Saigon. The U.S. quickly signaled its support for the new military leadership, which immediately formed a Military Revolutionary Council under the leadership of the popular southern General Duong Van Minh (often known as "Big Minh").

The North Vietnamese regime was initially puzzled at how to respond to the overthrow of Ngo Dinh Diem. He had been a tough opponent, but the widespread antagonism to him had provided fuel to the revolution. By contrast, the new military government, although inexperienced, appeared to have wide approval from the general populace in the South. At first, the DRV quietly signaled its willingness to start exploratory peace talks. When its overtures were rejected, Hanoi decided to take advantage of the inexperience of the new government in Saigon by escalating the war in the South. At a major meeting held in December, Party leaders approved a proposal to intensify pressure on Saigon by infiltrating regular units of the North Vietnamese armed forces down the "Ho Chi Minh Trail," through the mountains and jungles of central Vietnam and neighboring Laos and Cambodia. Hoping that the United States would not respond, Hanoi was now prepared to use North Vietnamese regular troops to achieve its objective of national unification.

Three weeks after the murder of Ngo Dinh Diem, John Kennedy was assassinated in Dallas. His successor, Lyndon Johnson, was anxious to avoid an escalation of the Vietnam conflict but, like Kennedy, was determined not to "lose" the war. But in the months following the overthrow of the Diem regime, the political and military situation in South Vietnam continued to deteriorate. In the political arena, the new military government was plagued with factionalism. "Big

> "Being stubborn and patient,
> not yielding an inch
> though physically I suffer,
> my spirit is unbroken."
> Ho Chi Minh   20th century

Minh" was soon replaced by his colleagues on the Military Revolutionary Council. The Saigon regime became a game of musical chairs, with military and civilian prime ministers following each other in office within months of each other.

The effects were soon felt on the battlefield, where the revolutionary forces continued to extend their control over the countryside. According to intelligence estimates, more than half the population were under the control of the revolutionary forces, and it was considered unsafe for Americans—now numbering more than 20,000—to travel outside the major cities. Equally ominous, U.S. intelligence was receiving reports that the infiltration of men and supplies from North Vietnam was running well above previous years. In fact, it was becoming evident that, unless the U.S. took drastic action, the fall of South Vietnam could take place in a matter of months.

In this context, the famous "Tonkin Gulf incident"

took place in August of 1964. American warships on an intelligence mission in the Tonkin Gulf off the coast of North Vietnam were allegedly attacked by North Vietnamese coastal craft. President Johnson claimed that the attacks had been unprovoked and asked Congress to give him the authority to take whatever action was necessary to protect U.S. lives and security interests in the area. Critics raised doubts about the administration's version of the incidents and some even questioned whether they had taken place. Nevertheless, Congress was stirred by patriotic fervor and approved the President's request. Lyndon Johnson was now armed with the authority to take further military action to prevent the spread of communism in Indochina. (The true facts and legal issues surrounding the Gulf of Tonkin incident and resolution are discussed in Chapters 2, 3, and 8).

The Tonkin Gulf incident suddenly brought the growing crisis in Indochina to the attention of the American people. The Johnson administration proposed that the civil war in Vietnam now was a vital issue in American foreign policy. American money and American lives might soon be invested in a Cold War struggle some 10,000 miles away.

With the crisis came controversy. At this stage in the struggle, most Americans accepted the rationale pre-

---

CHRISTMAS

The Hessian in his last letter home
said in part

" they are all rebels here
who will not stand to fight
but each time fade before us
as water into sand . . .

the children beg in their rude hamlets

the women stare with hate

the men flee into the barrens at our approach
to lay in ambush

some talk of desertion . . .
were it not for the hatred
they bear us, more would do so

There is no glory here
Tell Hals he must evade the Prince's levy
through exile or deformity

Winter is hard upon us. On the morrow we enter
Trenton. There we rest until the New Year . . ."

—Steve Hassett

sented by the Johnson administration that Vietnam, and Southeast Asia as a whole, were vital to U.S. national security interests. Still, some began to question whether increased involvement was in the overall American interest. On college campuses where students and professors organized "teach-ins" to bring public attention to the war, questions about the nature of the conflict and the U.S. role in precipitating the crisis began to be raised.

Much of the controversy centered around the origins of the problem. Was the growing conflict in South Vietnam an "armed attack" from the north, as the administration contended? Or was it primarily a civil war, provoked by the brutal policies of the regime of Ngo Dinh Diem, which drove desperate peasants, minority tribesmen, and urban intellectuals into the ranks of the NLF? Was the NLF itself a creature of Hanoi? Or was it an independent organization truly representative of the aspirations of the people in South Vietnam?

Other questions dealt with legal issues. Had the United States, or the DRV, broken the Geneva Accords? Had Diem been within his legal rights to refuse consultations on elections in 1955? Others were moral. Did the United States have any business in becoming involved in a bitter struggle where the issues, both moral and political, were sometimes less than clear?

Although some Americans found easy answers to such questions, most were uninformed or confused. Many Americans were persuaded by Cold War rhetoric and the experience of World War II that the United States had no choice but to aid South Vietnam in order to deter further aggression and prevent the entire region from sliding into the clutches of international communism. Others, recalling the enormous costs of Korea, were concerned greatly about getting bogged down in another land war in Asia. Still others found the lessons of both World War II and Korea irrelevant to the crisis in Indochina. To them, the conflict in Vietnam appeared to be less an attempt by Moscow or Beijing to spread the Red Tide throughout the Pacific than an internal revolution, fueled by human misery, political brutality, and a desire for social justice.

In 1964, such arguments were only beginning to be heard. They were certainly not the views of the majority of the American people. Yet the American public approached the growing crisis in South Vietnam with a profound sense of uneasiness, and a sense of foreboding that the worst was yet to come.

Discussion Questions

1. What nations and/or geographic features border Vietnam? What two areas of Vietnam are considered the "heartland" of the country?

2. Most of the population of Vietnam is composed of people known as the _____? They make up approximately ___% of the entire population. What groups make-up the remaining percentage of the population of Vietnam?

3. What were the major colonial powers of the Pacific region during the sixteenth and seventeenth centuries? What were their primary interests in the area now known as Vietnam and in the other Southeast Asian territories? Have any Asian countries been involved in the colonization or occupation of Vietnam over the course of history? If yes, which one(s)?

4. What did France consider its "mission civilisatrice" in Indochina? What were the positive and negative consequences of French colonial policy? What, if any, of these consequences do you believe the Indochinese people would have considered positive at the time?

5. What events of WW II contributed to the rise of the Communist Party in Vietnam? Who was its leader? What was (who were) the "Vietcong," the "NLF?" What were the objectives of these groups? Who controlled them, if anyone?

6. What was the major reason that the U.S. became involved in assisting the "Associated State of Vietnam" in the 1950s?

7. What was the major military strategy of the "Vietminh" in fighting the French in the 1950s? How does this strategy compare with that used to fight the American, South Vietnamese and allied troops during the 1960s and 70s?

8. What were the two major components of the Geneva Agreement of 1954? Were they adhered to by either side? If not, what happened, and why?

9. What do you believe were the major successes and failures of the Diem regime? What might have been done by him and his government that could have changed the outcome of the 1960s and 70s in Vietnam; in the American involvement in Vietnam?

10. Do you believe that the outcome of the Diem regime was what the Kennedy administration wanted? Why? What do you believe would have been the best American policy toward Vietnam during the periods of the Diem and "Big Minh" governments? Why?

11. What was the general, overall foreign policy context of American involvement in Vietnam, i.e., why were we there and why did we stay? What were the "pros" and "cons" of such a policy? If you had been President at the time, how would you have handled the situation in Vietnam?

Chapter 2

Jerold M. Starr

AMERICA AT WAR IN VIETNAM: DECISIONS AND CONSEQUENCES

President
Lyndon B. Johnson

Introduction

In 1967, historian Arthur M. Schlesinger Jr. called the Vietnam War a "nightmare" which "no President...desired or intended." Schlesinger explained, "In retrospect, Vietnam is a triumph of the politics of inadvertence [oversight]. We have achieved our present entanglement...through a series of small decisions."

In contrast, historian Barbara Tuchman has charged that "American intervention was not a progress sucked step by step into an unsuspected quagmire. At no time were policymakers unaware of the hazards, obstacles and negative developments." In Tuchman's view, the failure of U.S. policy lay in the "folly" of pursuing a goal "despite accumulating evidence that the goal was unattainable, and the effect disproportionate to the American interest.... "

In this chapter, we will study the evidence available to U.S. decision makers; the decisions they made; and the consequences those decisions had for United States involvement in Vietnam. You can make up your own mind as to whether U.S. leaders backed unawares into Vietnam or deliberately persisted despite many warnings.

Whether U.S. leaders knew what was going on in Vietnam is one question. What they were trying to do there is still another. Historian Sidney Lens has stated that the war in Vietnam was not an "accident," but "American policy drawn to its ultimate—and logical—conclusion." For Lens, that policy was to use military force in order to gain "access to raw materials" and markets for American goods in the Third World; that is, an "open door" for "western trade and investment."

Leslie Gelb and Richard Betts also have rejected any contention that the war was a "blind slide down a slippery slope." In contrast to Lens, however, they have said that the U.S. goal simply was "to contain communism in Vietnam." Accordingly, the "escalation of involvement...was the response to the progressive escalation of the price of keeping the commitment."

The question of U.S. goals in Vietnam is best considered within the framework of the five general reasons that leaders choose to commit their nations to war. You will find it easy to remember them as the Five P's: Power, Prestige, Principles, Profits, and Protection (of territory). Following are explanations of the five P's illustrated by statements made concerning U.S. interest in Vietnam.

1. **POWER** — Nations often go to war to increase their power or to prevent their enemies from increasing their power. Some nations do this by attacking weaker neighbors; others form alliances with other nations to build up their strength.

In April 1950, a National Security Report on Vietnam stated that, if the U.S.S.R. came to dominate even more areas of the world, it might mean "that no coalition adequate to confront the Kremlin with greater strength could be assembled...."

2. **PRESTIGE** — The desire to defend or advance a nation's prestige—that is, a nation's standing in the eyes of the world—is a second factor that may lead to war.

In January 1966, Assistant Secretary of Defense, John McNaughton, stated in a memorandum: "The present U.S. objective in Vietnam is to avoid humiliation...to preserve our reputation as a guarantor, and thus to preserve our effectiveness in the rest of world."

3. **PRINCIPLES** — Sometimes nations go to war to enforce cherished principles, such as ensuring human rights or the rights of vessels at sea.

At a speech at Johns Hopkins University on April 7, 1965, President Lyndon B. Johnson stated: "The central lesson of our time is that the appetite for aggression is never satisfied. To withdraw from one battlefield means only to prepare for the next. We must say in Southeast Asia—as we did in Europe—in the words of the Bible: 'Hither shalt thou come and no further.'"

4. **PROFIT** — Nations go to war for profit, that is, to advance their economic interests by protecting investments, securing raw materials, or gaining new markets for their exports.

In 1965, U.S. Ambassador to South Vietnam, Henry Cabot Lodge, was quoted as saying: "He who holds or has influence in Vietnam can affect the future of the Philippines and Formosa to the east, Thailand and Burma with their huge rice surpluses to the west, and Malaysia and Indonesia with the rubber, ore, and tin to the south.... Vietnam does not exist in a geographical vacuum—from it large storehouses of wealth and population can be influenced and undermined."

5. **PROTECTION** — When a nation is attacked or invaded by another nation, it usually will fight to protect its people and territory.

On March 31, 1968, President Johnson warned: "What we are doing now in Vietnam is vital not only to the security of Southeast Asia, but it is vital to the security of every American...."

It is important to note that going to war is often *not* the most effective way for a nation to achieve any of the above goals. Other policies may offer as much chance of success with less risk. For example, some in the State Department proposed that the U.S. need not establish a stronghold in Vietnam in order to oppose communist China's "wider pattern of aggressive purposes." In their view, a "unified communist Vietnam would reassert its traditional hostility to communist China." This, in fact, is what came to pass when China and Vietnam went to war briefly in 1979 over Vietnam's occupation of Cambodia.

It is also important to note that going to war may cause a nation to suffer losses, even when it is not defeated in battle. For example, in July 1965, Under-Secretary of State George Ball correctly forecast the loss of U.S. prestige because of its failure to triumph decisively in Vietnam:

I am concerned about world opinion.... If the war is long and protracted, as I believe it will be, then we will suffer because the world's greatest power cannot defeat the guerrillas.

U.S. efforts to hasten the end of that "long and protected" war, moreover, had their own costs to U.S. world prestige. On May 19, 1967, Assistant Secretary of Defense, John McNaugton, observed:

The picture of the world's greatest super-power killing or seriously injuring 1,000 non-combatants a week, while trying to pound a tiny backward nation into submission on an issue whose merits are hotly disputed, is not a pretty one. It will conceivably produce a costly distortion in...the world image of the U.S....

Now you have a clearer idea of why nations go to war and what they risk in the act. As we study the decisions that deepened America's involvement in Vietnam, remember the Five P's. How did they influence such decisions? Which of them seemed to be most important to U.S. leaders? What evidence was there that such goals were attainable? What indications were there that the war could cause the U.S. to lose any of the five P's? Were there alternative Vietnam policies that might have achieved U.S. goals with less risk?

Early American Involvement

On September 2, 1945, a frail man stood before a hushed crowd in central Hanoi and spoke these words: "We hold the truth that all men are created equal, that they are endowed by their Creator with certain inalienable rights, among them life, liberty, and the pursuit of happiness." The speaker was Ho Chi Minh, and he was declaring the independence of Vietnam. Later in the day, as the independence celebrations continued; American airplanes flew overhead in a display of friendship; United States Army officers joined dignitaries on the reviewing stand, and a Vietnamese band played the "Star-Spangled Banner."

Few people in Hanoi recognized the passage from the American Declaration of Independence or knew the American national anthem. But Ho Chi Minh, though a deeply committed communist, was a practical man. He allowed the United States to play a prominent role at the birth of modern Vietnam for a good reason. Seeking international support for his nation's independence, he feared that it would only be a matter of weeks before France, the former colonial ruler of Vietnam, returned in force. He was right.

For more than a half century before the outbreak of World War II, Vietnam had been part of the French colony of Indochina. Then, in 1940, world events swept

over Southeast Asia. Japanese forces moved down from China, taking over French Indochina. The Japanese pushed on, driving the Americans from the Philippines, the Dutch from Indonesia, and the British from Malaya. European colonialism in Asia had been challenged successfully—and by an Asian nation.

Throughout Southeast Asia, nationalists fighting European colonialism welcomed the Japanese. Ho Chi Minh, however, opposed replacing one colonial ruler with another. Aligning himself with the Allies (the United States, the Soviet Union, China, Great Britain, and progressive elements in France), he and his Vietminh revolutionaries worked for the defeat of Japan. In return, he expected to gain independence for his country after the war.

The defeat of Japan in 1945 gave Ho his long-awaited opportunity. At the time, however, Vietnam was in chaos. To disarm the Japanese forces still in the country, a Chinese Nationalist army had been dispatched to the northern part of Vietnam, while British troops had moved into the south. Meanwhile, rival Vietnamese groups were at each other's throats. More ominously, French merchants and officials still in Vietnam were calling for the return of the French army.

Late in 1945, fighting broke out in Saigon between French civilians and the Vietminh. To restore order, the outmanned British decided to transport French forces back into the region. Ho was disappointed when the United States agreed to the plan. Meanwhile, the Chinese Nationalists had arrived in the north, which they began to loot. Confronted with the Chinese presence, Ho concluded that he had no choice but to ask the French back—on the condition that they honor Vietnam's independence. France agreed to do so.

Distrustful of the French, Ho had at least found a way to rid his nation of the Chinese—Vietnam's traditional enemy. As he told critics of his plan:

You fools! Don't you realize what it means if the Chinese remain? Don't you remember your history? The last time the Chinese came, they stayed 1,000 years. The French are foreigners. They are weak. Colonialism is dying. The white man is finished in Asia. But if the Chinese stay now, they will never go.

Despite the agreement with the French, it was clear from the start that peace would not last. The French public, for one thing, opposed any kind of compromise with the Vietminh. Every French political party—from the most conservative to the communists—longed to restore the national prestige that had been lost to Germany and Japan during World War II. Reinstating the colonies to their prewar status seemed one way to do it.

The short-lived agreement between France and the Vietminh came apart at the port city of Haiphong. After a minor dispute late in 1946 over the collection of customs duties, French armored units attacked the city. Ships anchored in the harbor lobbed shells into Haiphong, and airplanes dropped bombs. When it was over, entire neighborhoods had been flattened; and at least 6,000 civilians had lost their lives. Meanwhile, the French moved toward Hanoi, once capital of all Indochina, and after bloody street fighting, took the city.

As rebellion raged throughout the region, the United States was just beginning to formulate its policy on Vietnam. At first, it looked as if President Franklin Roosevelt might support the movement for independence. In a memo to Secretary of State Hull in 1944, Roosevelt stated:

> I had for over a year expressed the opinion that Indochina should not go back to France but that it should be administered by an international trusteeship. France had the country—thirty million inhabitants for nearly one hundred years and the people are worse off than they were in the beginning.... France has milked it for one hundred years. The people of Indochina are entitled to something better than that.

At a press conference on February 23, 1945, Roosevelt again suggested that Vietnam might be made a "trustee" to be educated for "self-government" just as the U.S. had done in the Philippines. However, he never took any action to initiate such a plan.

In April 1945, G.H. Blakeslee of the U.S. State Department saw the dilemma of choice for the U.S. as between causing "French resentment" which would "impose a serious strain on our relations" or weakening "the traditional confidence of eastern peoples in the United States."

From October 1945 to February 1946, Ho Chi Minh sent at least eight communications to the President of the United States asking that Vietnam be allowed the chance to prepare itself for independence or asking for U.S. and United Nations protection against French aggression. Ho also approached other American officials with informal proposals for closer U.S.—Vietnamese relations. George M. Abbot, First Secretary of the U.S. Embassy in Paris, met with Ho on December 12, 1946, and reported that Ho said he "would continue to resist the French desire for...economic monopoly." Instead, Ho proposed that "Indochina offered a fertile field for American capital and enterprise" and he "hinted that the policy might apply to military and naval matters as well," including the naval base at Cam Ranh Bay. *So much for communism*

Ho had good reason for appealing to the United States. His Vietminh forces had cooperated with the Americans during World War II, providing them with information about Japanese troop movements and assisting downed Allied pilots.

Ho and military advisor Giap with U.S. forces during the Second World War.

Back in Washington, however, questions were raised about Ho's communism. Many of the experts contended that Ho was primarily a nationalist. For example, A. L. Moffat, Chief of the Division of Southeast Asian Affairs in the State Department, testified to the Senate Foreign Relations Committee:

> I have never met an American...who had met Ho Chi Minh who did not reach the same belief: that Ho Chi Minh was first and foremost a Vietnamese nationalist. He was also a communist and believed that communism offered the best hope for the Vietnamese people...the top echelon of competent French officers held almost unanimously the same view.

Some argued that, regardless of his communism, it was crucial that the U.S. recognize that Ho was the only leader in Vietnam who commanded the respect of the majority of the people. For example, here is Thurston Morton, Assistant Secretary of State for Congressional Relations under John Dulles:

> Whether we like the particular economic system or social system that he might develop or not, we must remember that he [Ho Chi Minh] is, indeed, considered by many peasants, the small people, little people of South Vietnam and North Vietnam as the George Washington of his country.

Still others argued that Ho's communism should not threaten the U.S. precisely because he was a strong nationalist and not aligned with the Soviet Union. Indeed, investigations by both the State Department and American officials in Saigon in 1948 found "no evidence" of any link, let alone a chain of command, between Ho Chi Minh and "Moscow, China or the Soviet Legation in Bangkok."

Still, American policymakers remained suspicious of Ho. Many viewed him as part of an alleged Soviet plot to dominate the world. France's efforts to hold on to its former colony had somehow become recast as a confrontation between the superpowers.

By the end of World War II, tensions had started to build between the United States and the Soviet Union. These tensions would soon grow into a bitter rivalry known as the cold war.

Early in 1946, George Kennan, a leading State Department expert on Russia, pointed out that in the future the United States would have to resist the Soviet Union's plans of world conquest. Kennan did not expect the communists to launch all-out war, as Hitler had done in 1939. He thought they would be more patient, taking control of any area of the world where the forces of democracy seemed weak.

Many western leaders believed that World War II might not have taken place if the west had forcefully opposed Hitler's expansionist aggression in the 1930s. As the Soviet Union strengthened its domination over the countries of eastern Europe, Kennan's policy of containment of communism became a cornerstone of American foreign policy.

In the first years after the end of World War II, Americans felt deep concern about communist gains in western Europe too, particularly in Italy and France. In France, economic problems and political instability were sapping the country's strength. Some French politicians warned that France's recovery would be set back by the loss of its Indochinese colony. That development, in turn, could play into the hands of the growing French Communist Party. In a conversation with the American ambassador to France in 1945, French President Charles De Gaulle warned:

> The Russians are advancing apace as you well know.... If the public here comes to realize that you are against us in Indochina, there will be terrific disappointment and nobody knows to what that will lead. We do not want to become communist; we do not want to fall into the Russian orbit, but I hope you do not push us into it.

Other events also influenced American policymakers. One was the takeover in 1949 of China by the communist forces of Mao Zedong. President Harry S. Truman quickly asserted that the containment policy, at first focused on Europe, would be extended to Asia. By late 1949, the United States faced its first tough decision in Vietnam. Leading figures in Truman's administration were urging him to send aid to help the French forces in Indochina. Consider their recommendation as you answer the following questions.

You Decide!

1. *Fact Check* What reasons did France give for fighting in Vietnam?
2. *Fact Check* According to American officials, what interests did the United States have in the region?
3. *Constructing a Valid Argument* What arguments would a supporter of American aid to France have been likely to offer?

4. *Constructing a Valid Argument* What reasons were there for rejecting aid to France?

5. *Making a Decision* If you were President Truman, what decision would you make? Why? Which of the Five P's was involved in your decision?

The Decision and Its Consequences

Following the advice of Secretary of State Dean Acheson, Truman asked Congress to give $15 million in aid to France in Indochina. Congress approved the appropriation in 1950, the first of the more than $2.6 billion worth of military and economic aid sent to the French over the next five years. Indeed, American assistance would become so crucial that by 1954 the United States was paying nearly 80 percent of France's military costs in Indochina.

It seems clear, in retrospect, that in the aftermath of World War II the State Department had submitted to the pressure of its European desk and the rising tide of anti-communism. On May 29, 1949, Secretary of State Acheson stated:

> [The] question [of] whether Ho [is] as much nationalist as commie is irrelevant. All Stalinists in colonial areas are nationalists. With achievement [of] national aims (i.e. independence), their objectives necessarily become subordination [of the] state to commie purposes and [the] ruthless

extermination not only [of] opposition groups but [of] all elements suspected [of] even [the] slightest deviation.

On March 2, 1950, Carlos Romulo, President of the U.N. General Assembly, sent a letter to Acheson contesting this view. He had met Ho Chi Minh personally and felt he was "a man who could make all sorts of trouble for Stalin," a man who would "not allow himself to be a tool of the Kremlin." Despite such appeals, the U.S. course was set. A month earlier (February 7, 1950), China and the U.S.S.R. had recognized Ho Chi Minh's Democratic Republic of Vietnam as an independent nation and Secretary of State Acheson had declared that such ties removed any "illusions" about Ho's "nationalist" nature and revealed "his true colors as the mortal enemy of native independence in Indochina."

Archimedes Patti, a Major in the OSS who acted as a liaison between Ho Chi Minh and the U.S. in Indochina in 1945, always felt that the U.S. had missed a golden opportunity back then. At a 1983 conference at the University of Southern California, Patti commented: "There is little doubt in the light of available documentation that Ho was forced into dependence upon Peking and Moscow by American opposition or indifference. No question in anybody's mind about that. We had him on a silver platter, by the way, and I speak on first hand. But we turned him down."

In late 1949, Secretary State, Dean Acheson (right) persuaded President Truman to earmark $15 million to aid the French forces in Indochina.

Eisenhower and Dienbienphu

There were others in the Truman administration who did not welcome the decision to aid the French. One American policymaker warned, "Whether the French like it or not, independence is coming to Indochina. Why, therefore, do we tie ourselves to the tail of their battered kite?" Most believed, however, that the commitment was limited and the risks were few. With the invasion of South Korea by communist North Korea in the summer of 1950, moreover, the United States seemed confirmed in its belief that the Soviet Union wanted to conquer all of Asia. The defense of Southeast Asia now assumed even greater importance.

In the early days of the conflict, most observers assumed that the French would easily defeat the Vietminh. French forces far outnumbered those of the Vietminh and were able to maintain control of the major cities and highways.

The Vietminh, however, had learned much from the success of Mao Zedong in China. The key lesson was that no military unit should confront the enemy unless the enemy was outnumbered. The result was that the Vietminh rarely fought any pitched battles. Instead, small bands of guerrillas lay in ambush along roads and trails, attacking the advancing enemy before disappearing into the jungle. They also moved at night, cutting off enemy supply and communications lines, and vanishing before dawn. Ho predicted how the war would be fought:

> It will be a war between an elephant and a tiger. If the tiger ever stands still, the elephant will crush him with his mighty tusks. But the tiger will not stand still. He will leap upon the back of the elephant, tearing huge chunks from his side, and then he will leap back into the dark jungle. And slowly the elephant will bleed to death. That will be the war in Indochina.

And so the war dragged on, year after year, with the Vietminh refusing to be lured into a major battle where they might be defeated. By the end of 1952 they had worn down the French, and there was no longer enthusiasm among the French public for what was being called "the dirty little war." In spite of the support of the United States, the war was costing France dearly, both in money and lives lost.

In 1953, however, there was a dramatic shift in French military strategy. General Henri Navarre's plan was to move a major part of the French army into northern Vietnam near Laos, creating an inviting target for the enemy to attack in force. When that happened, Navarre believed, the superior French troops would at long last defeat the Vietminh. So confident was Navarre of his plan that he boldly predicted victory, saying "Now we can see it clearly—like light at the end of a tunnel."

The place that Navarre chose for his showdown with the Vietminh was the remote village of Dienbienphu, located in a broad valley surrounded by jungle-covered hills. Twelve battalions of French troops, numbering 13,000, were dispatched to Dienbienphu in November, 1953. The Vietminh managed to move heavy artillery guns along jungle trails and positioned them in the hills overlooking the French position. By March 1954, some 50,000 Vietminh surrounded the French base. Another 20,000 were strung out along supply lines.

The attack on Dienbienphu began on March 13, 1954, when suddenly every heavy gun in the Vietminh arsenal opened fire on the French garrison. Telephone lines were cut, the airstrip was pocked with shell holes, and many French guns—foolishly left unprotected — were destroyed. Even more damaging, the airstrip was knocked out, making resupply impossible except by parachute drop.

Over the next two months, the Vietminh closed in on Dienbienphu. The Vietnamese forces dug tunnels right up to the edge of the French bunkers, emerging from them to engage in hand-to-hand combat. Slowly, one outpost after another in the valley was overrun, and the noose around Dienbienphu drew tighter. The French realized that they needed outside help—and soon.

Given the emergency, high-ranking French military officers flew to Washington, D.C. to plead for help. There they met with American officials, including President Dwight Eisenhower. The French requested American bombers to launch massive air strikes against the Vietminh. Unless the United States moved quickly, they argued, France would be driven from Indochina and the communists would score a major victory.

American policymakers had followed the siege of Dienbienphu with mounting concern. The United States had, after all, invested large sums of money in France's military efforts. There also was concern about what would happen in the event of a Vietminh victory.

Senator William Knowland (left), Vice-President Richard Nixon (center) and Senator Lyndon Johnson (right) discuss U.S. aid to France at Dienbienphu in 1954.

As President Eisenhower told the American public at a press conference in 1954, "The loss of Indochina will cause the fall of Southeast Asia like a set of dominoes." (This view later became known as the "domino theory.") Many top officials, including Vice President Richard Nixon, favored sending American warplanes—or even American troops—to Vietnam.

On the other side, several influential members of Congress, including Senator Lyndon Johnson, urged

> "I am against sending American GI's into the mud and muck of Indochina on a blood-letting spree to perpetuate colonialism and white man's exploitation in Asia."
>
> Senator Lyndon B. Johnson
> (Democrat-Texas) 1954

caution. Those opposed reminded the President that the United States had recently signed an end to the Korean conflict, and there was little public support for getting bogged down in another land war in Asia. They indicated that the lesson of Korea was that the U.S. should not go into war without allied support. However, Britain indicated that it did not want to get involved.

What, then, should Eisenhower do? You decide as you answer the following questions.

You Decide!

1. *Fact Check* Why did the French decide to fortify Dienbienphu?
2. *Constructing a Valid Argument* What were the main arguments of a supporter of France's request for American help?
3. *Constructing a Valid Argument* What reasons were there for not aiding France?
4. *Making a Decision* What decision would you make if you were President Eisenhower? Why? Justify your decision using one or more of the Five P's.

The Decision and Its Consequences

In the end, Eisenhower agreed with Army Chief of Staff Matthew Ridgway that American involvement in a major war in Asia would be a mistake, particularly without the help of our allies (and no such help was likely). Elected on a peace platform and having recently ended the Korean conflict, Eisenhower turned down the French request, stating: "If the U.S. were unilaterally to permit its forces to be drawn into conflict in Indochina and in a succession of Asian wars, the end result would be to drain off our resources and to weaken our overall defense situation." On May 7, 1954, Dienbienphu fell to the Vietminh. France's seven-and-a-half-year effort to regain its former colony had ended in bloody defeat.

In the Footsteps of Genghis Khan

There, where a French legionnaire
once walked patrol
around the flightline perimeter of the airfield
at Nha Trang,
ten years later I walked,
an American expeditionary forces
soldier on night guard duty
at Nha Trang,
occupied even earlier,
twenty years before
(a year more than my nineteen),
by the Japanese.

Unhaunted by the ghosts, living and dead
among us
in the red tile-roofed French barracks
or listening in on the old Japanese telephone line
to Saigon,
we went about our military duties,
setting up special forces headquarters
where once a French Foreign Legion post had been,
oblivious to the irony
of Americans walking in the footsteps
of Genghis Khan.

Unencumbered by history,
our own or that of 13th-century Mongol armies
long since fled or buried
by the Vietnamese,
in Nha Trang, in 1962, we just did our jobs:
replacing kepis with berets, "Ah so!" with "Gawd!
Damn!"

—**Jan Barry**

Honoring
the Geneva Accords

On the same day the red flag of the Vietminh went up over the former French command bunker at Dienbienphu, delegates from the nine nations involved in the wars in Asia assembled in Geneva, Switzerland. Their task was to find permanent peace settlements for Korea and Vietnam, both geographically divided by revolutions.

No settlement was found to the Korean situation. In fact, that country still is divided. As for Vietnam, the conference did worse, creating new problems.

The Geneva Conference was held under clouds of mistrust. The heads of the French and Vietminh delegations refused to speak with one another. The Vietminh were deeply suspicious of the motives of the Chinese. John Foster Dulles, the American Secretary of State, made headlines by pointedly refusing even to shake the hand of China's delegate, Zhou Enlai.

In this atmosphere, two key decisions were made. The first was a cease-fire agreement between the French and the Vietminh. In order to separate the two sides, a partition line was drawn at the seventeenth parallel, roughly dividing Vietnam in half. The French forces were to be regrouped south of the line, while the Vietminh were to assemble in the north. The U.S. did much to encourage and assist migration to the south.

Partition was seen by the delegates as a temporary measure designed to halt the fighting by separating the two sides. Elections to unify Vietnam would follow. After much haggling, France and the Vietminh agreed that in July 1956, free general elections would be held by secret ballot, under international supervision. The purpose of the elections was to choose a government for Vietnam as a whole. The United States and South Vietnam did not actually sign this agreement. However, the U.S. observer in attendance read a statement in which the U.S. endorsed the principle of a free election and pledged not to interfere with its implementation.

As both sides began withdrawing their forces north and south of the partition lines, the election question loomed large in the future. As a participant at Geneva, the United States found itself in a dilemma. In principle, the United States, as the world's leading democracy, favors free elections. Nevertheless, the best intelligence showed that Ho Chi Minh was the strong favorite to win the presidency of a unified Vietnam. A CIA intelligence estimate on August 3, 1954, stated that "If the scheduled national elections are held in July, 1956, and if the Vietminh does not prejudice its political prospects, the Vietminh will almost surely win."

The Joint Chiefs of Staff, in a memorandum on March 12, 1954, to the Secretary of Defense, had reached the same conclusion. "Current intelligence leads the Joint Chiefs of Staff to the belief," they wrote, "that a settlement based upon free election would [result] in the almost certain loss of the Associated States [South Vietnam, Laos, Cambodia] to communist control." President Eisenhower was advised that Ho's share of the vote could go as high as 80 percent.

What position, then, was the United States to take on the question of elections? You decide as you answer these questions.

You Decide!

1. *Fact Check*   What were the two main agreements reached at Geneva?

2. *Making A Decision*   If you were President Eisenhower and intelligence estimates showed that the Vietminh were likely to win free election in Vietnam, what would you do? Would you encourage the elections to go forward, or would you try to halt them? What part did the Five P's play in your decision?

The Decision and Its Consequences

The United States strongly backed the position of Ngo Dinh Diem, head of the new government in southern Vietnam, in rejecting all agreements made in Geneva. Diem had no intention of participating in his own downfall. However, he was able to stick with his refusal only because the United States backed him up. A National Security Council Policy Statement on August 20, 1954, stated clearly that the U.S. position was "to prevent a communist victory through all-Vietnam elections." In the words of Secretary of States Dulles, "The United States should not stand passively by and see the extension of communism by any means into Southeast Asia."

The election deadline passed, then, and it seemed as if Vietnam would be permanently divided, like Korea or Germany. From that time on, Americans viewed North and South Vietnam as two separate countries. For Ho Chi Minh and the Vietminh leadership, however, the feeling of betrayal was profound. They were determined to reunify Vietnam.

American Backing of Ngo Dinh Diem

When Ngo Dinh Diem was appointed Prime Minister of South Vietnam in 1954, most observers believed he faced a hopeless future. Having spent the last four years in exile in the United States and Europe, Diem was little known among the Vietnamese people. Many Americans, however, welcomed Diem's rise to power. Liberals recalled his courageous opposition to French rule. American Catholics liked the fact that Diem was a staunch Catholic. Administration figures applauded his fervent anticommunism. They recognized, however, that Diem was widely regarded as the creation of the United States and were eager, therefore, that he demonstrate strong leadership.

Diem surprised nearly everyone by doing just that. In his first weeks in office he survived a planned *coup d'état* (an effort to overthrow a government by force) by his chief of staff. He also faced down a challenge by the many political and religious factions that, with their private armies, stood in the way of effective rule in the south. Fighting raged in Saigon in the spring of 1955 between government forces and the Binh Xuyen, a powerful force of armed gangsters. To the surprise of most observers, Diem emerged as the victor.

Having secured power in Saigon, Diem now turned to the rest of South Vietnam. Taking advantage of a surge in popularity, he called for an election that would oust Emperor Bao Dai and allow the formation of a new government with Diem as chief of state. Rigging the election that he would have won anyway, Diem claimed victory by a 98.2 percent margin. Saigon, with roughly 405,000 registered voters, somehow cast 605,000 votes for Diem. Soon, he pushed through a new constitution giving him sweeping powers. The new president could override the decisions of the legislature in most matters; he could also deprive citizens of civil rights for "national security" reasons.

In order to further consolidate his power, Diem took steps to prevent the 1956 unification election. He ordered police to arrest people demonstrating for the elections or even explaining the Geneva Agreement to others. Diem then sealed the border between the two zones of the country, cutting off all trade relations and postal exchanges with North Vietnam.

Diem's next move was against those communists remaining in South Vietnam. He ordered the arrest of anyone who had fought against the French or who was even related to a former resistance member. Jealous neighbors or corrupt officials routinely denounced innocent people. Tens of thousands were imprisoned. Whole villages whose people were not friendly to the government were destroyed by artillery.

By 1957, most of the remnants of the Vietminh had been crushed. Those who survived retreated to remote areas where they eventually joined with other anti-Diem forces to form the National Liberation Front (NLF). Their numbers and organization grew. The Diem government mockingly called them the Vietcong, a name which stuck.

So complete was Diem's triumph that he paid a state visit to the United States in 1957, where he was greeted with enthusiasm. Already, however, there were ominous signs. Power rested firmly in the hands of Diem's corrupt and unscrupulous family. Allied to Diem's inner circle were wealthy landlords who opposed any hint of land reform.

Diem's land policy provoked widespread resentment in the countryside. When the Vietcong took control of villages, they distributed land among poor peasants at no cost. Diem, on the other hand, made peasants pay for land that the Vietminh had given them during the war with France. Finally, to expand his control, Diem replaced all previously elected village chiefs and village councils with handpicked outsiders. This deeply offended Vietnamese peasants who held to the traditional principle that "the power of the Emperor stops at the village gate." For many peasants the war of resistance against French-Bao Dai rule did not end, but was merely replaced by resistance to U.S.-Diem rule.

Opposition to Diem grew among the western-educated in the towns and cities of Vietnam as well. In 1956, opposition politicians risked arrest for trying to establish parties not authorized by Diem's people. In late 1957, Diem began to harass newspapers critical of his regime. In March, 1958, the government closed down the largest newspaper in Saigon. By 1959, "all opposition political activity had come to a halt."

Throughout this period, the U.S. Embassy "looked the other way from repressive police measures and political arrests unless these led to embarrassing news stories." Privately, however, U.S. officials acknowledged that Diem's "autocratic methods and his lack of communication with the Vietnamese people are a continuing cause of concern." In 1962, Senate Majority Leader Mike Mansfield submitted a private report on Vietnam to President Kennedy. His findings painted a gloomy assessment of Diem's support among Vietnam's peasants:

> Vietnam, outside the cities, is still an insecure place which is run at night largely by the Vietcong. The government in Saigon is still seeking acceptance by the ordinary people in large areas of the countryside. Out of fear or indifference or hostility the peasants are still without acquiescence [passive support], let alone approval of that government.

Soon the Buddhists joined the opposition, staging widely publicized demonstrations against the government. Since the days of the French, the Buddhist majority had been persecuted. During the colonial era the Catholic Church became the largest landowner in the country; and Catholics received the best government jobs, were favored in army promotions, and enjoyed other advantages. Buddhists charged that little

had changed under the Catholic Diem, and protests spread. Then, a dramatic event in 1963 heightened the tension. A Buddhist monk committed suicide by setting himself on fire on a busy Saigon street. An American observer, Roger Hillsman of the U.S. State Department, described the scene and its effect:

> And then suddenly a towering flame. And the priests and the nuns in the audience moaned and prostrated themselves toward this burning figure and he sat there without flinching, and the smell of gasoline and of burning flesh [were] in the air for ten minutes. The political effects of this were enormous. It was so dramatic. It hit the headlines all over the world. It had enormous political consequences outside of Vietnam and inside of Vietnam. People thought they saw the face of Buddha in the clouds.

The United States, during the Diem years, had gradually enlarged its presence in South Vietnam. It had sent advisers and military aid to help the Saigon government establish an army, called the Army of the Republic of Vietnam (ARVN). When Ho Chi Minh ordered immediate "armed struggle" against the Diem regime in 1959, however, fighting in the south spread and the need for more Americans became apparent.

The new administration in Washington, headed by President John Kennedy, appeared eager to help. Kennedy had once described South Vietnam as a "test of American responsibility and determination." Early

Buddhist Monks carrying Thich Quang Duc's remains and pictures of his suicide conduct a funeral procession through Saigon.

in his presidency he approved the training of advisers who would teach local forces "counterinsurgency" methods against guerrillas. Programs were immediately beefed up at the Special Warfare Center at Fort Bragg, North Carolina. The men of the U.S. Army Special Forces, nicknamed Green Berets because of their apparel, learned to fight guerrillas in Third World jungles and mountains. Soon they were being sent in increasing numbers to Vietnam.

By 1963, the year Kennedy was assassinated, there were over 16,000 American advisers in Vietnam. Many were secretly involved in armed combat, a fact carefully concealed from the American public.

By 1963, Ngo Dinh Diem had been in power for nine years. In that time, however, he had turned nearly every religious and political faction in South Vietnam against him. The United States was unhappy, too. Already it had sunk billions of dollars in Vietnam. Still, Diem resisted any American suggestions of land reform or economic development, seeming interested only in preserving power.

With public opposition to Diem at a high point and with the campaign against the Vietcong going nowhere, the United States demanded action. In a pointed hint to the Saigon government, President Kennedy told a television audience that "...it is their war. They are the ones who have to win it or lose it. We can help them...but they have to win it—the people of Vietnam."

Kennedy was not really prepared to withdraw from Vietnam, and Diem knew it. Still, the American administration was determined to apply pressure on him. With rumors of coup plans sweeping Saigon, a major decision would have to be made. Think about this situation as you answer the following questions.

You Decide!

1. *Fact Check* What early successes did Diem enjoy? What were his failures?
2. *Evaluating* In general, what should be the responsibility of a nation toward a faithful ally when that friend has become unpopular in his own country?
3. *Making A Decision* What position should Americans have taken regarding the rumored coup against Diem? Should the United States have continued to back Diem or should it have encouraged his overthrow? Explain your answer, using the Five P's to justify your decision.

The Decision and Its Consequences

In October 1963, Kennedy cut off aid to South Vietnam and told the American ambassador in Saigon that the United States would not "thwart a change of government." When informed of the President's decision, the rebel officers began making their final plans. On November 1, 1963, troops led by General Duong Van Minh ("Big Minh"), circled the presidential palace, while others occupied the radio station and police headquarters. Diem and his brother escaped from the palace but were captured the next morning. Locked inside an armored car, they were shot and stabbed repeatedly. Officials in Washington were stunned when they heard about Diem's brutal murder; Kennedy, upon hearing the news, was described as having "rushed from the room with a look of shock and dismay on his face."

In Saigon, meanwhile, crowds cheered as political prisoners were set free and as statues of the hated Diem were pulled down. Americans, hailed as heroes for having sponsored the coup, were applauded wherever they went.

While support for the Diem regime was deteriorating, there were signs that Saigon was prepared to re-evaluate its refusal to negotiate a peaceful settlement with Hanoi. However, Washington remained opposed to such an option. A Mission Report on October 2, 1963, by Secretary of Defense McNamara and Ambassador Taylor stated: "A further disturbing feature of Nhu [Diem's brother and cabinet officer] is his flirtation with the idea of negotiating with North Vietnam, whether or not he is serious on this at present. This...suggests a possible basic incompatibility with U.S. objectives."

Four days after Diem was assassinated, *The New York Times* reported that "President Ho Chi Minh of North Vietnam had made it known that he is prepared to endorse President De Gaulle's proposal to reunite North and South Vietnam." This proposal envisioned "a neutral country independent of western or Chinese communist or Soviet influence."

President De Gaulle had made his proposal to the U.S. on August 29, 1963. It was rejected immediately by the Kennedy administration on the grounds that it "was unrealistic as long as the communists maintained their aggressive pressure against South Vietnam."

In November, however, Ho Chi Minh had coupled his communication to the west with a request to the

National Liberation Front and the Vietcong that they "seek to popularize this program among the people of South Vietnam" as "the only realistic settlement of the war."

Eastern European diplomats, obviously sympathetic to the cause of communism in Vietnam, asserted that Hanoi was sincere in its desire for "a settlement on the basis of the French proposal." They explained that the war had pushed North Vietnam into dependence "largely on China for rice and for other foods to make up for a deficit in production." The increasing rivalry between China and the Soviet Union has led to "suffocating pressure" by China on North Vietnam; Hanoi is "fearful of being caught between" Moscow and Peking.

As a consequence, Ho Chi Minh wanted a guarantee signed by the United States, the Soviet Union, France, Britain, and Communist China that would "not only underwrite the neutrality of a reunited Vietnam but must also protect it against interference—from Peking, Moscow or Washington."

Whether or not Ho Chi Minh was sincere in supporting De Gaulle's proposal is not known. However, if Washington had responded positively, the resolution of the conflict most likely would have been taken to the Security Council of the United Nations. President Kennedy rejected that option.

On November 22, 1963, Kennedy was assassinated; and Lyndon Johnson succeeded to the presidency. Johnson also rejected the proposal for a neutral Vietnam. On March 20, 1964, with pressures mounting for a settlement, Johnson ordered Henry Cabot Lodge, U.S. Ambassador to Saigon, to "stop neutralist talk wherever we can by whatever means we can."

Charles De Gaulle warned that the U.S, could not win its way in Vietnam by force.

The Gulf of Tonkin Resolution

Events in South Vietnam were going from bad to worse. A military council supposedly ruled the country; but its twelve members quarreled and plotted constantly, accomplishing nothing. The well-disciplined Vietcong soon took advantage of the political vacuum created by Diem's assassination.

After a quick trip to Saigon late in 1963, Secretary of Defense Robert McNamara privately informed Johnson that there would be a communist victory in Vietnam within two or three months. He urged the immediate deployment of large numbers of American troops. Military leaders, such as Curtis LeMay, commander of the Air Force, called for the bombing of North Vietnam.

> "Tell the Vietnamese they've got to draw in their horns or we're going to bomb them back to the stone age."
> U.S. General Curtis L. LeMay
> May 1964

Such advice seemed too drastic to Johnson. Looking ahead to the presidential election in November 1964, Johnson knew that a war in Asia would be unpopular with the American voters. For the time being, he would send more aid and more advisers. Still the troubling fact remained that by the spring of 1964, the Vietcong controlled more than 40 percent of South Vietnam and more than 50 percent of its people.

An accidental President, Johnson craved election in his own right. He wanted to win big, and he did not want events in Vietnam to distract him or the American people. His conservative Republican opponent, Barry Goldwater, tried to draw the nation's attention to Vietnam. He charged that there was a war going on in Vietnam and that the United States was not doing enough to win it. In accepting the Republican nomination, Goldwater said:

> Yesterday it was Korea; tonight it is Vietnam. Make no bones of this. Don't try to sweep this under the rug. We are at war in Vietnam. And yet the President, who is the Commander in Chief of our forces, refuses to say, refuses to say, mind you, whether or not the objective over there is

victory, and his Secretary of Defense continues to mislead and misinform the American people.

During the campaign Goldwater said that, if necessary, he would send American combat troops to Vietnam. Johnson, shrewdly playing on public fears that Goldwater was a dangerous extremist, took a more cautious stand. He pledged that "we are not about to send American boys nine or ten thousand miles away from home to do what Asian boys ought to be doing." Meanwhile, he secretly began making plans to deal with the situation in Vietnam.

> "I am not going to be the
> President who saw Southeast Asia go
> the way of China."
> President Lyndon B. Johnson to Henry Cabot Lodge,
> U.S. Ambassador to South Vietnam
> December 1963

Under the Constitution of the United States, Congress has the exclusive power to declare war. In other words, the President, who serves as Commander in Chief, may request a declaration of war, but only Congress can approve it.

This separation of power was respected by America's early chief executives, who obtained congressional approval for military actions. In time, however, Presidents began acting on their own. William McKinley sent troops to China to put down the Boxer Rebellion without consulting Congress. Presidents Roosevelt, Taft, and Wilson followed suit in the Caribbean and Mexico. In more recent times, American forces fought in Korea without President Truman asking Congress to declare war.

Lyndon Johnson wanted similar authority in managing the Vietnam situation. Still, as a former member of Congress, he saw the advantages in getting legislative backing for his policies. During the 1964 campaign for President, he had his advisers come up with a draft of a Congressional resolution. The resolution would allow him to send American forces to any Southeast Asian country threatened by "aggression or subversion." The President alone would decide the seriousness of the threat. Johnson considered submitting the resolution to Congress in the spring of 1964. However, his aides warned that it would lead to a floor fight. The resolution was shelved for the moment.

Events soon provided Johnson with the opportunity to offer Congress his resolution. On the morning of August 2, 1964, the American destroyer *Maddox,* which had been monitoring naval shellings in the Gulf of Tonkin, claimed that it was attacked by three North Vietnamese PT boats. South Vietnamese gunboats had been bombarding the nearby island of Hon Me the evening before, and it is likely that the North Vietnamese thought the *Maddox* was part of the same hostile operation. The PT boats managed to get within two miles of the American vessel and were said to have fired two off-target torpedoes before the *Maddox* sank one of the boats and crippled the others.

President Johnson did not respond immediately to the alleged attack; but ordered the *Maddox* to return to patrol duty in the Gulf of Tonkin, this time accompanied by another destroyer, the *C. Turner Joy*. Further confrontation was expected.

On the night of August 4, 1964, both ships reported that they were under attack. The report was based on sonar and radar contacts and on the questionable visual sighting of torpedoes and searchlights. The captain of the *Maddox* later admitted that he was not absolutely sure any shots had been fired; and, in fact, no evidence has *ever* been presented that there was an attack. Johnson later joked, "For all I know, our navy was shooting at whales out there."

Although reports of the incident were fuzzy, Washington claimed at the time that the American warships

> "We are not about to send
> American boys nine or ten thou-
> sand miles away from home to do
> what Asian boys ought to be doing
> for themselves."
> President Lyndon B. Johnson, Akron, Ohio
> October 21, 1964

were under fire. American bombers roared into action, striking North Vietnamese coastal bases. Meanwhile, a broadened version of the previously prepared resolution was offered in Congress. The Gulf of Tonkin Resolution empowered the President to take "all necessary measures to repel any armed attack against the forces of the United States and to prevent further aggression." The resolution, said Johnson, "was like grandma's nightshirt—it covered everything."

Congress and the American people knew little about

what had actually happened in the Gulf of Tonkin. Secretary of Defense McNamara told Congress that the American vessels had been minding their own business on a routine patrol thirty to sixty miles off the shore of Vietnam when they were callously attacked. He urged passage of the Gulf of Tonkin Resolution to give the President the authority to defend American sailors.

The vote on the Gulf of Tonkin Resolution was scheduled for August 7, 1964. If you had been a member of Congress, how would you have voted?

You Decide!

1. *Fact Check*   What was the *Maddox* doing in the Gulf of Tonkin?

2. *Evaluating*   What advantages would the Gulf of Tonkin Resolution offer President Johnson in the years to come?

3. *Making a Decision*   Given only what the Johnson administration has told you about the Gulf of Tonkin incident, if you were a member of Congress how would you vote on the Resolution? Why? What emotional factors might influence your decision? Which of the Five P's?

The Decision and its Consequences

Congress stood behind the President, voting for the Gulf of Tonkin Resolution by overwhelming margins—416-0 in the House and 88-2 in the Senate. One of the dissenting senators, Wayne Morse of Oregon, predicted:

> I believe that history will record we have made a great mistake.... We are in effect giving the President war-making powers in the absence of a declaration of war.

Morse would be vindicated in 1970, when Congress repealed the Resolution.

The Request for Combat Troops

With passage of the Gulf of Tonkin Resolution, Johnson had the legal authority, granted by Congress, to wage war against North Vietnam. He also had countered Goldwater's demands for action, showing that he could take tough measures in a time of crisis. Johnson would win a landslide victory on election day, capturing a record 61 percent of the vote and sweeping huge Democratic majorities into both houses of Congress.

Reluctant to expand America's involvement, however, he delayed making a major decision. He waited to see what would happen on the battlefield and listened as his top advisers debated what course to take.

Virtually all the leading administration figures at this time were calling for action against the North Vietnamese. Many, like Assistant Secretary of State William

> "It would be a great humiliation for this nation to be defeated by a small nation of 16 million people."
>
> Senator Russell Long (Democrat-LA)
> February 26, 1964

Bundy, backed the regular bombing of North Vietnam. (Johnson had allowed only a one-day attack following the Gulf of Tonkin incident.) The Joint Chiefs of staff agreed, saying that such bombing would relieve the pressure on the South Vietnamese government, giving it time to gain strength. Some advisers went further, urging Johnson to send combat troops to Vietnam immediately.

On the other side, the U.S. Ambassador to South Vietnam, Maxwell Taylor, opposed an American land war in Asia. He feared that the bombing of North Vietnam would lead only to increased Vietcong attacks in the south, ending with direct American combat intervention. He doubted the effectiveness of the bombing campaign against North Vietnam, for the most part a rural society.

George Ball, the Under Secretary of State, went even further. He called for a political solution as a means of heading off further American involvement. "Once on the tiger's back," Ball wrote, "we cannot be sure of picking the place to dismount." Ball found little support in the administration for his view.

With Johnson delaying a decision, communist forces went on the offensive. Beginning in December 1964, they struck government outposts and villages throughout South Vietnam. The government in Saigon seemed powerless to halt the attacks. Its effectiveness was paralyzed by coups and counter-coups, demonstrations and protest rallies, and fighting between Catholics and Buddhists. More and more, South Vietnamese officials seemed dependent on the United States for advice and

Johnson, Westmoreland, Clifford and Rusk

leadership.

The situation grew worse when, on Christmas Eve, 1964, a bomb was planted in a Saigon hotel used by American officers. Two Americans were killed and 58 injured. Now, Ambassador Taylor joined other American officials in Vietnam in urging Johnson to order the bombing of North Vietnam. Again, the President hesitated.

Soon, the action shifted to the town of Pleiku, in the central highlands. Pleiku was the site of a South Vietnamese army headquarters, from which patrols were sent to attack communist infiltration routes from the north. Just outside the town was an American base with an airstrip and a fortified camp where a detachment of Green Berets were billeted. On the night of February 6, 1965, the Vietcong struck Pleiku. Several Americans were killed while they slept, and over a hundred were wounded. Ten aircraft were destroyed as well.

National Security Council adviser McGeorge Bundy, who was in South Vietnam at the time, urged Johnson to respond to the Pleiku incident; and now the angry President was ready to act. Within hours, bombing strikes against North Vietnam were under way. Johnson's bombing programs, known by such names as Rolling Thunder, would go on for the next three years.

As the air strikes began, Johnson was less than candid with the American people about the difficult situation in Vietnam. After the raids had begun, he told a press conference that they were simply a response to the Pleiku attack and did not signal a change in American policy. "I know of no far-reaching strategy that is being suggested," he said. The President did not want to alarm the public; nor did he want to risk Soviet or Chinese intervention by making warlike statements. As a result, the country was sinking deeper into war with few people realizing it.

The air war had another, more immediate effect. With American planes now flying daily missions, the American commander in Vietnam, General William Westmoreland, worried about Vietcong attacks against American airfields. The huge American base at Danang was especially vulnerable to attack, and Westmoreland wanted Johnson to send two Marine battalions to protect it. He was asking for the first American combat troops to be sent to Asia since the end of the Korean War.

Secretary McNamara and the Joint Chiefs of Staff went even further. They urged the President to put the nation on a war footing and to explain to the public the American role in Vietnam. Others held back. Ambassador Taylor, for one, strongly objected to using American combat troops in Asia, claiming that they would be no more effective than the French. "The white-faced soldier," he advised Washington, "armed, equipped, and trained as he is, is not a suitable guerrilla fighter for Asian forests and jungles."

Johnson, who had been deeply angered by the Pleiku attack, was under pressure to act. Consider his decision as you answer the following questions.

You Decide!

1. *Fact Check*   What conflicting advice about Vietnam did President Johnson receive from his advisers?

2. *Fact Check*   Why did General Westmoreland request the deployment of American combat troops in Vietnam?

3. *Constructing a Valid Argument*   What, in your opinion, was the best argument advanced by those who wanted Johnson to send combat troops to Vietnam? What was the best argument offered by those opposed to such a measure?

4. *Making A Decision*   If you were President Johnson, what decision would you make? Why? What part did the Five P's play in helping you reach your decision?

The Decision and Its Consequences

Early in March 1965, Johnson approved Westmoreland's request. He acted, however, without fully informing Congress or the American people. He suggested that the troops were there only to defend the Danang base, even hinting that they would soon be withdrawn. Three months later, when the news was disclosed by accident in a press release, the administration admitted that American troops were authorized to undertake offensive operations.

Escalation

With the decision to commit combat troops to Vietnam, a major corner had been turned. In the months and years that followed, the demand for more troops would be heard with frequency and the word *escalation* began to be used to describe the situation. That is, one side would raise the stakes and widen the war; and the other side would respond in kind.

The request for additional troops came almost immediately. Westmoreland wanted more manpower; and, in early April 1965, he got two Marine battalions. Not content merely to defend coastal installations, the Marines were soon patrolling the countryside in search of Vietcong.

Meanwhile, the instability of the government in Saigon continued. After numerous government shake-ups, two young officers took control in June 1965.

President Thieu (right) and Prime Minister Ky (left).

General Nguyen Van Thieu was made Chief of Staff, while Air Vice Marshal Nguyen Cao Ky became Prime Minister.

The situation in Saigon, along with increasing Vietcong dominance in the countryside, led Westmoreland to call for still more American troops. Late in July, in a television speech scheduled for midday when the viewing audience is small, Johnson announced that he had agreed to Westmoreland's request for 180,000 men immediately, with another 100,000 in 1966.

By the beginning of 1966, there were nearly 200,000 American soldiers in Vietnam. At the same time, the communists were also strengthening their forces. They stepped up recruitment efforts in the south, while additional troops made the long trek from North Vietnam along the Ho Chi Minh Trail. The Trail was a network of jungle paths crossing the most densely forested parts of southern Laos and northeastern Cambodia, leading to South Vietnam. Most of the troops in the south were part of the National Liberation Front, aligned with, but partly independent of North Vietnam.

As the escalation continued, some administration figures began having second thoughts about American policy. Chief among them was Robert McNamara. The Secretary of Defense was troubled by the failure of the bombing campaign to halt the movement of North Vietnamese troops south along the Ho Chi Minh Trail. Doubtful that even 600,000 Americans could guarantee victory, he was deeply aware too of the first stirring of antiwar protests at home. Desperately, he cast about for a way out, even suggesting that the Vietcong be invited to share political power in the south.

McNamara's *In Retrospect: The Tragedy and Lessons of Vietnam* was published in 1995. In it he states that by the mid-1960s it was clear that the South Vietnamese were unlikely ever to achieve political stability or the ability to defend themselves even with U.S. technical support. He notes several occasions where other officials issued warnings that were ignored as well as opportunities for settlement over the period 1963–65 which were sabotaged. He blames this on a "miserable failure to integrate and coordinate our military and diplomatic actions." Several times, just when Hanoi had been told to watch for signs of good faith, McNamara observes it was, instead, subjected to stepped-up bombing.

By 1967, McNamara's doubts had grown to the point where he bluntly told a congressional committee that the bombing of North Vietnam had failed. Viewing McNamara as disloyal, Johnson replaced him with Clark Clifford, a Washington lawyer and old friend.

Many others inside the Administration also were critical, but did not share it with Congress. In September 1967, CIA Director Richard Helms sent Johnson an "eyes-only" memo in which he reported the conclusion of a detailed agency study that refuted the domino theory. In Helms' view, a U.S. defeat or withdrawal "would not be permanently damaging to this country's capacity to play its part as a world power working for order and security in many areas."

Publicly President Johnson preached optimism and confidence, and for the most part he gave the military most of what it wanted—new targets in North Vietnam and more American troops in South Vietnam. But privately he too was troubled. He recognized that escalation was no guarantee of victory. He also feared that if too many Americans poured into Vietnam, he ran the risk of drawing the Chinese into the war. As Johnson and other administration figures recalled all too well, the Korean conflict had nearly ended in disaster when China had entered that war.

As the war ground on, and as 1967 came to an end, nearly 500,000 American troops were in Vietnam. About 9,000 Americans had been killed in that year, and there was no end in sight. Johnson and other key administration leaders continued to preach optimism. Secretary of State Dean Rusk described the North Vietnamese as "hurting very badly," while General Westmoreland said, "We have reached an important point when the end begins to come into view." Casting aside all caution, Vice President Hubert Humphrey pronounced, "We are beginning to win this struggle. We are on the offensive. Territory is being gained. We are making steady progress." Humphrey and the others were wrong; the war was deadlocked.

Throughout late 1967, the North Vietnamese were preparing a major offensive in the south. They had a number of reasons for doing so. First, they recognized that the war was deadlocked. Second, they suspected that American resources had been stretched thin. And third, they hoped to break down the alliance between the Americans and the South Vietnamese. They believed there was widespread resentment against the Americans and that the population was ready to rise up against the foreigners on their soil. Many of the attacks were planned against American targets, including the United States Embassy in Saigon, as if to demonstrate to the South Vietnamese people that the Americans were not all-powerful.

Information gained from captured documents, from prisoners, and from secret agents led Westmoreland to suspect that a communist offensive was in the making. Knowing what would happen—and where—was hard to determine. Expecting the main enemy strike to fall in the northern provinces, he rushed extra troops to the region. Vietcong guerrillas, meanwhile, were secretly moving into the cities and towns, often disguising

> *"I see the light at the end of the tunnel."*
> Walter W. Rostow, National Security Advisor
> December 1967

themselves as ARVN soldiers. Weapons were smuggled in on wagons and carts and even in fake funeral processions.

Tet, the Vietnamese New Year holiday, was traditionally a time of celebration, a time when warring parties would respect a cease-fire truce. This Tet would be different. On the evening of January 30, 1968, some 80,000 communist soldiers went into action. No fewer than 36 of 44 provincial capitals were hit, as were 64 district towns, countless villages, and 12 American bases. For the first time, North Vietnamese leaders had committed large numbers of troops to a single, nationwide campaign. For the first time, they had dared to enter the cities in force.

Saigon saw some of the heaviest action. Over 4,000 troops struck at carefully selected sites, occupying the radio station, bombarding General Westmoreland's headquarters, and blasting into the United States Embassy compound.

The White House tried its best to dismiss Tet. On February 2, 1968, President Johnson stated that the offensive was a "complete failure." Militarily he was perhaps correct, for in most instances the attackers were swiftly crushed, with the government regaining control of the great majority of towns and cities. Also, the communists had failed to touch off the expected popular uprising against the Americans. Finally, the Vietcong, in the forefront of the fighting, had suffered devastating losses. In the years to come, North Vietnamese regular troops would increasingly dominate the campaign in the south.

Without question, South Vietnam had suffered grievously too. Thousands of civilians had been killed in the fighting (many by American bombers), and entire neighborhoods were destroyed. Following Tet, one of every twelve South Vietnamese was a refugee, living in wretched camps and adding to the strain on the national economy.

The greatest impact of Tet, however, was felt in the United States. Television coverage of the fighting had painted a picture far different from the rosy reports offered by administration spokesmen. Most Americans had never imagined that the communists in South Vietnam would be strong or daring enough to attack the cities or assault the United States Embassy.

The shock of Tet came at a time, moreover, when there were growing doubts about America's role in Vietnam. More and more people believed it had been a mistake to send troops to Vietnam. The public had become polarized. Many people urged the Johnson administration to withdraw from Vietnam. A roughly equal number called for an escalation of the war effort to achieve victory. One thing is certain: after Tet public confidence in President Johnson's leadership was severely undermined. (see Chapter 7 for a detailed discussion of the impact of Tet on public opinion.)

The clearest expression of public dissatisfaction came the next month, in March, when Eugene McCarthy, a previously unknown Senator from Minnesota, came within 300 votes of defeating Johnson in the New Hampshire Democratic primary. Just to come so close to a sitting President of one's own party was unheard of in modern American politics—and in the uproar that followed, most people assumed that McCarthy actually had won.

U.S. troops defend the U.S. Embassy from its roof during the Tet Offensive.

President Johnson told a shocked nation: "I shall not seek, and I will not accept, the nomination for another term as president."

The challenge from within his own political party was not the only problem facing Johnson. In early February, General Westmoreland had sounded a note of alarm. "I desperately need reinforcements," he wrote the President. "Time is of the essence." The American commander offered a plan by which 206,000 men would be called to duty, roughly half of whom would be sent to Vietnam by May 1. The rest would be deployed later in the year, if needed, or they would be assigned to other locations.

To meet such a request, Johnson would have to take a step he had long avoided. He would have to call up the reserves (the part of the nation's armed forces not on active duty but subject to call in an emergency). He would, in essence, have to put the nation on a war footing— something he fervently hoped to avoid now that the presidential election was fast approaching. To turn down the request, however, would be to risk defeat on the battlefield.

You Decide!

1. *Fact Check* What was the Tet Offensive? What impact did it have on South Vietnam? On the American public?

2. *Constructing a Valid Argument* If you were urging President Johnson to send more troops to Vietnam, what would be your most effective argument?

3. *Constructing a Valid Argument* What, in your opinion, is the best argument for *not* sending additional troops to Vietnam?

4. *Making a Decision* If you were President Johnson, what decision would you make concerning the troop requests? What part did the Five P's play in your decision?

The Decision and Its Consequences

Greatly influenced by the advice of his new Secretary of Defense, Clark Clifford, Johnson informed Westmoreland that we would send him just 13,500 troops, and no more. Then, in a television speech on the night of March 31, 1968, he announced a bombing halt over most of North Vietnam. He also offered to open negotiations with the communists. Finally, the man who just four years earlier had won one of the greatest electoral victories in the nation's history, announced in his closing words that he would not seek re-election.

Richard Nixon and the Vietnam War

Barely ten weeks after Johnson's surprise announcement, Vietnam became this country's longest war— longer than the Revolutionary War, the Civil War, World Wars I and II, or Korea. Ever since December 22, 1961, when an army private was killed by Vietcong bullets in a Mekong Delta ambush, Americans had been fighting and dying in Vietnam. And the fighting was by no means over. Johnson's departure from the White House in 1969 did not, as it turned out, bring peace to Southeast Asia. The war dragged on for four long years. Despite Nixon's campaign claim to have a "secret plan" to end the war, millions more were to become casualties before he was willing to concede defeat.

When Richard Nixon came to the White House, he was determined to break new ground in foreign policy. Both he and his National Security Adviser, Henry Kissinger, agreed that the administration was limited in what it could do in Vietnam. Recognizing the impact of Tet on the American people, and hoping to open talks with both China and the Soviet Union, they sought a negotiated settlement to bring an "honorable" end to the war.

To reach such a settlement, Nixon and Kissinger believed that more force would pressure the North Vietnamese into making concessions at the on-going peace talks in Paris. For Nixon this was crucial, for he did not want to abandon South Vietnam completely.

To get the North Vietnamese to negotiate seriously, Nixon was determined "to do something on the military front, something they will understand." Not wanting to sabotage the peace talks by resuming the bombing of North Vietnam, he turned to Cambodia.

For years the Vietnamese communists had made

> *"Those who have had a chance for four years and could not produce peace should not be given another chance."*
>
> President Richard M. Nixon
> October 1969

good use of those areas of Cambodia closest to South Vietnam. Communist forces would routinely attack targets in South Vietnam and then retreat across the border to safety in Cambodia.

Now, late in February, 1969, Nixon agreed to the bombing of Cambodia. The raids, which would continue for fourteen months, were carried out in secrecy. Neither Congress nor even the Secretary of the Air Force or the Air Force Chief of Staff were informed.

The North Vietnamese delegates at the peace talks that had begun in Paris did not acknowledge the bombing of Cambodia. To do so would have been to admit that their troops were in that nation, a fact they had always denied. The peace talks dragged on, with the communists knowing that time was on their side.

Meanwhile, under intense domestic pressure to wind down the war, the Nixon administration announced a plan that came to be called Vietnamization. Under this plan, the size of the South Vietnamese armed forces was to be enlarged from about 850,000 men to more than one million. In addition, the United States would turn over to South Vietnam huge quantities of military equipment. As the South Vietnamese army was enlarged and strengthened, American combat forces were scheduled to be pulled out. Finally, a shield of American B-52s and other planes was made available in case of communist attacks.

Vietnamization went slowly at first and Henry Kissinger, for one, had doubts about the whole program. He was convinced that the American

troops served as a useful bargaining chip at the Paris peace talks. Frustrated that those talks continued to go nowhere, Kissinger now called for "savage punishment" against the North.

The administration was also under increasing pressure at home. Across the country, antiwar activists were planning a series of peaceful protest rallies called moratoriums (that is, a halt to "business as usual"). The first moratorium, held on October 5, 1969, drew an estimated one million people in Washington, New York, San Francisco, and cities across America. Nationwide, church bells tolled, while the names of American dead were read at candlelight services. A month later, even larger crowds gathered, demanding an end to the war.

As 1969 came to an end, the Nixon administration tried to paint an optimistic picture. More than 100,000 Americans had been brought home, with another 150,000 planned to be withdrawn in 1970. Under the Central Intelligence Agency's controversial Phoenix program, as many as 60,000 Vietcong organizers were killed.

For the communist guerrillas, weakened by Phoenix and by the devastating American bombing, victory on the battlefield remained a distant dream. Still, Nixon remained under constant pressure to reach an end to the conflict. Looking for a way to shorten the war, he again turned to Cambodia.

Ever since American bombers had begun to hit Cambodia, the situation there had grown worse. To avoid the American bombs, the North Vietnamese had

> *"I'm not going to be the first American president who loses a war."*
>
> President Richard M. Nixon
> October 1969

moved deeper into Cambodian territory. They had also begun to organize and train bands of Cambodian communists known as the Khmer Rouge.

Cambodian military officers, for their part, were growing restless. Many wished to do more to evict the North Vietnamese and the Khmer Rouge from their territory. Led by General Lon Nol, they overthrew the Cambodian leader, Prince Sihanouk, in March 1970, while he was out of the country.

Following Sihanouk's ouster, the country fell into chaos. Communist troops began pushing back the Cambodian army and Lon Nol, at the suggestion of American officials in Cambodia, pleaded with Washington for help. On April 14, 1970, eight days before announcing to the American public that "we finally have in sight the just peace we are seeking," Nixon received Lon Nol's message. Soon, administration figures were debating several plans, including the boldest—an American invasion of Cambodia.

You Decide!

1. *Fact Check*   Why was Cambodia important to the communists fighting in South Vietnam?

2. *Fact Check*   For what reasons did President Nixon consider taking action against communist forces in Cambodia?

3. *Analyzing*   List the possible steps that Nixon might have taken in Cambodia.

4. *Making a Decision*   If you were Nixon, what step, if any, would you take in Cambodia? Why? Which of Five P's played a part in your decision?

The Decision and Its Consequences

On the evening of April 30, 1970, Nixon announced in a televised address that American and South Vietnamese troops had been ordered into Cambodia to destroy enemy supply depots and camps. According to Nixon, this "incursion," as he called it, would shorten the war and save American lives. He painted the situation as one in which America's prestige had been challenged, saying: *rhetoric, semantics.*

> If when the chips are down, the world's most powerful nation, the United States of America, acts like a pitiful helpless giant, the forces of totalitarianism and anarchy will threaten free nations and free institutions throughout the world.

The invasion, however, was a disappointment. Although huge amounts of supplies were destroyed, North Vietnam was able to replace them in the months that followed. Meanwhile, the United States found itself responsible for the shaky regime of Lon Nol. Even worse, the response to Nixon's apparent widening of the war—when it was supposedly winding down—was bitter. Hundreds of college campuses exploded in protest. The demonstrations spread after the killing by national guardsmen of four youths—two demonstrators and two passers-by—on the campus of Kent State University in Ohio. A commission, named by the President to study the tense domestic situation, later found the split in American society to be "as deep as any since the Civil War" and argued that "nothing is more important than an end to the war."

American Withdrawal

The passionate outbursts that followed the invasion of Cambodia stirred Congress to action. On June 24, 1970, the Senate voted overwhelmingly to repeal the Gulf of Tonkin Resolution. A congressional amendment passed in that same year also banned the use of American ground troops in Cambodia or Laos. These votes, while symbolic of the erosion of support for the war, did not actually constrain the Nixon administration's conduct of the war.

As the fighting continued into 1971, intelligence reports indicated that the North Vietnamese were planning yet another big offensive. To block the expected influx of troops and supplies from the north, military commanders in Saigon decided on a surprise move. They would cut the Ho Chi Minh Trail by invading Laos. The invasion of Laos, which would be carried out by South Vietnamese forces with American air support, would be the first real test of Vietnamization.

An inexperienced force of some 30,000 South Vietnamese began a cautious advance into Laos on February 8, 1971. After the first ARVN units reached the Laotian town of Tchepone, the North Vietnamese launched a massive counter-attack. The ARVN began a withdrawal which soon turned into a rout. Photographs of the retreat showed desperate ARVN soldiers pushing their way onto helicopters that had been sent in to remove the wounded. Some soldiers even dangled from the landing gear of the departing choppers.

The Laotion setback was a major disappointment to military leaders in Washington and Saigon. And again, the response in the United States was furious, with big demonstrations protesting this latest expansion of the war. Nixon, who announced in a televised speech a few weeks after the Laotion disaster that Vietnamization had "succeeded," recognized in private that the South Vietnamese army simply was not capable of taking over the fighting.

The Laotian invasion also hastened a problem that had recently come to the attention of military commanders—the rapid decline in morale of the American troops still in South Vietnam. Throughout the war, Americans in Vietnam had fought well. But now, with troops being sent home under the Vietnamization program, no one wanted to be the last to die in a cause that had clearly lost its meaning. Orders were questioned or disobeyed, and in some cases troops flatly refused to fight. There was even a growing number of incidents called fragging—the attempted murder of officers with fragmentation grenades.

Many troops turned to drugs, and by 1971 the Defense Department estimated that 28 percent of all American troops in Vietnam had experimented with heroin or opium. In that year, four times as many soldiers required treatment for serious drug abuse as did those undergoing hospital treatment for combat wounds.

Morale problems gripped the officer corps too. Many, feeling betrayed by the withdrawal policy, resigned or only halfheartedly went through their paces. A major summed up the feeling of his fellow officers:

> We won the war, that's what kills us. We fought the North Vietnamese to a standstill and bolstered the South Vietnamese army and government. But we can't persuade anybody of that.

Morale both in the field and at home was also affected by the publication in *The New York Times*, beginning in June 1971, of excerpts from what were called the Pentagon Papers. This was a secret study, commissioned in 1967 by Robert McNamara, of the role of the United States in Vietnam. Daniel Ellsberg, who had worked on the report, had given it to the *Times*.

The huge collection of confidential government memos seemed to bolster administration critics who had long argued that the American public had been continually deceived about the real situation in Vietnam. Nixon, who feared that the publication of secret information would harm national security, tried to stop the *Times* from publishing further extracts. The Supreme Court, which heard the case, refused to intervene and allowed the Pentagon Papers to be published.

There were not many Americans left in Vietnam by 1972. Of the 70,000 troops remaining, just 6,000 were combat troops and their activities were restricted. The North Vietnamese seized the opportunity to launch another all-out offensive.

On March 30, 1972, more than 120,000 North Vietnamese troops, supported by Vietcong guerrillas, attacked locations throughout South Vietnam. The next day, Nixon ordered American aircraft to start massive raids against the North. A month later, he informed the nation that he had ordered a naval blockade of North Vietnam and the mining of Haiphong harbor.

"We believe that peace is at hand."
Henry Kissinger, U.S. Secretary of State
October, 1972

The air attacks took a heavy toll, and even though the communists made significant gains in the south, by the end of the summer they had been badly battered. Meanwhile, with a presidential election approaching in the United States, it appeared that Nixon was assured a big victory over his Democratic opponent, George McGovern, an antiwar Senator from South Dakota. For these reasons, the North Vietnamese decided to call off the attacks and compromise with the Americans. For the time being, they withdrew one of their main demands—the removal from office of the South Vietnamese President, Nguyen Van Thieu. A settlement seemed near.

Beginning in late September, 1972, Henry Kissinger and Le Duc Tho, the North Vietnamese negotiator, met for several weeks in Paris. Le Duc Tho proposed a plan under which North Vietnamese troops would be permitted to remain in South Vietnam after a cease-fire had been signed. In addition, a coalition government would

Henry Kissinger
and North Vietnamese
Politiburo member
Le Duc Tho sit across
from one another as they
initial the Vietnam
Peace Agreement.

be established with the task of arranging for elections.

In October, just before the American presidential elections, Kissinger dramatically told reporters that "We believe peace is at hand. We believe an agreement is within sight." The American public, amidst general relief, took this statement to mean that the Vietnam War was over. Nixon went on to win the election, scoring an easy victory over McGovern.

Kissinger's announcement, which had been intended to speed settlement, soon proved premature. The United States, which seemed ready to go along with the proposal, had not counted on the resistance of President Thieu to it. Deeply mistrustful of the North Vietnamese, Thieu feared that such an arrangement was simply the first step to a communist take-over. The South Vietnamese insisted on sixty new amendments to the agreement. Le Duc Tho left Paris in mid-December, suspending the talks.

Nixon, frustrated and furious because an agreement had seemed so near, now ordered preparation for massive raids on Hanoi to force the North Vietnamese back to the bargaining table. Fifty thousand tons of bombs were dropped in the controversial raids, which went on for twelve days in late December. Known as the Christmas bombing (though no aircraft actually flew on Christmas day), the attacks devastated their military targets. They also demonstrated to President Thieu that

→ but it was Thieu's fault!

the United States would make good on its promise to punish the North Vietnamese if they violated any settlement. *→ but no settlement was violated!*

The U.S. suffered the loss of many planes, but the Christmas bombing probably forced the North Vietnamese to agree to reopen negotiations in Paris. Meetings resumed early in January 1973 with both sides now convinced of the other's determination to reach an agreement. Within a short time the war was settled on terms that were little different from Le Duc Tho's earlier proposal. At the formal signing ceremony on January 27, 1973, the parties agreed to (1) a cease-fire, with communist and South Vietnamese forces holding the areas they occupied at the time of the agreement; (2) the withdrawal from Vietnam of all American troops; (3) and the release of all American prisoners of war (POWs) held in North Vietnam. With the signing, Nixon announced, "We have finally achieved peace with honor." *erm...*

Under the terms of the Paris settlement, about 150,000 North Vietnamese troops were allowed to stay in South Vietnam. It was clearly a matter of time before fighting broke out again, as the government of Nguyen Van Thieu well knew.

Thieu had placed great stock in a private assurance from President Nixon that the United States would "respond with full force should the settlement be violated by North Vietnam." But Congress, sick to death of Vietnam and eager to reclaim a role in directing American foreign policy, began taking measures of its own. On June 4, 1973, Congress passed a bill that blocked funds for any United States military activity in Indochina. Then, later in the year, it passed the War Powers Act, overriding Nixon's veto. The measure requires the Chief Executive to inform Congress within 48 hours of the deployment of American military forces abroad. If Congress does not approve the deployment within 60 days, the troops must be withdrawn.

Gerald Ford, who became President in 1974 when Richard Nixon resigned from office, urged Congress to increase military aid to South Vietnam. Instead, Congress began cutting back on aid, slashing a $1 billion appropriation in September, 1974, to $724 million. Ford promised to support Thieu, but there appeared to be less and less that he could do. The aid cuts, meanwhile, had a devastating impact on South Vietnamese morale.

South Vietnam's days were clearly numbered. As the communists strengthened their forces and made plans for the coming struggle, Thieu's government in Saigon wrestled ineffectively with problems of unemployment, corruption, and inflation. With the public uneasy, Buddhist demonstrators, long quiet, once again began marching against the government.

In early 1975 the North Vietnamese began cautious probes against government positions. To their surprise they scored easy victories, meeting weak resistance from the South Vietnamese. Seeing no threat of renewed American intervention, they decided to push ahead, and soon South Vietnam was on the verge of collapse. Hundreds of thousands of panic-stricken refugees joined retreating soldiers as they jammed roads and fled toward the coast or toward Saigon.

Every night, television newscasts in the United States showed viewers the chaotic scenes from South Vietnam. The desperate situation affected Americans in different ways. Some, who believed the South Vietnamese government to be hopelessly corrupt and inefficient, welcomed what appeared to be its speedy collapse. Others were shocked that an ally, which the United States had promised to support, was being abandoned.

President Thieu pleaded with the United States for a big increase in military and economic aid to his country. Gerald Ford, noting that the United States had already spent $150 billion in Vietnam, urged Congress to give Thieu $722 million in emergency military assistance, arguing that the amount requested was, by comparison, "relatively small." Congress was suddenly faced with a major decision.

You Decide!

1. *Fact Check* What were the terms of the Paris peace settlement?
2. *Fact Check* Why did the South Vietnamese request emergency support from the United States in 1975?
3. *Making a Decision* If you were a member of Congress, how would you vote on Thieu's request for emergency aid? Why? Which of the Five P's played a part in your decision?

The Decision and Its Consequences

Tired of having to bail out the Saigon regime and concerned with problems in the domestic economy, Congress refused to approve the requested appropriation. It eventually approved $300 million in "humanitarian" aid, but no more.

Thieu called Congress' action a betrayal. The

> *"If the Americans do not want to support us anymore, let them go, get out! Let them forget their humanitarian promises!"*
>
> South Vietnamese President Nguyen Van Thieu
> April 1975

knowledge that there would be no more military aid, no return of the B-52s appears to have paralyzed him, and throughout many of the final, crucial days he issued no orders. Without his leadership, the government came to a halt.

Despite Thieu's charges, it is highly unlikely that more U.S. military aid would have turned back the North Vietnamese in 1975. In fact, in the judgment of Thomas Polgar, CIA Station Chief in Saigon, "there was absolutely nothing that the South Vietnamese could do, short of American military intervention, to restore or even stabilize the military situation."

By April 30, 1975, a North Vietnamese armored column was inside Saigon, speeding through deserted streets toward the presidential palace. Thieu had fled the country just days before, leaving behind a caretaker government to surrender to the communists. After decades of fighting, Vietnam was once again a single nation.

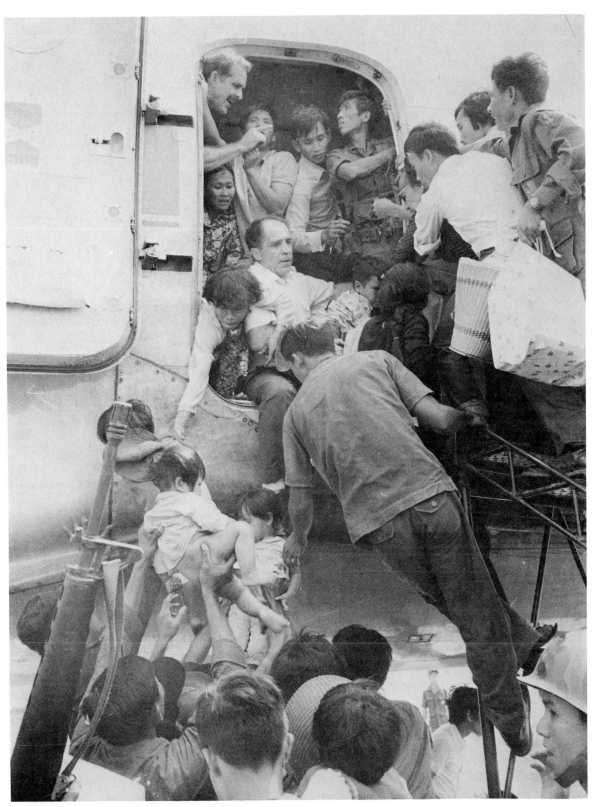

Americans and South Vietnamese flee in panic before advancing North Vietnamese forces.

'Hi, everybody! Look who's here!'

Discussion Questions

1. Which of the Five P's was most important in influencing American policy in Vietnam? Explain your answer.

2. How did geography explain, in part, American concerns about Southeast Asia? (You may want to examine a map of that region.) Consider political, economic, and strategic factors.

3. In what ways was the Vietnam War an extension of the Cold War?

4. Explain the following statement: "The real battle is for the hearts and minds of the Vietnamese people."

5. Choose one American President. Then explain how he used one or more of the following to justify his actions regarding policy in Vietnam.
   - domino theory
   - assertion that no American President had lost a war
   - belief that the 20th century was to be the "American Century"
   - expanded role and power of the presidency

6. Why did Ho Chi Minh look to the United States for assistance in his fight against the French? Considering that he was a communist, do you think he was sincere in his overtures? Explain your answer.

7. What did Maxwell Taylor mean when he said, "The white-faced soldier, armed, equipped, and trained as he is, is not a suitable guerrilla fighter for Asian forests and jungles."? Was Taylor correct? Explain your answer.

8. Should President Johnson have asked for a declaration of war by Congress in 1964? Why did he decide not to do so? What advantages would a declaration of war have given him? What disadvantages?

9. Why did the South Vietnamese government collapse within two years of the United States troop withdrawal? Should the United States have done more to prevent that collapse? Could it have done more? Explain your answer.

10. In general, did the United States back into Vietnam without being aware of what it was doing? Or did it deliberately move forward, ignoring the many risks involved?

Chapter 3   Millard Clements and Steve Cohen

WAS THE VIETNAM WAR LEGAL?

Introduction

Many countries have built memorials to soldiers killed while fighting under their flag. A war monument sits in a central space in many cities and towns throughout the United States. The Vietnam War, however, has posed a quandary for monument makers in this country. One memorial in Nantucket, Massachusetts demonstrates this difficulty. This small structure recognizes the citizens who served in the last three wars fought by the United States. The honorees include those who fought in World War II, those who took part in the "Korean Conflict," and those who served during the "Vietnam Era." The choice of words is quite significant. It points to an important question which lasted throughout the period in which U.S. citizens fought and died in Vietnam. Simply put, in a legal sense, was Vietnam a war at all?

Webster's Third New International Dictionary defines war as "a state of usually open and declared armed hostile conflict between political units (as states or nations)." Was the fighting in Vietnam "open and declared"? How has war been declared in the past? What does our Constitution say about the right to declare and wage war? Who decides if hostilities between nations have crossed the line between an "incident" and war? How much "armed hostile conflict" must there be before it can be considered a war?

These issues were important ones during the Vietnam War and still remain unresolved. Questions raised by the legality of the war in Vietnam deserve our scrutiny. Within a short time after troops were sent to Vietnam in large numbers, many Americans began to express serious reservations about our policy there. Within three years, even

Senator J. William Fulbright, who helped President Johnson achieve quick and easy passage of the Tonkin Gulf Resolution, complained publicly that he had made a regrettable mistake, never imagining it would be used as a declaration of war. The costs of that "mistake" were immense.

Throughout 1987, sensational disclosures of secret U.S. arms sales to Iran and funding of "Contra" rebels and mercenaries seeking to overthrow the government of Nicaragua became the subject of a full scale Congressional investigation.

By April 1991, half a million U.S. troops still were stationed in the Persian Gulf. Some had been there for over eight months. Iraqi troops had been driven out of Kuwait, but Saddam Hussein remained in power. The Middle East remained embroiled in conflict. Who and what will decide whether or not such conflicts escalate into new de facto wars?

Section 1
Historical Background

Legal arguments about when governments have a right to send armies to kill and destroy the property of those they call their enemies are as old as civilization.

Many have argued that killing people and destroying property may sometimes be necessary, just, and even wise. Declarations of war often express such a view. Other people have asserted that killing is always immoral and, as such, always improper for the State to undertake. In general, United States courts have refused to make decisions about the legality of war. The Constitution reserves to Congress the authority to declare and fund war. This means that if citizens do not like the way their representatives vote on matters of war and peace, their recourse is to vote for someone else in the next election. If the electorate cannot wait that long, they can initiate a recall of their representatives. In theory, therefore, they already have a remedy for such grievances. For this reason, judges in the U.S. have refrained from all appeals to decide issues of war and peace.

Political, economic, and moral considerations have clearly affected popular thinking about war. The following documents are just a sample of the kinds of codes and guidelines, rules and regulations, that have been devised at different times in history to deal with the realities of war.

Document Number One

"Thou shalt not kill," one of the Ten Commandments basic to Judaeo-Christian societies, would appear to prohibit participation in war. Making rules about when the Commandment could be broken and for what purpose fighting could be justified has long been a topic for scholars. By the thirteenth century, ideas about the rules of war were clearly stated by various Christian thinkers. One of the most famous explanations of war was offered by St. Thomas Aquinas, who was born in 1225 and died in 1274. Aquinas proposed the concept of a just war to explain why, in some cases, war was a proper undertaking for a practicing Christian:

IN ORDER FOR A WAR TO BE JUST THREE THINGS ARE NECESSARY.

FIRST, the authority of the sovereign by whose command the war is to be waged. First it is not the business of the private individual to declare war, because he can seek for redress of his rights from the tribunal of his superior. Moreover, it is not the business of a private individual to summon together the people, which has to be done in wartime....

SECONDLY, a just cause is required, namely that those who are attacked, should be attacked because they deserve it on account of some fault.

THIRDLY, it is necessary that the belligerents should have rightful intentions, so that they intend the advancement of good, or the avoidance of evil....For it may happen that the war is declared by the legitimate authority, and for a just cause and yet rendered unlawful through a wicked intention.

Document Number Two

The framers of the Constitution of the United States knew a great deal about war. Having suffered under British rule and having felt the lack of representation in Parliament as a major grievance, they fought a war to secure their independence; and they won. However, having experienced the devastation of war on their own soil, our forefathers were very concerned that no such costly commitment be undertaken again without a full public debate and widespread consent. They made the laws of the land very clear about the power to make war. Article I, Section 8 of the Constitution specified that the Executive branch of the government had to answer to the representatives of the people.

The Congress shall have the power to provide for the common Defense and general Welfare of the United States;

11) to declare War, grant letters of Marque and Reprisal, and make Rules concerning Captures on land and water;

12) to raise and support Armies, but no Appropriation of Money to that Use shall be for a longer Term than two Years;

13) to provide and maintain a Navy;

14) to make Rules for the Government and Regulation of the land and naval Forces;

Document Number Three

The development of what may be called the "modern laws of war" is based on the writings of Francis Lieber. Lieber was born in Germany in 1798 where he studied law and philosophy. He became a citizen of the United States in 1832. During the Civil War in the United States, he wrote what has been called the first systematic statement of the laws of land warfare. His thesis, usually called "The Lieber Code," was published on April 24, 1863, in Washington, D.C. as *Instructions for the Government of Armies of the United States in the Field by Order of the Secretary of War.* The Lieber Code has ten sections and many articles that deal with a wide range of topics such as military necessity, public and private property, prisoners of war, partisans, and civil war.

The argument of the Lieber Code is that the violence of war should be directed only toward armed enemies and that the conduct of war must be controlled or regulated by moral concerns. Lieber did not believe that "anything goes" should be the motto of warfare. A limit on permissible violence in warfare was part of his thinking. A sense of his language and argument can be found in these examples from the Lieber Code.

Article XIV
Military necessity, as understood by modern civilized nations, consists in the necessity of those measures which are indispensable for securing the ends of the war, and which are lawful according to the modern law and usage of war.

Article XVI
Military necessity does not admit of cruelty— that is, the infliction of suffering for the sake of suffering or for revenge, nor of maiming or wounding except in fight, nor of torture to extort confessions....It admits of deception, but disclaims perfidy; and, in general, military necessity does not include any act of hostility which makes the return to peace unnecessarily difficult.

Article LXVIII
Modern wars are not internecine wars, in which the killing of the enemy is the object. The destruction of the enemy in modern war, and indeed, modern war itself, are means to obtain

— — — — — continued — — — — — —

the object of the belligerent which lies beyond the war. Unnecessary or revengeful destruction of life is not lawful.

Article LXXI

Whoever intentionally inflicts additional wounds on any enemy already wholly disabled, or kills such an enemy, or who orders or encourages soldiers to do so shall suffer death, if duly convicted, whether he belongs to the Army of the United States, or is an enemy captured after having committed his misdeed.

Discussion Questions

1. What factors had to be present for Aquinas to consider a war to be just? What made war just in those circumstances?

2. Were Lieber's concerns the same as those that worried Aquinas? Were Lieber's reasons for his concerns the same?

3. How did Lieber distinguish between modern wars and earlier ones? Summarize Lieber's articles. Are they easy to understand? Are they complicated? If so, why?

4. What does "separation of powers" mean? Why did Congress reserve the power to declare war? Why didn't the Executive have the power to declare war? What are "letters of marque and reprisal?" Why are they mentioned in the Constitution of the United States?

5. How are military appropriations limited in Article I? Why?

6. Aquinas used some terms which were easy for him to define. Can you do so as easily? How does one judge "rightful intentions" or the "advancement of good" or the "avoidance of evil?" How did Aquinas know what was "rightful" or "good" or "evil?"

7. What does the old phrase that "all is fair in love and war" mean? Do you agree with it? Should wars be limited? Why or why not? If so, how? Who should do the regulating?

8. A Prussian general once made the case that war was

"merely the extension of diplomacy by other means." What did he mean by that? What is diplomacy? Should war fit into a special category of human behavior or is it merely another form of diplomacy?

Section 2
International Agreements in the Twentieth Century

The First World War was a watershed event in world history. The extent of the conflict, lasting from 1914-1918, the global scope of the war, and the huge number of casualties—ten million killed and twenty million wounded—shocked everyone. President Woodrow Wilson proposed a League of Nations to foster peaceful relations in the world. Wilson's concept was the first post-World War I attempt to prevent any such future war. Despite Wilson's strenuous cross-country tour of the United States to gain support for his dream, Congress did not vote to allow the United States to join that international body. Without the United States, the League was unable to stop the numerous border disputes between nations that lasted for nearly five years after the Armistice on November 11, 1918. Nevertheless, many hoped that when the consequences of the war were sorted out and economic stability returned, the League would help mediate international relations.

Other agreements were also made to help keep the peace. On April 6, 1927 for instance, the tenth anniversary of the United States' entry into the First World War, the Foreign Minister of France, Aristide Briand, proposed that the occasion be celebrated by an agreement between France and the United States to outlaw war between the two countries. Frank B. Kellogg, the Secretary of State of the United States, proposed that a treaty outlawing wars of aggression should include other nations as well. "The International Treaty for the Renunciation of War as an Instrument of National Policy" was signed by representatives of the United States, France, and forty-two other nations in August

1928. It is commonly known as the Kellogg-Briand Pact.

The nations that signed the pact announced that "in the names of their respective peoples that they condemn recourse to war for the solution of international controversies, and renounce it as an instrument of national policy in their relations with one another." They all agreed to settle disputes between them by "pacific means." The decade which began with the Great Depression sorely tried the well-meaning words of that idealistic agreement. It did not survive.

A new attempt followed the Second World War. The United Nations was "the last, best hope" of mankind in an era of new nation-states emerging from the collapse of old empires, increasing competition between capitalist and communist superpowers, and the spread of nuclear weapons. The United Nations Charter was signed by its original members on June 26, 1945 and went into effect on October 24 of that year. The original fifty-one United Nations have been joined by more than that number of new members since 1945. The United Nations Charter set up ways in which its signatories would strive to settle disputes through arbitration or mediation rather than armed conflict. Members, however, did retain the right to act unilaterally if necessary.

Document Number Four

The United Nations Charter contains one hundred and eleven articles within its nineteen chapters. As an international agreement, it has had the force of law in the global arena. Selected articles from the United Nations Charter follow.

Article 1
The Purposes of the United Nations are:

1. To maintain international peace and security, and to that end: to take effective collective measures for the prevention and removal of threats to the peace, and for the suppression of acts of aggression or other breaches of the peace, and to bring about by peaceful means, and in conformity with the principles of justice and international disputes or situations which might lead to a breach of the peace;

Article 2
3. All Members shall settle their international disputes by peaceful means in such a manner that international peace and security, and justice, are not endangered.
4. All Members shall refrain in their international relations from the threat or use of force against the territorial integrity or political independence of any state, or in any other manner inconsistent with the Purposes of the United Nations.

Article 33
1. The parties to any dispute, the continuance of which is likely to endanger the maintenance of international peace and security, shall, first of all, seek a solution by negotiation, enquiry, mediation, conciliation, arbitration, judicial settlement, resort to regional agencies or arrangements, or other peaceful means of their own choice.

Article 51
Nothing in the present Charter shall impair the inherent right of individual or collective self-defense if an armed attack occurs against a Member of the United Nations, until the Security Council has taken the measures necessary to maintain international peace and security. Measures taken by Members in the exercise of this right of self-defense shall be immediately reported to the Security Council and shall not in any way affect the authority and responsibility of the Security Council under the present Charter to take at any time such action as it deems necessary in order to maintain or restore international peace and security.

Document Number Five

Despite the idealistic notions of the United Nations and the fact that, unlike the League of Nations, the United Nations had the support and financial backing of the United States, armed struggle between states did not disappear after World War II. The European empires, already shaken by the difficult war against Germany, Italy, and Japan, soon faced incipient rebellions in their own overseas colonies. The Vietnamese nationalists declared their independence from France in September 1945, but soon were forced to confront the Europeans with guns instead of documents. Beginning in 1946, under the leadership of a nationalist and communist named Ho Chi Minh, the Viet Minh began fighting the French for control of their country.

The Cold War divided the world following World War II, and the colonial war waged by the French was turned into an anti-communist crusade. By 1950, following communist uprisings in Greece and Turkey and communist victories in eastern Europe and China, the United States began to send significant military aid to the French in order to forestall any further communist gain. Within four years, the United States government was paying eighty percent of the bill for the French military effort in Vietnam.

While the United States was doing the funding, however, the French were doing the dying. The "dirty little war" in Vietnam, as the French press referred to it, dragged on and grew ever more unpopular. In the spring of 1954, this dissatisfaction came to a head after the French suffered a surprising defeat at the Battle of Dienbienphu. Having lost this symbol of their strength in embarrassing fashion, the French were in a more receptive mood to leave Vietnam before things got worse. A negotiated settlement became a real possibility. An international conference in Geneva, meeting concurrently with the siege of Dienbienphu, placed Indochina on its agenda. When Pierre Mendes-France became Prime Minister of France in June 1954, he pledged that a solution to the Indochina problem would be found quickly or he would resign. Within a month, agreements were reached at Geneva.

In attendance at Geneva were representatives from Cambodia, the Democratic Republic of Vietnam (which became North Vietnam), France, Laos, the People's Republic of China, the State of Vietnam (which eventually became South Vietnam), the Union of Soviet Socialist Republics, the United Kingdom, and the United States. The Geneva Agreements accomplished a number of things. They established dates and times for the fighting to be halted—8:00 AM on July 27, 1954 in the north, 8:00 AM on August 1 in central Vietnam, and 8:00 AM on August 11 in the south. The agreements partitioned the country into two sections at the seventeenth parallel. North Vietnam was to be controlled by the Democratic Republic of Vietnam, which had been proclaimed by Ho Chi Minh in 1945. South Vietnam was led by officials from the newer State of Vietnam, which had been set up by the French in the midst of the war against the Vietminh. Elections were to be held within two years of the Geneva Conference in order to reunite the country under one government. The division at the seventeenth parallel was a stopgap

The Vietminh plant their flag after defeating the French at Dienbienphu.

French Prime Minister, Mendes-France, greeting the Chinese foreign minister, Zhou Enlai, at Geneva in 1954.

measure. In order to lower the risk of fighting between the newly-established sectors, neither side was to introduce new troops or weapons into its area.

The cease-fire agreement was signed by the major participants in the fighting, the Democratic Republic of Vietnam and France, and the Final Declaration was announced by the participating powers. The State of Vietnam and the United States, however, did not join the others in the Final Declaration. The United States had decided that it did not want to be a party to a decision which recognized the existence (even temporarily) of North Vietnam as a communist-controlled state, and which established the possibility of an all-communist Vietnam within two years. Rather, while acting as an observer at Geneva, the United States, under its representative W. B. Bedell Smith, Undersecretary of State, made its own unilateral statement. The United States announced that it had taken note of the agreements reached at Geneva on July 20 and 21, 1954, and had the following comments to offer.

The Government of the United States of America declares with regard to the aforesaid Agreement and paragraphs that (i) it will refrain from the threat or the use of force to disturb them, in accordance with Article 2 (Section 4) of the Charter of the United Nations dealing with the obligation of members to refrain in their international relations from the threat or the use of force; and (ii) it would view any renewal of the aggression in violation of the aforesaid Agreements with grave concern and as seriously threatening the international peace and security.

In connection with the statement in the Declaration concerning free elections in Vietnam, my Government wishes to make clear its position which it has expressed in a Declaration it has made in Washington, on June 29, 1954, as follows:—'In the case of nations now divided against their will, we shall continue to seek to achieve unity through free elections, supervised by the United Nations to ensure that they are conducted fairly.'

With respect to the Statement by the Representative of the State of Vietnam, the United States reiterates its traditional position that peoples are entitled to determine their own future and that it will not join in an arrangement which would hinder this. Nothing in its declaration just made is intended to or does indicate any departure from this traditional position.

We share the hope that the agreement will permit Cambodia, Laos, and Vietnam to play their part in full independence and sovereignty, in the peaceful community of nations, and will enable the peoples of that area to determine their own future.

Document Number Six

The fear of communism sparked the United States to take major initiatives after World War II. The United States stationed millions of troops overseas, fought a war in Korea, financed the French in Vietnam, and spoke out strongly at all international meetings. An additional step was taken less than two months after the Geneva Conference adjourned, when the United States and its allies in the region signed the Southeast Asia Collective Defense Treaty in Manila. The United States was the leading sponsor of the agreement whose signatories included Australia, France, New Zealand, Pakistan, the Philippines, Thailand, and the United Kingdom. The group itself became known as the South East Asia Treaty Organization, or SEATO. While South Vietnam was not an official signatory of the SEATO Pact, it was nonetheless covered in a separate "protective" protocol; so were Cambodia and Laos.

Dulles and Diem, 1956

Article IV

1. Each Party recognizes that aggression by means of armed attack in the treaty area against any of the Parties or against any State or territory which the Parties by unanimous agreement may hereafter designate, would endanger its own peace and safety, and agrees that it will in that event act to meet the common danger in accordance with constitutional process. Measures taken under this paragraph shall be immediately reported to the Security Council of the United Nations.

2. If, in the opinion of any of the Parties, the inviolability or the integrity of the territory or the sovereignty or political independence of any party in the treaty area or of any State or territory to which the provisions of paragraph #1 of this Article from time to time apply is threatened in any fact or situation which might endanger the peace of the area, the Parties shall consult immediately in order to agree on the measures to be taken for the common defense.

3. It is understood that no action on the territory of any State designated shall be taken except at the invitation or with the consent of the government concerned.

Article XI
Understanding of the United States

The United States of America in executing the present Treaty does so with the understanding that its recognition of the effect of aggression and armed attack and its agreement with reference thereto in Article IV, paragraph #1, apply only to communist aggression but affirms that in the event of other aggression or armed attack it will consult under the provisions of Article IV, of paragraph #2.

Discussion Questions

1. What does Article 33 of the United Nations Charter say? What does Article 51 declare? How do you define self-defense? How do nations define self-defense?

2. What was the political situation in Vietnam after the Geneva Conference ended? Who was in charge of what? What was the role of the French in Vietnam after the Geneva Conference ended?

3. Did the United States agree with the Final Declaration of the Geneva Conference? What did the Undersecretary of State have to say? What did the United States say that it would do? Why?

4. Based on Bedell Smith's statements, what role was the United States going to take in that region after 1954? Why would the United States take any interest in that area?

5. Compare the SEATO articles with Bedell Smith's statement. What role does the SEATO document foresee for the United States in Southeast Asia?

6. How does the SEATO agreement compare to the others discussed in this section?

7. Based on all of these documents, how would you characterize the foreign policy of the United States in Southeast Asia in 1954?

8. How do these agreements affect the actual foreign policy of the United States? Do they limit the freedom of action of U.S. governments? Do they make world security more likely? Why or why not?

9. Should the United States make agreements all over the globe? Should the United States undertake the role of world policeman? Why or why not? Justify your answer.

Vietnam Dream

Sometimes still   in my deepest sleep
Someone orders "Turn"   and we turn.
The ship swings lazily   like a log
Caught in a current,   and
The guns point to something I cannot see.

Then someone orders "Fire"   and we fire,
The first shell spinning out of the barrel
Like a football   thrown for a gain.
Where it touches the earth
Smoke puffs   like popcorn.

And then   all is still.
I have been ready now for years,
Waiting the order that never came,
The sneer of cold command,
The Jews lined up at the bathhouse door.

I cannot see beyond that moment
Whether   shaking my head   I turn
Away   or whether   when someone orders
"Kill"   I kill.

—Ron Carter

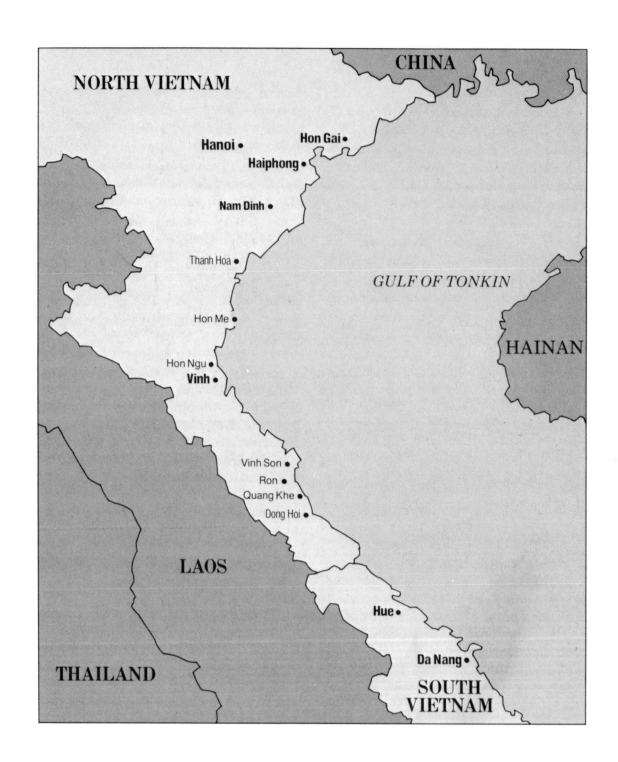

Section 3
The Vietnam War

By the time Lyndon Johnson became President following the assassination of President John Kennedy on November 22, 1963, the United States already was deeply involved in the policies of the Government of Vietnam (known as South Vietnam). Some 16,500 American military advisors were there; billions of dollars in aid had been sent, and millions of words of American advice had been offered. Yet, by the end of 1963, even Secretary of Defense Robert McNamara, an early proponent of American aid to South Vietnam, recognized in a memo to President Johnson that South Vietnam was in danger of "falling" to the communists.

President Johnson tried to follow in Kennedy's footsteps in Vietnam. He wanted to prevent the defeat of the South Vietnamese government of the moment (there were seven governments in office in the year following President Diem's murder in November 1963) but, at the same time, he did not want to look like a war hawk. Johnson sought bipartisan support for his middle-of-the-road course. During the spring of 1964, Johnson and some of his advisers drafted a resolution of support for the White House policies in Vietnam and intended to introduce it to Congress. However, these experienced politicians shelved the resolution when serious doubts were raised as to whether Congress would be willing to pass it. Johnson did not want a floor fight in Congress over the actions of the United States in South Vietnam. This resolution eventually reemerged in August 1964, following the government's reports of a military encounter in the Gulf of Tonkin between American and North Vietnamese vessels.

The White House claimed that the *USS Maddox* was fired upon by North Vietnamese PT boats on August 2, 1964. The *Maddox* was, according to government statements released at that time, in international waters and on a routine mission. To prevent further incidents, the administration announced that the *USS Turner Joy* had been sent to travel with the *Maddox*. On August 4, the United States reported that both ships had been fired upon in an unprovoked attack. The White House declared that there would be reprisals. The attacks on August 2 and August 4 led to the first American bombing raids over North Vietnam.

The U.S. destroyer Maddox

Document Number Seven

The announcement of the reprisals was timed to take place just as the raids themselves were taking place over North Vietnam. Secretary of Defense McNamara answered some questions from reporters shortly after the announcement. The reporters sought as much information as possible about the incidents in the Gulf of Tonkin. McNamara's response presented the Johnson administration's position on the incident.

Question: Mr. Secretary, I am sure there is no doubt in your mind that these PT boats came from, in fact, North Vietnam?

McNamara: There is none. The radar made it quite clear that they were coming from North Vietnamese bases.

Question: Mr. Secretary, can you give us the basic reasons for the Gulf of Tonkin patrol?

McNamara: It is a routine patrol of the type we carry out in international waters all over the world.

Question: Does it have anything to do with movements of junks, or whatever it is, back and forth?

McNamara: No. It has no special relationship to any operations in that area. We are carrying routine patrols of this kind on all over the world all the time.

Question: Mr. Secretary, do you have any idea why the North Vietnamese may have done this?

McNamara: None.

Question: What was the closest, roughly, that the attacking craft have come to the *Maddox* and *Joy*?

McNamara: We have had reports of torpedoes 100 and 200 yards off the beam of these ships. I can't tell you how close the attacking craft came to the vessels, although if they were firing automatic weapons they must have come closer than 800 yards at a minimum.

Question: Who opened fire first?

McNamara: It was quite clear that the PT boats initiated the attack.

Question: When was the last time that there were destroyers up there in the Tonkin Gulf?

McNamara: I prefer not to answer the question other than to say that we have been carrying on routine patrols in that area for months.

Question: How far up do you go, Mr. Secretary, before they turn back?

McNamara: I prefer not to answer that, either. We don't wish to identify the course of our operations in that area.

Question: Mr. Secretary, have there been any similar aggressive actions on the part of the North Vietnamese navy short of the torpedoing that we didn't bother to report before?

McNamara: No....I want to emphasize that these attacks both on Sunday and today...occurred in international waters. These destroyers were operating between 30 and 60 miles off the North Vietnamese coast.

Document Number Eight

Following the alleged attack on the *Maddox* and the *Turner Joy,* the resolution which had been written in the spring of 1964 was resurrected. It was quickly introduced into the House of Representatives and the Senate and was strongly supported by the testimony of Cabinet members. On August 6, Secretary of State Dean Rusk explained to the Senate Foreign Relations Committee in some detail why the Johnson administration sought passage of this resolution. In his prepared statement and in his answer to Senator Ervin's questions that follows, Rusk indicated that this Resolution was an important one.

Rusk: Mr. Chairman, I would like to add one comment to this statement, and that is that this resolution, and this consultation which the executive and the legislative branches are now having in the course of today, will in no sense be the last contact between the executive and legislative branches on these problems in Southeast Asia. There will continue to be regular consultations not only with committees but between the President and the congressional leaders, and on a bi-partisan basis. That has been the practice of Presidents in this postwar period.

Therefore, as the Southeast Asia situation develops, and if it develops, in ways which we cannot now anticipate, of course there will be close and continuous consultation between the President and the leaders of the Congress.

President Johnson meeting with National Security Council to discuss the Gulf of Tonkin incident. Defense Secretary McNamara is seated to his left.

The important aspect of this resolution is, I venture to guess, not so much in the constitutional field as in the broad political field here and abroad. We have, since 1945, been engaged in an effort to bring about a peaceful world situation. The main thrust of that has necessarily been to bring to a halt the kind of armed aggression and subversion and infiltration which have come, both as a matter of doctrine and as a matter of practice, out of the communist world.

We feel that it is very important that this country, on as unified a basis as possible, make it quite clear to the entire world that we are prepared to take the steps that may be required to insure the security of those to whom we are committed, and to bring such aggression to a halt. That is the primary purpose of this particular action today. And we very much appreciate the speed with which Congress has turned its attention to this problem and hope very much that a unified and prompt action can be taken.

We have never doubted the support of the American people for the policies that have been followed through three administrations over a period of a decade. But in the face of the heightened aggression on the communist side, exemplified by these latest North Vietnamese attacks, it has seemed clearly wise to seek in the most emphatic form a declaration of congressional support both for the defense of our armed forces against similar attacks and for the carrying forward of whatever steps may become necessary to assist the free nations covered by the Southeast Asia Treaty.

Ervin: Is it your position that we are now rendering such aid as we are rendering to Vietnam under an obligation assumed by us under the SEATO Treaty?

Rusk: Well, there are several aspects of this. In the first place, the President, we believe, has authority under aid programs and under his own responsibility as President and Commander-in-Chief to give assistance of the sort we have been giving there. Of course, all this assistance that is provided, the tangible assistance, is done on the basis of congressional appropriations which are fully discussed here.

We do believe that the obligations of the SEATO Treaty are both joint and several, and that the SEATO Treaty is a substantiating basis for our presence there and our effort there, although, however, we are not acting specifically under the SEATO Treaty.

Ceremony

The 'copter lays flat the rice stalks
as it first hovers and then rises over the water
with the pilot pulling back on the stick.
The abducted, a fulvous skinned farmer, watches
his hamlet shrink to a tear.

Another Vietnamese aboard, hands bound
behind his back, with the rope looped tight
around his neck, stares with suspicion.

Both wear black, worn shiny, silk pajamas.
The bound one has no shirt over his scarred,
emaciated chest, while the farmer wears a buttonless
US Army jungle shirt, with one sergeant stripe hanging
on the left sleeve. It is permanently sweat-stained.

The 'copter flies lazily 2,000 feet above the paddies.
Through an interpreter, the American Lt.
asks the farmer three quick questions.
He replies with the same quickness. He doesn't know.
He is only a farmer, a poor man with half a crop
and half a family. A poor man who knows nothing,
nothing. Two more questions are asked of him,
    knowing
he is only a farmer and cannot know. And nothing.
One more, with the threat of him being dropped
from the 'copter. Tears of fear and resignation fall.

Without ceremony, he is shoved over the side.
He seems to glide. His scream floats up to the ears
of the bound VC, whose muscles tighten against the
    ropes.
The water buffalo jumps at the splash, and the
sucking mud swallows the crumpled body, buries him
in the ground of his ancestors. The sun burns
in the sky—incensed.

Even before the questions are asked of the VC,
the Lt. knows he will talk. And the VC knows he
will not, because he knows the sun also burns for
him; his ancestors are also below. Already
the cricket's chirp fills his morrow.

    —Richard M. Mishler

Document Number Nine

The Tonkin Gulf Resolution, formally known as the Southeast Asia Resolution, was passed within a week of the incidents in the Gulf of Tonkin. The House of Representatives passed it unanimously, while the Senate had but two dissenters—Senator Ernest Gruening from Alaska and Senator Wayne Morse from Oregon. The Executive branch of the United States government later claimed that this resolution provided all the congressional consent needed for its policies in Vietnam.

THE SOUTHEAST ASIA RESOLUTION
To promote the maintenance of peace and security in Southeast Asia.

Whereas naval units of the communist regime in Vietnam, in violation of the principles of the Charter of the United Nations and of international law, have deliberately and repeatedly attacked United States naval vessels lawfully present in international waters, and have thereby created a serious threat to international peace; and

Whereas these attacks are part of a deliberate and systematic campaign of aggression that the communist regime in North Vietnam has been waging against its neighbors and the nations joined with them in the collective defense of their freedom; and

Whereas the United States is assisting the peoples of Southeast Asia to protect their freedom and has no territorial, military or political ambitions in that area, but desires only that these peoples should be left in peace to work out their destinies in their own way: Now, therefore be it

Resolved by the Senate and House of Representatives of the United States of America in Congress assembled, That the Congress approves and supports the determination of the President, as Commander in Chief, to take all necessary measures to repel any armed attack against the forces of the United States and to prevent further aggression.

Section 2.

The United States regards as vital to its national interest and to world peace the maintenance of international peace and security in Southeast Asia. Consonant with the Constitution of the United States and the Charter of the United Nations and in accordance with its obligations under the Southeast Asia Collective Defense Treaty, the United States is, therefore, prepared, as the President determines, to take all necessary steps, including the use of armed force, to assist any member or protocol state of the Southeast Asia Collective Defense Treaty requesting assistance in defense of its freedom.

Section 3.

This resolution shall expire when the President shall determine that the peace and security of the area is reasonably assured by international conditions created by action of the United Nations or otherwise, except that it may be terminated earlier by concurrent resolution of the Congress.

Johnson signing the Tonkin Gulf Resolution (left to right) Sen. Everett Dirksen (Republican-IL), Hon. John McCormick (Democrat-MA), and Sen. J.W. Fulbright (Democrat-AR)

Sen. Ernest Greuning (Democrat- AK) (left) and Sen. Wayne Morse (Democrat-OR) (right) cast the only dissenting votes to the Tonkin Gulf Resolution.

Document Number Ten

Within six months of the Gulf of Tonkin Resolution's passage, the United States' role in Vietnam had increased dramatically. Operation Rolling Thunder, the sustained bombardment of North Vietnam, had begun and, as bombers flew missions, American ground troops arrived in South Vietnam to protect American planes on American bases from enemy attacks. The ground troops had their missions evaluated and re-evaluated over the early months of 1965, and combat missions, known as "search and destroy" operations soon commenced. American and Vietnamese casualties grew accordingly.

With casualties came criticism. The earliest domestic opposition to the war was small, but the one query which was soon raised was whether or not these actions constituted a war. Was this a legitimate war? The United States government answered these early questioners of the war's legality by publishing a legal memorandum. Leonard C. Meeker, the Legal Adviser of the Department of State, submitted a memorandum to the Senate Committee on Foreign Relations on March 8, 1966. Entitled, "The Legality of the United States Participation in the Defense of Viet-Nam," Meeker's document concluded that the United States' actions in Vietnam were well within its legal rights. Meeker's conclusions follow.

> South Vietnam is being subjected to armed attack by communist North Vietnam, through the infiltration of armed personnel, military equipment, and regular combat units. International law recognizes the right of individual and collective self-defense against armed attack. South Vietnam and the United States upon the
>
> _ _ _ _ _ continued _ _ _ _ _ _

FEIFFER®

SENATOR, WHY DO YOU SUPPORT THE WAR?

SUPPORT THE WAR?! I'M **AGAINST** THE WAR!

I SPEAK IN THE SENATE AGAINST THE WAR!

I SPEAK ON TV AGAINST THE WAR!

I SPEAK TO THE PRESIDENT AGAINST THE WAR!

NOBODY IS MORE OPPOSED TO THE WAR THAN I AM!

THEN WILL YOU VOTE TO CUT MILITARY APPROPRIATIONS?

ARE YOU CRAZY? THERE'S A WAR ON!

request of South Vietnam, are engaged in such collective defense of the South. Their actions are in conformity with international law and with the Charter of the United Nations. The fact that South Vietnam has been precluded by Soviet veto from becoming a member of the United Nations and the fact that South Vietnam is a zone of a temporarily divided state in no way diminishes the right of collective defense of South Vietnam.

The United States has commitments to assist South Vietnam in defending itself against communist aggression from the north. The United States gave undertakings to this effect at the conclusion of the Geneva conference in 1954. Later that year the United States undertook an international obligation in the SEATO Treaty to defend South Vietnam against communist armed aggression. And during the past decade the United States has given additional assurances to the South Vietnamese Government.

The Geneva accords of 1954 provided for a cease-fire and regroupment of contending forces, a division of Vietnam into two zones, and a prohibition on the use of either zone for the resumption of hostilities or to "further an aggressive policy." From the beginning, North Vietnam violated the Geneva accords through a systematic effort to gain control of South Vietnam by force. In the light of these progressive North Vietnamese violations, the introduction into South Vietnam beginning in late 1961 of substantial United States military equipment and personnel, to assist in the defense of the South, was fully justified: substantial breach of an international agreement by one side permits the other side to suspend performance of corresponding obligations under the agreement. South Vietnam was justified in refusing to implement the provisions of the Geneva accords calling for reunification through free elections throughout Vietnam since the communist re-

gime in North Vietnam created conditions in the north that made free elections entirely impossible.

The President of the United States has full authority to commit United States forces in the collective defense of South Vietnam. This authority stems from the constitutional powers of the President. However, it is not necessary to rely on the constitution alone as the source of the President's authority, since the SEATO treaty—advised and consented to by the Senate and forming part of the law of the land—sets forth a United States commitment to defend South Vietnam against armed attack, and since the Congress—in the joint resolution of August 10, 1964, and in authorization and appropriations acts for support of the US military effort in Vietnam—has given its approval and support to the President's actions. United States actions in Vietnam, taken by the President and approved by the Congress, do not require any declaration of war, as shown by a long line of precedents for the use of United States armed forces abroad in the absence of any congressional declaration of war.

Document Number Eleven

Meeker's memorandum had been prompted by an earlier document prepared by the Lawyers Committee on American Policy Towards Vietnam which had questioned the legality of the American intervention. Following Meeker's publication of his assertion that the intervention was legal, the Lawyers Committee invited a group of academic authorities on international law to serve as a Consultative Council for them. Their completed document was published in 1967 and called *Vietnam And International Law*. Its subtitle was *The Illegality of United States Military Involvement*. Some of its conclusions follow.

The policy of the United States in Vietnam has been to use military force in violation of the Geneva Accords of 1954, the Kellogg-Briand Pact of 1928 and several rules of general international law. In the pursuit of this policy, the United States has ever more openly claimed for itself and the Saigon regime the right to consider the Geneva Accords of 1954, which regulate the internal and international position of the whole of Vietnam, as non-binding, while at the same time insisting that the other side is bound.

In particular, the following salient points emerge:

1. The United States claim to be acting in "collective self-defense" on behalf of South Vietnam is contrary to the well-established meaning of the rule laid down in Article 51 of the United Nations Charter to define the situations in which the right of collective self-defense may be lawfully exercised.

2. The United States military intervention in Vietnam therefore also violates the fundamental prohibition of the use of force proclaimed in Article 2(4) of the Charter as a Principle of the United Nations.

3. The United States has refused for more than a decade to abide by the basic Charter obligation contained in Article 33(1) to seek the settlement of international disputes by peaceful means.

4. The United States has refused to make proper use of the elaborate machinery created by the Geneva Accords of 1954 for the purpose of preventing any improper developments in Vietnam. The United States, furthermore, abetted and supported the systematic disregard of these obligations by the Saigon regime.

5. The State Department contends that an armed attack by North Vietnam upon South Vietnam occurred before February 7, 1965, the date on which the United States started overt war actions. This contention itself implies that the use of force by the United States in Vietnam during the four-year period between 1961 and early 1965 was illegal. The State Department agrees with the position of this analysis that armed attack must have taken place to justify the use of force by the United States under the principle of "collective self-defense."

The tenor and logic of the State Department Memorandum of March 4, 1966 provokes a concern that exceeds the conflict in Vietnam. Its manner of interpreting facts and its interpretations of international law pose serious dangers for the future. We consider that it is a professional duty to oppose the acceptance of the reasoning and principal conclusions contained in the State Department Memorandum.

The logic of the Memorandum challenges the basis of world legal order by weakening the foundations of the United Nations with respect to the regulation of force used by nations.

The United States has acted in disregard of the principles and purposes set forth in the United Nations Charter. The United States has abandoned the standards and procedures of international law to such an extent as to imply that "international law is irrelevant in the Vietnam case."

Document Number Twelve

By the fall of 1967, there were nearly half a million members of the United States Armed Forces in South Vietnam. Opposition to the war was still a minority opinion in the United States, but the policies of the Johnson administration were under increasing attack. One of the most relentless critics was Senator J. William Fulbright of Arkansas. As Chairman of the Senate Foreign Relations Committee, Fulbright had shepherded the Tonkin Gulf Resolution through the Senate in August 1964. However, he had changed his mind about the wisdom of the President's policies. He now was convinced that the Vietnam War was a mistake, and he tried to change government policy by reexamining the Tonkin Gulf incident and the resolution that had followed.

In the summer of 1967, Fulbright held hearings on Vietnam. Attorney General Nicholas Katzenbach was one of the government officials who testified before the committee. Below are excerpts of his interrogation on August 17, 1967.

Katzenbach: A declaration of war would not, I think, correctly reflect the very limited objectives of the United States with respect to Vietnam. It would not correctly reflect our efforts there, what we are trying to do, the reasons why we are there, to use an outmoded phraseology, to declare war.

Fulbright: You think it is outmoded to declare war?

Katzenbach: In this kind of context I think the expression of declaring a war is one that has become outmoded in the international arena.

Katzenbach: The combination of the two [SEATO and the Tonkin Gulf Resolution], it seems to me, fully fulfill the obligation of the Executive in a situation of this kind to participate with the Congress, to give the Congress a full and effective voice, the functional equivalent of the constitutional obligation expressed in the provision of the Constitution with respect to declaring war.

Fulbright: They [the administration] did not ask for a declaration of war. They do not have one yet.

Katzenbach: That is true in the very literal sense of the word.

Fulbright: It is quite true, not only literally, but in spirit. You haven't requested and you don't intend to request a declaration of war, as I understand it.

Katzenbach: ....That is correct, Mr. Chairman, but didn't that [Tonkin Gulf] resolution authorize the President to use the armed forces of the United States in whatever way was necessary? Didn't it? What could a declaration of war have done that would have given the President more authority and a clearer voice of the Congress of the United States than it did?

Katzenbach: Now the language of that resolution, Mr. Chairman, is...as Congress knew full well, a very broad language.

Fulbright: Yes.

Katzenbach: And it was explained in the debate. You explained it, Mr. Chairman, as head of this committee.

Fulbright: But I misinterpreted it.

Katzenbach: You explained that resolution and you made it clear as it could be what the Congress was committing itself to, and that resolution provides—

Fulbright: No, I didn't.

Katzenbach: That it stays in existence until repealed by a concurrent resolution.

Fulbright: I not only didn't make it clear, obviously, it wasn't clear to me. I did make statements that I thought this did not entail nor contemplate any change in the then existing policy, and, of course, there has been very great change in it. I think it is perfectly proper to examine the resolution simply because it is the latest example of the application of this problem or misapplication of the declaration of war. But in the question of Congress setting or determining the broad question of waging of war as opposed to the repelling of an invasion or an attack, a specific attack in this case, this is where I think I went astray, and, we did, in making the language much too broad, particularly that portion to repel any aggression in the future, not just this one.

Katzenbach: ....The situations surrounding declarations of war as such have changed rather dramatically since 1789, as a matter of history and as a matter of practice. You find sometimes that some provisions of the Constitution have to adjust, and there are mechanisms for their adjustment in the world around them.

The declaration of war traditionally had the Congress participate in a situation that was rather total, where you were taking on a foreign nation rather totally, not for limited objectives. In the present case, the Congress did have an opportunity to participate in the decision involved in what was in effect a major military action. At least I thought there had been the effort, embodied in these resolutions and in other ways, to give the Congress an opportunity to participate in the functional way that was contemplated by the Founding Fathers, but without the declaration of war, which I think would be misleading and which I think would be wrong in a situation where you have limited objectives.

Document Number Thirteen

President Johnson soon backed up Mr. Katzenbach's arguments. On August 18, 1967, in a live televised news conference, the President gave his reasons for proposing the Gulf of Tonkin Resolution, what rights that Resolution had given him, and what Congress could do if it now wanted to object to the Resolution that it had so overwhelmingly approved in August 1964.

The President's answer was in response to a question posed by reporter Sarah McClendon.

I have given a lot of thought and concern and attention to attempting to get the agreement of the Congress on the course that the government followed in its commitments abroad.

As a young Senator, I recall very vividly hearing Senator Taft speak on several occasions about President Truman's intervention in Korea. He frequently said, in substance, that while he thought what the President did was right, he did it the wrong way; that he should have consulted the Congress and he should have asked for their opinion.

Under the Constitution, the Congress has the right to declare—declare—war. It was never intended that the Congress would fight the war, direct the war, take the bombers off the ground, put them back on it, ground them. But it has the responsibility to declare the war.

Senator Taft thought that President Truman, before he committed our troops in Korea, should have asked the Congress not necessarily for a declaration, but for an opinion—for a resolution.

President Eisenhower followed that policy in several instances, asking the Congress for an opinion. He discussed it with the leaders before he submitted the resolution.

Back in May and June 1964, before the Tonkin Gulf, we considered what we should do in order to keep the Congress informed, to keep them in place, and to keep them in agreement with what our action should be there in case of contingencies. There was very active debate in the government, as I remember it, back as far as May and June of that year. Then we had the Tonkin Gulf.

After the Tonkin Gulf we responded to the action with appropriate measures.

But after that, we felt that we should point out that there was likelihood there would be other instances. We could see the problem developing in that area. So we asked the leadership of the Congress to come to the White House.

We reviewed with them Senator Taft's statement about Korea, and the actions that President Eisenhower had taken, and asked their judgment about the resolution that would give us the opinion of the Congress.

We were informed that a resolution was thought desirable. So the members of the Executive and Legislative branches talked about the content of that resolution.

A resolution was drafted. That was reviewed with the leaders on, I believe, August 4, 1964.

I sent a message up to the Congress shortly afterwards and asked for consideration of a resolution. Some of the members of the Congress felt that they should amend the resolution, even after amendments had already been put into it by members, to provide that if at any time the Congress felt that the authority delegated in the resolution should be withdrawn, the Congress, without waiting for a recommendation from the President—he might differ with them—could withdraw that authority by just passing a resolution which did not require the President's veto. They could do it by themselves.

That suggestion was made to me by a prominent Senator. I readily accepted.

So the machinery is there any time the Congress desires to withdraw its views on the matter.

We stated then, and we repeat now, we did not think the resolution was necessary to do what we did and what we are doing. But we thought it was desirable. We thought if we were going to ask them to stay the whole route, and if we expected them to be there on the landing, we ought to ask them to be there on the takeoff.

I believe that every Congressman and most of the Senators knew what that resolution said. That resolution authorizes the President—and expressed the Congress' willingness to go along with the President—to do whatever was necessary to deter aggression.

We are, as I say, trying to provide a maximum deterrent with a minimum loss. We think we are well within the grounds of our constitutional authority. We think we are well within the rights of what the Congress said in its resolution.

The remedy is there if we have acted unwisely or improperly.

Document Number Fourteen

The key questions remained. Was the Tonkin Gulf Resolution the equivalent of a Declaration of War? What did it allow the President to do? Could the President's power be limited? If so, how? Did the President need any Congressional consent whatsoever?

Even after the President's lengthy answer on August 18, confusion reigned among supporters and opponents of administration policy in Vietnam. Katzenbach went through some rough interrogation from conservative Republican Senator Burt Hickenlooper from Iowa. The issue was: who declares war?

Hickenlooper: Do you consider we are at war today in Vietnam?

Katzenbach: Will you tell me in what sense you mean the word?

Hickenlooper: I am not defining a sense.

Katzenbach: I would say, in popular terms, clearly we are at war there, in popular terms.

Hickenlooper: If we are in a war, how long have we been at war there?

Katzenbach: As far as the United States is concerned, I think we have been in what would in a popular sense be called war since such time as we sent American military units directly to engage enemy units.

Hickenlooper: Which was really in 1961 when we sent large units in?

Katzenbach: I would think so, Senator. It is a very difficult question because if you look at the tradition of this we probably would have committed things that would have been called acts of war before this.

Hickenlooper: I do not want to be nitpicking on this. What I am trying to get at is this: We got into war, in the general sense of the term, by the order of the President prior to the Tonkin Bay Resolution. I am trying to lay my premise here; and you can comment on it all you want to. I may be wrong, I did not know.

If that is the case, if we got into war by order of the President prior to the Tonkin Bay Resolution, why did we need the Tonkin Bay Resolution?

Katzenbach: Senator, we did not get into war prior to the Tonkin Bay Resolution. That is the reason I interrupted you, because the North Vietnamese—

Hickenlooper: Well, what were we in before the Tonkin Bay Resolution? I don't know.

Katzenbach: We were involved before that in efforts to assist the government of South Vietnam to put down an insurgency movement which they had which was supported, financed, helped, directed, and so forth and so on by North Vietnamese. It was subsequent to the Tonkin Gulf Resolution that North Vietnam used regular military forces to come across the demilitarized zone and down the Ho Chi Minh Trail to engage in support of the insurgency movement there, with its own army, military forces; indeed, to invade and to commit an act of aggression against South Vietnam. That came subsequent to Tonkin.

Hickenlooper: I understand it is your contention that the President has the power, did have the power, to order these troops into Vietnam?

Katzenbach: Yes, sir.

Hickenlooper: Not only into South Vietnam, but the bombing of North Vietnam?

Katzenbach: That is correct, Senator.

Hickenlooper: Without the Tonkin Bay Resolution?

Katzenbach: As a constitutional matter, I believe that he could have.

Hickenlooper: That is where the confusion, of course, arises, because the only thing that the Constitution says about war as far as the President is concerned, is that he is Commander-in-Chief...[and] that the Congress has the power to declare war. It has the power to raise and support armies, but no appropriation of money to that use shall be for a longer term than two years....Now, the Commander-in-Chief does not do those things. Under the normal acceptance of the term he runs the show after Congress has done those things.

Katzenbach: I think it is an important point to make, Senator, because they have been doing these things through Vietnam.

Hickenlooper: Yes. Precedent is piling upon precedent until we finally accept it as a fact, which I am not willing to do myself....

In connection with the thesis that the President has the right to order troops into a foreign country...and commit them to battle, without resolution of the Congress or without authority of the Congress, does Congress have the right to pass a proper measure, a joint resolution or something else, to bring those troops out of that country contrary to the wishes of the President?

Katzenbach: I very much doubt that it has the power to do that. It would seem to me that that would be an invasion of the Commander-in-Chief —

Hickenlooper: Do you mean to take the position that this Congress cannot order the American armies and troops out of a foreign country if it wants to?

Katzenbach: As a constitutional matter I would not take that view. I think you raise a much closer question if it refers to support of them under the appropriations act. On that I think as a practical matter it is perfectly obvious Congress can do this.

Hickenlooper: Do what?

Katzenbach: Can get the troops out of Vietnam if it chooses to do it.

Hickenlooper: I am not talking about any round-the-corner operation by withholding funds....We can withhold funds from the President of the United States to pay his salary or to pay the employees that he has. Yes, we have the purse strings over here in the Congress. But I think it is a difficult doctrine for me to agree to, that the Congress cannot control the President...from the standpoint of the use or the withholding of the troops of this country abroad. I simply cannot go along with that doctrine.

Document Number Fifteen

The debate over the legality of the war was not completed in 1967. Nor were the protagonists on either side of the issue satisfied when the administration was forced to admit in 1968 that the incident in the Gulf of Tonkin had not been the clearly unprovoked assault originally portrayed. The *Maddox* had not just been on a "routine" mission but was providing coverage for South Vietnamese bombing missions only about twelve miles away. Moreover, the August 4 assault, the government unhappily admitted, probably had never taken place. Opponents of the U.S. intervention in Vietnam did not rest after the resolution based upon the alleged incidents in the Gulf of Tonkin was repealed in January 1971. For, even with the Vietnamization of the war, and the decrease in casualties suffered by U.S. forces, the continuation of any American military presence in Vietnam still provoked great divisions within the country.

The "incursion into Cambodia" ordered by President Nixon in April 1970, renewed questions of the powers of the Presidency. The legality of sending American troops into another Southeast Asian nation coupled with the Ohio National Guard shootings of Kent State University students provoked demonstrations on hundreds of college campuses across the nation. Twenty-five percent canceled some classes. More than 100,000 people marched in protest in the nation's capital. Members of Congress also were outraged.

Although U.S ground forces were not part of the South Vietnamese invasion of Laos in 1971, American planes and supplies were used in that assault . Talk of a bill to limit the President's authority to send troops wherever he wanted to, while preserving the President's ability to protect national security, led to action. Following the 1973 peace treaty, which removed United States combat troops from South Vietnam, Congress passed a War Powers Act, which dealt specifically with the ways in which the escalation of the number of U.S. forces in Vietnam had occurred. This act limited the Executive's power to maintain troops overseas without congressional approval. President Nixon immediately vetoed the measure claiming that it stripped necessary and legitimate power from the Presidency. Despite Nixon's vocal opposition, the War Powers Act was passed over his veto. The vote was 75-18 in the Senate and 284-135 in the House of Representatives.

WAR POWERS ACT

Purpose and Policy

It is the purpose of this joint resolution to fulfill the intent of the framers of the Constitution of the United States and ensure that the collective judgment of both the Congress and the President will apply to the introduction of United States Armed Forces into hostilities, or into situations where use of such forces in hostilities is clearly indicated by the circumstances, and to the continued use of such forces in hostilities or in such situations.

Under Article I, Section 8 of the Constitution, it is specifically provided that the Congress shall have the power to make all laws necessary and proper for carrying into execution, not only its own powers but also all other powers vested by the Constitution in the Government of the United States, or in any department thereof.

The constitutional powers of the president as Commander-in-Chief to introduce United States forces into hostilities, or into situations where imminent involvement in hostilities is indicated by circumstances, are exercised only pursuant to:

1. A declaration of war

2. Specific statutory authorization

3. A national emergency created by an attack upon the United States, its territories or possessions, or its armed forces.

Key Requirements

1. The President is required in every possible instance to consult with Congress before and after introducing armed forces into hostilities or into situations where imminent involvement in hostilities is clearly indicated by the circumstances.

2. In the absence of a declaration of war, the President shall report reasons and justifications to Congress in writing within forty-eight hours after the introduction of armed forces and periodically thereafter.

3. The President shall terminate any use of armed forces within sixty days from the date of his report unless Congress gives him specific authorization by declaration of war or otherwise.

4. The President is not to infer authority to introduce armed forces into hostilities or into situations where involvement in hostilities is clearly indicated by the circumstances from any law or treaty unless specifically authorized by Congress.

5. Nothing in the Resolution is intended to alter the constitutional authority of the Congress, the President, or the provisions of existing treaties; or to grant the President additional authority to introduce armed forces into hostilities or into situations wherein involvement in hostilities is clearly indicated by the circumstances.

Discussion Questions

1. How did Secretary of Defense McNamara describe the attack on the *Maddox?* What issues disturbed the reporters? Did his statements in 1964 withstand scrutiny a few years later?

2. What points did Secretary of State Rusk make in his prepared statement? What did the SEATO Treaty say about responding to attacks? Why did Rusk think that a congressional resolution would be a good idea? Was it, in his opinion, a necessary step? Why or why not?

3. What was the message of the Southeast Asia Resolution? What were the aims of the United States in that part of the world? How does the resolution relate to the SEATO Treaty? Is the resolution the equivalent of a declaration of war? Why or why not?

4. What did Meeker's memorandum say? How did he defend the legality of American intervention in Vietnam? What legal arguments did he make? What questions particularly concerned him?

5. What did the Lawyers Committee say in answering Meeker? How did they approach the question of the legality of the war in Vietnam? How did they answer Meeker's arguments? Which conclusion did you feel was the more convincing? Why? Does legality matter? Why or why not?

6. Where do Katzenbach and Fulbright agree in Document 12? Where do they disagree? How did Katzenbach see the Gulf of Tonkin Resolution? What did Fulbright say about it? What did Katzenbach say about the meaning of declarations of war? Do you agree? Why or why not? Reread Document 2. Did Katzenbach's interpretation reflect an accurate reading of the Constitution? Defend your answer.

7. Why did President Johnson feel that the Gulf of Tonkin Resolution was so important? Did Johnson think that the resolution had given too much power to the President? What do you think? Had the Executive branch of government usurped the power of the Legislative branch? Did it have to because of the facts of life in the twentieth century? Is the Constitution outmoded

War Powers in the Gulf and Elsewhere

Whatever the course of events in the Persian Gulf, one of Congress's first acts as it returns from recess should be to amend the War Powers Resolution.

There is something wrong with a resolution that imposes time deadlines for completing military actions. But there is also something wrong with one that allows the president to commit tens of thousands of American troops without formally consulting Congress, let alone winning its approval. This is precisely what the framers of the Constitution—and of the War Powers Resolution—set out to avoid.

Both conservatives claim that any congressional participation in the decision to deploy troops fetters the president's "implied" powers as commander in chief. But the intent of the framers could hardly be clearer: Except when the president is repelling "sudden attacks," he is meant to assume strategic control of the forces only after an explicit congressional declaration.

Some liberals claim that giving the president a 60-day blank check is an unconstitutional abdication of Congress's power to declare war, but in theory Congress can cut off funds over the president's veto. In fact, one section of the War Powers Resolution—the section permitting Congress to order the president to withdraw troops from combat by concurrent resolution—might already be invalid under a 1983 Supreme Court decision.

The problem with the War Powers Resolution, suggests Harold Koh of Yale Law School, is not that it's unconstitutional, but that it's badly drafted.

First, the resolution requires the president to consult with Congress "in every possible instance," but allows the president to be the judge of when that is "possible." Second, it requires consultation with Congress before sending troops abroad, but does not specify how many members must be consulted or how far in advance. Third, the resolution permits the president to file three different types of "reports" to Congress on committing forces abroad. Yet the law's 60-day clock for removing the troops runs automatically only after a report of "imminent hostilities" is submitted. Simply by his choice of report, the president can evade the resolution's substantive requirements.

The unintended result of the War Powers Resolution is to reverse the constitutional division of power. Congress, by timid inaction, can cause troops to be withdrawn over the commander in chief's objection. And the commander in chief, by extravagant word games, can commit troops without congressional authorization. But the purpose of the resolution—to 'insure that the collective judgement of both Congress and the president will apply" to the pursuit of war—is sound.

The amendment to the War Powers Resolution, proposed by Sens. Robert Byrd of West Virginia, Sam Nunn of Georgia, John Warner of Virginia and George Mitchell of Maine, would correct the resolution's most obvious flaws. It would create a permanent consultative group, composed of the majority and minority leaders of both houses of Congress and the chairmen and ranking members of the Foreign Affairs, Foreign Relations, Armed Services and Intelligence committees.

The amendment would require the White House to consult regularly with the group, not only hours before or hours after deciding to deploy troops. It would allow the consultative group to introduce a joint resolution for expedited consideration, either specifically authorizing troops or specifically disengaging them, regardless of the president's report. And it would repeal the requirement that troops automatically be withdrawn within 60 days if Congress does nothing at all.

The Byrd-Nunn amendment should appeal to the president as well as to Congress. By removing the automatic cutoff of troops, it removes the incentives for enemies to use the peculiarities of American law as a military asset, delaying their attacks until after the war-powers clock has expired. At the same time, by ensuring an early resolution of support, it buffers the president against national recrimination once the initial enthusiasm of deployment has faded.

If Congress passes the Byrd-Nunn amendment, President Bush should sign it. There has been an odd dichotomy between word and deed in the president's dealings with Congress in foreign affairs. In practice, he has informally consulted with congressional leaders. But by more fully availing himself of Congress's war powers, Bush would strengthen the nation's staying power in the difficult weeks ahead.

Jeff Rosen
The New Republic
September 1990

in this case? Explain your answer.

8. What was Senator Hickenlooper trying to find out from Attorney General Katzenbach? What did they disagree about? Compare their versions of the Constitution to Document 2. With whom do you agree? Why?

9. What did the War Powers Act establish? What problems was that piece of legislation trying to solve? Has it been used since its passage? When?

10. Did the War Powers Act limit the powers of the President as President Nixon claimed that it would? Did the War Powers Act change the Constitution or did it return things to their traditional balance? Explain.

Persian Gulf War

We will learn in Chapter 4 that the lack of a formal declaration of war by Congress imposed significant constraints on the government's ability to conscript many of its best men into the armed services. And we will learn in Chapter 7 that the U.S. public reacted slowly and with caution to the Johnson administration's commitment in Vietnam. Within four years, by a margin of 63 percent to 26 percent, Americans polled by Gallup agreed that they would have opposed U.S. involvement in Vietnam had they known the costs and the casualties involved. The U.S. suffered almost 400,000 casualties in Vietnam and finally was forced to withdraw in 1973.

Casper Weinberger, Secretary of Defense under President Reagan, said he learned an important lesson from Vietnam. In 1984 he was quoted as saying, "If we decide it is necessary to put combat troops into a given situation, we should do so wholeheartedly, and with the clear intention of winning....Before the U.S. commits combat forces abroad there must be some reasonable reassurance we will have the support of the American people and their elected representatives in Congress." These are prudent words. If people believe a war is just and necessary, they are capable of extraordinary sacrifices. However, in a democracy, we must never take the support of the people for granted.

It is the responsibility of political leaders to convince the representatives of the people of the need for war and the great risks it entails. That is why our founding fathers made certain that any such hazardous commitment as war would require a full public debate and declaration by Congress. Moreover, our system is based on the idea that citizens are able to influence decisions on such matters through their elected representatives. The denial of such opportunity in Vietnam provoked serious distrust in the political process among many Americans.

Since the end of World War II, several U.S. presidents have skipped over Congress and claimed constitutional authority as commander-in-chief of the nation's armed forces to commit Americans to battle. U.S. entry into the Korean War was called a United Nations "police action." However, most of the troops were American. We know that Congress did not knowingly authorize Presidents Johnson and Nixon to wage war in Vietnam. Similarly, the U.S. has dispatched troops to the Suez Canal and Lebanon and attacked Libya, Grenada and Panama without prior approval from Congress.

On August 2, 1990, Saddam Hussein, President of Iraq, ordered his troops into Kuwait, a small oil-rich emirate (kingdom) on the Persian Gulf. During the Ottoman Empire, the emirs of Kuwait paid tribute to their overlords in Baghdad. The modern state of Kuwait was carved out of Iran proper by the British in 1916. In 1958, Iraq overthrew its British-imposed monarchy. Three years later, Britain granted independence to Kuwait. Iraq never recognized the border and three times—1961, 1973, and 1976—massed troops on the border threatening to take the territory by force.

In the early 1970s Iraq went to war with the U.S. backed Shah of Iran over control of the Shat el Arab; an inlet of the gulf and Iraq's only access to the River Basra. CIA assistance to Kurdish rebels in northern Iraq forced Iraqi troops to battle on two fronts and led to their surrender in 1975. In 1980, Iraq invaded Iran again to redress its earlier "humiliation" and to "regain control" of the Shat el Arab.

From 1980-88, Iraq waged war against Iran on its eastern front. Some observers claimed that Kuwait took advantage of the situation by pumping oil from Iraq's

Rumaila field that dips into the disputed border area. Burdened with debts from the war, Iraq tried for several months in 1990 to persuade Kuwait and Saudi Arabia to limit oil production by adhering to agreed-upon production quotas. Kuwait refused, forcing oil prices down.

After the August 1990 invasion of Kuwait, Iraq moved quickly to occupy and annex the entire country. Claiming that Saudi Arabia was in immediate jeopardy, President Bush dispatched U.S. troops to defend its border with Iraq.

In the months that followed, Bush rallied world opinion and engineered a United Nations sponsored economic embargo against Iraq. At the same time, he built up U.S. forces in the Gulf to over 200,000 troops, more than enough to deter any attack.

As 1990 drew to a close, Bush talked about going to war with Iraq to liberate Kuwait, destroy Iraq's armed forces, and depose Saddam Hussein as head of state. He proposed increasing U.S. troop strength to over 500,000 to enable him to accomplish such objectives.

Over that same period, many Americans began to question Bush's policy in the Persian Gulf, particularly his long-standing military assistance to Iraq and refusal to sanction Hussein for human rights abuses. On October 17, 1990, U.S. Secretary of State James Baker advised the Senate Foreign Relations Committee that the Bush administration did not feel obliged to get congressional approval for war against Iraq. On October 26, eighty-two members of the U.S. House of Representatives signed a "Statement of Concern" in which they demanded that the administration not undertake any Middle East offensive "without the full deliberation and declaration required by the Constitution."

On November 20th, the Center for Constitutional Rights filed a lawsuit in federal court to prevent Bush from ordering an offensive attack in the Persian Gulf without the prior authorization of Congress. Fifty members of Congress joined the suit. The congressional group, led by Rep. Ron Dellums (Democrat-CA) asked the court for an injunction to bar Bush from an offensive strike against Iraq unless he first obtained approval from Congress, and for a declaration stating that under the Constitution only Congress has the power to declare war.

On November 29th, the U.N. Security Council passed resolution 678 on a 12-2 vote, setting January 15, 1991, as the deadline for Iraq to abide by previous resolutions calling for its unconditional withdrawal from Kuwait or face military force.

On December 13, 1990, U.S. District Judge Harold Greene ruled that it would be premature to order President Bush to ask Congress for a declaration of war against Iraq. In his view, the President's commitment to that course of action was not yet definite and a majority of Congress had not argued that the administration was abridging its power to decide on war. However, Judge Green did affirm that the constitution reserves the right to declare war to the Congress and the courts do have jurisdiction over such matters.

On December 29th, Congressional Democrats threatened to cut off funds for operation Desert Shield if President Bush did not seek congressional approval. On January 8th, Bush asked Congress to vote to support the use of force against Iraq. On January 10th, Congress opened debate on resolutions dealing with the Persian Gulf. On January 12th, Congress approved the use of force by votes of 250-183 in the House and 52-47 in the Senate.

On January 16th, U.S. forces started the war against Iraq with a major bombing campaign. The bombing continued for six weeks, with 100,000 sorties making it the most concentrated air war since Vietnam (See Chapter 10). On February 23rd, Gen. Norman Schwarzkopf launched the coalition troops ground offensive. Two days later Saddam Hussein announced that Iraq's occupation forces would withdraw completely from Kuwait. General Schwarzkopf recommended to President Bush that he "continue the march" to Baghdad to annihilate Iraq's armed forces, but on February 27th, President Bush declared victory over Iraq and ordered U.S. troops to cease fire. Kuwaiti troops raised the emirate's flag in Kuwait City.

The weakness of the War Powers Amendment was revealed by Bush's ability to mobilize and station half a million U.S. troops in the gulf without the consent of Congress; a force almost equal to the peak of the Vietnam War. New legislation clearly is required here if the intent of the framers of the U.S. Constitution is to be honored.

Still, the President did seek authorization to use

military force from the Congress, a decision crucial to the support he enjoyed for the war. Before U.S. forces went into combat in mid-January, polls indicated that Americans were almost evenly divided over whether to commence the fighting or give sanctions and diplomacy more time to work. After the air attacks began on January 17th, support for sanctions and diplomacy dropped to about 15 percent and criticism by members of Congress ceased entirely.

Despite America's impressive military rout in the Persian Gulf, it is clear that the region is still fraught with conflict. Since 1945, the U.S. has been involved in five wars in the Middle East. Today, Israel and Palestine are more apart than ever on any resolution of their differences, the principal obstacle to peace in the region for over forty years. In fact, more Israeli civilians and soldiers were stabbed to death by Palestinians in the two weeks after the war than were killed in six weeks of Iraq's scud missile attacks. Kuwaiti troops immediately began carrying out tortures and executions of Palestinians, Iraqis, and others suspected of betrayal. Kuwaiti citizens were very critical of the failure of their leadership to provide economic relief and commit themselves to desired political reforms. Before the invasion only 40 percent of Kuwaiti residents had citizenship rights and only 60,000 males (3% of the population) were allowed to vote. Although political parties are outlawed in Kuwait, by late April 1991, opposition groups were staging joint rallies against the al-Sabah family's almost total control of the country.

Iraq was plunged into a civil war, with Shiite Muslems in the south (55% of Iraq's population) and Kurdish rebels in the north (20% of Iraq's population) attacking Hussein's forces. President Bush decided to let Hussein use his combat helicopters and other tactical advantages to put down the rebellions explaining that he didn't want to risk the country being splintered into factions and vulnerable to external control like Lebanon. Also, the Shiites were thought to be too closely allied with Iran which has been antagonistic to the United States since the overthrow of the Shah by Muslim fundamentalists. U.S. troops held their position while the rebellions were ruthlessly crushed and hundreds of thousands of Kurds fled to Turkey and Syria. President Bush was criticized for his decision,

but reiterated his desire for a quick withdrawal of American forces. Finally, Bush was moved to set up refugee relief camps guarded by U.S. soliders in order to combat the 600 daily deaths from starvation and disease that the Kurds were suffering. Observers speculated that the camps would delay the U.S. troop withdrawal and could lead to the "quagmire" the President seemed determined to avoid.

Syria's power in the region has been enhanced by its participation in Bush's "international coalition" of forces. Syria has a 400,000 man army, a 370-mile border with Iraq, and occupies much of Lebanon. Syrian troops have persecuted both leftist and rightist Lebanese forces, assassinated key political figures, and engaged in widespread smuggling and drug trafficking. President Hafsez al-Assad has sponsored international terrorism, including the 1987 plot to blow up an El Al jet carrying more than 300 passengers at London's Heathrow Airport.

In early April 1991, the U.N. Security Council passed a cease-fire resolution that imposed a heavy burden of restitution on Iraq while eliminating its capacity to make war on its neighbors. However, President Bush was resigned to allowing Hussein, the man he called "Hitler," to remain in power. The U.S. expressed the hope that, in time, Hussein's own political organization would remove him. The alternatives seemed to be one of Hussein's own generals, perhaps even his son-in-law, Hussein Kamil Majid. Know-ledgeable observers have considered them all "ruthless" and "likely to be just as tyrannical."

During the transition, many U.S. troops remained in Iraq for months. While many world leaders called for a demilitarization of the region, the Bush administration authorized multi-billion dollar arms sales to Saudi Arabia, Egypt, Israel, Turkey, and other countries.

On March 20, 1991, the U.S. Senate passed a bill to provide a first installment of $42.6 billion toward the war effort. In time, this payment was covered by contributions from U.S. allies. The Pentagon claimed a total war bill of $70 billion, but other authorities disputed the calculations. As U.S. leaders and citizens began to reassess the costs of the war, what actually was gained, and the continued potential for conflict in the region, perhaps some were moved to ask "are our foreign policy objectives as clear as they could be? Have we seriously considered alternatives to military force in all situations?"

In this context, it must be noted that the economic embargo against Iraq was working. On December 5, 1990, CIA Director William Webster, testifying before the House Armed Services Committee, said U.N. sanctions were blocking 90 percent of Iraqi imports and 97 percent of its exports. While he felt that the Iraqi military could have weathered sanctions "for as long as nine months," he said the Air Force would have been compromised within three to six months and that shortages of "various critical lubricants" would eventually disable ground units. On January 5, 1991, leading economists stated that the sanctions had lowered Iraq's GNP by 40 percent or more, by far the greatest impact international sanctions had ever had on a country. The sanctions had reduced Iraq's Ministry of Trade's monthly allocation of staple food items to the population by over 60 percent. Whether the sanctions ultimately would have brought about Iraq's withdrawal from Kuwait without the devastation of the war (see Chapter 10) is a question that can never be answered.

Conclusion

Immediately after the Persian Gulf War, Republicans in Congress threatened that in the 1992 elections they would punish Democrats who voted for continued sanctions over immediate force. The sagging U.S. economy turned out to be a more important issue in the elections which put Bill Clinton, in his youth a Vietnam War protester, into the White House. Still, some observers worried about the effect such an offensive would have, if successful, on the willingness of members of Congress to debate U.S. foreign policy and vote their consciences. The abdication of Congress in decisions of war and peace would be a direct threat to our constitutional system of government.

Beyond even that great challenge is that of a world without war. Do you agree with the sentiments expressed in the United Nations Charter? Are they practical in today's world? What would it take to establish enforceable international law? Would this be desirable? What risks might there be? Can the nations of the world ever join together to outlaw war? In a world in which nine nations can make nuclear weapons and two of them have deployed 50,000 such instruments of annihilation, these questions have never been more urgent.

Final Questions

1. This chapter has investigated the question of whether the Vietnam War was legal. Does a war have to be declared? Did the Gulf of Tonkin Resolution serve as a legitimate substitute for a declaration of war? Did the SEATO Treaty make such a declaration unnecessary? Do both of them do that job? Neither of them? Does it matter?

2. Does the Vietnam War fit Aquinas' definition of a "just" war? What does that concept mean to you? Has technology affected the way we think about war? If so, how?

3. Are there any lessons to be learned from this debate over the legality of the war in Vietnam? What are they?

4. Through the 1980s the United States supported the "Contras" in their fight against the legally established and popularly elected government in Nicaragua. Was that a war? If American advisors had gone there in large number, would that be a war? American ground troops? Would the War Powers Act then have been in effect? Should the United States undertake such actions without a Congressional declaration of war? Why or why not?

5. Reread the second paragraph of this chapter. How would you now answer the questions which were raised?

WHO FOUGHT FOR THE U.S.

Who Fought In The War

Who are the soldiers who fight in their nation's war? Who will be the nameless men to serve under the famous generals whose names we all learn? From what cities, towns, and villages do they come? What fate awaits them? Would you become a soldier? Why would you fight in a war?

Imagine yourself an 18-year old high school senior just prior to graduation. The time is the late 1960s and the war in Vietnam is going strong. How do you plan your future? What are your goals? A local college? A major university? A good job? Your own car? Do you have a girlfriend? Plans for marriage? Perhaps you are considering a tour of military service, even a military career. Add to this dilemma of choice the prospect of being sent across the world to Vietnam to fight in an increasingly unpopular war with a rising casualty rate. What would you do?

In this chapter, we will look at the choices that young American males were willing and able to make regarding service in Vietnam and what consequences this had for the composition of our armed forces and the combat effectiveness of our troops. Before we do, however, let us briefly review the chain of events, largely ignored by the American people, that eventually led to service in Vietnam for millions of their sons.

YEAR-END U.S. TROOP STRENGTH AND BATTLE DEAD, 1961 -1973

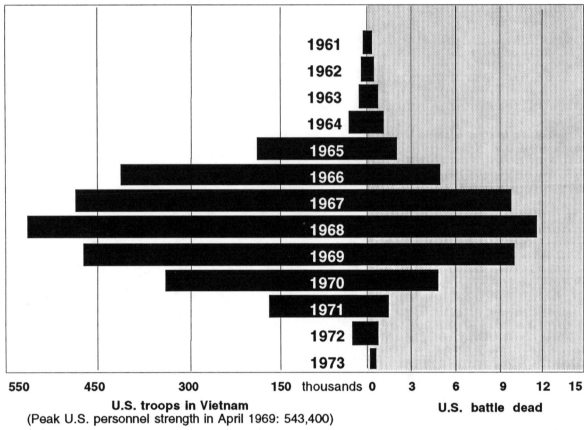

| 550 | 450 | 300 | 150 | thousands 0 | 3 | 6 | 9 | 12 | 15 |

U.S. troops in Vietnam
(Peak U.S. personnel strength in April 1969: 543,400)

U.S. battle dead

As discussed in the first three chapters, the war between France and Ho Chi Minh's Vietminh was settled by the 1954 Geneva Accords. This agreement ended about 100 years of French rule in Vietnam. It called for elections to unify North and South Vietnam under one government in 1956. Fearing Ho Chi Minh's popularity, especially in the more unified North, South Vietnam's President Ngo Dinh Diem refused to permit such elections to be held. He was supported in this decision by the Eisenhower administration. On January 3, 1957, the International Control Commission reported that neither North nor South had honored the Geneva Accords. It was war again in Vietnam.

On November 8, 1960, John F. Kennedy was elected President of the United States. At the time, the U.S. had 685 military advisors in South Vietnam. On December 20, 1960, the National Liberation Front of Vietnam (NLF) was formed and accelerated guerrilla actions throughout the south.

In May 1961, President Kennedy assigned U.S. Special Forces (Green Berets) to Vietnam. Early in 1962 Kennedy established the American Military Assistance Command in South Vietnam. By year's end there were 4,000 U.S. military advisors in Vietnam.

South Vietnam's President Diem proved to be a ruthless and unpopular leader. He had to put down two attempts to overthrow him by members of his own army. During May and June 1963, the Buddhists staged huge demonstrations against the government. Several priests set themselves on fire to express their protest. One such dramatic suicide provoked demonstrations all over Saigon.

President Kennedy assigned the U.S. Central Intelligence Agency (CIA) to consult with a group of mutinous South Vietnamese generals seeking to oust Diem. On November 1, 1963, Diem was assassinated. Thousands cheered the news, but Saigon was still divided.

On November 22, 1963, President Kennedy himself

was assassinated. While a nation mourned, President Lyndon B. Johnson assumed the reins of government. By the time of his death, Kennedy had increased U.S. troop strength in Vietnam to about 20,000. The Air Force had flown 7,000 missions. Nevertheless, the NLF exercised some degrees of control, including taxation, in more than two-thirds of the villages and all but three of South Vietnam's forty-four provinces. President Johnson would now have to decide what course the U.S. would take in Vietnam.

Johnson was advised that defending an independent non-communist state in South Vietnam would take many more U.S. troops. However, the Constitution of the United States requires a declaration of Congress to establish a state of war. It was precisely the purpose of our founding fathers to demand a thorough public debate before such a hazardous commitment could be made. President Johnson escaped this condition by using the authority implied by the August 7, 1964, "Gulf of Tonkin Resolution" to wage war in Vietnam. (See chapters 2 and 3 for a fuller discussion of this decision and its legal implications.) This maneuver proved to be a double-edged sword. The lack of a formal declaration of war by Congress meant that Johnson was not free to mobilize all forces for a total commitment. Rather, he was faced with the challenge of raising an army within the constraints of a peace-time military conscription policy that allowed numerous deferments from service.

President Johnson turned to the member countries of the Southeast Asia Treaty Organization (SEATO), established in 1954 to defend all member states (including Cambodia, Laos, and South Vietnam) against aggression by communist nations. While Pakistan declined to participate, three SEATO member countries did send combat troops. For several years Thailand provided over 11,000 troops, Australia almost 8,000, and New Zealand over 500. Total "third nation" forces reached 70,000 in 1969, more than the 39,000 sent to Korea, but fewer than were needed. They had a combined total of 5,000 deaths during the course of the war. Such support was costly, however. The U.S had to pay Thailand about $50 million per year and the Philippines about $39 million per year in compensation for their assistance.

France and Great Britain refused to provide any military support to the U.S. In fact, President Charles DeGaulle and Prime Minister Harold Wilson actively counseled the U.S. against prosecuting the war and worked for years to promote a negotiated settlement. The only country outside of SEATO to send troops was South Korea. Its contingent of almost 50,000 soldiers was spread across the coastal area of the northern half of the country. Local inhabitants considered the South Koreans the most brutal force in the war. Between 1965 and 1970, South Korea charged the U.S. $1 billion for this military assistance.

The failure to convince most of our allies to send troops to Vietnam meant that the brunt of the fighting had to be carried by American and South Vietnamese soldiers. The government placed a one-year limit on tours of duty in Vietnam to encourage enlistment. American troops in Vietnam increased to 125,000 in 1965, 358,000 in 1966, and a peak of 543,000 in 1969. Thereafter, the number of U.S. troops in Vietnam declined as President Richard M. Nixon's "Vietnamization" program transferred more responsibility for the ground fighting to the South Vietnamese. Nevertheless, the one-year limit required such a frequent turnover of troops that, by the time the last American soldier left Vietnam, 2.15 million had served. By 1973, all U.S. troops were gone; and on April 30, 1975, the war ended with victory by the combined forces of North Vietnam and the NLF.

The Early Years: Volunteers and Victories

During the early years of the U.S. military buildup, most of the soldiers sent to Vietnam were professionals or volunteers. They trained together and were sent by troop ship across the Pacific to fight together. The professional soldiers, especially the non-commissioned officers (NCOs), looked forward to the opportunity to gain combat experience. Morale was high and some observers commented that this was one of the finest fighting forces ever assembled.

The first major battle took place in the fall of 1965 in the Ia Drang Valley of the Central Highlands. Some 1,500-1,800 North Vietnamese Army (NVA) soldiers were killed in action there, contrasted to fewer than 300 soldiers of the U.S. Army's First Cavalry Division. The more than five-to-one kill ratio reflected the competence of the American forces.

"Vietnam: The War is Worth Winning," stated an editorial headline in the February 25, 1965 issue of *Life* magazine. The editorial went on to note that "there is a reasonably good chance the present phase of the war can be successfully wound up in 1967 or even in late 1966....The war in Vietnam is...about the future of Asia. It is very possibly as important as any of the previous American wars of this century."

At the time of the editorial, there were about 200,000 Americans in Vietnam. Some 125,000 had been there less than six months and about 50,000 were engaged in combat. About 1,400 had been killed and 6,000 wounded. Casualties were small enough and volunteerism high enough to give credibility to the administration's reassurances that a successful war effort could be managed without great public sacrifice. In a 1966 survey of high school sophomores, only 7 percent said the draft or Vietnam were problems that concerned them.

The Troop Buildup and the Draft

By the end of 1966, there were 400,000 American troops in Vietnam. The casualty toll had reached over 5,000 Americans killed in action and 16,000 wounded. Many of the enlisted men already had served their one-year tour of duty and were now rotating back to the States to be reassigned to other units. Their slots increasingly were being filled by soldiers recruited through the Selective Service System. As more soldiers were needed, more reliance was placed upon the draft.

By December 1966, the draft call was up to 40,000 men each month. Many of these soldiers were assigned to combat units upon their arrival, knowing only those people they had met in-flight. They lacked the security of serving alongside guys from basic training. Many of these draftees simply did not want to be there and a lot of them were being sent straight into combat. Morale problems began to surface. By 1970, draftees comprised 39 percent of the troops but almost 55 percent of the combat deaths.

Almost everyone of the Vietnam generation, whether or not they served in the military, was emotion-

President Nixon's draft lottery in action

ally affected by the war. As one author noted, "Vietnam was the most divisive time of battle in our country since the Civil War." It's easy to imagine yourself a hero when there is no immediate threat, but young Americans were being killed in Vietnam. Moreover, the only way to survive such a situation was to be willing to kill, an act that does not come easily to most. Many young Americans simply were not moved to such great sacrifice by the cause of Vietnam. The issue for almost all male youth, then, was whether to enlist or how to avoid the draft. For millions, this meant a confrontation with their local Selective Service ("draft") board.

Established in 1917 for World War I, local draft boards were authorized to grant deferments and exemptions to individuals who were conscripted in their area. By the 1960s, the Selective Service System included about 4,000 local draft boards. These boards were staffed by unpaid civilian volunteers, usually older white, middle-class men who were veterans of World Wars I and II.

As the war ground on, these local boards found themselves less and less able to meet their quotas of soldiers for Vietnam. A major reason was that there were numerous deferments and exemptions from military service built into the peacetime Selective Service law enacted in 1948. In addition to deferments for reasons of family, health, and religious principles, the law also provided deferments for occupations considered to be "in the national interest," especially those in the fields of health, education, religion, and agriculture. The following is a list of Selective Service classifications that could be assigned:

I-A   Available for military service

I-A-O   Conscientious objector available for noncombatant military service only

I-C   Member of the armed forces of the United States, the Coast and Geodetic Survey, or the Public Health Service

I-D   Member of reserve component or student taking military training

I-O   Conscientious objector available for civilian work contributing to the maintenance of the national health, safety, or interest

I-S   Student deferred by statute (High School)

I-Y   Registrant available for military service, but qualified for military service only in the event of war or national emergency

I-W   Conscientious objector performing civilian work contributing to the maintenance of the national health, safety, or interest

II-A   Registrant deferred because of civilian occupation (except agriculture or activity in study)

II-C   Registrant deferred because of agricultural occupation

II-S   Registrant deferred because of activity in study

III-A   Registrant with a child or children; registrant deferred by reason of extreme hardship to dependents

IV-A   Registrant who has completed service; sole surviving son

IV-B   Official deferred by law

IV-C   Alien

IV-D   Minister of religion or divinity student

IV-F   Registrant not qualified for any military service

V-A   Registrant over the age of liability for military service

Of the 26.8 million Vietnam era draft-age men, some 15.4 million, over 57 percent, were deferred, exempted, or disqualified from military service. Another 570,000, or 2 percent, committed draft violations. Over 200,000 were reported to federal prosecutors. Of these, 8,750 were convicted, 3,250 of whom went to prison. Another 3,000 went into hiding. Up to 100,000 fled the country. All of these young men also might be considered casualties of the war. For purposes of the war effort, however, the relevant figure is that almost 60 percent of the eligible population escaped military service entirely during the Vietnam era.

How to Avoid Vietnam

One course to avoid military service was to do so on principle by claiming conscientious objection. This course usually required extensive documentation by religious authorities. Moreover, almost all of the 172,000 young Americans who did qualify for such classification had to work for two years in low-paying community-service jobs outside of commuting distance from their homes. About a thousand individuals were convicted for refusing to do alternative service, a federal crime (see Chapter 7 for further discussion of this issue).

A more popular way to stay out of Vietnam was to go to college. Virtually every student who maintained satisfactory progress toward his degree was classified II-S, whereby the "registrant [was] deferred because of activity in study." If the student flunked out or was graduated, he again became eligible for the draft. Of course, the student could go to graduate or professional school and continue his deferment for another several years. Enrollment in colleges and universities increased by 6-7 percent during the war. Much of this increase was due to increased federal aid to an expanding system of higher education, patronized by a growing middle class, eager to provide advantages for their children. Nevertheless the effect was to reduce the pool of draft-eligible males by several hundred thousand.

In the early years most students were in favor of the war. For example, in 1965 only 6 percent of those polled favored immediate withdrawal of American troops from Vietnam. Pro-war students picketed university teach-ins, sometimes shouted obscenities, even physically attacked participants. Conservative students petitioned for support of U.S. policy in Vietnam at campuses all over the country. Blood drives for U.S. soldiers were organized at Ohio State, Stanford and other campuses. However, none of this implied a willingness to enlist. A 1967 Gallup Poll showed that most students acknowledged that the draft discriminated against the poor, but two-thirds disagreed with a proposal that the proportions of college and non-college youths drafted should be the same.

Like the general public, student opinion turned decisively against the war after the Tet Offensive early in 1968. Between 1967 and 1969, the proportion of students calling themselves "hawks" on the war shrank from one in two to one in five. By 1969, a majority of all students thought the war was a mistake and favored immediate withdrawal of American troops from Vietnam.

Still, there was a sizeable minority who continued to support the war. Moreover, even on campuses with a strong peace movement, most students were unwilling to give up draft deferment programs and off-campus employment opportunities with the military. For example, in 1969, a majority of students at Brown, Northeastern, and Tufts (all New England schools) still supported the continuation of ROTC on campus, although in the last case without academic credit. A May 1970 Harris Poll showed that a larger plurality (37%) of all college students favored permitting ROTC with academic credit on campus than favored its complete removal (25%). Even more dramatic were the findings from the same poll that 72 percent believed that companies doing defense business should be allowed to recruit on campus and that 70 percent agreed that "school authorities are right to call in police when students occupy a building or threaten violence." College

As we counsel young men concerning military service, we must clarify for them our nation's role in Vietnam and challenge them with the alternative of conscientious objection. I am pleased to say that this is the path now being chosen by more than seventy students at my own alma mater, Morehouse College, and I recommend it to all who find the American course in Vietnam a dishonorable and unjust one. Moreover, I would encourage all ministers of draft age to give up their ministerial exemptions and seek status as conscientious objectors. These are the times for real choices and not false ones. We are at the moment when our lives must be placed on the line if our nation is to survive its own folly. Every man of humane convictions must decide on the protest that best suits his convictions, but we must all protest.

—Rev. Martin Luther King Jr.

campuses certainly were major centers for the storm of protest against the war. However, they also were safe sanctuaries for all students: hawks, doves, and those concerned just with their own careers.

Another strategy for avoiding military service was to go into an occupation that was draft-deferred, like medicine, teaching or the ministry. A 1970 survey by Kenneth and Mary Gergen of 5,000 students at 39 colleges and universities found that one in three had altered their career plans, many for the purpose of seeking a draft-exempt occupation. Between 1968 and 1971, occupational deferments rose by over 270,000 (124%).

Hardship deferments were granted to men who were the sole means of support for their dependents. Many men chose to marry and have children in order to avoid the draft. These strategies were known as "marrying out" and "babying out". Between 1968 and 1971, such "dependency" deferments rose by almost 420,000 (11%).

Perhaps the greatest prize for those who wished to avoid Vietnam was a IV-F classification, in which "the registrant [was] not qualified for military service." This usually was granted for reasons of illness or disability and could be obtained by failing the induction or pre-induction physical examination. Some peace organizations even counseled young men on ways to fake various illnesses. Attorneys provided draft counseling for fees ranging from $200 to $1,000 and for anyone who found a competent lawyer, avoiding the draft was virtually assured.

Draft counselors directed men to certain boards in order to obtain exemptions. Baskir and Strauss report: "By far the most popular place to go for a pre-induction physical was Seattle, Washington. In the latter years of the war, Seattle examiners separated people into two groups: those who had letters from doctors or psychiatrists, and those who did not. Everyone received an exemption, regardless of what the letter said."

Many of these physicians charged big fees for letters to draft boards. Antiwar doctors or medical students were well known to university students. According to Baskir and Strauss, "A careful exam by a knowledgeable specialist and an equally careful choice of a pre-induction physical site guaranteed an exemption for nine clients out of ten." Individuals could be exempted for orthodontic work as well. A dentist in Los Angeles put braces on anyone who could afford them for a cost

of between $1,000 and $2,000.

If the above options were not available, there were many ways to fail the physical examinations. Some faked homosexual tendencies, starved themselves to obtain an underweight disqualification, or even mutilated their own bodies by slicing off a part of their thumb or shooting themselves in the foot.

Finally, one could lower one's chances of seeing combat in Vietnam by choosing a branch of the service more removed from the action, like the Coast Guard, Navy, or Air Force. The best assignments were the Reserves and National Guard. There was a four-to-six month active duty obligation, yearly summer camps, and monthly meetings over a six-year period. More than one million Vietnam-era males became guardsmen or reservists, almost all of whom stayed home; only 15,000 (1.5%) were sent to Vietnam. Studies by the Pentagon and National Guard indicated that between 70 and 90 percent of all reservists and guardsmen were draft-motivated. It was a very popular choice for college-trained men.

Figure 1 displays the various choices made by all members of the Vietnam generation.

In 1969, both to equalize the combat burden and to remove the threat of conscription as a motivation for protest, President Nixon established a lottery system for the draft. The lottery was based on the random selection of days of the year. The first date selected was September 14, which meant that local draft boards were required to select first all the eligible males born on that day for the January 1970 draft. Exemptions and deferments were still allowed. However, a low ranking draft number gave many young men reassurance of not being drafted and allowed everyone to plan the months ahead with more certainty.

Hardship, occupation, and student deferments were abolished by 1971. However, by that time, it made much less of a difference. The war was being turned over to the Vietnamese and draft quotas were sharply reduced. Fewer men now faced military service in Vietnam.

Throughout the war, many individuals took positive action to avoid military service. These men were much more likely to be from the higher classes of American society. They were able to escape military service by obtaining exemptions and deferments often unknown and unavailable to individuals lacking education and money.

1. The Vietnam Generation

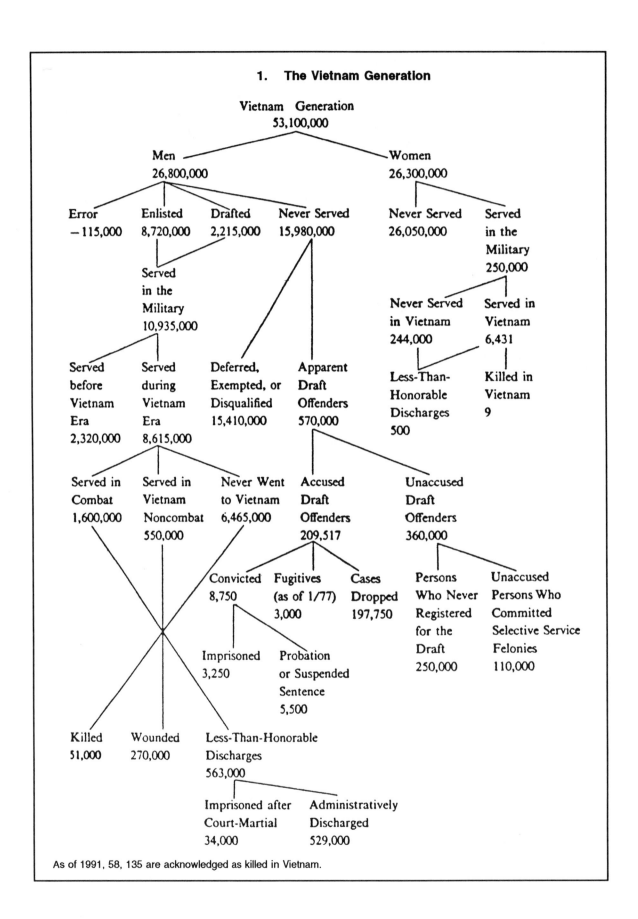

As of 1991, 58, 135 are acknowledged as killed in Vietnam.

Who Fought For The U.S.

During 1968-69, at the height of the American involvement in the war, there were 543,000 troops in Vietnam. You were much more likely to serve in the military, be sent to Vietnam, and see combat if you were from a lower-income family and without a college education.

Clearly, most of the alternatives for avoiding the draft and combat in Vietnam were restricted to those with money and education. Poor boys don't go to college or train to be doctors, teachers, or ministers. Poor boys don't go to psychiatrists or orthodontists for expensive treatment. Poor boys don't worry that much about their careers, and many are likely to be raised in a home where military service is valued and enlistment encouraged.

In some areas, these inequities were especially acute. A congressman from northern Wisconsin, for example, took a survey and found that of 100 draftees from his district, every one had come from families with an annual income of less than $5000. A study in Chicago found that men from low-income neighborhoods were three times as likely to die in Vietnam as men from high-income neighborhoods. Those from neighborhoods with low educational levels were four times more likely to die in Vietnam as those from neighborhoods with high educational levels.

One study of enlisted men found that a high school dropout had a 70 percent chance of being sent to Vietnam; a high school graduate had a 64 percent chance, and a college graduate, a 42 percent chance. A 1965-66 survey found that college graduates made up only 2 percent of all draftees. Another study by a Harvard University graduate found that only 56 of 1,200 Harvard students had served in the military, only two of whom were sent to Vietnam. James Fallows, at the time a Harvard University student, reflects: "During the five or six years of the heaviest draft calls for Vietnam, there was the starkest class division in American military service since the days of purchased draft deferments in the Civil War." Fallows says he and his Harvard classmates avoided service through a variety of devious tactics while the working-class men from Chelsea responded to the call. He asks "why all the well-educated presumably humane young men...so willingly took advantage of this most brutal form of class discrimination—what it signifies that we let the boys from Chelsea be sent off to die."

Given the widespread class discrimination in military service, it was to be expected that the sons of U.S. political leaders would be spared the sacrifice of Vietnam. Indeed, a 1970 report showed that 234 sons of senators and congressmen were of draft age during the war years, 1965-1970. More than half, 118, received deferments. Of those remaining, only 28 were sent to Vietnam and only 19 (8%) saw combat. None were killed and one was wounded. Barry Goldwater Jr. did

Table 1. Likelihood of Vietnam-Era Service			
	Military Service (%)	Vietnam Service (%)	Combat Service (%)
Low-Income	40	19	15
Middle-Income	30	12	7
High-Income	24	9	7
High-School Dropouts	42	18	14
High-School Graduates	45	21	17
College Graduates	23	12	9

his "alternative service" in the House of Representatives. It is tempting to speculate whether Congress' long and active support for the war might have been compromised had their children and grandchildren been exposed to the same risks as those of their less fortunate constituents.

Racial Minorities in Vietnam

During the war, as today, many blacks volunteered for military service, especially in the Marine Corps, in hopes of escaping the ghetto and bettering themselves. Many of these men were assigned to combat in Vietnam. Since the poverty rate among blacks in the U.S. is three times that among whites, black youths also were much more likely to be drafted into the military, assigned to Vietnam, and killed in combat. A final reason for this discrimination was that few blacks were assigned to decision making roles on local draft boards. In 1967, only 216 of 16,632 draft board members (1.2%) were black.

Blacks and Hispanics comprised 31 percent of all combat troops at the beginning of the war. In 1965, blacks accounted for 24 percent of all Army combat deaths. This was almost twice their share of the relevant population. As the government expanded its draft call, the black casualty rate declined proportionately to 20 percent in 1967 and 14 percent in 1968. By the end of the war, blacks accounted for 10.3 percent of all armed forces who served in Vietnam (11.9% of the Army). Although they were more likely to have been involved in heavy combat than white soldiers (37% to 25%), they constituted 13.5 percent of all combat deaths, a figure slightly greater than that of draft-eligible black males in the general population.

Hispanics also served and died in large numbers. One of two Hispanics in Vietnam served in combat and one of five were killed in action. General S.L.A. Marshall noted, "In the average rifle company, the strength was 50 percent composed of Negroes, Southwestern Mexicans, Puerto Ricans, Guamanians, Nisei, and so on. But a real cross-section of American youth? Almost never." This discrimination was reinforced by

both the Armed Forces Qualification Test (AFQT) and by a program called Project 100,000. The AFQT was designed to weed out potential recruits who lacked the skills needed by the military. While too low a score on the test served to bar entrance into the service for some, a low but passing score channeled many into non-technical positions in combat units.

Project 100,000 was a plan to extend opportunities for military service and promotion by providing remedial programs for those who would otherwise fail the AFQT because of their lack of formal education. Of course, it also was a plan to meet draft quotas without removing other deferments. As mentioned, while the Project did increase the numbers of minorities eligible for military service, their relatively low scores on the AFQT condemned them to a combat role in Vietnam. A total of 354,000 men were recruited into the military under the program, 41 percent of whom were black and 40 percent of whom were assigned to combat units. Their casualty rate in Vietnam was almost twice as high as that of Vietnam veterans as a whole. Project 100,000 was terminated in 1972 when many fewer American soldiers were being called to Vietnam.

The data show clearly that the military in Vietnam consisted overwhelmingly of lower-income males with a high school education or less. A significant portion of this group included whites from rural areas in the south and blue collar communities in the north, and blacks and Hispanics of Puerto Rican and Mexican descent. Included in this figure were significant numbers of almost illiterate men recruited from city streets and country roads. This volatile mix of traditional racial enemies had consequences that will be discussed in the next section.

Black Against White in Vietnam

Back home in the U.S.A., blacks were waging an assault on institutionalized racism. Ghetto riots and militant rhetoric provoked a white backlash which increased racial tensions and incidents of violence. Ultimately, the American people's problems with racism at home also came to haunt them in Vietnam, provoking discord among the troops and conflict with the Vietnamese and undermining any effort to promote the ideal of democracy as an alternative to communism.

There is never a convenient time for war. However, the war in Vietnam worked a special hardship on the black community. As the war escalated, it took media coverage and public attention away from the issue of civil rights reform. The war demanded more and more of the national budget. Black youths were serving and dying in disproportionate numbers.

In the early 1960s, the main student civil rights organization was called the Student Nonviolent Coordinating Committee (SNCC). As early as 1965, many SNCC leaders had come to the conclusion that Vietnam and segregation were "part of the same system" of racist oppression. Sammy Younge Jr., a student at Tuskeegee Institute, was killed while trying to use a "whites only" restroom at a gas station in Alabama. Three days after Younge's murder, SNCC issued its first official statement opposing the war in Vietnam. The statement pointed out that Younge's murder had taken place at a time when the United States was sending black youths to Vietnam to fight for the "freedom of others, while in our own country, many government officials openly avow racism."

Also in 1966, SNCC boycotted a White House conference on civil rights supported by the National Association for the Advancement of Colored People (NAACP) and the Urban League, on the grounds that "an administration that was obliterating human rights in Vietnam could not further them within the United States." Congress on Racial Equality (CORE) leader Lincoln Lynch stated that to support the war, so "suffused with conscious racism, is to support the racism on which it feeds." Julian Bond gave up his seat in the Georgia legislature rather than disavow SNCCs staunch opposition to the war.

By 1967, despite severe admonitions from national leaders, Martin Luther King Jr. began linking Vietnam and civil rights. King charged that the social programs needed to advance the cause of needy minorities were being sacrificed to the escalating costs of the war. He bemoaned the poor "paying the double price of smashed hopes at home and death and corruption in Vietnam." And he challenged ministers to present the "alternative of conscientious objection" to young men seeking counseling on military service.

By 1968, the Black Panther party had moved to the forefront of what had now become the Black Power movement. Its ten-point program for social change

ONE MAN SAID "WE SHOULD FIGHT FOR FREE ELECTIONS IN MISSISSIPPI AND ALABAMA, NOT IN VIET NAM."

SOME NEGROES ARE WORRIED BECAUSE SO. MANY OF US SUFFER FROM THE WAR.

included the following provision: "We believe that black people should not be forced to fight in the military service to defend a racist government that does not protect us. We will not fight and kill people of color in the world who, like black people, are being victimized by the white racist government of America."

By 1969, this attitude had become widespread in the black community. Journalist Wallace Terry interviewed 392 black enlisted men in Vietnam and found that 64 percent believed that their fight was in the United States, not in Vietnam. About a third advocated immediate withdrawal of U.S. troops. Marine PFC Reginald Edwards told Terry, "We fought for the white man in Vietnam. It was clearly his war. If it wasn't, you wouldn't have seen as many confederate flags as you saw...an insult to any person that's of color on this planet." The saying, "No Vietnamese ever called me Nigger," became a popular way for black soldiers to say, "It's not my war." By the end of the decade, the symbols of black nationalism were evident throughout the U.S. military: there were black power salutes and handshakes, Afro hairstyles and soul music.

Many blacks identified with the Vietnamese who also were treated as inferiors. Vietnamese civilians who worked on American bases prepared the food, hauled the garbage, cleaned the buildings, and carried the baggage. They did all the dirty work, for which they received very little pay and were treated with suspicion and contempt by many soldiers. Black soldier Gerald Bayette saw the situation this way:

The first thing that caught my attention while waiting for my bags at the airport was the Vietnamese. They were the ones unloading the plane, carrying the bags to where we were waiting. All during which the American soldiers who were supervising (of course) ordered them to hurry up while making derogatory remarks about Asians in general. I thought about the airport and train stations in the States, where menial jobs such as baggage carrying are handled by the brothers, who must take the same devil's abuse in order to provide for their families. It disgusted me.

Despite reservations about racism in Vietnam, black soldiers distinguished themselves in combat; and, as in previous wars, traditional racial antagonisms melted in the heat of battle on the front lines. One black GI reflected: "You couldn't think just white or just black—you had to think for everybody. That was one of the things that the war did for me. It started me thinking about men in general, instead of whites or blacks—even though a lot of whites forgot about that after they got back to the States. It taught them a lot of lessons. Some whites never forgot. And a lot of blacks never forgot it either." Here is one of many such examples, offered by black soldier, Harold "Lightbulb" Bryant:

There was another guy in our unit who made it known that he was a card-carrying Ku Klux Klan member. That pissed a lot of us off, cause we had gotten real tight. We didn't have racial incidents like what was happening in the rear area, 'cause we had to depend on each other. We were always in the bush.

Well, we got out into a fire fight, and Mr. Ku Klux Klan got his little ass trapped. We were going across the rice paddies and Charlie just started shootin'. And he jumped in the rice paddy while everybody else kind of backtracked.

So we laid down a base fire to cover him. But he was just immobile. He froze. And a brother went out there and got him and dragged him back. Later on, he said that action changed his perception of what black people were all about.

In the rear, however, hatred between blacks and whites tore U.S. troops apart and frequently exploded into violence. Certainly, there is plenty of evidence of official discrimination and black defiance of such in the military. Even by October 1971, blacks constituted 14.3 percent of the enlisted men but only 3.6 percent of the officers in the U.S. Army. Racial confrontation in the military started to become a serious problem around 1967-68, about the time that ghetto riots and black militance were on the rise back home. In 1968, forty-three black GIs at Fort Hood refused to go on "riot duty" at the Democratic National Convention in Chicago. In 1970, seven black soldiers from the 176th Regiment disobeyed orders to go on patrol duty, claiming their lives were being deliberately endangered by racist officers. In 1972, racial incidents on the USS Constella-

ONE NEGRO MAN SAID: "WHY SHOULD WE FIGHT FOR A COUNTRY THAT HAS NEVER FOUGHT FOR US?"

ONE SAID "WHY ARE WE ALWAYS FIRST CLASS CITIZENS ON THE BATTLEFIELD, AND SECOND CLASS CITIZENS AT HOME?"

tion caused a training exercise to be canceled. When the ship returned to port, 122 black sailors (joined by eight white sailors) raised their fists in protest.

A 1971 Congressional Black Caucus study found that half of all soldiers in confinement were black. A 1971 NAACP study showed that a white first offender was twice as likely to be released without punishment as a black first offender. This study also found that blacks received 45 percent of all less-than-honorable discharges, a rate more than three times their share of enlisted men.

In many units, blacks and whites chose to eat in separate groups and sleep in separate buildings. Such separation further fueled mistrust and hostility. Given the lack of confidence in military justice, the tension of the war and the ready availability of weapons, it was, perhaps, inevitable that such hostility would erupt into deadly violence. In addition to beatings, stabbings and shootings, there were "fraggings"— attempts to kill or injure by tossing a fragmentation grenade. Fraggings most often came from angry troops against overzealous platoon leaders who pushed them too hard. However, sometimes they occurred in racial confrontations. A racial incident at Cam Ranh Bay led to a fragging in which 31 were injured. The insult "nigger" led to a brawl at Puloi near Saigon in January 1971. By midyear, 154 assaults by Americans on Americans had been recorded. Between 1969 and 1971, there were 600 fragging incidents in Vietnam in which 82 Americans were killed and 651 wounded by each other. (see Chapter 5 for more discussion of this issue). This theme of self-destruction in the U.S. Army is featured dramatically in the Academy Award winning film, *Platoon*.

OK Corral East
Brothers in the Nam

Sgt. Christopher and I are
in Khanh Hoi down by the docks
in the Blues Bar where the women
are brown and there is no Saigon Tea
making our nightly HIT—'Hore Inspection Tour'
watching the black   digging the night sights
     soul sounds   getting tight

the grunts in the corner raise undisturbed hell
the timid white MP has his freckles pale
as he walks past the high dude
in the doorway in his lavender- jump suit
to remind the mama-san quietly of curfew
     he chokes on the weed smoke
     he sees nothing his color here
and he fingers his army rosary   his .45

but this is not Cleveland or Chicago
he can't cringe any one here and our
gazes like brown punji stakes impale him

we have all killed something recently
we know who owns the night
and carry darkness with us

     —Horace Coleman

Americans Against Vietnamese

Also treated in *Platoon* is the racism expressed by many U.S. soldiers against the Vietnamese people themselves. Of course, the official publications of the U.S. Military Assistance Command in Vietnam advocated humane treatment of the Vietnamese people as the most effective way to win their hearts and minds:

Remember that we are special guests here; we make no demands and seek no special treatment.

Join with the people! Understand their life, use phrases from their language, and honor their customs and laws.

Treat women with politeness and respect.

Make personal friends among the soldiers and common people.

Always give the Vietnamese the right-of-way.

Be alert to security and ready to react with your military skill.

Don't attract attention by loud, rude, or unusual behavior.

Avoid separating yourself from the people by a display of wealth or privilege.

Above all else you are members of the U.S. military forces on a difficult mission, responsible for all your official and personal actions. Reflect honor upon yourself and the United States of America.

Indeed, there were many soldiers who displayed respect, even affection, for the Vietnamese. Such GIs volunteered their labor and resources to social relief organizations. Some married Vietnamese women and/or adopted Vietnamese orphans. These were the exception, however.

As with all wars, the terror of life and death promoted a racist contempt that served to dehumanize the enemy and make killing morally defensible. Many soldiers were instructed in this attitude in basic training. Marine PFC Reginald Edwards reports:

The only thing they told us about the Viet Cong was they were gooks. They were to be killed. Nobody sits around and gives you their historical and cultural background. They're the enemy. Kill, kill, kill. That's what we got to practice. Kill, kill, kill.

Rifleman Haywood T. Kirkland agrees:

Right away they told us not to call them Vietnamese. Call everybody gooks, dinks. They told us when you go over in Vietnam, you gonna be face to face with Charlie, the Viet Cong. They were like animals or something other than human. They ain't have no regard for life. They'd blow up little babies just to kill one GI. They wouldn't allow you to talk about them as if they were people. They told us they're not to be treated with any type of mercy. That's what they engraved into you. That killer instinct. Just go away and do destruction.

Once in combat, there were other factors that heightened this racist hostility. Compared to the U.S., Vietnam was perceived as a poor and backward country. Moreover, many GIs felt that the Army of the Republic of Vietnam (ARVN) showed less skill and courage in combat than the Vietcong, an observation that reinforced American cynicism toward the Vietnamese. The heat and rain, mud and leeches, insects, bad food, and long hours caused fatigue and irritation among the troops.

As if that weren't enough, there was the peculiar nature of the war itself. In contrast to the image many had of European wars, there were relatively few sustained confrontations between uniformed troops to gain or defend strategic territory. The enemy infiltrated the population and practiced hit-and-run tactics that frustrated GIs in the field. Many soldiers were killed or mutilated by land mines and booby traps with no enemy in sight. Frustration and rage built up within them. Finally, their ignorance of the language and culture made GIs vulnerable to terrorism by seemingly innocent villagers who were working with the NLF. Here is one soldier's story:

I met this girl in a village store...I guess she was the only Vietnamese I ever got close to. By then I spoke a little of their language and I found out she was studying English and Math. I said I would help her and kinda started to hang around the place when I was free....Once, the last time, I brought a flower: it helped me forget.

One day we were on this patrol, it was rainy and suddenly we were caught in an ambush. Our guys returned the fire. We hit them hard and then called in the gunships for support....

Then, maybe thirty minutes after, the firing stopped and we moved out to look for the wounded and to take a body count. There was a bunch of bodies all around, all VC. One of them was my little girl friend, now dead, bullets through her chest and head. She had an automatic near her, I was shocked, she was a VC. Who the hell were our friends? Who were our enemies? I never felt more confused than at that moment.

Given the consequences of such deception, perhaps it was healthy for American GIs to be suspicious toward all Vietnamese. Unfortunately, this attitude frequently degenerated into an indiscriminant disdain. Commonly used terms like "dinks" and "slopes" expressed a general racist contempt for all Vietnamese people. Army medical officer Gordon Livingston recalls numerous examples of fairly routine American mistreatment of Vietnamese civilians, e.g., "driving tracked vehicles through rice paddies; throwing C-ration cans at children from moving vehicles; running truck convoys through villages at high speeds on dirt roads (if the people are eating rice at the time it has to be thrown away because of the dust)...."

The "gook syndrome" sometimes exploded into violent atrocities committed by GIs against innocent civilians as well as enemy soldiers (see Chapter 6 for a fuller discussion of this issue.) As with all wars, some brutal men trained in weapons of violence took advantage of the opportunity to attack others with impunity. Incidents like the following illustrate the depths of inhumanity to which many young American boys were plunged in Vietnam:

'We had this gook and we was gonna skin him,' a grunt told me. I mean he was already dead and everything, and the lieutenant comes over and says, 'Hey asshole, there's a reporter in the TOC, you want him to come out and see that? I mean, use your fucking heads, there's a time and place for everything.' 'Too

Guerrilla War

It's Practically impossible
to tell civilians
from the Vietcong.

Nobody wears uniforms
They all talk
the same language,

(and you couldn't understand
 them even if they didn't).

They tape grenades
inside their clothes,
and carry satchel charges
in their market baskets.

Even their women fight;
and young boys,
and girls,
It's practically impossible
to tell civilians
from the Vietcong;

after a while,
you quit trying.

—W.D. Ehrhart

bad you wasn't with us last week,' another grunt told me, coming off a non-contact operation, 'we killed so many gooks it wasn't even funny.'

Of course, for every GI who took ghoulish pleasure in such revenge against the enemy, there were more who were sickened by the cruelty. Many came to doubt seriously whether the war could or should be won. In 1971, a survey of men on their way to Vietnam found that almost all had serious criticisms of U.S. military policy in Vietnam. However, they were divided over whether to get out or step up the war. Forty-seven percent considered the war a mistake and 40 percent thought America was not fighting hard enough to win.

Once in Vietnam, such doubts grew worse. More and more U.S. soldiers came to question the purpose of the war and the ethics of their own participation. From 1964 to 1972, more than 500,000 cases of soldiers "absent without leave" (AWOL) were reported. Deserters numbered 93,250—three times that of Korea. Fewer than 3,000 deserted while in Vietnam. Some 20,000 men deserted after serving their year in Vietnam while in post-combat stateside military assignments. For many, desertion clearly was a protest against the war or an expression of delayed stress reaction. Like the draftees, deserters were drawn disproportionately from the ranks of poor blacks and blue collar whites with little education.

All American troops were withdrawn from Vietnam in 1973. The memory of crack U.S. troops winning key victories was now a distant thought. The war had lost all sense of moral purpose for too many. Could we justify the terrible expense when we had so many unsolved problems at home? Did we offer a moral alternative when we couldn't even overcome the hate among ourselves?

It must be understood that war has a political, economic, and social dimension as well as a military one. Superior firepower will not by itself win the battle for hearts and minds. If you can win that battle, there is much less need for superior firepower. Noting the terrible contradictions in the behavior of U.S troops in Vietnam, Livingston asked, "How can we presume to influence a struggle for the political loyalties of a people for whom we manifest such uniform disdain is to me the great unanswered, indeed, unanswerable question of this war." Livingston also recognized the parallels to the "racist" treatment of black people back in the U.S. and warned, "the price of our lack of perception is defeat abroad and, if not corrected, may be the dissolution of society at home."

Indeed, things seemed to be falling apart everywhere. The promise of Lyndon Johnson's Great Society Program had been squandered on the huge war budget and American cities were aflame with protest. More and more GIs wondered what they were supposed to be fighting for. Explanations by the White House were no longer convincing.

Certainly, some soldiers continued to fight with valor on the fields of battle. The Nixon years (1969-73) witnessed 20,000 Americans killed, 110,000 wounded, and more than 500 captured or missing in action. However, for many, given the plan for disengagement, heroism seemed futile. No one wanted to be the last soldier killed in Vietnam. By now, volunteers were a minority and desertions were on the rise. Morale was low and alcohol and drugs were abundant. The enemy seemed to be everywhere. After nine years of American bloodshed and body bags, Vietnam would be left to the Vietnamese.

Who Fights Today

In 1973 the U.S. abolished compulsory military conscription and instituted a professional volunteer army. Among the arguments for the change were that compulsory service violated civil liberties and an all-volunteer army was less likely to suffer from internal dissension. Among those opposed were that the public would be less watchful over White House use of military force in U.S. foreign relations, that the poor, especially racial minorities, would shoulder an unfair share of the defense burden, and that the overall quality of the troops would suffer.

Throughout the 1980s, high unemployment, especially for youth, rising government military subsidies, and a relatively peaceful international scene encouraged higher enlistments. During this period, opportunities for the advancement of blacks increased greatly. By 1986, blacks constituted ten percent of Army officers and seven percent of generals. Gen. Colin L. Powell became the first black man to chair the Joint Chiefs of Staff.

In February 1991, as the ground war in the Persian Gulf became more imminent, the White House reassured a worried public that it would not be necessary to bring back the draft. At the time, black men and women stationed in the Gulf totalled 104,000, 25 percent of the Americans deployed in the region and 30 percent of all Army troops. This represented over twice their 12 percent share of the U.S. population.

A *New York Times*/CBS poll found that 55 percent of black respondents opposed the Persian Gulf War compared to only 27 percent of white respondents. Reporting in the *Chronicle of Higher Education*, Michele N-K Collison found black students at Temple, Duke, Syracuse, Howard and other universities to be critical of the war. Rallies and teach-ins stressed the greater risk of casualties for blacks, an even larger component of the infantry, and the diversion of money to the war that could have been used for social problems afflicting black Americans.

Almost all students interviewed had a family member or friend in the Gulf and they were concerned for their safety. A student at Temple called it "a poor man's army." A residence hall coordinator at the University of California at Davis said "black students have a choice between the streets and the Army." Many students criticized President Bush as hypocritical for asking "black troops to fight for freedom in the gulf" while refusing "to sign a civil-rights bill that would outlaw discrimination against black citizens."

Clearly, criticisms by black Americans during the Vietnam War concerning U.S. value commitments, budget priorities, and racial justice were still relevant during the recent Persian Gulf War. The racial climate within the military has improved, but economic opportunities for black people in America remain bleak.

Reporter: What does it do to a guy when he survives all of this as you have?

PFC: Makes you scared. It really does. I was up there the day after on the 20th talking to a sergeant that I know, just trying to console him. He wasn't hit that bad, but it sure makes you feel better when you have somebody to talk to. I was talking to him when mortars started coming in. It's just impossible to describe how scared these guys are when mortars were coming in and there's nothing they can do.

—Interview with unidentified U.S. soldier, as reported in *Vietnam Remembered.*

"I wanna go to Vietnam
I wanna kill a Vietcong
With a knife or a gun
Either way will be good fun

But if I die in the combat zone
Box me up and send me home
Fold my arms across my chest
Tell my folks I done my best"

—Army marching cadence

Soldiers marching into combat sing and shout brave words. Inside, the feelings are quite different. Here are two such portraits—an American and a National Liberation Front soldier.

"A Pawn in the Game: The Vietnam Diary of Sgt. Bruce F. Anello," U.S. Army, killed in action in Vietnam, May 31, 1968

1967

Oct. 21. It seems like a year I've been gone already, but it hasn't even been a month. The ocean is a tiring object, but on occasions it has its beautiful times. Especially at night, but always I wish I didn't have to watch it alone.

Nov. 9. Our ambush—with the rain beating on my helmet. Not a drop coming in, so it trickles around my neck and soaks into my skin. While my finger's on the trigger frozen with fear and from the wind . . . haven't fired a shot yet. Nor has one come my way. Just frustration and harassment . . .

Nov. 21. Lost respect for a bunch of people today. For no reason they tore down this hootch, burnt it, trampled down their garden, ripped out their trees and there wasn't even any suspected enemy. I told him I hope someone kicks in his TV tube while he's over here . . .

Dec. 10. *How can I describe an ambush? . . . darkness comes, and the clouds turn black with threatening rain, and the moon can barely seep through. It's the signal to move to the trail where the man died yesterday. An eerie feeling creeps into your whole being as the beautiful trees of daytime turn into laughing demons from the cold night wind.*

Dec. 24. *Christmas Eve—Ho ho! Today I fought a war. Instead of the Yuletide burning, it was a village. Instead of Christmas light it was artillery. Instead of the white snow , it was rain. Instead of warm smiles, it was a weary frown. Instead of bells ringing out, it was bullets. Instead of laughter, it was mother's pain, it was a man saying, "I'm going home." Instead of peace and good will, it was war and sorrow. But be still, for today Christ was born . . .*

1968

Jan. 12. *Even here they hound me about a haircut. Like they don't have nothing else to worry about. A guy in our platoon shot a civilian today. He personally was sorry. But the platoon sarge said we should have burnt his I.D. and put a grenade in his pocket. The squad leader put a note on him when the chopper took him away, saying he didn't have an I.D. and he ran.*

Jan. 14. *A letter came—from Mary even. Today Jan. 14, declared as a new holiday. It was so beautiful I cried. I can't even express how it made me feel. A lot of words wouldn't mean half enough of how good I feel. I was gonna read the envelope for* *three days, then open it, read the heading for the next three days, and one sentence per 3 days. It should last me until the next letter.*

Feb. 12. *. . . I admire the spirit of the V.C. But who wouldn't have spirit? They have a cause to die for, it's their country. We have nothing to gain. We don't even want the country. So what is to win—when we have nothing to win?*

Feb. 24. *Seems every other thought is of being home. Yet, it's still a long time to go. It only depresses me. But it's hard not to think about it. You wake up in the morning, thinking about what it would be like in a warm bed. You start cooking some cans and you wonder what it would be like to sit at a table with a cup of coffee. You brush the dirt off your clothes and you wonder how a warm shower would feel . . . Then the man tells you to pack up and sling it all on your back. And you wonder what it would be like to be free, instead of always fighting for it . . .*

Mar. 1. *The captain has no faith in his men whatsoever. The lieutenant said, "If you have any opinions, keep them to yourself." A self-made god. The captain is even higher than God. He told us: "Don't ask me why I tell you something to do, if you don't you'll die."*

I got to get out of here. The man drives you insane. I'm no longer fighting the enemy. My mind just seems to be fighting the army . .

Mar. 10. *I'm really digging this new company. Digging foxholes* *every night. Digging rice out of crocks. Digging a place to sleep . . .*

Mar. 20. Looking back through the pages, I can now make a statement on all the facts I have thus far collected: . . .that is. I've been here for 6 months and still don't know what the hell we're fighting for . . .

April 4. It seems the latest fad is to build up a kill record. Since our platoon got in that battle, we've killed 45 V.C. The other platoons are jealous so now they kill anybody—just to match our record. I've seen—skip it. I'll write about that later. I can say I've seen brutality to the utmost. Grossness, ridiculous and senseless killing. And no conscience whatsoever. I get the usual statement handed down since the cavalry and Indians. "The only good gook is a dead gook."

April 24. The sweat runs down my forehead, as I lie in my mud hole. Ants crawling up my legs. Mosquitoes buzzing around my ears. It's so dark the bushes take odd shapes and play on the imagination. Every fiber in my body feels like a leech . . .

May 2. Walking on point today, I saw a man about 20 years old, so I yelled "La day" (meaning come here). He turned and saw me. His eyes went big—and he tore off running—so I shot him. He ran a hundred yards down some trails with his guts in his hand . . . The thought of what I did made me sick . . . I'm not proud of what I did.

March to the Front Line (2:35) Words and Music by Huy Quang

Since the days we began to oppose *Giac My**
They have killed our brothers, sisters, and parents
We cannot sit still.
We must march to the front lines.
We must have courage,
To protect our village homes.
Avenge the blood of our kin.
Cast off the American yoke.
Their puppet troops burn our homes,
Our granaries.

We must rise together against them,
Until victory.
Blood for blood, we'll fight to the last.
All our people, we'll work together.
After our victory,
We'll return to our village homes.
But blood will flow as long as the Oppression is here.

*Giac My means American aggression.
—1971 by Paredon Records

Diary of an Unknown Soldier from the *National Liberation Front of Vietnam*

It is May 1st. *I am writing because something very important happened that suddenly changed my life: this morning at half-past seven, I turned up to report and comrade Lan told me: "Get ready to go into the army." I think writing may help me to understand the feelings that seized me. A kind of joy and excitement, I admit. But, at the same time, something like terror and pain. Because I shall have to leave my wife, Can, this be love that is so sacred to me. We were married only four months ago and have been together so little. In accepting this separation, I am making a great sacrifice and denial. Dying does not frighten me: if my death helps my people, then I am ready to die. But to be parted from Can makes me suffer so much. Too much.*

May 3. *Can, your heart is in your eyes. A broken heart. But someday there won't be a single American devil left in this country. If it were not for the Americans we would not be kissing each other goodbye.*

May 8. *Today it is my turn to do the cooking and I have to find water. But after marching for two nights on end my legs are almost broken. Every movement I make causes terrific pain; I have never been good at sports . . . I miss Can terribly. I think of nothing else and count the days we've been separated.*

May 10. *We have no rice and cannot buy any here because there is none. All we have eaten is the little rye and we have slept on empty stomachs. We shall have no rice until tomorrow evening and only then if things go well. Hunger is an ugly thing and I have no wish to write.*

May 26. *I have been feeling ill for sixteen days and did not write . . . For six hours I have been cutting wood. But that is nothing compared with the leeches. The moment we set foot in the jungle and in this damp climate we met our worst enemy—leeches. Curse them. They are everywhere; they cling to the first man they see. Although we are careful to cover every part of our bodies, they still manage to attack us* and every time I feel a prick I know what it is. I take off my shoe and invariably my foot is covered with blood. Disgusting.

June 1. I have been in the army for nearly a month and all we do is train: to creep forward on hands and knees, to roll into holes, even to climb trees and hide among the leaves. These exercises are hard, and harder still because of the heat; even the wind that blows from Laos is hot. But this hard life has strengthened our ability to bear it. It has actually restored my enthusiasm . . . Tomorrow is a day of rest and I have asked permission to visit my home; my parents live not far from here. I was allowed to because I had volunteered to go to South Vietnam . . . I feel wild with happiness; I shall see my mother and the rest of my family.

June 2. I have seen my relatives but not my Mother. Oh, Mother, how sad. When we arrived it was half-past eleven at night and my heart was beating fast . . . You had gone to Dong Noi that morning. Dearest Mother, you will suffer so much when they tell you I came and did not find you. I suffered as well . . . I was thinking of you, Mother. Perhaps I shall not have another chance like this one . . . Even now the tears are falling on the paper. How sad it was, Mother. We have never been lucky, the two of us . . .

Dec. 30. *When we saw a house, Li and I took off our equipment and went in to ask for food. The owner gave us a pan of freshly cooked potatoes and a bunch of bananas. We ate until we nearly burst and called Nuoi and Mai to give them the rest. We wanted to pay him, but the good man refused. He even offered us a cup of hot water to help us digest the food. His kindness put us into a good mood . . .*

Jan. 18. *Only a few days more and we shall celebrate Tet . . . Suddenly we have been ordered not to stop in houses, not even to go inside them. Something new is in the air. We must keep silently marching. So while other people are gaily celebrating Tet we shall have to hide quietly in the wood. I remember the last Tet. Can and I spent it together. We were happy.*

Jan. 23. *Suddenly we heard planes and someone shouted: "They're bombing us." A second later a plane dived straight above us, then came a terrific explosion and fragments of the bomb hit everywhere. One passed at four centimeters from my head. I heard it whistling. What mysterious laws govern a man's life and survival? . . .Clearly it is not my destiny to die here. Where is it written that I am to die?*

Jan. 29. *We got up very early and had breakfast before dawn. Everything is ready. I wrote a letter to Can and gave it to a* *friend who has just come back from Thailand and I hope he can manage to get it to her. Can, my dearest Can. Perhaps the end is waiting for me, but there will never be an end to our love. Even if I die or you die it will not end. Can, my dear Can. Now we must go. The commander is calling and telling us to . . .*

(Oriana Fallaci, the Italian journalist, picks up the story from here.)

Feb. 19. The diary stops here. He must have died five or six days later, on the outskirts of Saigon. Or else he may have died on Jan. 29 itself, in a bombing raid like the one I went on with Capt. Andy in the A-37. I can't think of anything else. And I keep wondering: does Can know about his death? Perhaps she has just received his last letter and is writing to him at his new address . . .

—Oriana Fallaci, *Nothing, And So Be It,* translated by Isabel Quigley, New York: Doubleday & Co., Inc. 1972

Discussion Questions

1. Recount the events leading up to large-scale involvement by United States forces in the Vietnam War. In what ways was waging the Vietnam War under the Tonkin Gulf Resolution a "double-edged sword?"

2. Were the soldiers who served in the Vietnam War in the earlier years different from those who served in the later years? In what ways?

3. How would each of the following individuals most likely react to the fact that 60 percent of the eligible draft-age population avoided military service during the Vietnam War: someone who was against the war; someone who was for the war; a veteran of WWII?

4. Since deferments could be obtained in so many ways, why do you think so many young males were still drafted?

5. What is meant by the term "poverty draft?" How could such an unfair means of selecting soldiers for the military occur in a democracy?

6. Describe relations between blacks and whites in Vietnam during the war. Did blacks see any relation between racism in Vietnam and racism in the US?

7. Did black and white soldiers differ in their perceptions of the Vietnamese people? How?

8. To what extent do you believe the "Nine Rules For Personnel of U.S. Military Assistance Command, Vietnam" were followed by U.S. troops. Do you think these rules were realistic? Why or why not?

9. Why is the enemy dehumanized during wartime? Is this necessary for success in a war effort? What role, if any, did racism play in this process?

10. Compare and contrast the themes of the American and National Liberation Front marches. Now compare and contrast the diaries of the American and NLF soldiers. What are the similarities and differences between the countries? Between the marches and the diaries?

Chapter 5   **Joe P. Dunn and Jerold M. Starr**

HOW THE U.S. FOUGHT THE WAR

Introduction

During April 1975, millions of Americans watched the communist takeover of Saigon on television. Triumphant North Vietnamese troops advanced rapidly on the city while the Army of the Republic of (South) Vietnam (ARVN) fled in panic. Because the airport was no longer safe, helicopters were forced to lift off from the roof of the American Embassy to take those chosen for rescue to aircraft carriers off shore. Some of those not chosen clung to the helicopter's skids in a desperate effort to escape.

This is what the American commitment had come to in Vietnam. Many wondered how the world's mightiest military power had not been able to conquer a small, less developed country in Southeast Asia. Years later, millions of Americans—especially those who fought there—find this very hard to understand or accept.

The Vietnam War was basically different from past U.S. wars. Debates over U.S. war strategy produced more controversy than consensus. William Westmoreland, the Commanding General of U.S. Forces in Vietnam from 1964-1969, commented: "The longest war in our history, it was the most reported and most visible to the public—but the least understood." Marine General Lewis Walt remarked: "Soon after I arrived in Vietnam it became obvious to me that I had neither a real understanding of the nature of the war nor any clear idea as to how to win it."

Vietnam was difficult to grasp for many reasons. In previous wars, one could look at a map of the territory held by each side, see who was advancing or retreating, and assess the war's progress. But Vietnam was "a war without fronts." Not until the final days in 1975 could anyone look at a map and tell who was winning. From the Demilitarized Zone (DMZ) which divided the country, through the mountainous Central Highlands, to the coastal plane and the delta in the southernmost part of the country, the varied South Vietnamese terrain meant that the war itself differed from one area of the country to another.

The nature of the war also changed dramatically over time and is best understood in terms of the following distinct stages: (1) 1961-1964, (2) 1965-1967, (3) 1968, (4) 1969-1970, (5) 1971-1973, (6) 1973-1975. Vietnam veterans use their location and year in country to designate their particular Vietnam War experience.

The 100 or so advisors in place when President John F. Kennedy took office in 1961 grew to 16,300 by the time of his death in November 1963. As the U.S. changed its primary mission to a combat role, the number of troops grew proportionately—from 23,000 to 184,000 by the end of 1965; 385,000 by the end of 1966; 485,000 by 1967; 536,000 by 1968—and reached a peak of 543,000 in early 1969. Then, with Vietnamization, troops declined to 475,000 by the end of 1969; 336,000 by 1970; 158,000 by 1971; 24,000 by 1972; to fewer than 250 personnel by mid-1973.

Vietnam was the longest and most unpopular foreign war in American history. It ranked second in fiscal expense and a close third in casualties. Depending on one's criteria, between 2.15 and 3.14 million Americans served at some time and place in the Second Indochinese War. More than 58,000 died, and more than 300,000 were wounded.

The South Vietnamese provided even more manpower and suffered more casualties. The Republic of Vietnam Armed Forces (RVNAF) grew from 514,000 at the beginning of 1965 to almost 1.1 million by the end of 1972. Over this period, some 170,000 ARVN troops were killed, three-fourths of the Allied total. Other countries also sent forces. The South Korean contribution reached a peak of 50,000 of its best troops in 1970. Australia, New Zealand, and Thailand sent smaller military contingents, and the Philippines dispatched a small number of civilian personnel. Total "third nation" forces reached 70,000 in 1969, and had a combined total of 5,000 deaths during the course of the war.

As Chapter 10 makes clear, both the U.S. and Viet-nam suffered tremendous losses in lives, treasure, and spirit. Stanley Karnow calls it the war nobody won. Certainly America lost. Everybody agrees on the motto "No More Vietnams," but this means different things to different people. That makes it all the more imperative that citizens keep an open mind and try to understand what happened, what went wrong, and what might have been the alternatives.

The Legacy of World War II

The victory over fascism in World War II established the United States as the world's dominant military and industrial power. It was seen as a triumph of the American way of life, a nation growing into true greatness. Americans cheered their brave soldiers returning from the war. However, many felt the war had been won as much in the factories as on the battlefields. In this view, it was the superior capacity of American industry to produce more and better weapons and equipment that prevailed in the long run.

The dominance of corporate leaders among U.S. foreign and military policymakers assured a friendly climate for this point of view. Over the period 1940-1967, the major corporations and investment houses provided 70 of the 91 individuals who held top positions in the Departments of Defense and State, the three military services, the Central Intelligence Agency and the Atomic Energy Commission.

This ethic of technology and managerialism pervaded American society through the 1950s. On the home front an army of "organization men" in "gray flannel suits" supervised the growth of the American economy. On the front lines U.S. soldiers, better trained and better equipped, defended U.S. vital interests around the world.

The military and the new national security policymakers placed high reliance upon technological superiority, particularly America's nuclear arsenal and unsurpassed fleet of jet fighters and bombers. The Korean conflict demonstrated to many the dangers of conventional land war in Asia. Through the mid and late 1950s, air power and nuclear weapons were emphasized at the expense of the infantry. Thus, the U.S. entered the Vietnam era with unquestioned faith in the superiority of high-technology warfare, an arrogance about its ability to "manage" many conflicts across the globe, and little regard for its foes in less developed Asia. All of these factors would contribute to its failure.

The Advisory Role: 1955 - 1960

From 1950-1954, the U.S. poured almost $4 billion into France's futile effort to defeat the Vietminh guerrillas. President Eisenhower and major U.S. officials criticized the French Army's leadership, organization, strategy, tactics, and training of the Vietnamese. Military leaders especially disapproved of what they perceived as France's lack of will to fight. General J. Lawton Collins said the U.S. had "to put the squeeze on the French to get them off their fannies." One Marine colonel boasted that "two good American divisions with the normal aggressive American spirit could clean up the situation in the Tonkin Delta in ten months." These assertions ignored the determination of the Vietminh and their broad-based political support.

Following the French defeat, U.S. advisors took over the training of the RVNAF and sought to structure the Army of the Republic of (South) Vietnam (ARVN) into a copy of the U.S. Army, capable of fighting a mid-intensity, conventional war against North Vietnam. The strategy was to use "high volumes of firepower to minimize casualties." Vietnamese General Staff objections that the French were defeated by a guerrilla, not a conventional, army were swept aside. Instruction in counterinsurgency was minimal. American advisors were not trained to speak Vietnamese on the premise that their tour of duty was too short to make that worthwhile. In sum, the U.S. set up a huge official bureaucracy in the midst of a revolutionary political situation with little or no knowledge of the society and culture of the area.

By 1959, the ARVN had seven standard divisions and four armored cavalry regiments, reminding one U.S. advisor of a lighter firepower model of a World War II division. ARVN training was essentially the same as that of U.S. soldiers back home. The American Tables of Organization and Equipment were translated into Vietnamese and issued. ARVN soldiers were put through standard American training exercises, including a 25-mile march with 50-pound pack that was too arduous for the much smaller Vietnamese.

By the late 1950s, the U.S. clearly had adopted South Vietnam as a client state, pouring hundreds of millions of dollars into the country to subsidize the government

TYPICAL ARMY COMBAT UNITS IN VIETNAM	
Squad:	about 10 men under a staff sergeant
Platoon:	4 squads under a lieutenant
Company:	4 platoons under a captain
Battalion:	headquarters and 4 or more companies under a lieutenant colonel or major
Division:	approximately 15,000 men, including headquarters, 3 brigades with artillery and other combat support, under a major general

and the military. Betraying their own provincialism, U.S. officials tried to transform Vietnam into a western style society. Although the Geneva Accords (1954) limited outside uniformed military personnel in Vietnam to 342, the U.S. was now up to 700. By the end of the decade, despite this build-up, U.S. advisors still insisted the guerrillas were no real threat.

The Counterinsurgency

The nature of the advisory role changed in the early 1960s. After two years of organizing, the National Liberation Front (NLF) was officially established in South Vietnam in December 1960. President Kennedy feared that Indochina was a prime theater for Soviet-sponsored "wars of national liberation." Influenced by his reading of *The Uncertain Trumpet* (1960) by former Army Chief of Staff Maxwell Taylor, Kennedy believed that the U.S. must prepare to meet this global challenge.

Kennedy extended Taylor's proposal for a more "flexible military response" to include low-intensity warfare and assigned this counterinsurgency role to the Army Special Forces. He gave them more money and manpower. Over the objections of Army leadership, Kennedy further authorized the Special Forces to don the green beret to identify themselves as an elite corps.

Given the President's strong endorsement, the Army was now obliged to give more attention to counterinsurgency. However, the top leadership remained committed to conventional warfare. General Lyman Lemnitzer, Chairman of the Joint Chiefs of Staff (1960-1962), said "the new administration was 'oversold' on the importance of guerrilla warfare." General George H. Decker, Army Chief of Staff (1960-1962), boasted that "any good soldier can handle guerrillas." General Earle Wheeler, Army Chief of Staff (1962-1964), dismissed the political dimensions of the conflict with the statement "the essence of the problem in Vietnam is military." Even General Taylor considered counterinsurgency "just a form of small war," and characterized the Army's reaction to Kennedy's directives as "...something we have to satisfy. But not much heart went into the work."

McNamara and Westmoreland

Kennedy expanded the RVNAF from 150,000 to 200,000 troops and sent more U.S. advisors. American commitment was widened further when the Military Assistance Advisory Group (MAAG) was upgraded to Military Advisory Command—Vietnam (MACV) in February 1962.

The President appointed Robert McNamara, former President of the Ford Motor Company, to be his Secretary of Defense. McNamara's passion for statistical precision made him the perfect model of the new military manager. Vietnam was just another problem to be "managed" successfully. Officials proclaimed that the RVNAF were improving and the political situation stabilizing.

But American senior advisors attached to ARVN units told another story. Lieutenant Colonel John Paul Vann produced particularly pessimistic reports. Vann believed that ARVN training and the pacification program were failures. He stated that South Vietnamese political and military leaders were corrupt, and even accused the ARVN of avoiding the enemy in the field. His message was that the war was being lost.

Back in the U.S. in June 1963, Vann learned that his and other critics' reports were being suppressed by MACV headquarters. He scheduled a briefing with the Joint Chiefs, but Chairman Taylor sided with MACV and canceled it. Forced to resign from the Army for personal reasons, Vann soon returned to Vietnam and, in time, became the highest ranking civilian advisor in the country. Until his untimely death in a helicopter crash in 1972, he was recognized as one of the most knowledgeable individuals about the war.

Lacking appreciation of the revolutionary nature of the challenge, U.S. policymakers were optimistic about solving what they saw as essentially a military problem. Despite talk about winning hearts and minds, U.S. leaders never persuaded South Vietnamese President Diem to undertake the social, economic, and political reforms needed to win support for his government. He failed to address the needs of the many landless farmers and his village security program of strategic hamlets was widely resented.

In November, Diem was killed in a U.S. approved coup. Kennedy was assassinated three weeks later. Lyndon Johnson inherited a political and military quagmire with no end in sight. For the next year and a half, Saigon governments came and went in a series of coups, and the war effort virtually stopped.

The U.S. Enters Into Combat: 1965-1967

Using the authority of the Tonkin Gulf Resolution instead of an official declaration of war by Congress, President Lyndon B. Johnson sent U.S. forces into combat in Vietnam in 1965. Already committed to an ambitious program of social reforms, Johnson was reluctant to jeopardize support by plunging the country into a full-scale war. He also was mindful of strong public opposition to sending American troops to fight in another land war in Asia, especially given North Vietnam's mutual defense pact with China. He expressed confidence that a great power like the United States could manage the war in Vietnam long enough for the ARVN and the South Vietnamese government to establish themselves.

Vietcong soldiers advance along a small irrigation waterway.

Against the U.S., the Vietcong followed the same strategy of protracted warfare that the Vietminh had used to defeat the French. Because of their disadvantage in manpower and firepower, Vietcong guerrillas avoided any direct engagements where they did not have a numerical superiority. Instead, they practiced hit-and-run tactics to drag out the war, undermine the morale of U.S. forces and exhaust the patience of the American public. This also gave the Vietcong time to win the ideological battle for the hearts and minds of the people.

In response, U.S. military leaders planned a "war of attrition" against the guerrillas. The goal was to destroy the enemy in the field at a rate fast enough to reach the "cross-over point," that is, the point at which casualties would exceed additions to the enemy force. At that point, the enemy was supposed to recognize that victory was not possible and quit the fight. General Westmoreland predicted that the cross-over point would be reached in late 1967 or early 1968.

To ensure the success of its war plan, U.S. commanders developed three separate but related strategies. First, the U.S. Army and Marine Corps would conduct "search and destroy" missions, large-scale ground combat operations designed to accelerate the pace of combat and casualties. Second, U.S. troops would destroy villages friendly to the enemy. As one U.S. General

explained to *The New York Times* correspondent, R. W. Apple, "You've got to dry up the sea the guerrillas swim in—that's the peasants—and the best way to do that is blast the hell out of their villages so they'll come into our refugee camps. No villages, no guerrillas: simple." The final effect of this campaign would be to create "free fire zones" where anyone in the area was "automatically suspected" of being Vietcong or a Vietcong sympathizer and fired upon.

Third, the U.S. Air Force and Navy would conduct an extensive bombing campaign in North Vietnam to undermine support for the guerrillas and cut off the flow of men and supplies to the south. A major target was the "Ho Chi Minh Trail," the major overland supply route from north to south. The Trail was 250 miles long, ran through Laos, and included an estimated 6,000 miles of roadways, pathways, streams, and rivers down which soldiers and supplies could move. This became especially important by 1966 when the People's Army of (North) Vietnam (PAVN) began sending entire regiments into battle in the south. It was reasoned that, once guerrillas were cut off from their supplies and reinforcements, their number would be decreased that much faster.

Counting Kills

Some critics of U.S. policy warned that the French also had fought a war of attrition and they had lost. But

AUTH Tony Auth, Philadelphia Inquirer

U.S. leaders were certain they would succeed where the French had failed. In 1962, Douglas Pike responded to a MACV general's remark that the goal in Vietnam was "to kill VC, pure and simple," by explaining that the French had killed many of the enemy and still lost. The general replied, "Didn't kill enough Vietcong." Each military unit's Order of Battle section kept detailed records of enemy units and even individual personnel by name. Great computers in Saigon tracked Vietcong recruits, defectors, North Vietnamese infiltration, and allied captives.

The most important measure of progress in the war was the number of enemy killed, popularly known as the "body count." The pressure for producing a high body count ran from the Pentagon and White House down to small field units. The success of a leader was determined by how many enemy were killed under his command. A low body count often meant removal from command.

Faced with such pressures, many resorted to falsifying reports. Marine Lt. Col. John Buchanan reveals, "We claimed that for every American that was killed, we killed 13 NVA's. Some of those enemy were old women and children. Sometimes we would count shin bones and body parts. War is not an exact science, and everybody exaggerates." Robert Mall, an enlisted man, reported that in his unit "a weapon captured was counted as five bodies. In other words, if you shoot a guy who's got a gun and you get that gun, you've shot six people."

In 1974, Douglas Kinnard, Brigadier General in Vietnam, polled all the other U.S. generals who had served in the war. Some 64 percent of the 173 responded. Sixty-one percent of the respondents said the body count was "often inflated." As for careerism as a factor in command, 87 percent considered it a problem, 37 percent said it was "serious."

Westmoreland believed the enemy was preparing to move beyond guerrilla tactics to larger scale operations. This would give U.S. units, with their superior firepower, a chance to engage and kill the enemy in greater numbers. He sought increased U.S. forces to conduct search and destroy missions. The plan was for the infantry to "hump the boonies" to make contact with the enemy in the field and then call in artillery barrages, helicopter gunships, fighter-bombers and airmobile reinforcements to

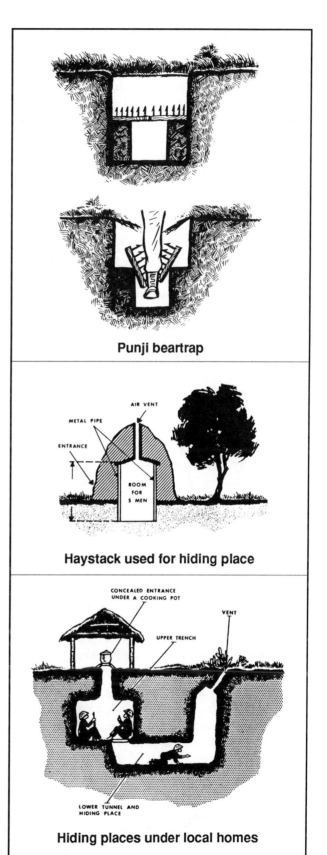

Punji beartrap

Haystack used for hiding place

Hiding places under local homes

destroy them with minimal American casualties. As General Glen A. Walker explained to reporters, "You don't fight this fellow rifle to rifle. You locate him and back away. Blow the hell out of him and then police up."

To support the attrition strategy, Westmoreland presided over the construction of an elaborate infrastructure of roads, military installations, air fields, ports, artillery firebases, etc. While a remarkable engineering accomplishment, Westmoreland's strategy required a great many soldiers to be involved in construction projects rather than combat.

A number of large-scale operations in 1966 and 1967, which sought to accelerate the attrition strategy, looked good on paper. They uncovered caches of weapons, munitions, and supplies; destroyed tunnel complexes; and produced high body count. However, they also had heavy social and political costs, such as those detailed in journalist Jonathan Schell's *The Village of Ben Suc*, an account of how a whole village of "Vietcong sympathizers" was bulldozed and its people forcibly relocated. Such tactics did not help and probably hurt the U.S. war effort.

It was already evident by late 1966 that the attrition strategy was failing. The U.S. and South Vietnamese could not kill the enemy as fast as the Vietcong could recruit replacements or the North Vietnamese march troops down the Ho Chi Minh Trail. Despite American efforts to search out the enemy and engage them in combat, most contacts were brief with only a small number of enemy killed.

For the most part, the NVA/VC forces dictated when and where they would fight. One study reported that almost 90 percent of all combat engagements were initiated by the enemy. The guerrillas learned to strike quickly, in the words of a Marine medic "kill a couple of people and split before anybody got there." They avoided the massive U.S. firepower by slipping into the villages, fleeing to impenetrable jungle, disappearing into tunnel complexes, or crossing the border into Laos and Cambodia, which were off limits to American ground action until late in the war.

Methods Backfire

A more controversial aspect of search and destroy was that many soldiers believed it was premised on the use of ground troops as bait for Vietcong ambushes.

Captain Michael O'Mera explained to Congress:

> They made their ground units bait by sending them into the swamps, into the jungles, into the rice paddies where they would search for the enemy and at night set up in a night-logger or a combat-patrol position, and from this position they were most likely to get attacked. This is where the enemy would most likely hit them. They were bait.

As the war progressed and this suspicion spread, many troops began to resist. By 1968, some units even faked night patrols, going outside the camp a few hundred yards and spending the night there rather than going further out to set an ambush. This attitude became known as "search and avoid." Other soldiers sought a way out of the war by shooting, injuring or exposing themselves to disease.

The most serious reaction was called "fragging" because soldiers would use fragmentation grenades to warn or kill commanders who seemed too willing to risk their charges' lives on hazardous assignments. Dr. Charles Levy, a psychiatrist assigned to the 3rd Marine Division, estimated that over 500 attacks occurred in the first eight months of 1969, whereas the official figure was 96 for the entire year. Victims were classified as either wounded or killed in action by enemy forces, not U.S. troops. Sociologist John Helmer found that 58 percent of the combat vets he interviewed replied "yes" to the question "Did you ever personally know of a fragging incident in your unit directed against NCOs (sergeants) or officers?"

It was widely known that ten thousand dollars was offered for fragging Major General Melvin Zais, commander of the 101st Airborne (Airmobile) Division, for ordering an attack on "Hamburger Hill" in May 1969, when his troops took very heavy casualties for no apparent strategic advantage. One of his men explained, "Every time we radioed him our position, he flew overhead in a copter and we got hit." Nobody collected the reward. The army acknowledges 600 cases of fragging over 1969-1971. The actual number will never be known, but search and destroy operations for U.S. troops were soon phased out.

Another problem with the search and destroy operations was that, while troops were rewarded for producing a high body count, there was no reliable method for certifying the identities of many of those suspected or

killed. This was an enormous problem in a revolutionary war in which almost anyone could be friend or foe.

The dilemma of whether or not to shoot plagued GIs in the field and still haunts many suffering from post-traumatic stress disorder today. Some went by the book and only fired on those carrying a weapon. Others fired at anything that ran. Given the rewards for reporting a high body count, however, everyone's moral dilemma was covered by what came to be called the "meer gook rule," that is "if it's dead and it's Vietnamese, it's VC." The massive killing of innocent civilians by U.S. troops drove more and more neutral Vietnamese into the ranks of the Vietcong.

Other tactics had their own costs. The use of antipersonnel bombs offended sensibilities all over the world. Napalm bombs burned up available oxygen and asphyxiated those in the area. The bombs also spit out a jelly-like gasoline that clung to the flesh and burned to the bone. Other bombs scattered a broadside of steel pellets or barbed-wire steel splinters that were useless against military installations but deadly against humans. Unfortunately, it was often the slow and weak—women, children and the elderly—who suffered from the attacks.

The bombing, bulldozing or burning of villages believed to be friendly to the Vietcong caused the enemy logistical problems. And the massive defoliation campaign, almost eighteen million gallons of herbicides sprayed over 4.5 million acres of forest and cropland, deprived the Vietcong of food and of ground cover from which to launch ambushes. However, these extreme methods also caused much suffering to the innocents.

The chemical warfare program damaged U.S. esteem in world opinion, provoked protest at home, and turned more Vietnamese against the Americans. One study found that three of four peasants whose crops had been poisoned said they hated the U.S. and South

Rules of Engagement or "Organized Butchery"?

"...we were fighting in the cruelest kind of conflict, a people's war. It was no orderly campaign, as in Europe, but a war for survival waged in a wilderness without rules or laws; a war in which each soldier fought for his own life and the lives of the men beside him, not caring how he killed in that personal cause or how many or in what manner and feeling only contempt for those who sought to impose on his savage struggle the mincing distinctions of civilized warfare—that code of battlefield ethics that attempted to humanize an essentially inhuman war. According to those 'rules of engagement,' it was morally right to shoot an unarmed Vietnamese who was running, but wrong to shoot one who was standing or walking; it was wrong to shoot an enemy prisoner at close range, but right for a sniper at long range to kill an enemy soldier who was no more able than a prisoner to defend himself; it was wrong for infantrymen to destroy a village with white phosphorus grenades, but right for a fighter pilot to drop napalm on it. Ethics seemed to be a matter of distance and technology. You could never go wrong if you killed people at long range with sophisticated weapons. And then there was that inspiring order issued by General Green: kill VC. In the patriotic fervor of the Kennedy years, we had asked, 'What can we do for our country?' and our country answered, 'Kill VC.' That was the strategy, the best our best military minds could come up with: organized butchery. But organized or not, butchery was butchery, so who was to speak of rules and ethics in a war that had none?..."—Philip Caputo, *A Rumor of War*. New York: Holt, Rinehart and Winston, 1978: 33-4.

Gliding Baskets

"Eight Six Foxtrot—Eight Six Foxtrot.
This is One One Zulu. Over."

    The woman in blue
    Carried the weight swiftly, with grace,
    Her face hidden by her
    Conical rice straw hat.

"One One Zulu—this is Eight Six Foxtrot. Go."
"Roger Eight Six. I have Fire Mission.
Dink in the open, Grid: Bravo Sierra,
Five Six Niner, Four Six Five, Range:
Three thousand, Proximity: Eight hundred. Over"

    The two heavy baskets
    Balanced on tips
    Of the springing Chogi stick
    Glided close to the hard smooth path.

"Read back, One One Zulu."
"Roger Copy, Eight Six."
"Shot, on the way, wait."
"Shot out, Eight Six."

    A sighing 105 mm round slides through its parabola
    Then the explosive tearing at the steel which surrounds it,
    And the shrapnel catches the gliding baskets,
    And they crumple with the woman in blue.

near An Trang
August 14, 1969

—Frank A. Cross Jr.

Vietnamese governments. Some already were opposed, but others were provoked by the assaults on their villages. Thus, the U.S. military's own tactics were causing them to lose the important political battle for the hearts and minds of the people.

As the war dragged on, it became clear that U.S. strategy was stalemated by the enemy's clever and tenacious defense. As long as it was willing to stay the course, the U.S. could control militarily any area it chose. However, it could never establish sufficient political control over enough of the country to leave the fighting to the ARVN, let alone to neutralize the insurgency. The question was how long the American public and its representatives in Congress would tolerate the escalating costs of this stalemate.

North Vietnam could not conquer the South as long as it was defended by U.S. troops. However, its interest in the struggle was deeper and longer standing than that of the U.S. As Premier Pham Van Dong explained to Bernard Fall, they were willing to fight for decades, even centuries, as they had done against the Chinese. He predicted that the U.S. would become frustrated with the long, inconclusive war and eventually give up. Thus, the NVA/VC did not have to win, but merely to keep from losing.

The Air War: 1965-1967

Most American leaders disputed Dong's prediction of eventual NVA/VC victory. They believed that their bombing campaign would make the war too costly for the North Vietnamese. The air war campaign, called "Rolling Thunder," had three related objectives: (1) to break the will of North Vietnamese leaders to support the Vietcong in the south, (2) to destroy North Vietnam's industrial base, and (3) to stop the flow of men and supplies to the south.

The unit of measurement for bombing missions is called the "sortie," one flight by one plane. Throughout 1965, the sortie rate climbed, from 3,600 in April to an average of 5,500 a month by the end of the year. Ambassador Maxwell Taylor explained that U.S. air attacks would escalate until leaders in the North came to see a "vision of inevitable, ultimate destruction if they do not change their ways!" Some 134 targets in North Vietnam were bombed in 1965, many of them more than once.

On the advice of Secretary of Defense McNamara, President Johnson stopped the bombing from December 1965 through January 1966. The purpose was to persuade the American public and world opinion that the U.S. was serious about peace and willing to "give North Vietnam a face-saving chance to stop the aggression." However, when war planners assessed the campaign, they were forced to conclude, "the idea that destroying or threatening to destroy North Vietnam's industry would pressure Hanoi into calling it quits seems, in retrospect, a colossal misjudgment."

In 1966, rather than abandon the air war, the U.S. developed a new plan for attacking North Vietnam's petroleum-oil lubricants (POL) facilities, that is, gasoline supplies. According to the Joint Chiefs of Staff, attacks on such facilities would damage the DRV "capability to move war supporting resources within the country and along the infiltration routes to SVN [South Vietnam]...." The air strikes wiped out 80 percent of the storage areas in Haiphong Harbor and completely destroyed the large "tank farm" in Hanoi. In August, the

Corporal Charles Chungtu, U.S.M.C.

This is what the war ended up being about:
we would find a V.C. village,
and if we could not capture it
or clear it of Cong,
we called for jets.
The jets would come in, low and terrible,
sweeping down, and screaming,
in their first pass over the village.
Then they would return, dropping their first bombs
that flattened the huts to rubble and debris.
And then the jets would sweep back again
and drop more bombs
that blew the rubble and debris
to dust and ashes.
And then the jets would come back once again,
in a last pass, this time to drop napalm
that burned the dust and ashes to just nothing.
Then the village
that was not a village any more
was our village.

—Bryan Alec Floyd

U.S. Defense Intelligence Agency declared that 70 percent of North Vietnam's known bulk-storage capacity had been destroyed as well as seven percent of its smaller sites.

More Failure: More Escalation

Despite such widespread destruction, the CIA estimated that North Vietnam still had a POL storage capacity of about 90,000 tons, or almost three times the 32,000 tons it needed to sustain the war effort.

At McNamara's request, the Institute for Defense Analysis (IDA) evaluated the effectiveness of the air strikes on POL facilities. It concluded that "as of July 1966, the U.S. bombing of North Vietnam had had no measurable direct effect on Hanoi's ability to mount and support military operations in the south at the current level."

The reason for this, quite simply, was that Vietcong and NVA forces in the south had little need for gasoline supplies. They did not have that many trucks, let alone armored divisions, airplanes or helicopters. Besides, the VC received relatively few supplies from the north. They got their money, dry goods and food from people in the south. Most of their weapons were either captured in ambushes or purchased on the black market. Even if you included all North Vietnamese regular troops operating in the south, the CIA estimated the total need for supplies to be no greater than 100 tons a day. This could be conveyed in just 50 truckloads. Supplies also were carried on bicycles and the backs of porters, and floated down streams in 55-gallon drums. In the analysis of Air Force Major Earl H. Tilford Jr., "a hundred tons of supplies proved to be too small a trickle for air power to shut off."

The IDA's analysis highlighted what it saw as the fundamental flaw in the U.S. air strategy: North Vietnam had "basically a subsistence agricultural economy" that presented "a difficult and unrewarding system for air attacks." There were few manufacturing plants and most regions were nearly self-sufficient in food and other basic goods. Finally, the study group concluded, "The indirect effects of the bombing on the will of the North Vietnamese to continue fighting...have not shown themselves in any tangible way."

Rejecting the basic logic of this analysis, Westmoreland and the Joint Chiefs of Staff argued that the only problem with the air war was that planners had restricted too many targets close to population centers.

They insisted that the U.S. should be less concerned with U.S. public and world opinion and impose only those minimum restraints necessary to avoid indiscriminate killing of the population.

President Johnson gave the green light to escalate the air war again. In October 1966 alone, 12,000 sorties were flown. For most of 1967, pilots were allowed to strike almost any target but Haiphong Harbor and parts of Hanoi. However, in August, McNamara had to admit to Congress that "the enemy operations in the south cannot, on the basis of any reports I have seen, be stopped by air bombardment—short, that is, of the virtual annihilation of North Vietnam and its people." Of course, U.S. leaders rejected such a course. All civilized nations agree that modern wars are to be fought for high principle or rational gain, not annihilation of a whole people.

Failure Again

As for the other objectives, Johnson's advisors were very negative. McGeorge Bundy concluded that "Ho Chi Minh and his colleagues simply are not going to change their policy on the basis of losses from the air in North Vietnam." In fact, he stated, no intelligence estimate over the last two years had even made such a claim. And Walt Rostow, another key Presidential advisor, was now saying, "We have never held the view that bombing could stop infiltration."

A second IDA study confirmed that, as of October 1967, U.S. bombing of North Vietnam still had not reduced the flow of men and supplies to the south nor "weakened the determination of the North Vietnamese leaders to continue to direct and support the insurgency in the south."

In sum, the U.S. command responded to reports that the bombing campaign was not effective in achieving its objectives by increasing the scope and intensity of the bombing. In 1965, 25,000 sorties dropped 63,000 tons of bombs; in 1966, 79,000 sorties dropped 136,000 tons; and in 1967, 108,000 sorties dropped 226,000 tons. It finally became clear that the problem was not one of scale but of basic concept.

According to Tilford, "The Air Force was hurt badly in Vietnam. We lost 2,257 aircraft. More than 2,700 airmen perished and many remain missing." The Rolling Thunder campaign itself "cost us $10 for every $1 worth of damage inflicted on North Vietnam."

Ironically, U.S. air losses were greater than neces-

North Vietnamese supplies moving south on bicycles.

sary precisely because the objectives of the campaign were unrealistic. In the absence of any confirmed strategic value, U.S. commanders concentrated on producing big numbers, in a manner similar to the body counts.

The monthly limits on bombing missions were transposed by the Air Force and Navy into "production quotas." Each commander was evaluated on whether or not his unit reached their "quota" of sorties. The pressure to keep flying sorties continued into the hazardous flying weather of December through mid-May. Pilots who complained that bad weather made bombing missions both futile and dangerous were confronted with arguments for bureaucratic self interest. One officer told Air Force Captain Richard S. Drury:

Obviously you don't understand the big picture, Captain. If you knew what was really going on you'd see why you're going out there. It's simply a matter of dropping ordnance [bombs and rockets] and flying sorties. The more we drop the better we do and also the Defense Department looks at what we used during this time period and projects our future finances and allotments on that figure. If we cancel flights then we drop less ordnance, use less fuel and oil, and get less next time.

Early in the war, the competition between Air Force and Navy commanders over sortie rates led to many planes being sent on missions with very few bombs, thus risking more pilots and planes than necessary. Tilford concludes, "the large maintenance toil needed to support our sophisticated aircraft enforced a managerial mindset in which quantitative measures, like sortie-generation rates, in-commission rates, and bomb damage assessments became an end unto themselves."

Pacification: 1967

In 1967, as confidence in the bombing strategy waned, the U.S. finally began to pay serious attention to pacification. McNamara persuaded the South Vietnamese to put up to 60 percent of ARVN infantry battalions into what was called Revolutionary Development operations. An Office of Civil Operations and Rural Development (CORDS) was created under Robert Komer, a hard-driving, outspoken manager nicknamed

"Blowtorch." Employing South Vietnamese, South Koreans and Thais, CORDS activities included resettling refugees, village security, local political participation, encouraging enemy defections, and other projects.

The training and successful operation of local paramilitary units was an important part of the village security program. Some American critics accused these regional forces (RF) and popular forces (PF), derisively called "Ruff-Puffs," of general ineptitude, cowardice and infiltration by the Vietcong. Clearly, the Ruff-Puffs had minimal training, poor leadership, and little combat support such as communication radios, mortars, artillery support, air resources, or even ammunition. Yet they were a prime target for communist attacks and suffered a large percentage of South Vietnamese casualties. It also should be acknowledged that they accounted for 30 percent of enemy kills. One observer called them the unsung heroes of the war.

The *Chieu Hoi* program to encourage defectors from the enemy was the most successful pacification effort. Between 1965-1972, 50 billion propaganda leaflets were distributed in the two Vietnams, Laos, and Cambodia. This program produced more than 200,000 defectors, including about 120,000 enemy combatants, without any loss of life. Comparatively inexpensive, the program had one of the best cost/benefit ratios of any activity undertaken. *psychological warfare.*

Despite its success, the program provided many examples of American cultural ignorance. Many messages were written in literary Vietnamese rather than peasant vernacular. This conveyed an elitist tone and alienated the common people. Vietnamese interpreters often translated American phrases literally which distorted the message. One leaflet used a picture of a bikini-clad Vietnamese woman to appeal to communist soldiers. The Vietnamese just considered the whole thing to be in bad taste.

The most controversial pacification project was the Phoenix Program to eliminate the Vietcong infrastructure (VCI) who operated undercover in the government, military, and business communities as well as the villages. The program was run by the South Vietnamese with U.S. technical and logistical support coordinated by the CIA. Some 81,000 people were arrested and interrogated. Torture often was used to extract confessions. According to figures from the Saigon government, 33,000 were sentenced to prison, 26,000 were killed and 22,000 changed their allegiance to the South

Vietnamese government.

Unfortunately, the program often was subverted by other interests. Some South Vietnamese used Phoenix to settle family feuds, wipe out debts, or eliminate personal enemies. An intelligence officer in the U.S. Army attached to Phoenix reported: "When I arrived in the district I was given a list of 200 names of people who had to be killed. When I left after six months, we still hadn't killed anyone on the list. But we'd killed 260 other people."

Phoenix's record is mixed. In some provinces, it was very successful in virtually eliminating the VCI. In others, it accomplished nothing. Leadership, commitment, and local conditions varied tremendously. Postwar interviews with communist leaders revealed that they considered Phoenix a very devastating program. Whatever the program's flaws, it is clear that in a revolutionary war, targeting the hidden infrastructure—counterinsurgency—is an essential element of strategy.

Counting the Enemy

By the middle of 1967, the number of NVA soldiers in the south was less than three percent of North Vietnam's available manpower. One study in late 1968 showed that if enemy forces continued to sustain the unusually high level of casualties inflicted in the first half of that year, it still would take a minimum of 15 1/2 years to eliminate the enemy. In summary, the attrition strategy was doomed to fail.

However, Lyndon Johnson did not accept this logic. He believed that the U.S. could make the costs so heavy for North Vietnam that in time they would abandon the Vietcong, and then the guerrillas could be eliminated. Johnson and military strategists failed fully to appreciate the revolutionary dimensions of the conflict and continued to underestimate the indigenous strength of the Vietcong.

In late 1966 and early 1967, a debate raged among the CIA, military intelligence, and the Joint Chiefs over who should be counted as Vietcong combatants. Should part-time personnel engaged in auxiliary tasks be included alongside trained, armed guerrillas? From his study of captured enemy documents, CIA analyst Sam Adams argued that the number of Vietcong was much higher, in fact, almost double what MACV listed. If these higher numbers were correct, most of the claims of progress were invalid. This would be politically damaging to support for the war.

Chairman of the Joint Chiefs, General Earle Wheeler, did not want these higher estimates released to the press. General Westmoreland concurred. After the war, a television documentary accused Westmoreland of covering up the higher numbers even from the President. General Westmoreland brought suit, but later dropped it in the middle of a widely publicized trial. Both adversaries claimed that their positions had been upheld.

In the fall of 1967, CIA, military intelligence, the ambassador to South Vietnam, and others agreed to accept the MACV estimates as official. Soon afterward Westmoreland reported to President Johnson that the tide of the war was shifting to the U.S. In a speech to Congress and the American people, the General professed to "see the light at the end of the tunnel" and predicted that the U.S. would start to withdraw troops in the next couple of years.

The War Turns Bad: 1968

Within a few weeks there were indications of a major communist build-up around Khe Sanh, an isolated Marine outpost 14 miles south of the DMZ and six miles from the Laotian border. The siege of Khe Sanh began in late January. It lasted for 77 days and was the most controversial battle of the war. Johnson feared an American Dienbienphu and got a written "guarantee" from each member of the Joint Chiefs of Staff that the base would be held. He had a model built in the war room in the White House basement and studied the situation daily. The media also watched developments closely. Walter Cronkite called the battle of Khe San a "microcosm of the war."

When it was over, an estimated 10,000-15,000 North Vietnamese had been killed, as contrasted to fewer than 250 Americans. Westmoreland called Khe Sanh "one of the most damaging, one-sided defeats among many that the North Vietnamese incurred." General Lewis Walt called it "the most important battle of the war." Westmoreland added that Khe Sanh "discredited" the "myth of General Giap's military genius."

General Dave Palmer disagreed. He saw Khe Sanh as a diversionary tactic that "accomplished its purpose

Friendly Fire

I looked toward the spot where the fire fight had begun, and saw a dark figure running toward me. His rifle was pointed directly at me. I remember feeling fear deep inside that this Vietcong was about to kill me, and when he was almost on top of me, I raised my rifle, pointed it, and fired three times at his head and chest. The figure fell right in front of me.

Someone ran out and dragged the body back. He screamed, "Somebody has just shot the Corporal—" They said his name. I realized then that I had just killed one of my own men....

In October, I went out on a patrol. I'd killed the corporal and had to make up for it. As we were crossing a rice dike, we were suddenly hit by a tremendous burst of automatic fire. It went on for an hour, and a strange feeling of relief and excitement—and victory—swept over me. But it turned out that we'd been attacked by the South Vietnamese, the ARVN. "They thought you were the Vietcong," the major told me. And then he put me in for a medal....—Ron Kovic, "On the Eve of the Tet Offensive." In Lynda Rosen Obst. *The Sixties.* Reprinted in The New York *Times Magazine*, November 13, 1977.

magnificently." Indeed, Giap later revealed that the North Vietnamese did not regard Khe Sanh as important, let alone another Dienbienphu. In his view, the Americans made Khe Sanh important because they felt their prestige was at stake. However, as soon as the battle was won, Khe Sanh was evacuated. As for Giap, diversion, indeed, was his game. During the 77 days of battle in the wilderness, the communists launched their biggest coordinated offensive of the war—and it was in the cities.

At dawn on January 30, 1968, the first day of the annual Tet (lunar New Year) truce, the Vietcong, with NVA support, attacked 36 of the 44 provincial capitals, five of the six largest cities, 64 of the 242 district capitals, 50 hamlets, and 23 military bases and airfields.

The fighting during Tet was intense. It was a decisive military victory for the U.S. The assault was beaten back and the attackers suffered enormous casualties. Although probably inflated, MACV estimated 40,000 enemy deaths at a cost of 1,000 Americans killed. Many of the Vietcong infrastructure surfaced and were killed. The people's uprising for which the communists hoped did not occur. The Vietcong were so badly damaged that the NVA was forced to assume the major burden of the fighting from then on.

On the other hand, the communists scored a significant psychological victory in the offensive. Despite the heavy price in lives, they definitely called into question the U.S. and South Vietnamese governments' ability to protect their own people. The attack on the U.S. Embassy and size and coordination of the whole assault impressed many war weary Americans and Vietnamese and dealt a severe blow to public support for the pacification program.

After years of optimistic reports, people were shocked at the boldness and scale of the enemy offensive. Moreover, much of the action took place in Saigon and other major cities where film crews could cover it without the interference of MACV. The result was more scenes of combat, disorder, and violence than the public had ever seen. Many more Americans expressed concern over the large and growing number of American casualties. While small when compared to that of the communists, they were much larger than the U.S. public was prepared to tolerate in a war with unclear objectives and of questionable morality. As it turned out, 1968 was the peak year for U.S. casualties in the war—14,615 killed and 46,800 wounded.

The U.S. Destroys Hue to Save It

Cronkite: "If the communists' intention was to take and seize the cities, they came closer here at Hue than anywhere else, and now, three weeks after the offensive began, the firing still goes on, here on the new side of the city, and across the Perfume River to the old side, the Citadel."

"Probably, a week before this offensive began, the army of North Vietnam, with Vietcong support, began moving into the mountains south of here, one day's march away. And then the day before the offensive began, January 30th to 31st, they began that march toward the city. Meanwhile, another regiment of the NVA were moving in from the north, into the city, the old Citadel, from the north, and they swept quickly through it, too, except for a small corner in the northeast of the Citadel held by the South Vietnamese Army headquarters."

"It was a tough fight. It was house-to-house, door-to-door, room-to-room. They found they couldn't get into the doors and the windows; the North Vietnamese Army held them too tightly and had booby-trapped them as well. They had to blast their way in with plastic charges placed against the sides of the houses. It was such a tough fight that although the American Army hoped not to use heavy weapons and air strikes against this old city, they finally had to bring them in to win the battle."

"The destruction here was almost total. There is scarcely an inhabitable building in the city of Hue. Whatever price the communists paid for this offensive, the price to the allied cause was high, for if our intention is to restore normalcy, peace, serenity to this country, the destruction of those qualities in this, the most historical and probably serene of all South Vietnam's cities, is obviously a setback. Now, a job no one dreamed we were going to have to undertake. It is now the rebuilding of an entire city, and the lives of the people in it".—CBS Television, "Who, What, When, Where, Why: Report from Vietnam by Walter Cronkite." February 27, 1968.

Abrams salutes his departing predecessor, General Westmoreland, during a brief farewell ceremony at Tan Son Nhut airbase.

Reassessment After Tet

In the wake of Tet, Johnson realized he lacked the support to continue the war indefinitely. When Westmoreland requested 206,000 more troops to join the 525,000 already in Vietnam, Johnson ordered a review of U.S. Vietnam policy by a group of experienced statesmen he called "the wise men."

Headed by the new Secretary of Defense, Clark Clifford, the group heard reports by the Departments of Defense, State and others that the Vietcong numbered many more than previously reported. Some intelligence organizations estimated that North Vietnam had so many young people in its population that, if necessary, it could send more than 100,000 men to war each year forever. The International Security Agency of the Department of Defense concluded, "Even with the 200,000 additional troops requested by MACV, we will not be in a position to drive the enemy from SVN or destroy his forces."

A key memorandum to Johnson advised against the increase because the Saigon leadership showed no willingness or ability "to attract the necessary loyalty or support of the people." As such, a large U.S. troop increase would only "intensify the belief of the ruling elite that the U.S. will continue to fight its war while it engages in backroom politics and permits widespread corruption."

Johnson denied Westmoreland's request and began turning more of the war over to the ARVN. As explained by Secretary of Defense Clifford on July 15, 1968, "We are interested in doing all we can to accelerate the development of the ARVN. We intend to give preference to the ARVN forces, even at the expense of our forces." This was to be the beginning of the Vietnamization program later concluded under President Richard M. Nixon.

Johnson's Peace Proposal

On March 30, 1968, two months into the Tet Offensive, President Johnson made a startling address to the nation. He announced that he would not seek his party's nomination for re-election so that he would not be an obstacle to successful peace negotiations. He stated further that he was limiting bombing to the southern part of North Vietnam as an inducement for peace talks. With bad weather forecast, Johnson really wasn't giving much away. In fact, he advised U.S. ambassadors abroad that they "should make it clear [to U.S. allies] that Hanoi is most likely to denounce the project and thus free our hand after a short period."

To Johnson's surprise, Hanoi accepted the offer. *whoa!* Late in October 1968, Johnson halted all bombing over the north and entered into negotiations with North Vietnam. He hoped this gesture would help his Vice President, Hubert Humphrey, win the November election for President. However, Richard Nixon, whose campaign advertised a "secret plan" to end the war, was elected.

Vietnamization: 1969-1973

Once in office, Nixon extended Johnson's plan to train ARVN troops to take the place of U.S. ground troops in the field. He called it "Vietnamization." Despite reservations, U.S. advisors organized a crash training program for the ARVN, complete with massive supplies of equipment and matériel. For the first time, all ARVN were issued the M-16 rifle, the weapon of U.S. forces since 1966.

In 1970, Cambodian leader, Prince Norodom Sihanouk was overthrown in a *coup d'état* led by General

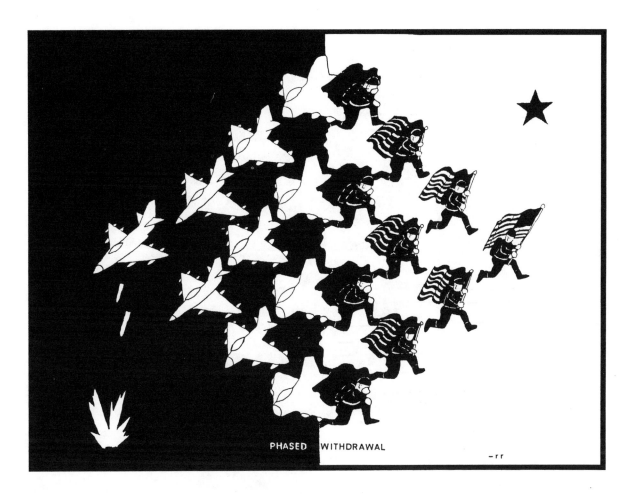

PHASED WITHDRAWAL

—rr

Lon Nol and supported by the U.S. In May, Nixon ordered an "incursion" into Cambodia as part of the search for the communist party headquarters for South Vietnam (COSVN). While COSVN was never found, the incursion was judged a military success. U.S. forces killed more than 2,000 enemy troops, cleared 1,600 acres of jungle, destroyed 8,000 bunkers and captured huge weapons and munitions caches.

On the other hand, the Cambodian incursion further undermined support for the war. College campuses erupted in protest over the widening of the war. Four students were killed by National Guard troops at Kent State University in Ohio in early May. Congress began to put funding restrictions on the war. Moreover, a disastrous February 1971 incursion by the ARVN into Laos dampened enthusiasm for the Vietnamization process.

There also were long-term consequences of the assault on Cambodia that eventually proved disastrous to the people of that tiny country. The incursion was preceded by about 3,600 secret B-52 bombing raids

over the period March 1969 to May 1970. The bombing triggered a low-level communist insurgency along the eastern frontier. The rebels, called Khmer Rouge, gained in size and determination. The bombing also drove nearly two million people from the countryside into Phnom Penh where they later became victims of Khmer Rouge leader Pol Pot's forced exodus. The "secret bombings" eventually led to the "killing fields" of Cambodia.

Bombing Widens

While Nixon was winding down the ground war, he widened the air war. Not wanting to destroy his new image with the American public as a peacemaker, Nixon said the air war would be essentially defensive in nature. Under this plan, reconnaissance planes were to be sent out and, when fired upon, backed up by other American war planes. U.S. planes flew 37,000 such "protective reaction strikes" against North Vietnam in 1969. What was unknown to Congress and even much of the military was that this apparent reduction in the

Ruins of a section
of a hospital in Hanoi,
hit by a B-52 bombing
attack during the 11
days of Linebacker II

North Vietnamese
delegates resume
secret peace
negotiations with
U.S. representatives
in January, 1973.

U.S. war effort was linked to secret bombing campaigns over Cambodia, already discussed, and over Laos.

Two different air wars were fought over Laos from 1968 through 1972. The first, called "Barrel Roll," was over a north plateau region called the Plain of Jars. It was directed at encampments of the NVA and Pathet Lao, a guerrilla force of about 35,000 men who were the Laotian equivalent of the Vietcong. Some villages also were bombed. The second bombing campaign was carried out in southern Laos against the Ho Chi Minh Trail used by the North Vietnamese to move men and supplies into South Vietnam. Over the course of this campaign U.S. forces dropped a total of 2.2 million tons of bombs.

On March 31, 1972, North Vietnam launched the largest offensive since Tet 1968, a conventional invasion across the DMZ by 120,000 NVA troops led by Soviet tanks and artillery. The U.S had only 100,000 military personnel, including 6,000 combat troops, left in Vietnam. Nixon responded with the largest bombing campaign of the war (code named Linebacker), the mining of Haiphong Harbor, and a naval blockade of North Vietnam.

Almost all oil storage facilities and 70 percent of electrical power generating capacity in the north were destroyed. The new laser-guided smart bombs smashed many bridges and railroads. Interdiction reduced overland imports form 160,000 to 30,000 tons a month. Mining the Haiphong Harbor cut seaborne imports from 250,000 tons a month to nearly zero.

Air power alone took 120,000 North Vietnamese lives. Troung Nhu Tang of the Vietcong's Provisional Revolutionary Government explained that as the summer went on, it was obvious that the losses were more than could be sustained and that the territorial advances could not be held. Negotiations to get the Americans out of the war were imperative.

U.S. Disengagement: 1972-1973

By October 1972, the negotiating teams in Paris produced a peace treaty agreeable to the U.S. and North Vietnam. South Vietnamese President Thieu charged the U.S. with betraying his government and opposed the agreement. After his re-election, Nixon instructed Kissinger to address Thieu's concerns. On November 20th, Kissinger presented Hanoi's Le Duc Tho with sixty-nine amendments to the agreement demanded by Thieu.

"Traitors!"

The peace talks resumed, but broke down completely on December 13th. Two days later Nixon gave Hanoi an ultimatum to return to the table within 72 hours. When it passed, he unleashed the most intensive bombing of the entire war, known as Linebacker II. In eleven days, 740 B-52 and 1,000 other aircraft sorties dropped over 20,000 tons of bombs on the Hanoi-Haiphong area.

Hanoi's air defense, bolstered by an estimated 850 Soviet-made SAMS (surface-to-air missiles), had been much improved. The U.S. Air Force acknowledged 15 B-52s and 11 other aircraft shot down, 33 aviators killed and 33 captured. The North Vietnamese claimed over 1,600 of their people killed and thousands wounded.

This brought forth a storm of protest from world leaders, including the Pope. China and the Soviet Union threatened to withdraw support from the negotiations unless the bombing raids were stopped. Members of Congress made it clear they would impose legal constraints upon return from Christmas recess. Nixon's popularity rating fell to 39 percent overnight.

Hanoi's air defenses now were crippled, but so was the Nixon Presidency. Both nations were war weary and world leaders demanded a settlement. On December 30, 1972, by mutual agreement, Nixon stopped the bombing and the North Vietnamese delegation returned to the negotiating table. Nixon quickly surrendered most of the changes demanded by Thieu. On January 27, 1973, the Paris Accords were signed, ending America's longest war.

North Defeats South: 1973-1975

The ordeal was just beginning for South Vietnamese leaders, however. The treaty allowed North Vietnam to maintain almost 150,000 troops in the south. It also placed restrictions upon the amount of aid that South Vietnam could receive, although no restrictions were placed upon aid for North Vietnam. The American public was relieved to see this long nightmare come to an end. The Thieu administration in the south was angry and apprehensive.

The U.S. turned over immense amounts of equipment and matériel to the South Vietnamese prior to the treaty, and promised more. Thieu had an army of over one million and the third largest air force in the world. Nixon pledged continued support and guaranteed that U.S. troops would return if the treaty were violated by North Vietnam. Still, the North Vietnamese were dug

in and the ARVN could not expect to maintain the same level of firepower as when the U.S. was involved.

By the beginning of 1975, over 300,000 North Vietnamese troops with 700 tanks were poised to take over the south. Aided by strategic lapses by Thieu, North Vietnam's spring offensive triumphed on May 1, 1975. Some criticized the U.S. for abandoning its ally. However, few would claim that anything short of U.S. reentry into the war would have forestalled the final outcome.

Conclusion

In the wake of this defeat, many Americans have been tempted to look for scapegoats in Congress, the media, the universities, and the anti-war movement. A poll by Louis Harris in 1979 found that 73 percent of the public and 89 percent of Vietnam-era Veterans agreed: "The trouble in Vietnam was that our troops were asked to fight in a war which our political leaders in Washington would not let them win."

One well-known conservative critic of the U.S. war plan in Vietnam is Colonel Harry Summers (retired). For him "the most frustrating aspect of the Vietnam conflict" is that the U.S. armed forces won "every major battle of the war, yet North Vietnam, rather than the United States, triumphed in the end."

Summers believes the problem was that America's basic strategy was flawed. In his view, the U.S. should have been much less concerned with the Vietcong and pacification. Instead, it should have defined the war as a conventional confrontation between North Vietnam and the United States and its ally in the south. Having done this, President Johnson should have rallied public support for a full declaration of war. This would have enabled Johnson to raise taxes, call up the reserves, place a cordon across Laos and invade North Vietnam, with no restriction on bombing. Summers claims that China and the Soviet Union would have stayed out of the fight and the U.S. would have won the war.

Other experts contend that Summer's proposals would have been impossible to implement politically or militarily. Moreover, Summers' conjecture about the responses of China and the Soviet Union cannot be proven. Such actions carried the potential risk of a much greater and more devastating war.

As the discussion of public opinion polls in Chapter 7 makes clear, from the start, most Americans did not want to risk American boys in a land war in Asia, were very concerned about China coming into the war, and did not think the South Vietnamese government could be saved.

Contrary to Summers, others have said that the fundamental flaw in the U.S. war plan was that U.S. leaders defined the conflict too narrowly in military terms. As Tilford reminds us, "Basic strategy courses teach that war is more than a contest between armed forces. It is a struggle between nations that incorporates economic, cultural, social, and political, as well as military, dimensions." In Vietnam, there was far too little knowledge of the local political situation, far too little appreciation of the determination and appeal of the enemy, and far too little attention to counterinsurgency and pacification.

In 1984, journalist William Broyles Jr. returned to Vietnam where he had served as a Marine lieutenant during the war. Broyles interviewed several Vietnamese generals and soldiers about their strategy. Asked why they persisted despite the enormous firepower against them, many responded in paraphrases of the simple but powerful slogan of Ho Chi Minh: "Nothing is more important than independence and freedom." Americans viewed the war through the prism of Cold War ideology as between communism and capitalism. For most Vietnamese, however, race and nation were much more important forces.

Still, Broyles persisted, American helicopters were extremely mobile and artillery and B-52s awesomely destructive. How could the Vietnamese win against all that? The Vietnamese answer was that they prevailed by turning America's superior military strength against her. One soldier replied, "We learned to build special shelters, to decoy your artillery and planes with sham positions, to tie you to your firebases and helicopters so that they worked against you."

Military technology, by itself, cannot prevail. Winning or losing depends primarily on the motivation of the troops, nourished by the support of the people. When people believe in a cause, they are capable of extraordinary sacrifices; and, soldiers are capable of extraordinary courage. In South Vietnam, however, that was not the case. The ARVN had little public support, especially in the countryside, and suffered a high rate of desertion (more than 20 %). It also abandoned or sold a great many U.S. manufactured weapons to the insurgents. Fewer than one in ten generals in the survey by Gen. Kinnard saw the ARVN as "an acceptable fighting force."

The U.S. military didn't have much support in Vietnam either. In an interview with the *New Republic* magazine, President Thieu himself stated: "The main reason the Vietcong remain so strongly entrenched is that people...still believe there is little difference between the French whom they called colonialists and the Americans whom they call imperialists."

To win the crucial battle for hearts and minds necessary to govern South Vietnam, the U.S. and its allies had to win the loyalty of the people with social, political and economic reforms. At the very least, they needed to broaden the popular base of the government by bringing in the Buddhists and the "Third Force" advocates for democratic reforms. They also needed to implement programs to redistribute land so as to reduce hunger and malnutrition. Perhaps the above would not have been sufficient; but there is no question that they were necessary.

In areas under their control, the communists won the support of many peasants by giving them land to farm. Also, as John F. Kennedy's advisors warned him, the communists were able to appeal to the force of nationalism in mobilizing people against the "white faces" with guns.

The war in Vietnam showed clearly that technology could be overcome by human ingenuity and determination. The communists persisted despite twice the per capita battle death rate as Japan in World War II. In fact, only a handful of countries in the past 100 years have accepted such tremendous losses. Tilford proposes that perhaps *the* most important factor in the war was "enemy determination":

> The North Vietnamese had decided that they were not going to be defeated. If U.S. air strikes knocked down a bridge, hordes of peasants mobilized to repair the destruction caused by the bombs, to build fords, or to put in an underwater bridge. The bombing may even have strengthened the resolve of a people who were culturally inured to adversity.

Many in the military understood this U.S. foreign policy disaster all too well. During the war, playwright

Arthur Miller was invited to speak at West Point. After his talk, he went to a reception at a young colonel's house. Miller reports: "Some eight or ten officers, all of them Vietnam veterans and their wives, sat around until three that morning unburdening themselves, trying to make it clear to me not that they were losing the war because they had one hand tied behind their backs, but because they were trying to fight a political and moral conflict with explosives. The war, despite all the bravery of their men, had somehow shamed the service."

When it was all over, Kinnard asked the generals who had commanded in Vietnam whether the war was worth the effort in view of the casualties and the disruption of American politics and society. More than half (53%) said the war either had not been worth it or should not have progressed beyond an advisory effort.

As we shall see in Chapter 12, radical, liberal, and conservative perspectives still compete with each other in U.S. foreign and military policy debates. They all agree, however, that political leaders must inform the public of the likely costs of a foreign war before making such a commitment. Public support is essential. Few wars are cheap and, as the Soviet Union learned in Afghanistan, many can be long and frustrating. No nation should go to war unless it is willing and able to bear its costs.

Because war is not just a conflict between soldiers, but involves entire nations, an effective war plan must have social, political, and economic as well as military aspects. This means that we need to understand the cultures and political environments of the countries in which we are involved.

Leaders should not deceive the public and its representatives in order to manipulate consent to war. Eventually the truth will come out, and disengagement is far more costly and difficult than initial avoidance. The public needs a cause it can believe in for its sons to march off to war, and that cause must be solidly based in clearly stated national principle and interest.

American power is not infinite. It must be exercised with great care and only where our vital national interests clearly are at stake. Few today believe that Vietnam ever qualified by these standards.

Discussion Questions

1. In what ways did industrial leaders influence U.S. military policy?

2. "Rules of Engagement" are the rules that govern the conditions under which U.S. forces could fire on a suspected enemy. Do such rules make sense in a guerrilla conflict?

3. After 1968, many American soldiers in Vietnam resisted the war effort. How did they do this and what is your opinion of their actions?

4. Why were many Vietnamese hostile toward the government of South Vietnam? What role did ARVN (Army, Republic of Vietnam) play in this relationship?

5. What were the goals of the Strategic Hamlet Program? How did it work? Why did the program fail?

6. During wartime, should we permit the military to lie to political leaders and the public in the name of national security? If not, what can we do to prevent it? What might be the consequences?

7. In the spring of 1967, General William Westmoreland announced that the "cross-over point" had been reached. What did he mean? Was this assertion wrong? Why?

8. What is meant by the statement "the airwar could destroy the land, but it could not defeat the people"? If this statement is true, why do you think that we continued the bombing for so long?

9. In what ways were U.S. efforts to "win" the war in Southeast Asia counterproductive? Do you think that U.S. civilian and military leaders have learned any lessons from the experience in Southeast Asia? If so, what are those lessons?

Chapter 6   **Jerold M. Starr and Christopher W. Wilkens**

WHEN WAR BECOMES A CRIME:
THE CASE OF MY LAI

What Happened at My Lai?

The men of Charlie Company began to stir at first light. Their sleep that night had been fitful because every man was thinking about the attack the next day. It was a chance, at last, to bring some hurt to their enemy. The men collected their weapons, a triple load of ammunition and grenades, extra water, and medical packs. Some wrote last wills and testaments before boarding the helicopters. The first lift rose into the sky at 0655 hours (6:55 a.m.) towards the hamlet of My Lai-4. The men were quiet as the choppers churned through the early morning sky. In the distance they could see the first fall of the artillery on the edge of the village.

The morning of March 16, 1968, dawned hot and humid, as it usually does in Quang Ngai Province. The village of Son My simmered in the early morning heat. Suddenly, the shelling began. The people took refuge in their homemade shelters. The shelling stopped, and they heard the approaching helicopters. They knew that American soldiers would soon enter the village, as had happened on many other occasions. A few began to leave their shelters to wait.

Thirteen-year-old Tran Huyen, like many boys in the hamlet that morning, was out walking the water buffaloes. He usually stayed with them for five to seven days before returning to the village. He had been out two days when he saw twenty-five helicopters flying towards the hamlet. He was not alarmed because it was common to see American helicopters in the area.

Lieutenant William J. Calley Jr. and his First Platoon were in the first lift of the attack. Their orders were to secure the landing zone and make certain there were no enemy troops left in the area to fire on the second lift twenty minutes later.

Touch down was at 0722 hours (7:22 a.m.). The ships flared out over a rice paddy about 150 meters from the edge of the village. First platoon jumped out and began setting up a defense perimeter. Initial confusion arose when one gunship pilot called in a "hot LZ" (landing zone under enemy fire). However, company commander Captain Ernest Medina radioed that the landing had been smooth and that his men had come under no fire. PFC Charles Hall confirmed, "I did not hear any bullets crack by my ears like you normally hear...nothing was happening...."

In the village all was quiet. Nguyen Thi Doc was just beginning a morning meal with thirteen members of her family, including nine grandchildren. She heard the Americans "come down from the sky" but thought nothing of it: "they had been in the village before and always brought us medicine or candy for the children. If we had known what they came for this time, we would have fled."

The second lift of troops landed on schedule and the thirty odd men of Lieutenant Calley's First Platoon lined up and moved into the village. They were tense and prepared for heavy enemy fire. As they moved through the village, they followed the physical terrain, breaking into smaller and smaller groups. PFC Paul Meadlo remembers someone calling out that there was a "gook" over there. Sergeant Mitchell said to shoot him and somebody did. The massacre was on. Sergeant Charles West recalled later:

"When the attack started, it couldn't have been stopped by anyone. We were mad and we had been told that only the enemy would be there when we landed.... We were going in for a fight and for our dead buddies....We started shooting everything and everybody we saw....It was like our ammunition would never run out...."

Nguyen Thi Mai, thirteen, was in her hut with her family when she heard the Americans enter the village and begin shooting. She remembers everyone rushing out and scattering in different directions. Mai and her father began running toward the rice paddies. They had almost made it to the fields when they were confronted by three American soldiers, spread out in front of them about ten meters apart. She recalls painfully:

"When we saw the soldiers, we stopped running. My father knelt down on his knees and put his hands over his head. I stood in front of him. I wanted to stand between the soldiers and my father. They did not say anything. Then they looked at my father and me. They shot him and walked away."

"A bullet went through my father's chest and blood came out. He was still breathing. I cried and held him in my arms. He looked at me but could not talk. Then he stopped breathing."

"I cried and stayed a while with my father. Then I went to look for a place to hide in the fields."

Mai's whole family was killed that morning.

PFC Michael Bernhardt remembers coming into the hamlet and seeing his fellow soldiers "doing a whole lot of shooting....But none of it was incoming. I'd been around enough to tell that. I figured that we were advancing on the village with fire power." The raging fever in the other members of his platoon shocked Bernhardt. He watched one soldier fire clip after clip at everything he saw, laughing all the time. Bernhardt felt sick about what he was seeing, but also felt helpless to do anything but stand and watch. All through that bloody hour his rifle was slung muzzle down. He felt he had no reason to shoot. He told a reporter during the investigation later...."I found out that an act like that, you know, murder for no reason, could be done by just about anybody."

Lieutenant Calley set some of the men to work gathering people together in groups in a central location. PFC Meadlo describes what happened next....

"Calley issued orders to push the people into a ditch. Three or four GIs complied. Calley struck a woman with his rifle as he forced her into the ditch. Lt. Calley began to shoot into the ditch and ordered the others to join in....We pushed seven or eight more people into the ditch and began to fire into the people there....I guess I shot twenty to twenty-five people in the ditch...men, women, kids, babies....Mothers were grabbing their kids and kids were grabbing their mothers....I didn't know what to do...."

Pham Phon and his family hid in their shelter when the shelling began. When it stopped, Phon told his wife and three children to come out and walk slowly toward

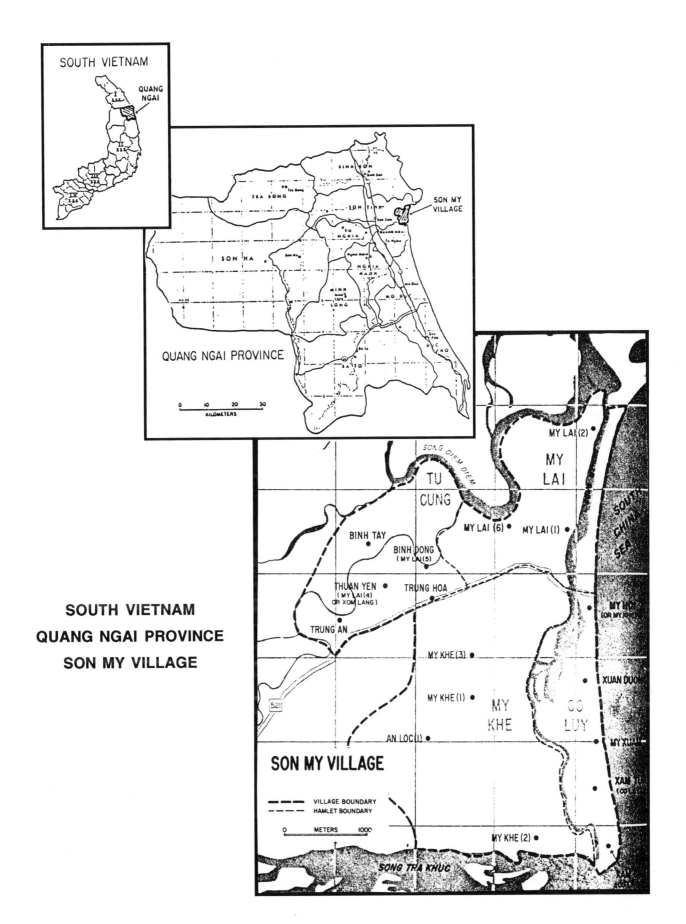

**SOUTH VIETNAM
QUANG NGAI PROVINCE
SON MY VILLAGE**

SOUTH VIETNAM

QUANG NGAI PROVINCE

SON MY VILLAGE

147

the Americans. They knew they shouldn't stay inside the house or bunker. And they knew it was imperative not to run. The three children smiled and shouted, "Hello! Hello! Okay! Okay!"

The Americans pointed their rifles at the family and sternly ordered them to walk to the canal about a hundred meters away. When they reached the canal, Phon saw "a lot of people who were grouping there," many of whom were crying. Sensing disaster, his quick thinking saved his family's life:

"I tell my wife and my kids, slip into the canal when GI not looking. We watch for our chance and we do that. So then the GI begin to shoot at the standing people and at the sitting people on the banks of the canal. They fall into the canal and cover us with their bodies. So they were not wounded, myself, my wife and my two sons. My little daughter, only seven years old, she was wounded in the arm when the GIs shoot into the canal when they heard the people groaning and making much noise."

During the subsequent investigation, Phon was asked whether the GIs had acted on their own, without a leader. He replied, "No, there was a leader....He was a small man, small like a Vietnamese. He waves his hand like that and then he shoot his gun and then all GIs shoot their guns."

Robert Maples, a machine gunner, was ordered by Calley to fire into the ditch, but he refused. He watched as others fired round after round and even tossed grenades into the ditch until everyone was believed dead.

Warrant Officer Hugh C. Thompson was piloting one of the circling helicopters. He and his gunner, Larry Colburn, noticed the large numbers of dead and wounded Vietnamese civilians. He started to mark the location of the wounded with smoke so they could be found and treated. One of the first wounded that he marked was a little girl. A group of soldiers then walked over and riddled her body with automatic weapons while she lay on the ground. Thompson later identified the man that did the shooting as Captain Ernest Medina.

Thompson was furious. He radioed the troops on the ground to find out what was going on. He reported to headquarters about the unnecessary shootings taking place in the village. His message was recorded on tape. At one point he decided to drop down and evacuate some of the wounded. He and his crew chief spotted a group of a dozen to fifteen children. He ferried the

children to the hospital and returned to My Lai.

Thompson landed again, having spotted a small child lying by himself. As he started toward the child, he saw Calley also approaching the child. Thompson motioned Calley toward him. They met near the helicopter. They exchanged words. Calley motioned with his rifle. Obviously angry, Thompson approached the waist gunner on his aircraft. He told the gunner to aim his weapon "at that officer" and if the officer attempted to interfere, to shoot him. Thompson then went back, picked up the child and carried him back to the helicopter. He flew the child to the hospital. Calley walked over to his radio operator and said, "That guy isn't very happy with the way we're running this operation. But I don't care. He's not in charge." Hugh Thompson would later receive the Distinguished Flying Cross for his actions that day at My Lai-4.

Ronald Haeberle, the Army photographer assigned to the mission, was at My Lai-4 nearly the whole day. His photographs were released nearly two years later and shocked millions of Americans. As he moved through the village, he took pictures of dead Vietnamese piled on top of each other; pictures of dead children clinging to their dead mothers; pictures of GIs burning hooches, buildings, and food supplies.

The official Army account of the Brigade attack that day claimed a body count of over one hundred twenty-eight Vietcong and listed both individual and crew-served weapons as captured. Charlie Company was credited with fifteen VC dead and the capture of three individual weapons. The company also was credited with the capture of a radio and documents on the outskirts of the hamlet of My Lai-4. The report went on to add that one American soldier had been killed and one wounded during the fighting.

In actuality, Charlie Company had suffered only one casualty; one of the men had shot himself in the foot. He later testified that he had done it to get out of the village before any more killing took place. As for enemy presence, PFC Bernhardt "didn't remember seeing one military age male in the entire place, dead or alive." And the three rifles found were American. The "body count" was over three hundred, by Captain Medina's estimate. It would later be shown that the count was much higher: more than four hundred at My Lai-4 and another one hundred plus by Bravo Company at My Khe-4 to the north of My Lai. In all, the two companies had killed well over five hundred unarmed Vietnamese civilians in less than four hours.

The next day, young Tran Huyen returned from walking the water buffaloes. He met some of the survivors and, now very alarmed, "ran into the hamlet." He recalls:

"It smelled very much. I saw that everything had been burned. I saw arms and legs and pieces of heads lying around. I ran to my house and saw it was burned down. I lifted the ashes and found my grandfather....I could not understand what had happened. Why American soldiers wanted to kill everyone in the village."

"My mother and father and brothers had already been buried by my relatives when I arrived. I went to their graves. I cried....I still cry when I think of that day."

Discussion Questions

1. Are there times when it is important to obey orders without question or hesitation? Give examples.
2. Is obedience instinctive to human beings or is it socially conditioned? Can people be taught to disobey orders that cause unnecessary suffering to others?

For three weeks during the Tet offensive of January, 1968, communist soldiers occupied the city of Hue. They arrested and executed thousands of those considered "enemies of the people," that is leaders allied with the government of South Vietnam. Some were buried alive in mass graves. Editorial cartoonist Tony Auth comments on the dilemma for many Vietnamese.

Victims are People First

Who were the people of My Lai and what could they have done to provoke such brutality? My Lai was more than just a war zone. It was a traditional farm village that traced its history back to the early 17th century. The beauty of its land and beaches were well known, as were its bountiful rice harvests and abundant catches from the sea. Within the hamlets themselves, there grew a handicraft market of wood, bamboo, ivory and metals. The village of Son My became an educational and Buddhist religious center for that part of Quang Nagi Province. From its earliest times it was strongly nationalistic, opposed to western missionaries and traders. When necessary, this opposition took the form of armed resistance.

During World War II, the Vietminh resistance forces in the area cooperated with the United States and actively opposed the Japanese occupation. When the war ended, the people welcomed Ho Chi Minh's declaration of an independent Vietnam. When the French returned in 1946, the Vietminh again organized resistance in the area. In 1955, with the French finally driven out, the Vietminh declared themselves representatives of the people of the village. They organized a new people's council that encompassed all four hamlets. They took land from some absentee landlords and gave it to those peasant farmers who had no land. The Vietminh also imposed taxes on the wealthy land owners and businessmen in the area. Representatives of the government of the Republic of (South) Vietnam occasionally visited the area, but had no influence over the people. In 1960, however, the U.S. sponsored government of President Ngo Dinh Diem challenged the leadership and reforms enacted in the village of Son My. The wealthy land owners were brought back to reclaim the land taken from them and government tax collectors were bribed. By this time, the Vietminh had been replaced by the National Liberation Front (NLF). The Army of the Republic of Vietnam started to organize a militia to keep the NLF reformers out of the village. To make matters even worse, Diem appointed a Catholic Archbishop and his brother as the religious and political leaders of Quang Ngai Province. Repression of the people grew and, with it, increasing opposition to the "U.S. puppet" government of President Diem and his two hated brothers.

At this time, NLF representatives moved back in to challenge the government for control. They arrested the government's representatives and formed a people's council and a people's court to carry out public trials. Representatives and supporters of the Saigon government were removed from the village. A campaign was launched to educate villagers about the "people's cause." By 1964, the forces of the Saigon government had been routed and Vietcong and NLF forces moved freely throughout the Son My area. When U.S. forces arrived in 1965, Quang Ngai Province became one of the first areas of operations. The U.S. Marine Corps launched Operation Starlight and soon communist and U.S. forces were engaged in open warfare with the civilian population caught helplessly in the middle.

As they had always been, peasant farmers in the area were concerned primarily with the survival of the village. Therefore they cooperated as much as possible with all political and military forces operating in the area. Whenever a new force came to the area, the peasant farmers greeted them with a smile. All requests were considered and, when possible, satisfied. The villagers did not protest when their food was confiscated. They did not resist when their young men were taken to fight in the war. Both sides took advantage of this situation. Some of the young men of the village were in the Army of the Republic of (South) Vietnam. The elders and villagers gave out as little information as possible without being insulting. They tried to remain neutral because they would have to answer to both sides. They provided support only when it was necessary to save the village as a whole.

Discussion Questions

1. If you were responsible for the safety and welfare of the village, how would you relate to the military forces in the area?
2. If, as some people argue, the war in Vietnam was immoral, does that mean that American soldiers who served in Vietnam also were immoral? If, on the other hand, you think the war in Vietnam was moral, does that mean that everything that American soldiers did was moral? Can we take different positions on these questions?
3. Do you think it is possible for the Vietnamese people today to forgive those who committed atrocities against them? Why might they be willing to do that? Would that be alright?
4. What does My Lai teach you, if anything, about how you should conduct your life? About moral values? Individual responsibility?

The Laws of War

"Okay," you might say, "My Lai was terrible, but didn't General Sherman say 'War is Hell'? Isn't all fair in war?" Actually, that is one of those cliches that probably has never been true. The civilized world has written records of attempts to establish laws of warfare that go back 2,500 years or more. Such laws pertain to both the issue of adequate justification and of proper conduct. Codes of conduct are concerned with preserving standards of morality. Among other things, they seek to reconcile the killing of others with the prohibition against murder common to all human societies.

Wars are not fought because ordinary people are instinctively aggressive. On the contrary, any nation going to war must first figure out how to recruit and motivate its troops. Neither is war inevitable. Wars are fought as a result of political decisions made by national leaders. And they base such decisions on their calculation that their nation's interests—whether power, prestige, profits, principles and/or protection of territory— are more likely to be advanced by going to war than by not going to war.

Laws concerning humanitarian treatment for the defeated make it possible for leaders to concede a losing fight and, thus, limit unnecessary casualties on both sides. Neither the winner nor the loser has any interest in fighting to the last man. For war to make any sense at all, there must be spoils for the victor to enjoy. The obvious purpose of laws of war, then, is to keep war as a legitimate last resort for leaders to choose in settling

For All My Brothers and Sisters

This is not easy to write about   it involves
the ignorant peasants shot by the A-
merican soldiers   these peasants were so
ignorant they had no names   so primitive
in nature they were all indistinguishable
from one another   so like dumb animals
their language was babbling nonsense   and when
they died all you could remember was their
gestures   clinging together in the ditch

Dick Lourie

LAST TRAIN TO NUREMBERG

Words and Music by
PETER SEEGER

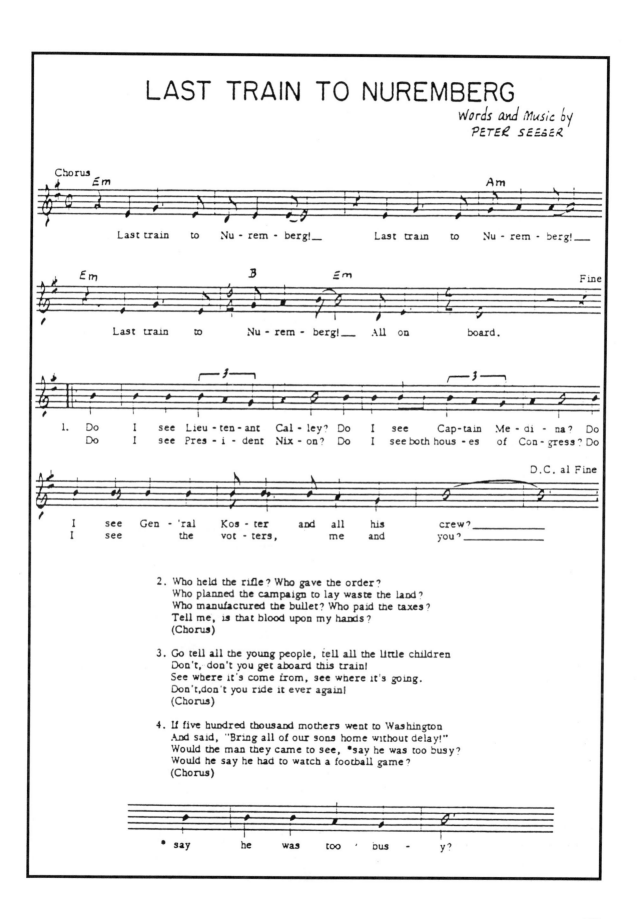

Last train to Nu - rem - berg!__ Last train to Nu - rem - berg!__

Last train to Nu - rem - berg!__ All on board.

1. Do I see Lieu - ten - ant Cal - ley? Do I see Cap - tain Me - di - na? Do
Do I see Pres - i - dent Nix - on? Do I see both hous - es of Con - gress? Do

I see Gen - 'ral Kos - ter and all his crew?_____
I see the vot - ters, me and you?_____

2. Who held the rifle? Who gave the order?
Who planned the campaign to lay waste the land?
Who manufactured the bullet? Who paid the taxes?
Tell me, is that blood upon my hands?
(Chorus)

3. Go tell all the young people, tell all the little children
Don't, don't you get aboard this train!
See where it's come from, see where it's going.
Don't, don't you ride it ever again!
(Chorus)

4. If five hundred thousand mothers went to Washington
And said, "Bring all of our sons home without delay!"
Would the man they came to see, *say he was too busy?
Would he say he had to watch a football game?
(Chorus)

* say he was too bus - y?

disputes. The development of what may be called "modern laws of war" is based on the work of Francis Lieber. Born and raised in Germany, Lieber became a citizen of the United States in 1832 at the age of 34. His major work, "the Lieber Code," was published on April 24, 1863, during the time of the American Civil War.

The basic argument of the Lieber Code is that the violence of war should be directed only toward armed enemies and that the conduct of war should always be regulated by moral concerns. Certainly the American Civil War, an especially cruel conflict that took the lives of almost a half-million Americans, makes the logic of limiting war's destruction very apparent. Among other things, the Lieber Code prohibits attacks on disabled enemies and torture to extort confessions, while requiring medical treatment for captured wounded enemy.

Today's international laws of war are contained in a series of treaties called the Hague and Geneva Conventions. The United States Senate has ratified these treaties so they are established in U.S. law. These laws set limits to what soldiers in war may do. U.S. Army Field Manual 27-10 is the basis for instructing all U.S. soldiers in the laws of warfare during basic training. Some of the actions that are outlawed under international law are as follows:

- murder of civilians and prisoners of war

- ill-treatment of civilians and prisoners of war

- acts of rape

- deportation of civilian populations for slave labor

- killing of hostages or other terroristic acts

- plunder of public or private property

- any destruction of cities, towns or villages not justified by military necessity

What If You Are Ordered To Commit A War Crime?

During World War II, Nazi military forces and their agents committed terrible crimes against innocent civilians. They slaughtered six million Jews, half the total population of Jews in the world, as well as millions of Catholics, communists and other "undesirables." The horror of this holocaust shocked the world. After the war, the victorious nations put many Nazi leaders on trial in Nuremberg, Germany for war crimes. The common defense of these leaders—that they were not personally responsible for their crimes because they were only following orders—led to the formulation of the Nuremberg Principles. These principles hold:

"The fact that a person acted pursuant to an order of his government or a superior officer does not relieve him from the responsibility under international law, provided that a moral decision or choice was in fact possible for him."

"A higher law sometimes requires men to give their allegiance to humanity rather than to the state."

The United States Army incorporated these principles into its own Uniform Code of Military Justice. For example, the code specifies that the "orders of his superiors" that a soldier "must obey" themselves must be "lawful." The code also states that "every violation of the rules of war is a war crime."

With respect to the subject of this Chapter, the U.S. Army has clearly defined the shooting of unarmed civilians as a grave violation of the Geneva Convention of August 12, 1949. A 1968 MACV (Military Army Command in Vietnam) directive requires a soldier to report as soon as possible to his commanding officer any "incident or act thought to be a war crime...." Moreover, persons discovering war crimes are required to "preserve physical evidence, to note the identity of witnesses present at the time, and to record the circumstances and surroundings." All this information is to be "made known to officials of the Saigon Command and forwarded to headquarters as soon as it is practical."

High ranking officers in the American and South Vietnamese military command knew if what people were saying happened at My Lai were true, it would constitute serious war crimes for which some soldiers would have to be tried. In fact, it was considered so horrible that many tried to cover it up completely. And they almost succeeded.

Discussion Questions

Do you agree that, if nations are going to have wars, they need laws of warfare? If you do not, what would you propose instead? If you do, make a list of laws you would include.

Now look at the laws you listed and see if you covered the following:

1. How should civilians be treated? What if they are suspected enemy agents? enemy sympathizers?

2. What should be the rules of interrogation? Should torture be allowed? What if the suspect refuses to talk?

3. How should an unarmed or wounded enemy officer be treated? What about an unarmed or wounded enemy soldier?

4. Do prisoners of war have any rights? What about food? shelter? medicine? What if your own troops don't have enough?

5. Would you allow the use of chemical weapons, like Agent Orange? Why? Why not?

6. What about bombing? Should bombing of enemy bases be allowed? What about factories? What if there is a danger that hospitals and/or schools might be accidentally destroyed? Should anything be done if they are?

7. Should any particular weapons be outlawed? What about "cluster" bombs that spray metal fragments for hundreds of yards or napalm that spreads a gasoline jelly that eats away at the flesh?

The Cover-up

My Lai was the biggest action in the Americal Division's area of operations. So it was no wonder that the sky over My Lai was filled with C&C flights (command and control flights). All commanders were tied into the command net and could hear all the radio "traffic" from the attacking companies while the action developed.

As Charlie Company moved out of the hamlet, Major Charles Calhoun, Task Force Barker's Executive Officer, told Captain Medina to go back and recount the civilian dead. Medina complained that it was late and he wanted to get into a night defensive position before dark. Suddenly, General Koster came on the radio and said to cancel the last order because it was too late in the day. He then asked Medina how many civilian dead were counted during the action. Medina reported twenty-five to twenty-eight.

What Medina did not know was that all radio "traffic" from the day's action had been recorded at Brigade Headquarters. In addition, Warrant Officer Thompson had filed a complete report at his headquarters, the 123rd Aviation Battalion, describing what he had seen and his conversation with Calley. Rumors of what happened in the hamlet of My Lai-4 began to spread throughout the whole Division.

Medina was advised of Thompson's complaint and called his platoon leaders together. He told them that there probably would be an investigation of some kind. He asked them not to talk about what had happened with anyone outside the company. He promised that he would back them up to the fullest. Still, some of the men were worried. One warned the Vietnamese interpreter to "look casual" and "be cool" or "it could be very dangerous for you."

On March 17, Colonel Henderson, the Brigade Commander, initiated a routine investigation of the incident. Medina's men reported there were no indiscriminate killings during the attack. Thompson and his gunner, Larry Colburn, both reported what they saw, but Henderson showed little interest. For the rest of the year, Charlie Company settled back into its operational routine. Calley was relieved of platoon command. He requested and received a transfer out of the company. Very few of the men talked about the attack any more. However Thompson's "official" complaint could not be ignored completely. People were talking. At Chu Lai, the Americal Division's main base, General Koster began to receive inquiries from both Saigon and Washington about the rumors. He sent the inquiries to Henderson and ordered a formal investigation.

The reports all came to Koster's desk. Civilian deaths were acknowledged, but they were attributed to errant artillery and gunship strikes. There was no mention of unnecessary shootings of civilians. Koster forwarded these reports to Saigon and Washington.

Major General Samuel W. Koster

Ronald L. Ridenhour

Headquarters, apparently satisfied, filed the reports. No one seemed to notice that none of the survivors of My Lai-4, nor any of the men of Charlie Company had ever been interviewed.

The South Vietnamese military, on the other hand, had talked to survivors and others in the area and they knew most of what had happened that day. These reports were sent to Saigon, but they were suppressed. President Thieu's office was concerned with not antagonizing the Americans and not arousing anti-American feelings among the South Vietnamese.

It took the persistence of a young helicopter door-gunner, Ron Ridenhour, to bring the story of the massacre to public light. Ridenhour wrote letters to at least thirty congressional leaders and Pentagon officials asserting his belief that "something rather dark and bloody did indeed occur some time in March 1968 in a village called 'Pinkville' in the Republic of Vietnam." After months of being ignored, he decided to go public. His story was picked up by journalist Seymour Hersh. In his own investigation Hersh discovered that Ron Haeberle had made up a slide show from his personal collection of pictures from the My Lai-4 attack. Both Ridenour and, subsequently, Hersh, offered the story to most of the nation's major media. All refused. Hersh finally sold the story to Dispatch News Service. After they broke the story on November 13, 1969, nearly every major news agency gave it prominent coverage.

Directed by President Nixon, Secretary of Defense Melvin Laird ordered Secretary of the Army Stanley Resor to conduct a full and "total" investigation of the incident. It was discovered that Army files and after-action reports on the incident had been either destroyed or deliberately misfiled by high ranking officers. Army radio logs also were altered for that day to further cover up what had happened. Eventually, the Army would charge twenty-five men either with participating in the killing of Vietnamese civilians or in the subsequent cover-up. Congress was briefed and a report was made to the world press. It took twenty months for the American public to learn about the attack on My Lai-4.

Discussion Question

History offers examples of other tragedies, such as the Holocaust, which were possible because people were indifferent to the suffering. Do you agree or disagree that people who do not speak out when they witness war crimes are accomplices to those crimes?

The Court-Martial

When news of the My Lai Incident became more wide spread, Calley was pulled back to Fort Benning. Army Intelligence and Army Criminal Investigation agents began to criss-cross the nation to find witnesses. In all, nearly four hundred people were interviewed regarding what they knew about My Lai-4.

On September 6, 1969, Calley was formally charged with violating Article 118 of the Uniform Code of Military Justice. His court-martial began on November 12. He was charged with one hundred nine counts of murder of the estimated more than four hundred killings in My Lai.

Every attempt was made to ensure that Calley would be tried by a jury of his peers. Like Calley, four of the

On-scene investigation in the My Lai area.

six jury members had been graduated from OCS at Fort Benning. Five had served in Vietnam for at least one full tour. All were combat veterans who had received awards for valor under fire. The trial judge, military defense lawyer and two civilian lawyers were combat veterans.

The trial brought out the shortcomings of Calley's preparation prior to being shipped overseas. At one point he was questioned about his instruction in the rules of warfare, as outlined in the Geneva Convention of 1949, which specifically outlawed "willful killing, torture, or inhuman treatment...."

■ ■ ■

Calley: "I know there were classes. Nothing stands out in my mind what was covered in those classes."

Question: "Did you learn anything in those classes of what the Geneva Convention actually covered as far as rules and regulations of warfare were concerned?"

Calley: "No, sir."

Question: "Did you ever receive any instructions on taking prisoners?"

Calley: "Yes, sir. Treat them with respect, humility. Don't humiliate them. Keep them silent. Keep them separated and keep them closely guarded, sir."

On the other hand, Calley saw obedience to orders as absolute:

Question: "Did you receive any training in any of those places that had to do with obedience to orders?"

Calley: "Yes, sir. It was to be assumed that all orders were legal, that a soldier's job was to carry out all orders to the best of his abilities. You could be court-martialed for refusing an order....You could be sentenced to death for refusing an order in the face of the enemy...."

Question: "...Were you ever required in any way, shape or form to make a determination of the legality or illegality of an order?"

Calley: "No, sir. I was never told that I had a choice."

Question: "If you had a doubt about an order, what were you supposed to do?"

Calley: "If I questioned an order, I was to carry out my mission first and then come back and make my report....If I was given a mission I was expected to carry it out immediately...."

■ ■ ■

George Latimer, Calley's defense lawyer, appealed to the jury to consider the peculiar horrors of this war of attrition against guerrilla forces in Indochina:

"Lieutenant Calley and his platoon were inadequately trained and instructed for this type of combat. The unit was understrength and it was the first time some of the men had been under fire. They were led to believe that their attack would be bitterly resisted by the enemy. The accused had knowledge of many atrocities committed by the enemy on American and South Vietnamese servicemen and civilians in the area. Many of the soldiers operating in the Quang Ngai area had been killed and others ruined for life by having their arms and legs blown off by mines...."

"Thus it was that Charlie Company, with Calley's the lead platoon, stormed into My Lai on March 16, 1968, with a feeling of revenge and reprisal."

During the course of Calley's trial, many members of his platoon, now mostly discharged veterans, testified as to what had happened in the village that day; what Calley had done and what he had ordered his men to do. Medina testified that he felt Calley had exceeded his orders during the attack on the village. Meadlo and Bernhardt gave the most damaging eyewitness accounts of the events. Ron Haeberle's photographs were the most dramatic physical evidence introduced. After all testimony had been heard and all ninety-one witnesses called, the jury retired to consider a verdict. The jury took thirteen days to arrive at a verdict. While he waited, Calley was interviewed for a book by John Sack. During this interview, Calley reflected on the forces that had contributed to his frame of mind that day in My Lai:

"...So that was us: Charlie Company and we were in Vietnam now....There seemed to be no nice sections

Captain Ernest Medina

Lieutenant General William R. Peers

anywhere. I felt superior there. I thought, I'm the big American from across the sea. I'll sock it to these people here...."

"After my second, my third, my fourth, my fifth, my tenth, my twelfth, my twentieth—ambush, I still hadn't had a VC in my killing zone, and I had had perfect ambush sites too....Charlie was combat infantry! *We want to kill!*"

"Not half as much as our colonel did. He kept asking us, 'Any body count?'"

"No, sir."

"'No body count?'"

"Nobody there to shoot at."

"'You better get on the stick sometime.'"

"Yes, sir."

"I thought, oh, forget it, Colonel. What do you really want of me?...do you kill everyone in South Vietnam? And say, 'We have won, we are going home.' I imagine so: just everything in today's society is 'How many thousands? How many millions? How many billions?' And everything was in Vietnam; was numbers and I had to furnish them. So television could say, 'We killed another thousand today,' and Americans say, 'Our country's great.'"

"The body count—damn. I did what every lieutenant had to: I finally got us a body count...."

"If you're a GI who has lost eighteen friends in a mine field with a Vietnamese village a few hundred meters away—well. You think, Why didn't the Vietnamese signal us? Why didn't the Vietnamese tell us, 'Hey there's a mine field there.'....At last it dawned on me, these people they're all the VC...."

"I had now found the VC. Everyone there was VC. The old men, the women, the children—the *babies* were all VC or would be VC in about three years. And inside of VC women, I guess there were a thousand little VC now. I thought, Damn it, what do I do?...Chop up all these people?"

Reflecting on the reasons for the war, Calley became philosophical:

"We weren't in My Lai to kill human beings, really. We were there to kill ideology...an intangible idea."

"To destroy communism. Now, I hate to say it, but most people know a lot more about communism than I do. In school, I never thought about it. I just dismissed it: I looked at communism as a southerner looks at a Negro, supposedly, *It's evil, It's bad*...."

"As for me, I like Christianity....A man with a little paddy says, 'I like something else, and I'm happy too'. I ask would communism hurt him? It wouldn't hurt him a damned bit! Compared to a war, communism would be a godsend. The horrors of war came together at My Lai on March 16, 1968. And maybe someday the GIs who went there will say, 'Now the world knows what war is. And now the world really hates it. And now there is No More War.'"

As for his own guilt or innocence, Calley clearly had learned much since his arrest:

"...I'm different now. I said a long while ago, if Americans told me 'Go massacre one thousand communists,' I will massacre one thousand communists. No longer: today if America said, 'Go to My Lai. Kill everyone there,' I would refuse to. I'd really say, 'It's illegal, and I can't be a part of it.' Of course to kill everyone in My Lai isn't the only illegal thing we do. To evacuate them is illegal too—is against the Geneva Convention. I've learned. So is kidnaping them. To burn their houses is very illegal, and I don't know why the Judge didn't say, 'A reasonable man would realize it.' One shouldn't burn a Vietnamese village. It is against the Uniform Code of Military Justice, Article CIX. It doesn't carry death, but it does carry five years at Leavenworth. Hell, to just be in My Lai with an M-16 and some ammunition is illegal too....I now think, to go to Vietnam is illegal too."

On March 29, 1970, the jury reached its verdict. It found Lieutenant William J. Calley Jr. guilty of the murder of at least thirty-three "oriental human beings, occupants of the village of My Lai, whose names and sexes are unknown, by means of shooting them with a rifle."

The jury then sentenced Calley to be dishonorably discharged from the Army with forfeiture of all pay and allowances and committed to Leavenworth Prison for life. After the announcement of his sentence, Calley was taken away to the post stockade.

On April 1, 1970, Calley was placed under house arrest based on orders from the Commander-in-Chief, while the case was placed under review and appeal. In September, President Nixon reduced Calley's sentence to twenty years. The case was appealed to various courts for more than three years. In the end all appeals were denied. However, after the final appeal,

Lieutenant William J. Calley Jr.

Pentagon news conference, March 17, 1970.
Left to right: General Peers, Secretary of the Army Stanley Resor,
Army Chief of Staff William C. Westmoreland

the court recommended that President Nixon grant a parole to Calley, and so he did. Calley was released from prison in 1974, after serving three years of a revised twenty-year sentence.

Discussion Questions

Calley was tried in a military court. What do you think was the basic issue of the trial?

1. Whether or not Calley was acting under orders from his superiors.

2. Whether or not Calley actually did kill civilians.

3. Whether or not Calley believed everyone in the village was the enemy and therefore had to be destroyed.

4. Whether or not there was active encouragement or implied approval by his superiors for this kind of action.

5. Whether or not Calley is still responsible for his action even if he is acting under orders.

Americans React

When the My Lai massacre finally was exposed, Americans reacted in very different ways. Some refused to believe that it had, in fact, occurred. Some even blamed the media for trying to undermine the war effort. Some felt deeply ashamed for their country. Others felt that we should not blame ourselves for the actions of a few. Some accused the men of war crimes. Others urged that the men not be punished because they were only following orders. Some warned that any soldier was capable of such atrocities and that we must be vigilant against them. Others lamented that, as a nation, we probably would learn nothing from the event. Here are some of the letters sent to *Life* magazine in response to its report on My Lai:

There are outfits where a tone of violence, and inexcusable violence, is established....We really fool ourselves if we think there isn't a little SS in every army—just waiting for some fatheaded colonel or general to bring it out.

Tim Carmichael
Ajijie, Mexico

■ ■ ■

I think the whole thing has been blown up out of all proportion....There is an obvious campaign waged to show the United States as immoral.

Harry Fletcher, 44
Montgomery, Alabama professor

■ ■ ■

We as a people are also on trial and should not try to placate our conscience by scapegoating any or all of those directly connected with the alleged act. Every German I met right after the Second World War said he fought on the Russian front and Hitler was to blame for everything. If the My Lai massacre proves to be true, it will be further evidence of what this war is doing to all of us, not just the soldiers.

Mark Hatfield
U.S. Senator, Oregon

■ ■ ■

I gave them a good boy and they made him a murderer.

Mrs. Anthony Meadlo
mother of Paul Meadlo

■ ■ ■

If the principles of the Nuremberg war trials mean anything at all—if America means anything at all—then these men who killed women, children and old men should never be allowed to hide behind the excuse that "I was just following orders."

Truman R. Clark
Conshohocken, Pennsylvania

■ ■ ■

Under no circumstances do I think a person placed in the situation of being required to kill should be punished because he killed the wrong people.

Jerry Cramm, 19
Oklahoma City student

Having been a Marine, a devoted American, a true believer in our great country, I took the massacre as one would the death of his child. The picture in your issue was like a knife in my heart.

Roger R. Eckert
La Mesa, California

■ ■ ■

I think we'll forget all about it as soon as another crisis comes along. We don't have very long memories as a nation.

Mrs. Better Vickers, 51
Montgomery, Alabama housewife

■ ■ ■

As a nation we can deplore our mistakes. But I do not believe that our national conscience should make us hang our heads in shame. That would be blaming all for the actions of a few.

Erik Jonsson
Mayor of Dallas

■ ■ ■

During the trial of Lieutenant Calley, many enlisted men and fellow officers gave him moral support. Some called to him to "Hang in there!" or "Hang tough!" because "We're behind you!" His case was discussed openly in Congress and was a part of President Nixon's weekly briefings. For many, Calley's trial seemed to be a trial on the justice of the war itself.

One national survey (see Table 1) found that Americans disapproved of Calley being brought to trial by a margin of 58 percent to 34 percent. Among those disapproving of the trial, 83 percent agreed, "It is unfair to send a man to fight in Vietnam and then put him on trial for doing his duty." About two-thirds of the trial critics also considered the trial "an insult to our fighting men" and "unfair" to Calley who was seen as a "scapegoat" being "blamed for the failures of his superiors."

Among those who approved of the trial, over half (53%) asserted, "Even a soldier in a combat situation has no right to kill defenseless civilians." Nearly half emphasized the importance of personal responsibility and preserving the "honor" and discipline of the Army. Some 45 percent (15% of the total sample) agreed: "The trial helps to make clear the immorality and cruelty of the Vietnam War and of the way we are fighting it." Most revealingly, about two-thirds of the total sample thought that "most people" would "shoot all inhabitants of a Vietnamese village suspected of aiding the enemy, including old men, women and children." More than half said that they personally would do so in such a situation.

When Calley's court-martial found him "guilty of premeditated murder," *Newsweek* conducted its own national survey (see page 166). Almost four in five Americans disapproved of the verdict. When probed, however, only 20 percent said they objected because they thought what happened at My Lai "was not a crime." The vast majority (71%) objected to Calley "being made the scapegoat for the actions of others above him." Four of five considered the sentence of life imprisonment to be "too harsh." Most revealing was the belief by half of those surveyed (over two-thirds of those with an opinion) that "the incident for which Lieutenant Calley was tried was a common one." What many probably did not know was that 122 other American servicemen also were convicted by court-martial of murdering Vietnamese civilians.

Perhaps they did, because a staggering one in three Americans polled felt that "high government and military officials should be tried" for "war crimes in Vietnam." The fact that so many millions felt that way toward their own leaders during a time of war makes a very powerful statement about the mood of the American people after six to seven years of fighting in Vietnam.

Discussion Questions

1. In which way(s) did the reactions of the American public to My Lai reflect the debate over the war generally? Did any of the reactions address other concerns? What were they?

2. Why do you think that so many in the U.S. were reluctant to apply the same standards to our conduct in the war in Vietnam as our leaders applied to the Germans at Nuremberg in 1945?

3. Are there consequences to our nation's standing in the world if we are hypocritical with respect to the Nuremberg principles and other international codes, like Geneva, in our conduct of war? Despite our great sacrifice, did the United States lose world respect in Vietnam, not as much for losing as for how it fought the war?

4. Who is responsible?

a. The soldiers? They are required to obey orders. Can they judge when an order is illegal? Was a moral

"I WONDER IF THAT INCLUDES EX-PRESIDENTS?"

During Calley's court-martial, Secretary of Defense Melvin Laird announced that all U.S. servicemen, even those already separated/discharged from service, would still be held liable for their actions if charges were filed against them for war crimes committed in Vietnam.

TABLE 1

ATTITUDE TOWARD TRIAL OF LT. CALLEY

"There has been a good deal of discussion about whether or not Lt. Calley should have been brought to trial in the first place. Considering what you have seen, heard or read, do you approve or disapprove of Lt. Calley having been brought to trial?"

Approve 34% (N=301)   Disapprove 58% (N=521)   Don't know 8%(N=69)

Reasons	Agree with (%)	Most important (%)
Among respondents approving of trial:		
a. Even a soldier in a combat situation has no right to kill defenseless civilians and anyone who violates this rule must be brought to trial	53	27
b. The trial helps make clear the immorality and cruelty of the Vietnam war and the way we are fighting it	45	20
c. To preserve its honor, the Army has to bring to trial anyone accused of breaking its rules of warfare	45	14
d. The trial helps to put across the important idea that every man must bear responsibility for his own actions	48	18
e. Many other U.S. soldiers have been tried for crimes in Vietnam; it would be unfair to let Lt. Calley off without a trial	40	8
f. None of these or don't know	14	14
Among respondents disapproving of trial:		
a. It's unfair to send a man to fight in Vietnam and then put him on trial for doing his duty	83	45
b. The trial keeps us from facing the real issue: what's wrong with the war and the way it's being fought, not just the actions of an individual soldier	43	9
c. The trial is an insult to our fighting men and weakens the morale of the U.S. Army	64	11
d. The trial used Lt. Calley as a scapegoat: one young lieutenant shouldn't be blamed for failures of his superiors	67	15
e. Many other U.S. soldiers have done the same kinds of things as Lt. Calley; it is unfair to single out one man and put him on trial	69	15
f. None of these or don't know	3	5

TABLE 2

RESPONSES ON ITEMS ASSESSING ATTITUDES TOWARD CALLEY'S ACTION

ITEM	Total Sample (N = 989) (%)
a. What would most people do if ordered to shoot all the inhabitants of a Vietnamese village suspected of aiding the enemy, including old men, women and children:	
Follow orders and shoot	67
Refuse to shoot them	19
b. What would you do in this situation:	
Follow orders and shoot	51
Refuse to shoot them	33
c. Assuming it is true that Calley received orders to shoot, what should he have done:	
Carry out	61
Refuse to carry out	29
d. Overall opinion of Calley's action:	
Right—what any good soldier would do under the circumstances	29
Wrong—but hard for him to know right or wrong in this situation	39
Wrong—clear violation of military code	6
Wrong—violation of morality regardless of military code	17
e. Calley's actions were justified if the people he shot were Communists:	
Agree	37
Disagree	51
f. Calley's actions justified because better to kill some South Vietnamese civilians than to risk the lives of American soldiers:	
Agree	47
Disagree	39
g. In World War II it would have been better to kill some German civilians than risk the lives of American soldiers:	
Agree	53
Disagree	29
h. In terms of rights and wrongs, how did Calley's actions compare with the bombing raids that also kill Vietnamese civilians:	
Similar	56
Different	32

A *Newsweek* Poll On Calley's Fate
April 12, 1971

Newsweek commissioned the Gallup Organization to poll the U.S. public reactions to the Calley verdict. Telephone interviews surveyed a representative cross section of 522 Americans. The full questionnaire and its results:

Do you approve or disapprove of the court-martial finding that Lieutenant Calley is guilty of premeditated murder?

Approve	9%
Disapprove	79%
No opinion	12%

(If you disapprove) do you disapprove of the verdict because you think what happened at My Lai was not a crime, or because you think many others besides Lieutenant Calley share the responsibility for what happened?

Not a crime	20%
Others responsible	71%
Both	1%
Other	7%
No response	1%

Do you think Lieutenant Calley is being made the scapegoat for the actions of others above him, or not?

Yes	69%
No	12%
No opinion	19%

Do you think the Calley sentence of life imprisonment is fair, or too harsh, or too lenient?

Fair	11%
Too harsh	81%
Too lenient	1%
No opinion	7%

Do you think the incident for which Lieutenant Calley was tried was an isolated incident or a common one?

Isolated	24%
Common	50%
No opinion	26%

Some people have suggested that the U.S. is guilty of war crimes in Vietnam for which high government and military officials should be tried. Do you agree or disagree?

Agree	32%
Disagree	47%
No opinion	21%

choice possible for soldiers at My Lai? The Nuremberg Principles state: "The fact that a person acted pursuant to order of his government or of a superior does not relieve him from responsibility under international law, provided a moral choice was in fact possible for him."

b. The officers? They gave the orders and set examples of conduct for the soldiers. Were the officers only carrying out higher orders? In 1946 an International Tribunal found nineteen Nazis guilty of war crimes. Their defense was that they were following higher orders. The Tribunal ruled there is a point, even in war, at which obedience must defer to morality. The Nazis were convicted and sentenced to death or imprisonment.

c. The higher chain of command? Did they look the other way when informed of massive killing of civilians? Like General Yamashita, can they claim they did not order these actions? In 1945 the United States brought Japanese General Yamashita to trial because the men under his command had committed war crimes against Filipino citizens. His defense was that he had not ordered his soldiers to do what they did. Nevertheless, Yamashita was held responsible for his men's actions, and he was convicted and executed.

d. The policymakers? Are the policymakers accountable for what happened at My Lai, as the Nuremberg Principles held Nazi policymakers responsible? Is My Lai an isolated incident or part of the national policy?

e. The American public? By supporting the war with their votes and taxes were members of the public indirectly supporting the continuation of war crimes? If a citizen believed this were true, did (s)he have a responsibility to withhold taxes and otherwise obstruct the war effort? Where does personal responsibility begin and end?

How Could It Have Happened?

Twenty years have passed since the My Lai massacre. It would serve little useful purpose to dwell on questions of personal blame and guilt for what can never be undone. However, there is much that can be learned from this event that may help us to limit, if not completely prevent, any such future crimes against human-

ity. What we need to do is to identify those factors that contributed to a situation in which patriotic American boys were suddenly capable of the wholesale slaughter of innocent civilians. Were there warning signs that could have been detected? Were there factors that could have been controlled? Can we prevent any future My Lai massacres? To answer these questions we must review the history of Charlie Company leading up to My Lai.

In terms of background, the men of Charlie Company were fairly typical of American troops in Vietnam. Most were between eighteen and twenty-two years of age. Only a few had been to college, and some had not even finished high school. Nearly half were black and a few were Mexican-Americans.

Company Commander Medina was a career Army officer. During training in Hawaii, Medina's hard-core style of command earned him the nickname of "Mad Dog." Charlie Company became the best company in the battalion, winning nearly every competitive award at Schofield Barracks. As they shipped out for Vietnam, in December of 1967, they considered themselves the toughest outfit in the battalion.

Twenty-four-year-old William Calley had flunked out of junior college and had failed to make it in the business world. He enlisted in the Army just ahead of his draft notice. Nevertheless, the Army decided to send him to Officer Candidates School. His marks were "average," and he was graduated from Fort Benning OCS. Despite being deficient in map-reading and other skills, he received passing evaluations and was commissioned a Second Lieutenant. He was assigned as the leader of First Platoon, Charlie Company before it shipped out for Hawaii.

Former members of Calley's platoon remember him as an ineffectual leader, always trying to impress Medina, but usually messing things up. Many remember Medina calling Calley, "sweetheart," over the radio nets when Calley became confused and asked for directions. While in Vietnam, Calley was constantly challenged in his platoon by Sergeant Cowen. Most of their arguments ended with Calley saying, "I'm the Boss!" Calley's orders may not have been popular, but they were obeyed.

In Vietnam, Charlie Company's assigned task was to "search and destroy," that is, to make contact with the enemy and to destroy him with superior fire power. The command officers were expected to attain the proper "kill ratio," at the time which was three Vietcong for

The bodies of women and children lay piled on a road leading from My Lai.

every American. American commanders knew that those combat officers with the highest "body counts" of enemy dead were the ones who received the highest fitness reports for promotion. This command was passed from the top all the way down to the "grunts" in the field. A soldier could win a three day pass in-country with a confirmed VC "kill."

The area of "Pinkville" (Son My village) was considered to be a "free fire zone" or an area where all civilians were automatically suspected to be either VC/NLF or their supporters. Tens of thousands of tons of bombs, rockets, napalm, and artillery shells were poured into "free fire" zones in and around the "Pinkville" area, destroying nearly 70 percent of all the homes. Despite, or perhaps because of all of this, the Vietcong continued their undisputed control of the area.

The soldiers of Charlie Company learned quickly that their area of operations was infested dangerously with mines, booby traps, and snipers. The men of Charlie Company grew frustrated and terrified about when the next explosion might take place. Most came to blame the villagers for their troubles. They suspected the women and children were placing the mines and booby traps. The village elders would not tell them where the enemy soldiers were, nor where the mines were located. The men could recount how civilians had walked through a dried out rice paddy without incident, but the following American patrol would hit a mine that killed or wounded one of their soldiers. Resentment grew to the point that all the GIs saw the Vietnamese civilians as their enemies and not as allies or even neutrals.

The behavior of the men in the company began to change. Once, they had stopped civilians to check their papers, question them, and let them go. Now, they beat civilians to get information. When patrols moved into the villages, the men began to vandalize homes and intimidate people with weapons to get information. The men of First Platoon saw both Medina and Calley beat civilians. Their noncommissioned officers did not stop or report such abuse. As the losses to mines and booby traps continued to grow, so did the frustration and anger of the men.

On February 25, 1968, Charlie Company suffered its worst day in the war. The company had walked into a well laid mine field north of My Lai. Six men were killed and twelve wounded. It shook the confidence of the men to their very core. Almost all blamed the villagers of My Lai who "knew" that the mine field was there but did nothing to warn the company. One of the few who thought otherwise was PFC Bernhardt. He remembered that South Korean Marines had set up a base camp there and surrounded it with mines. He assumed they simply had not cleared the area before they left. However, as he recalls, "the guys in the company did not want to hear that....They were all gung ho, all for the Army. It was easier to blame the VC or the Vietnamese civilians."

About this time, at least two members of Charlie Company began to assault and abuse Vietnamese women. Some of the younger members of the company were troubled by this, but apparently no punishment was ever meted out. On one occasion a number of soldiers accosted a woman working in a rice field in a supposedly friendly area. As Bernhardt remembered, "They took her and her baby into the bushes....They raped her and killed her....I guess they killed her baby too."

The behavior of the men toward the villagers had become so barbaric that the elders were moved to send a complaint to the province capital. The complaint was forwarded to Lieutenant Colonel Barker, who sent it on to Medina for action. Medina called the company together and told his men that they would have to "cool it" in dealing with the civilians. He then reassured them that they would soon get their chance at the enemy...."once and for all."

It was March 15, 1968, at LZ Dotti. Medina called his company together to give operation orders for the following day. Intelligence reports indicated that the Vietcong 48th Local Force Battalion, one of the enemy's best units in the area, had established a base

> *...the longer you're in Vietnam...the more inhumane you become. You forget about the world. You forget about paved streets, flushing toilets and colored TV sets. All of a sudden you're out in the jungle. The most ruthless men are there, the guys who are firing and raping and all this sort of thing, are the legs (army slang for infantrymen). It's a crime not only on the young American kid for turning him into one of these monsters; it's also a crime on the Vietnamese people.*
>
> —Vietnam Infantryman's letter home

camp in the hamlet of My Lai-4. Charlie Company's mission was to destroy the VC 48th Battalion. The company was to destroy the village as well. The assault began at 0730 hours (7:30 a.m.). There was a preparatory artillery barrage on the village. Helicopter gunships poured prep-fire into the village too. By then the women and children were on their way to market at Quang Ngai City six miles to the south. This left a main force fighting unit of some 250 to 280 enemy soldiers in the village area. "You will be outnumbered two-to-one during the assault," Medina told his men. "You can expect a hot LZ, but I have every confidence that you will all prove equal to the task and do your duties."

Medina used a stick to sketch his plan of attack in the sand. Following the preparatory artillery barrage, First Platoon, under Calley, led the way into the village area. Calley's platoon swept through the southern end of the village chasing the enemy to the east. Second Platoon, led by Lt. Brooks, did the same in the northern end of the village chasing the enemy east. Alpha Company was the blocking force and trapped the enemy between the two forces. Third Platoon and the Weapons Platoon followed in "mop-up" operations. Medina, himself, accompanied the Third Platoon to the center of the village for control purposes. In closing the company meeting, Medina repeated the orders he had received from headquarters.

"You are to aggressively close with the enemy...and destroy his fighting capabilities. Any structures, food supplies, and local materials that could be used by the enemy are to be destroyed, as well....You are to burn the houses....Kill the livestock....Destroy the rice....Leave nothing alive behind for the enemy to use in the future...."

According to many members of Charlie Company, that night as they prepared for the mission, they all seemed to have the same idea from the briefing either implicitly or explicitly....NOTHING WAS TO BE LEFT ALIVE IN MY LAI-4 THE NEXT DAY.

Discussion Questions

1. Suppose you were a member of this company. How would you feel? Scared? Afraid to admit you are scared? Angry? At whom? Enemy soldiers? All Vietnamese? The Army? The American people?
2. What are your obligations to your fellow soldiers? What can you do about it?
3. What factors in the situation contributed to the likelihood of the massacre? Were they inevitable? What were the alternatives?
4. Was there any time where the growing blood lust of Charlie Company could have been stopped?

Factors Contributing to the Massacre

Psychiatrist William Gault studied the problem of how the average man in Charlie Company came to internalize and then act upon what he calls an "irresistible image of slaughter." In his interviews, Gault discovered that many soldiers in Vietnam had committed or witnessed slaughter. Often such brutal acts were merely mentioned by the men in passing. This led Gault to consider the factors in a combat situation that increased the likelihood of atrocities against civilians. The factors Gault lists are:

1. The enemy is everywhere.

The weary, overburdened U.S. infantryman in Vietnam saw immediate physical threat everywhere. He could not distinguish farmer from terrorist, innocent youth from Vietcong spy. Moreover, in this war of mines and booby traps, in this land of swamps, dysentery, and malaria, he felt that the country itself might kill him at any moment.

2. The enemy is not human.

Some armies have adopted this conviction officially. American soldiers regularly referred to the Vietnamese as "gooks" and "dinks." Some soldiers felt that the individual dead enemy was "not like you and me, but more like a Martian or something."

3. No personal responsibility.

GI's often felt that killing someone was not their personal responsibility. For example, orders may come down from battalion and company command to destroy enemy strongholds in a given area. Finally, a squad is directed to wipe out a cluster of suspicious huts. The entire squad simultaneously directs a torrent of small arms fire and rifle grenades through the flimsy thatch of the buildings. When a rifleman, picking through the rubble, discovers the corpses of a mother and her children, he doesn't take individual responsibility.

4. The pressure to act.

A rifleman's business is to use his rifle. A combat unit that does not get a chance to fight becomes restless. Frequently, however, infantry units in Vietnam suffered casualties from mines and snipers without getting a chance to face the enemy. The frantic soldier became so avid to avenge the suffering of his fellows that eventually he would shoot at anyone or anything.

5. The natural dominance of the psychopath.

During a brutal war, civilized customs are left behind. Violent, restless, men—psychopaths—find themselves in a world suited to their character. Their actions are often admired and they become leaders.

6. Firepower.

Today's rifleman carries a light-weight M-16 that spits ten strangely small bullets in one second at bone-shattering velocity. He doesn't aim; he points in the enemy's general direction and opens up a torrent of destruction. It serves also as a grenade launcher, making every soldier a miniature artilleryman. Terrified and furious teenage soldiers have only to twitch their fingers and what was a quiet village is suddenly a slaughterhouse.

Discussion Questions

1. Following are remarks made by some of the soldiers who were witnesses at My Lai. See if you can match them up with the factors Gault has listed:

    a. We were told to do it, and we did it.

    b. You give these people names to depersonalize them. They become dinks and slopes and slants and gooks, and you begin to say, and believe, "The only good dink is a dead dink."

    c. Pretty soon you get to hate these people. You don't know which are your enemies and which are your friends. So you begin to think they're all your enemies.

    d. Our officers said: "This is your chance to get back at them for killing your buddies."

    e. The Vietnamese are a funny people. They don't care if they live or die.

    f. It seemed like it was the right thing. Everyone was doing it.

    g. The Lieutenant told me: "If you don't kill her, you can be shot yourself."

    h. Our orders were that this was a search and destroy mission. The area was full of VC. Everyone was to be killed.

    i. Even if they were considered beasts, a water buffalo or a piglet would have fared better. Even if only one infant had been killed, that would have been enough.

2. Which of the factors listed by Gault were a necessary condition for My Lai? Which of these was the most important condition?

3. Would you consider any or all of Gault's factors to constitute a moral justification for the actions of American soldiers at My Lai? Do they explain such behavior? Is an explanation of human behavior useful, even if it does not justify the actions taken? Why?

REFLECTIONS ON A VISIT TO THE SOVIET UNION

by Steve Bentley

The Afghansi (Soviet veterans of the war in Afghanistan) have organized themselves into "clubs" similar in structure to VVA Chapters or VFW Posts....They gather at these clubs wearing camouflaged clothing and black sweatshirts that question the government's "official" estimate of 15,000 dead. Here they drink and talk and sing their songs about the war they have known and the pain they share.

It was at such a gathering that John Cashwell and I sat down with fourteen Afghansi vets on a Saturday morning this past September. We talked for hours. The initial tension giving way to laughter at the incredible parallels—and then someone said, "Tell us about your Lt. Calley"....

We talked about the reality of war and the emotional constriction that takes place; how, when surrounded by death and fear, the adrenaline can take you over what James Jones called "the thin red line" / I talked about the progression of madness and the truth that lurks in phrases like "kill 'em all and let God sort 'em out" or "Bomb Hanoi, Bomb Saigon, Bomb Disneyland, Bomb Everything"....

We'd tried to cover all the bases and still they continued to press about Calley. I began to feel we were under attack. My anxiety increased. John was also very uncomfortable and he tried to change the subject, but they brought it back, "What had become of Lt. Calley? What was he doing today?"....

I felt myself flush with a kind of crazy collective shame, as if I were cast in the role of defending Calley and America at one and the same time. I couldn't help thinking, "These commie bastards are busting our balls; they're telling us that when all is said and done, things aren't the same at all—we're less than them."

I'd had enough. I came straight out with it. "What's going on here? Do you guys feel different from us? Are you saying this kind of thing didn't happen in Afghanistan?" Andrey interpreted the question and there was a long silence. John and I scanned the faces of these young men as they stared into the table we sat around. Time passed and then a man to John's right began to speak. "There were 23 of us on patrol outside an Afghan village. We were ambushed and 19 were killed. The next day we returned to the village and killed all the males—old men and child alike." A short silence and then Peter began. "It was the same for all of us. It happened time after time and day after day in village after village. We are all Lt. Calleys. We all carry this burden in our hearts." Looking from Peter to John and myself, the boys around the table all nodded repeatedly in solemn, wet-eyed affirmation. Then it became clear to me why so many questions about Calley. Their question really was "How do we live with these memories of what we have done? We have these holes in our souls that no one understands. What will become of us? What further price must we pay?"

Just so—this is the moral pain so often found at the heart of those Vietnam vets still haunted by Vietnam. The intensity of this unfinished business varies as do the circumstances, but the guilt and shame over something seen and/or some action taken or not taken remains the same. Tens of thousands on all sides of both conflicts share the pain.

Maine *VVA Quarterly*, 1990, Vol. 2, No. 2

Update on My Lai Veterans

In 1988 the Associated Press distributed an article about the present whereabouts of those charged with war crimes in My Lai. Here is what they found:

Captain Ernest Medina (acquitted), 52, owns a real estate company in Marinette, Wisconsin;

Lt. William L. Calley Jr. (the only man convicted), 45, works in his father-in-law's jewelry store in Columbus, Georgia;

Corporal Kenneth Schiel (charges dismissed), 41, is a patrolman in Corunna, Michigan;

Sergeant Kenneth Hodges (discharged at the convenience of the government), drives for the V.A. in hometown of Dublin, Georgia. Alcoholism led to two divorces. Married for a third time he says he has been sober since 1985;

Sergeant Charles Hutton (barred from reenlistment), 39, repairs televisions in Monroe, Louisiana. He says he overcame a drinking problem resulting from his struggle with the burden of My Lai;

Paul Meadlo (testified under immunity at Calley's court-martial), 41, of Terre Haute, Indiana, whose foot was blown off the morning after the massacre, is a laid off factory worker;

Spec. 4 Robert T'Souvas (charges dismissed), 39, was a bum who was shot to death in 1987 by his girlfriend under a Pittsburgh bridge where they lived. They were arguing over a bottle of vodka;

Jim Bergthold (charged according to the article, but not mentioned in the book *The My Lai Inquiry* by General Peers who headed up that inquiry), 41, has not worked since 1985 because of PTSD. His family left him seven years ago because of his drug and alcohol abuse.

Conclusion

American Soldiers became capable of atrocities when they interpreted Vietnamese neutrality as betrayal and defined them as the enemy. This became a self-fulfilling prophecy. Crimes against civilians in Vietnam were not only immoral, they also undermined the U.S. war effort by driving more and more neutrals into the ranks of the enemy. Certainly one can sympathize with the terror of U.S. soldiers not being able to distinguish friend from foe in a strange land ten thousand miles from home. Even though humane treatment of civilians sometimes put a soldier's life at risk, it was his duty to remain civil in his dealings with the people.

A soldier's duty is not to stay alive by any means necessary. Such logic leads to combat avoidance, even desertion. A soldier's duty is to follow orders and be prepared to die if called upon. Such an order might be to charge a well-defended enemy position where many casualties can be predicted. Or it might be to not abuse civilians even if they might be suspected of collaborating with the enemy. Again, soldiers who showed no discipline and violated the military code by abusing Vietnamese civilians only increased the size and determination of the opposing forces.

We recognize that a certain number of wartime atrocities are inevitable, if only because some brutal men are drawn to war, trained in modern weapons, and put into situations where they can attack others with impunity. Therefore, we must learn how to train troops and monitor troop actions so as to minimize the influence of such men.

It is clear that war crimes are much more likely to occur in "wars without fronts" like Vietnam. Unfortunately, Vietnam is a clear case of the emerging pattern of modern warfare. Within weeks of the historic developments signaling the end of the Cold War with the Soviet Union in 1990, spokespersons for the U.S. Army and U.S. Air Force announced new missions to combat "instability" in Third World "trouble spots" through "low-intensity conflict" (e.g. guerrilla warfare, counterinsurgency, pacification), rapid deployment forces (e.g. the 1989 invasion of Panama) and surprise bombing raids (e.g. Libya in 1987). This means that the problem of war crimes could get worse.

Some think that all war is a crime and that it is futile to make and enforce rules of conduct. We do not argue for war. However, we have established that, in past wars, the actions of soldiers have been regulated by moral concerns. And we do argue that world civilization demands no less of us in the future.

Chapter 7

Jerold M. Starr with Charles Di Benedetti

TAKING SIDES: THE WAR AT HOME

How The Public Saw The War

Throughout the Vietnam War, pollsters closely monitored the public's opinions on the issues. Many in politics watched the polls closely, especially President Johnson, who carried clippings of favorable polls with him to impress critics.

Experts note that public opinion on international issues is influenced greatly by official policy and can change very quickly. Most Americans just don't pay much attention to events far from home. In March 1966, with nearly 400,000 U.S. troops fighting in Vietnam, only 47 percent of the public could identify Saigon as the capital of the South; 41 percent, Hanoi as the capital of the North. A year later, more than half still did not have "a clear idea" what the war was about. Thus, in the early years of the war, large segments of the public simply endorsed the President's policies. Erikson and Luttbeg explain:

> Because most political events are remote from people's everyday lives, people willingly view these events
> through the interpretation of their leaders. Also, since people want to believe that their political system
> is benign rather than corrupt or evil, they readily find reassurance from optimistic interpretations of the
> existing order and resist voices that tell them otherwise.

University of Michigan researchers Philip Converse and Howard Shuman noted a pronounced tendency for public opinion on Vietnam to swing behind the President, whether the initiative was toward escalation or withdrawal. In early 1964, a majority of Americans expressed dissatisfaction with Johnson's handling of the war in Vietnam. However, after Johnson called for a resolution to permit him to respond to the alleged attacks on U.S. ships in the Gulf of Tonkin, his support zoomed to 85 percent. In May 1966, the public was split on whether to bomb Hanoi and Haiphong. A month later, when the U.S. began bombing in those areas, those in favor surged to 85 percent.

In March 1968, the Gallup Poll asked if we should stop bombing the North in exchange for Hanoi's offer of peace negotiations. The public opposed the proposition by a margin of 51 percent to 40 percent. When, only weeks later, Johnson announced he was restricting the bombing of North Vietnam to encourage peace talks, 64 percent of the public voiced approval.

Although the President usually could count on a lot of people agreeing with whatever he said or did, the cause never really gripped enough people; and support for the war in Vietnam began to dwindle when casualties mounted.

Even as the first U.S. troops were being sent into combat in 1965, few Americans had faith in the ability of South Vietnam's leaders to govern. When asked by Gallup a year later, "Do you think the South Vietnamese will be able to establish a stable government or not?" 48 percent of the public said no; only 32 percent, yes. From 1966 to 1972 two of three Americans consistently advised Gallup that the government in South Vietnam would not be strong enough to "withstand communist pressures" after U.S. withdrawal.

Neither did the public foresee an eventual U.S. military victory. According to Gallup, in 1966, only 17 percent expected an "all-out victory" for the U.S. A year later it was 14 percent, with 70 percent predicting a compromise ending. Most thought the war would last for many years.

Reflecting the legacy of Korea, several polls over 1965 and 1966 showed clear majorities that wanted to see the United Nations take over from the United States, either to fight or settle the war. In fact, Johnson was criticized for neglecting that option by a margin of nearly two to one.

Although strongly hostile to a communist takeover of South Vietnam, most Americans were prepared to make the anticipated political compromise. When asked in 1966 how they felt about a settlement of the war involving free elections "which would result in the communists being part of the government," 47 percent were in favor; 41 percent, opposed. Two years later 60 percent were willing to accept an electoral outcome resulting in "a neutralist South Vietnam, neither on the side of the U.S. nor the communists." Only 20 percent were opposed.

As for fighting the war, many in the public shared Johnson's concern about possible intervention by communist China. In June 1966 the public was fairly split on the question of whether China would enter the war. When asked in April 1967 whether China would send troops "if North Vietnam shows signs of giving in," 42 percent said yes and 36 percent said no. As the first Marines were sent into combat at Da Nang Air Force Base in 1965, the Harris Poll put it to the American public:

All in all, what do you think we should do about Vietnam now? We can follow one of three courses: carry the ground war into North Vietnam, at the risk of bringing Red China into the

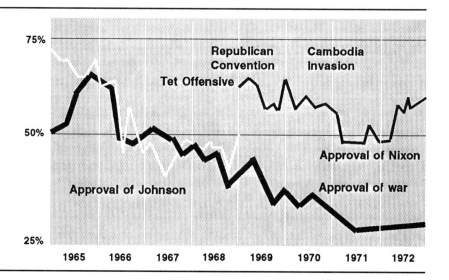

POPULAR SUPPORT FOR VIETNAM WAR AND TWO PRESIDENTS

fighting, try to negotiate and withdraw our support and our troops from South Vietnam or continue to try to hold the line there to prevent the communists from taking over South Vietnam. What do you favor?

Those who said the U.S. should "hold the line" outnumbered those who wanted to negotiate 49 percent to 38 percent. Only 13 percent said we should "carry the war to the North." After a summer of optimistic battle-field reports, those in favor of an all-out offensive increased to 30 percent, while those in favor of negotiating fell to 11 percent. Most importantly, the Johnson policy of steering a middle course had even greater support than before, a solid 59 percent majority of those polled.

Faced with the prospect of a long and inconclusive war, Americans favored a strategy that would minimize the loss of U.S. lives. From 1966 to 1970, two of three supported U.S. bombing of North Vietnam. When observers in Vietnam reported that the effect of the bombing was to "unite North Vietnam," the public rejected the claim, 52 percent to 24 percent. When Harris asked in March 1967 whether the U.S. should stop the bombing to seek negotiations, 63 percent said no; 15 percent, yes.

Sending troops to Vietnam was another matter, however. From 1966 to 1969, two of three Americans stated they would prefer to see the burden of the fighting transferred from U.S. troops to the South Vietnamese. This margin was identical to that of a similar poll on the Korean War conducted in November 1952.

By 1967, a majority of the public was opposed to any increase in U.S. troop strength in Vietnam. Nevertheless, troop size steadily grew to a peak of 543,000 in 1969. The number of U.S. casualties increased proportionately. As the toll mounted, more and more people grew impatient with the war and critical of Johnson's handling of it.

Those who thought "the United States made a mistake in sending troops to fight in Vietnam" increased from 24 percent in 1965, to 32 percent in 1966, to 40 percent in 1967. Those who approved of Johnson's handling of the war shrank from 50 percent in March 1966 to 33 percent in July 1967.

The Tet offensive of winter 1968 was the event that turned public opinion decisively against the war. News that communist forces had infiltrated major cities throughout the south and blasted into the American Embassy in Saigon hit the public like a bombshell.

Those in favor of the war fell from 62 percent to 41 percent. For the first time in the war, the "doves" were in the majority, practically doubling their numbers in one month, from 23 percent to 43 percent.

By July 1969, 63 percent of the public agreed that they "would have opposed U.S. involvement in Vietnam had they known the cost and casualties involved." Only 26 percent had no regrets. By November 1969, "doves" outnumbered "hawks" 55 percent to 31 percent, and President Nixon was forced to establish a draft lottery to equalize the burden and neutralize mounting draft resistance. In 1970, opponents of the war won their first policy victories when Congress repealed the Gulf of Tonkin Resolution and passed the Cooper-Church Amendment limiting Presidential action in Cambodia.

As 1971 began, almost 75 percent of Americans said they wanted their congressmen to "vote to bring all the troops out of Vietnam even at the risk of a Red take-over." The Nixon administration could not even win approval for bombing in Cambodia and Laos. Americans disapproved by a margin of two to one because they felt the bombing would prolong rather than shorten the war.

By 1972, almost 90 percent of those with an opinion felt, "U.S. participation in Vietnam had weakened our position throughout the world." By then, 75 percent were willing to state that "further military action in Southeast Asia should require a vote of approval by Congress." U.S. forces finally withdrew from Vietnam the following year.

Looking at the evidence as early as 1966, public opinion analyst Seymour Martin Lipset concluded, "The great majority of the American people desire peace in Vietnam, do not want war with China" and "anticipate a negotiated peace rather than...the defeat of the Vietcong." While "the dominant attitude seems to be not to let Vietnam 'go communist'," there is "a willingness to negotiate directly with the National Liberation Front."

It would be another seven long years before the U.S. government would conclude such negotiations and withdraw all American troops from Vietnam. During that period, more and more Americans came to care deeply about the issue, and many found ways to demonstrate their concern. The next few years would witness the largest movement against government war policies in U.S. history.

War Protest in America

Masses of citizens have protested all wars in U.S. history. Several churches in the U.S. oppose war as a matter of doctrine. Many in the north rioted to protest conscription for the Civil War. Two major pacifist organizations—the War Resisters League and Fellowship of Reconciliation—were formed to protest conscription for World War I. Throughout the 1930s, German-Americans actively opposed U.S. intervention in what was to become World War II. The polls showed Korea to be very unpopular with the American people. However, no war in U.S. history provoked so much active opposition as Vietnam.

To be sure, especially in the early years, most Americans said they supported U.S. policy in Vietnam. Many of those who backed the war flew flags in front of their homes, stuck flag decals on their car windows or put stickers on their car bumpers with messages like "America: Love It or Leave It" or "Support Our Boys in Vietnam." They also bought records like "The Ballad of the Green Berets" and, later, POW bracelets. However, there were few pro-war rallies held and those that were rarely drew as many as 10,000 people. Generally, people who supported the war were silent; and their numbers thinned as casualties mounted.

Those opposed to the war, on the other hand, conducted numerous mass demonstrations that increased in size through the years. After a major demonstration at the United Nations in New York on April 15, 1967, most of the ones that followed were held in the nation's capital, Washington, DC. These included marches and rallies of hundreds of thousands on October 21, 1967, October 15, 1969, November 15, 1969, May 9, 1970 and April 24, 1971.

The movement against the war in Vietnam had no organizational base nor ideological consensus. It included hundreds of *ad hoc* groups rooted in every kind of community and with little in common except opposition to the war. Actually, it would be more accurate to characterize the movement against the war as a movement of diverse movements rather than a unified force. In fact, this movement only came together physically at the national demonstrations. The last one, April 24, 1971, still stands as the biggest in U.S. history. Estimates of crowd size range up to a million people. Here

is a description by activist Fred Halstead of what you would have seen, had you been there:

"Buses bringing demonstrators that morning were backed up for twenty miles—all the way to Greenbelt, Maryland. Uncountable numbers of cars and buses filled with demonstrators didn't get to Washington until after the march and rally were over....

"After the first contingents reached the Capitol, I ascended its steps and turned to gaze upon the spectacle of Pennsylvania Avenue jammed with marchers as far as the eye could see. It stayed that way for hour upon hour, long after the grounds of the Capitol were packed with people. The continuous overflow took over every available patch of space in the general area....

"Almost every element of the American population had its representation. Present were older veterans of earlier wars, along with Vietnam vets and GIs. There was an all-Black contingent and a Third World Section embracing Blacks, Latins, Asian-Americans, Iranians, and Palestinians, each bearing their own banners. There was also a group of left-Zionists. In the procession in addition were a delegation of Native Americans; religious groupings; students from scores of colleges; political parties and organizations; hundreds of local and regional antiwar committees and coalitions; pacifists; gays; lesbians; Women's Strike for Peace; Another Mother for Peace; Women's International League for Peace and Freedom; the National Welfare Rights Organization; Business Executives Move for Peace; professional bodies of doctors, teachers, lawyers, and law and medical students; multitudes of government workers; a contingent of reservists and national guardsmen; high school students; handicapped people and others....Tens of thousands of trade unionists marched, their affiliations identified by placards and banners, in many cases defying top union officials."

Although the peace movement clearly included people from all social backgrounds, most participants were white and middle class. And, although the movement included people of all ages, the most militant and publicized opposition came from college students.

This is not because students were more critical of the war than other Americans. On the contrary, opinion against the war was strongest among women and the aged and the black and poor who were being asked to make the greatest sacrifice. However, few such people felt confident about speaking out, let alone trying to change government policy. Others did not join demonstrations because they were offended by the appearance and manner of many youthful protesters.

Young people were involved because war affects their interests directly. Also, students have the time, energy, and freedom from economic responsibilities to participate in public events. Throughout this century, issues of war and peace have been debated on college and university campuses. In the 1930s, hundreds of thousands of students spoke out against U.S. entrance into the growing war in Europe. Once President Roosevelt declared war, however, organized opposition ended and thousands of college men rushed to enlist. What was new in the 1960s was growing opposition to the government while the nation was "at war."

Students Protest The War

The principal student group to oppose the war in Vietnam called itself Students for a Democratic Society (SDS). Started in the early 1960s, many original members came from professional families and thought of themselves as young intellectuals with possible futures in politics. Some had their first experience with activism as volunteers for the Student Nonviolent Coordinating Committee's campaign against racial segregation in the south.

SDS called itself "New Left" because it was infused

with a sensibility that clearly distinguished it from the labor-oriented "Old Left" of the 1930s. This New Left rejected all ideologies as worn-out dogmas, bureaucratic organization as rigid and alienating, and "strategic" politics as corrupt. Instead, it tried to build a movement around the principles of cooperation, openness, and the direct participation of equals. "What we seek," declared several of its spokespersons in the spring of 1965, "is a thoroughly democratic revolution, in which the most oppressed aspire to govern and decide, to begin to practice their aspiration, and finally carry it to fulfillment by transforming decision-making everywhere...."

By the end of 1964, SDS membership stood at about 2,000 students on some 75 campuses. Within four years it would grow to a peak of about 40,000-100,000 on 350-400 campuses. The turning point in the popularity of SDS was its decision to challenge U.S. policy in Vietnam.

In March 1965, SDS organized the nation's first Vietnam "teach-in" at the University of Michigan. That semester there were teach-ins on campuses all over the country. One at Berkeley drew 12,000, but the largest was a national teach-in which included representatives from the State Department and was televised via closed circuit to 100,000 students on 100 campuses.

SDS followed the teach-ins by sponsoring the first national demonstration against the Vietnam War in April. The demonstration attracted 20,000-25,000 marchers, received national publicity, and brought chapter applications and memberships from a broad spectrum of American youth looking for a way to stop the war.

SDS remained the largest student political organization in the country until its break-up in 1969. It promoted many issues, advised campus leaders, and became the symbol of students against the war. However, its success was due largely to the fact that it had little or no central organization or program. Local chapters were independent and open to anyone. Meetings often had no chair nor agenda and ran for hours. Decisions usually were made by consensus. As a consequence, while SDS "travelers" helped to keep the pot boiling, developments on each campus took their own course.

Despite the events organized by SDS, however, those openly opposed to the war were a small minority on the campuses in 1965. One poll showed only six percent of all U.S. students favored the immediate withdrawal of U.S. troops from Vietnam. The teach-ins were picketed by pro-war students who waved banners and shouted obscenities at the speakers. Some physically attacked speakers.

Led by Young Americans for Freedom, conservative students gathered petition signatures from thousands of their peers around the country in support of U.S. policy in Vietnam. Blood drives for U.S. soldiers were organized at Ohio State, Stanford, and other campuses.

In August 1965, President Johnson announced that monthly draft calls would double. Undaunted, SDS responded with a program to encourage conscientious objector applications. On October 15, the first "International Day of Protest" was held. David Miller burned his draft card at a New York City rally while SDS staged a sit-in at the Ann Arbor, Michigan draft board office. When the newspapers publicized the SDS draft resistance call, the Justice Department threatened a federal investigation. Even liberal organizations were critical. SDS dropped the plan, but the publicity produced a boost in SDS chapters, from 100 to 180.

In the spring of 1966, General Lewis Hershey, Director of the Selective Service System, announced that some students would have to be drafted. The plan was to terminate deferments for those with a low class standing and those who failed a soon-to-be administered Selective Service Qualification Test. Hershey called for the cooperation of all college and university administrations in implementing the plan.

SDS responded by distributing its own test of knowledge of the Vietnam War to students at nearly 800 campuses in May. At several schools, SDS chapters called on university administrations to withhold cooperation with the Selective Service System. Sit-ins against class rank were staged by students at Wisconsin, Stanford, Oberlin, City College of New York, and elsewhere. Students at the University of Chicago closed down the administration building for the first time in the school's history. As mentioned, however, most campuses still were quiet.

CRACKS IN THE ESTABLISHMENT

The American foreign-policy-making elite also became divided over Vietnam. One visible example was the conflict between Dean Rusk, Secretary of State, and J. William Fulbright, Chair of the Senate Foreign Relations Committee.

Both Rusk and Fulbright were deeply patriotic southerners. Both were political moderates who supported the United Nations and Washington's Cold War to contain Soviet expansion. However, both also shared fundamental differences over America's involvement in Vietnam.

The clash between the two men occurred most vividly in February 1966, when Fulbright's Senate Foreign Relations Committee held three weeks of nationally-televised hearings on President Johnson's Vietnam policy. The gentle but direct Rusk was the administration's star witness. Mindful of the diplomats' failure to prevent war in the 1930s, Rusk said he saw the war in Vietnam as an act of aggression by North Vietnam and its communist allies against the democratic government of South Vietnam. He insisted the United States was obliged to counter the aggression and avoid any acts of appeasement. If America failed to hold the line in Vietnam, Rusk warned, the communists would continue their assaults on an ever shrinking free world until the U.S. had no choice

Senator J. William Fulbright

Secretary of State Dean Rusk

but to surrender or set off World War III. Vietnam, Rusk contended, was a vital test case of America's will to confront the challenge of international communism.

Fulbright saw Vietnam more as a test of America's wisdom than of its will. Fulbright declared the war in Vietnam a civil war, only marginally related to U.S. security interests. He criticized U.S. military escalation for threatening to provoke war with China, possibly leading to World War III. He dismissed Saigon's military rulers as "tinpot autocrats" and he insisted that, if anyone was to "save" Vietnam, it should be the Vietnamese. America, according to Fulbright, had neither the resources nor the interests sufficient to reverse a communist-led, anti-colonial, revolutionary war taking place on the borders of China. He urged the President to quit military escalation, withdraw U.S. forces into protracted coastal enclaves and negotiate U.S. withdrawal and an international settlement of the conflict.

Rusk and Fulbright typified the debate that eventually undermined consensus, even civility, among the nation's policy-making establishment. For his dissent, Fulbright was ridiculed as "Senator Halfbright" and estranged from political friends. For his doggedness, Rusk was dismissed as a political dolt who learned nothing and forgot everything. When his term of office ended, he was denied the prestigious business and teaching positions the Eastern Establishment normally accorded to those in its service.

Rise of Draft Resistance

Over the summer of 1966, a series of meetings were held by young men who had pledged themselves to resist induction into the armed services. Several were members of student political groups that had not yet taken a stand on this issue. They soon called themselves The Resistance. In Chicago in December 1966, The Resistance held a national "We Won't Go" conference, attended by more than 500 people from dozens of organizations. Soon after, *The New York Times* published an open letter to the White House from 100 student organization presidents and college newspaper editors warning that "unless this conflict can be eased, the United States will find some of her most loyal and courageous young men choosing to go to jail rather than to bear their country's arms." Spurred on by The Resistance, the SDS National Council also resolved in December 1966 to organize draft resistance. The resolution criticized the Vietnam War for suppressing the right of the Vietnamese people to self-determination, opposed conscription as coercive and undemocratic, and urged formation of local anti-draft unions to help organize those who wanted to resist.

Over the next several months anti-draft unions sprang up from coast to coast, some started by SDS, some independent. Local groups picketed and leafleted at induction centers and counseled draft age youths. Some helped organize the burning or turning in of draft cards. Such leaders risked prosecution by the Justice Department for violation of the National Selective Service Act, which forbids anyone "to counsel, aid or abet another to refuse or evade registration or service in the armed forces" on threat of five years' imprisonment and a $10,000 fine. Organizers hoped to clog the system with so many cases that conscription would grind to a halt.

As 1967 began, half of all college students still called themselves "hawks." Throughout the year, SDS broadened its analysis to include the issue of military connections to the universities. In addition to draft resistance, SDS chapters organized actions to protest or disrupt the appearance of recruiters for the military or war contractors like Dow Chemical, the makers of napalm. There also were efforts to expose and eliminate university-based defense research.

The poet, Allen Ginsberg, at the "Human Be-In" in San Franciscos' Golden Gate Park.

I-FEEL-LIKE-I'M-FIXIN'-TO-DIE RAG
by Joe McDonald

Come on all of you big strong men,
Uncle Sam needs your help again,
Got himself in a terrible jam
Way down yonder in Viet-Nam,
Put down your books and pick up your gun
We're gonna have a whole lot of fun

CHORUS:
And it's one two three what are we fighting for?
Don't ask me—I don't give a damn,
Next stop is Viet-Nam
And it's five-six-seven open up the Pearly Gates
Well, there ain't no time to wonder why
Whoopie, we're all gonna die.

© Copyright 1965 Alkatraz Corner Music

These issues mobilized students concerned with educational reform as well as those concerned with the war. When linked symbolically with the life-style of the "peace and love" counterculture, the student anti-war movement finally took on a life of its own.

On April 15, 1967, between a quarter and a half million people marched in New York City against the war. More than 150 burned their draft cards. Speaking to another 65,000-100,000 in San Francisco at the same time, David Harris called for a mass turn-in of draft cards by October 16th.

Throughout 1967 The Resistance broadened its base and organized a Stop the Draft Week for October 16-21. Over the course of the week, nearly a thousand cards were collected to present to the Justice Department. On the last day, 75,000 people gathered for a demonstration and teach-in on the steps of the Pentagon. There was a second draft card turn-in on October 27, 1967, a third on April 3, 1968, and a fourth and final one on November 14, 1968.

Campuses Erupt

Over the 1967-68 academic year, there were protests at more than 75 percent of U.S. universities and almost half of all colleges. Indeed, 1968 can be said to represent the turning point in the student protest movement. In January 1968, the Johnson administration indicted Dr. Benjamin Spock, Rev. William S. Coffin Jr., Michael Ferber, Mitchell Goodman and Marcus Raskin on charges of conspiring to persuade young men to resist the draft. The four convictions were later reversed on appeal and the trial served to rally, rather than intimidate, those committed to draft resistance.

In February 1968, the Tet offensive belied the Johnson administration's optimistic predictions and turned public opinion decisively against the war. Johnson was challenged in the Democratic primaries by Senators Eugene McCarthy and Robert Kennedy.

Both candidates attracted many young moderates, eager to stop the war, but opposed to the rising militance in the movement. A survey of 1,228 McCarthy volunteers in Milwaukee found that 80 percent were college students from middle class homes. Half considered

themselves some kind of Democrat and a fourth called themselves Independents. Not especially radical nor alienated, they were united only in their opposition to the war. They had rallied to McCarthy as a peace candidate seeking to win the presidency over Johnson's Vice President, Hubert Humphrey, and Republican candidate Richard Nixon, both of whom supported the war.

On April 14, 1968, Martin Luther King Jr. was assassinated. Blacks rioted in 138 cities in 36 states. There were more national guard and federal troops called than in all the riots of 1967. Tens of thousands of citizens were arrested. Frustration grew within the movement and, with it, despair that the conventional tactics of public education, petitioning Congress, and peaceful demonstrations could end the war and bring justice to racial minorities and poor whites.

Spearheaded by SDS, awareness grew on campus after campus about university contracts with the defense establishment and the lack of policy on the needs of minorities. Fewer students saw the war as a mistake. More saw it as an expression of American imperialism. Fewer students saw the university as a privileged retreat. More saw it as an important cog in the war machine. Protests were organized for more black studies, students and faculty, and against military research centers, ROTC, and recruiters for military contractors.

Many of these protests featured more militant tactics such as burning draft cards, blockading or occupying buildings, and even "trashing" property. The police response to such incidents, and to long-haired youth generally, became more violent. Police brutality itself served to intensify the hostility of activists and to incite bystanders to moral outrage and sympathy for the protesters.

As they became aware of this pattern, the more militant organizers adopted a strategy of confrontation to provoke police overreaction and force fence-sitting students and faculty to take sides. There were protests at three out of four universities and colleges over the academic year 1968-69. Consistent with the theme of peace, only three percent featured any violence. In many cases the peace activists were the objects, rather than agents, of the violence.

While less than one in ten students endorsed violence "as a general tactic," by 1968 a substantial majority would "sometimes" justify such non-violent civil disobedience as sitting in or blockading buildings, shielding political prisoners (like deserters and draft resisters), resisting or disobeying the police, or giving ultimatums to those in authority.

The proportion of protests featuring non-violent physical obstruction rose from nine percent in 1967-68, to 16 percent over 1968-69, to a peak of almost 20 percent over 1970-71. In 1968-69, police and national guardsmen were called in to break up protests at 127 campuses and made over 4,000 arrests. In the first six months of 1969, about 1,000 students were expelled from school. Legislatures in most states of the union passed tough new laws against campus demonstrations. The war was coming home.

The protest at Columbia University in the spring of 1968 was the worst at that time. Students challenged the administration over Columbia's affiliation with the Institute for Defense Analysis (IDA), a "think tank" of twelve member institutions organized in 1965 to channel university research into war technology. *Ramparts* magazine described Columbia as "a key base of operations for IDA's controversial Jason division" which studied everything from the use of tactical nuclear weapons in Vietnam to biological warfare to counterinsurgency weapons for use in the U.S. and abroad.

Students called for severing all Columbia ties with IDA and stopping a new student-only gymnasium which would have forced clearance of a black residential area. For months, the Columbia administration ignored appeals by the students to negotiate. Finally, the students occupied several buildings in the administration complex. The week-long sit-in was cleared by police, resulting in 148 injuries and 707 arrests of students, faculty, administrators and spectators. Students and faculty struck. The SDS campaign shut down the university in May 1968, and the administration agreed to withdraw Columbia from IDA that June. In February 1969 the administration suspended plans for the new gym.

A commission report, prepared under the direction of the distinguished attorney Archibald Cox, charged the Columbia administration with "authoritarianism" and the police with "acts of individual and group brutality." It also called for ways to be found to bring students into the policy-making process.

Meanwhile, the war ground on. In June 1968, just after winning the California Democratic primary, Robert Kennedy was slain by an assassin's bullet. Johnson's Vice President, Hubert Humphrey, had not

BATTLE OF THE HOLLYWOOD STARS

In 1964, Bob Hope conducted the first of eight annual Pentagon-sponsored Christmas tours for servicemen in the Pacific and Indochina. Alongside old show business friends like California Senator George Murphy and Governor Ronald Reagan he became one of the entertainment world's leading defenders of the Vietnam War.

"Listen," Hope told one interviewer in the spring of 1964, "if the Commies ever thought we weren't going to protect the Vietnamese, there would be Vietnams all over....Like it or not, we've fallen heir to the job of Big Daddy in the free world." Convinced of the righteousness of the war, Hope blasted antiwar dissidents as "traitors" who were "giving aid and comfort to the enemy."

Cowboy star John Wayne also was an active supporter of the War in Vietnam. He insisted the war was "damned necessary" to stop communist expansion. In fact, his only problem with the war was that it was not larger. "If we're going to send one man to die," he told an interviewer, "we ought to make it an all-out conflict."

In his 1968 film, *The Green Berets*, Wayne told the public that the war was a noble cause. Many were offended by what they saw as a less than truthful telling of what it was like in Vietnam. The film played to millions, but lost money.

Other entertainers risked their careers to oppose the war. Paul Newman and Joanne Woodward were early critics.

Jane Fonda in Hanoi.

Bob Hope and Jill St. John performing for U.S. troops.

Donna Reed organized a southern California-based group called Another Mother for Peace. Singer Barbra Streisand raffled off personal renditions of her songs to raise money for the antiwar movement.

No Hollywood performer became more identified with antiwar activism than Jane Fonda. During 1970-71, she and a few others, including actor Donald Sutherland and singer Country Joe McDonald, formed the Free the Army antiwar troupe. They toured towns near major U.S. military bases to promote antiwar protest within the armed forces.

In July 1972, Fonda visited U.S. prisoners of war in North Vietnam and made at least ten antiwar broadcasts over Radio Hanoi. Returning to the U.S., she and her new husband, activist Tom Hayden, organized the Indochina Peace Campaign (IPC). Traveling throughout the U.S., the IPC supported the presidential candidacy of George McGovern and put on programs to educate American audiences about the political and military struggle in Vietnam. After the 1973 Paris peace agreements, the IPC worked to end all U.S. aid to the South Vietnamese government.

Fonda was attacked by prowar activists. Her films were boycotted and the legislatures of Colorado and Maryland tried to bar her from their states. However, Fonda's career flourished nonetheless. She won critical acclaim, including an Academy Award, for her performances in a number of films, many of which addressed social problems like Vietnam Veterans' wounds and the hazards of nuclear power plants.

competed in the primaries, and the two peace candidates had won them all. McCarthy lacked the delegates to win on the first ballot and insiders predicted accurately that Johnson, Mayor Daley of Chicago (the site of the convention), AFL-CIO President George Meany and other power brokers in the Democratic Party were going to control the convention and hand the nomination over to Humphrey.

Most groups in the anti-war movement chose not to go to the convention. Chicago police had a reputation for being rough and, this time, Mayor Daley was prepared with barbed wire, tanks, and troops armed with M-1 rifles. Everyone feared for the safety of those who went.

About 2,000-3,000 militants showed up to protest the convention and the war. A later commission study revealed that one in six was a police undercover agent, some of whom were there to make trouble. The organizers had been denied a permit for participants to sleep in Grant Park, and most had no place else to go.

POLICE RIOT AT 1968 CHICAGO CONVENTION

We were the alternate delegates to the 1968 Democratic convention, and our forum was the street. Our plenary session convened along Michigan Avenue across from the Conrad Hilton Hotel. The police challenged our right to assemble, but we stood firm, literally bloodied but righteously unbowed, and told the TV cameras that "the whole world was watching."

The police moved just after midnight. A squad car buzzed our line, speeding away from a few haphazardly tossed rocks. A second car probed, and some, but not all, of our people cheered as a window disintegrated.

Then they charged.

The helmeted wave flowed across the park, lofting tear gas and smoke bombs and waving night sticks over their heads. They romped on the spot where the hippies had danced. They had no use for the "peace-creep dope-smoking faggots," and they told us so with a scream that said it all.

"Kill! Kill! Kill!"

When they were about 25 yards away, most of us took the hint. Some of us didn't take it fast enough.

"Walk! Walk!" said the ever-concerned clergy in our midst before they were smashed to the ground.

"Help! Help!" screamed a girl as the police tossed her into the park lagoon.

"Oh, my God!" moaned a boy as a gas-station attendant, frenzied by the herd stampeding past him, broke his arm with a baseball bat.

Allen Ginsberg stood across the street from the carnage...still trying to center the crowd with a series of desperately bellowed Ommmmmm's. Around him, the flowers were dying everywhere.

Some, though, were sprouting thorns. Abbie Hoffman had said that Yippies were hippies who'd been hit over the head, and the affinity groups that coalesced out of the chaos took him at his word. I watched a hulking *Seed* street seller, who could have played the biggest droog in "A Clockwork Orange," hurl a trash can through the window of an occupied police car. I was amazed by his boldness. I was depressed by the end of a dream. I understood as the peace signs turned to fists.

Abe Peck, former editor of *The Seed*, Chicago's underground newspaper, and now a writer for The Chicago Daily *News.*

Linda Rosen Obst. *The Sixties.* New York: Random House, 1977. Reprinted in *The New York Times Magazine,* November 13, 1977:40-2.

The demonstrators were angry about the refusal of both major parties to heed the voice of the people and stop the war. Many shouted obscenities at the police. Some threw rocks, sticks and even human feces. The police abandoned all restraint and attacked anyone and everyone. Demonstrators chanted, "The whole world is watching," while police clubbed and arrested them. Assessing the evidence of police assaults on newsmen, photographers, convention delegates and residents as well as demonstrators, a commission report later termed the event a "police riot."

Some of these scenes were televised. While the "battle of Chicago" shocked many viewers into sympathy with the demonstrators, most sided with the police. More than half of those polled felt the amount of force used was "the right amount or not enough." Only one in six thought there had been too much force. Many blamed the media for giving too much (or any) coverage to the demonstrators.

A Chicago policeman clubs demonstrators in Chicago's Lincoln Park during the Democratic Convention in August, 1968.

BLACK AMERICA AND VIETNAM

Growing up in East St. Louis, Illinois, Harold Bryant had his left ear pierced at the age of nine, as his father had before him. His grandmother said all male warriors in her ancestral tribe in Africa wore pierced ears, so when Bryant enlisted in the Army in 1965 at the age of 20, he went "wearing the mark of the African warriors I descended from."

Bryant did a one-year tour as a combat engineer who saw action from the Central Highlands to Cambodia. After his army discharge, he specialized in counseling black combat veterans. Looking back on his war experiences, Bryant said, "America should have won the war, but they wouldn't free us to fight. With all the American GIs that were in Vietnam, they could have put us all shoulder to shoulder and had us march from Saigon all the way up to the DMZ. Just make a sweep. We had enough GIs, enough equipment to do that."

Boxing champion Muhammad Ali saw Vietnam another way. Born and raised in Louisville, Kentucky, Ali (a.k.a. Cassius Clay) won a gold medal at the 1960 Rome Olympic games at the age of 18. Four years later, he defeated Sonny Liston to become the world's professional heavyweight champion.

In February 1966, as the Army sought to reclassify him for the draft, Ali, now a Black Muslim, declared that his religious beliefs required that he not fight in a white man's army against other people of color. To one reporter's question, he simply stated: "I ain't got no quarrel with the Vietcong."

Politicians and the media screamed for Ali's punishment. One Georgia lawyer launched a "Draft That Nigger Clay" cam-

Muhammad Ali stands outside the federal courthouse in Houston on April 27, 1967.

paign. Ali was unmoved. In April 1967, he refused induction into the Army on the grounds it violated his First Amendment rights to free exercise of his religion. He was sentenced to the maximum five years in prison and a $10,000 fine. Various state and national boxing commissions stripped him of his title and his license to box. For the three years that his case was under appeal to the U.S. Supreme Court, Ali was not allowed to practice his chosen profession.

In 1970, the court ruled in Ali's favor. In 1971, he tried to regain his title, but was beaten by new champion Joe Frazier. Three years later he won the crown back from George Foreman. Ali avenged his earlier loss to Frazier in two successful title defenses and reigned for several more years. He became one of the greatest champions of all time and a symbol of black pride all over the world. He never regretted his decision to refuse to serve in Vietnam. As he put it, "No Vietnamese ever called me nigger."

Escalation of Repression

From 1968 on, the Federal Bureau of Investigation (FBI), Central Intelligence Agency (CIA), National Security Agency (NSA), Internal Revenue Service (IRS), and Pentagon Intelligence launched massive counterintelligence campaigns against all kinds of political dissenters, especially those in the anti-war and civil rights movements. Such measures included wire taps, mail openings, office burglaries, personal harassment (e.g., trying to break up marriages, get people fired from their jobs, etc.), physical assaults, and the extensive use of undercover agents to entrap activists into using violent means in order to discredit them and justify further repression by the government.

These efforts were accelerated at the urging of the Nixon White House. In 1970, the FBI added 1,000 new agents and 702 new supporting personnel. FBI chief, J. Edgar Hoover, ordered investigations of SDS and "every black student union or group" on every college campus. These probes started more than 10,000 new FBI files in themselves. Over the entire period, 1960-1974, the FBI is known to have conducted more than 500,000 separate investigations of persons and groups considered to be "subversive" of the U.S. government. Not one of these led to a prosecution.

The CIA, whose charter prohibits it from domestic surveillance, nonetheless compiled 13,000 files on 7,200 American citizens. The IRS special unit conducted surveillance on 2,873 groups and 8,585 individuals. But no one could approach Army Intelligence for sheer exhaustiveness. Going after what one of their people called "anyone who could be considered, by any stretch of the imagination, to be left of center," the Army compiled computerized dossiers on roughly twenty-five million Americans—including many church leaders and Congressmen.

None of these spy efforts ever turned up anything the government could use. A 400-page report released by the U.S. Justice Department in 1976 concluded that there is "no firm evidence that senior communist intelligence services in the Soviet Union, China or Eastern Europe ever made any active attempt to incite American dissidents." Moreover, "the Cubans and North Vietnamese gave relatively little support."

Despite the lack of evidence, from 1969-1973, the U.S. Justice Department indicted scores of activists around the country on grounds of violating the Federal Anti-Riot Act of 1968. The defendants were accused of being conspirators who had crossed state lines with the intention to incite violence.

The evidence was always found wanting and no single defendant went to prison as a result of conviction in these conspiracy prosecutions. Nevertheless, the prosecutions did accomplish the purpose of tying up movement leaders in lengthy legal battles and draining the movement's financial resources. Expenses for any one trial ran between a half million and a million dollars. Many cases were thrown out of court when it was revealed that the key witness for the government was not only an FBI undercover agent, but the individual who had introduced the group to the idea and, sometimes, provided the material for committing violence, usually some sort of bomb.

Division and Debate

Their backs now up against the wall, activists debated passionately over the course of the movement. Some argued that activists should concentrate just on stopping the war. In their view, the war was an evil that, with enough public pressure, could be stopped. To attempt to promote broader social changes, indeed a revolution, would only further confuse and divide people. Others argued that the war was only a symptom of a "sick" system based on militarism and materialism. Until the system was changed, there would only be more Vietnams.

Those who sought to promote a revolution were themselves divided. There were basic disagreements over who would lead this revolution. Some looked to all peoples of color, including Third World nations and U.S. racial minorities also oppressed by "internal colonialism." Others looked to blue-collar workers, especially those in the factories. Some looked to the "new" working class of college-educated labor being trained for positions in government and the new service industries. Others looked to all young people turned off by the system and seeking a new way of life.

These debates had implications for where to organize, what language to use, and what tactics to employ. Basically, the socialists and communists argued that it

McCARTHY LOSES 1968 NOMINATION AND THE WAR GOES ON

Eugene McCarthy

With Kennedy gone, we learned that, except for the California delegation, two-thirds of his people were not really interested in making a fight on the issue of the war. They were interested in power. One group would have been for Bobby had he favored the invasion of China. The other consisted of political hangers-on who'd been left out of the Humphrey-Johnson organization. With his death, it became clear that both groups would support the party position.

Nevertheless, I spent the whole summer working for their support. I went to state conventions, party meetings and the rest. I worked hard in those states Kennedy had won, and in those where he and I together had pulled a substantial majority of the vote. Indiana was a prime case of what happened. Between us, Kennedy and I had 70 percent of the primary vote. Yet, at the convention, McGovern got a few votes, I got a few votes. The other 80 percent of Indiana went to Humphrey.

The choice was between pragmatics—elect a party Democrat—and having some integrity with respect to what had happened in the primaries. We filed protests against 20 delegations before the credentials and rules committees, on the grounds that our support was unrepresented. We fought every way that we could, all through the summer and at the convention.

...Anyone could see that we didn't have the votes.

...If we had won in California, and if Bobby hadn't been shot—if you start to speculate on that, you are off into another world.

Certainly we could have carried the convention in opposition to the war, and whoever was nominated would have taken that issue to the country. Had it not been for the assassination of Robert Kennedy and for the rules of the Democratic Party in 1968, the war in Vietnam might have ended three years earlier.

Sen. Eugene McCarthy

(Democrat-MN)

Linda Rosen Obst. *The Sixties.* New York: Random House, 1977. Reprinted in the New York *Times Magazine,* November 13, 1977:40-2.

Robert Kennedy

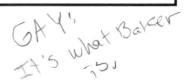

was necessary to educate and organize people slowly until they were moved to act on their own behalf. Seeking to appeal to workers and minorities, they rejected the drugs and dress of the counterculture. The anarchists, on the other hand, argued that it was necessary to provoke confrontations with authorities that would demonstrate to young people that all authority was against them and needed to be challenged. They used music and drugs to appeal to students and youthful drop-outs.

Most activists, including the revolutionaries, were concerned primarily with stopping the war. However, even here there were tactical debates. Should they back candidates for office and petition members of Congress? Should they withhold taxes and advocate draft resistance? Should they stage mass demonstrations in the capital? Should they organize small demonstrations in cities and towns all over the country? Should they challenge college administrations to withdraw from the war effort?

While the more ideologically oriented youth debated how to make a revolution, the draft resistance movement spread. Young men and their attorneys began to challenge the restrictiveness of the Selective Service law. On April 1, 1969, a Boston judge ruled that basing eligibility for exemption only on religion constituted a violation of the Constitution. Before the year was out, the Supreme Court had concurred with this interpretation in the case of Elliot A. Welsh, by a vote of 5-3.

A survey from the period demonstrated the significance of this distinction. Some 71 percent of draft resisters explained their action as bearing "moral witness as an expression of personal convictions." However, only 17 percent said they were acting "in accordance with certain religious beliefs."

Selective Service Director, Curtis Tarr, was willing to expand the definition of religion to include any system of personal belief, but still insisted that such objection must be to all wars, not just Vietnam or wars like it. This gave the nation's 4,000 local draft boards more discretion in individual cases, but still ruled out selective opposition as legitimate grounds for seeking a conscientious objector classification. In 1969 it was reported that more Selective Service prosecutions were in process in federal courts than any other criminal cases except auto theft, immigration and illegal drugs. By February 1970, an estimated 50,000-100,000 18-year-olds had failed to register for the draft.

During the "Chicago 8" conspiracy trial in the fall of 1969, the Weatherman collective came to town to demonstrate their opposition. The Weatherman ("You don't have to be a weatherman to know which way the wind is blowing") sought to organize alienated youth to disrupt the system. When Judge Julius Hoffman handed out severe sentences for contempt of court, the Weatherman showed their contempt by running wild in the streets and trashing property.

After Chicago, the Weatherman and other small militant sects became convinced that armed struggle was necessary to resist fascist repression in America. They threw themselves into more violent opposition to the war. Seeking to purge themselves of "white skin privilege" and to demonstrate their commitment to Third World revolution, they began to bomb symbolic targets, including police headquarters, the Pentagon, the State Department, and branches of the Bank of America. In every case they warned people in danger and no one was hurt.

The effect of this spiral of violence was to convince many hippies of the futility and peril of political reform. Thousands decided to head for the hills and founded rural communes where they could escape repression and plant the seeds of a better society. By 1970, at least a half-million youth were living in urban and rural communes and practicing alternative life-styles.

While the vast majority of college youth were relatively conventional in politics and life-style, most were now opposed to the war. By 1969, only one in five students called himself a "hawk." According to the American Council on Education, over 1969-70, four-fifths of four-year institutions and two-thirds of all institutions had protests. A Gallup poll in 1969 showed that 28 percent of U.S. students had participated in at least one demonstration. To be sure, most of these protests were concerned with issues other than Vietnam. By this time, however, the war had played a major role in creating a general climate of protest against authority.

At the same time, most students were also critical of the tactics and some of the demands of the militants. A poll of three New England universities (Brown, Northeastern and Tufts) found that a majority supported ROTC on campus, although without academic credit. A 1970 Harris Poll showed that a larger plurality (37%) of all college students favored ROTC on campus with academic credit than favored its complete removal

(25%). Moreover, despite the protests against Dow Chemical, 72 percent believed that companies doing defense business should be allowed to recruit on campus; and 70 percent agreed that "school authorities are right to call in police when students occupy a building or threaten violence."

Violence Comes Home

On April 30, 1970, President Nixon announced the "incursion" of U.S. troops into Cambodia. Protests erupted on campuses across the nation. According to one count, there were class strikes called at twenty new schools every day. On May 2, protesters at Kent State University (Ohio) burned down the school's ROTC building. Governor Rhodes banned all further demonstrations. Two days later many students challenged the ban by congregating on the Commons. The area also was congested by students coming from and going to classes.

The Ohio National Guard was dispatched to the scene and ordered the students to disperse. Some students shouted obscenities and threw rocks. Guardsmen fired tear gas into the crowd. Then, suddenly, still some distance away, several guardsmen turned around and fired into the crowd. Four students were killed and nine wounded.

During the four days that followed the Kent State

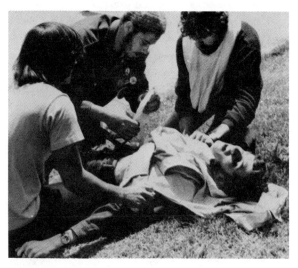

Students try to staunch the flow of blood from William K. Schroeder, one of four students killed by National Guardsmen at Kent State.

killings, there were class strikes at a hundred or more schools each day. On May 9, more than 100,000 protested in Washington, D.C. By May 10, there were strikes at 448 campuses; many completely closed down.

Ten days after the killings at Kent State, there were disturbances at Jackson State College, a black school in Jackson, Mississippi. On the night of May 14, students threw bricks and bottles at passing white motorists; a truck was set ablaze; and city and state police, called to protect firemen, were harassed by the crowd. Police fired a fusillade into a girls' dormitory. Two people

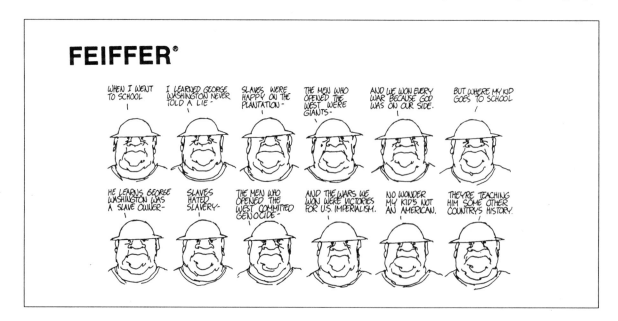

were killed and 12 were wounded.

The protest spread to other schools; many suspended classes in memory of those killed at Jackson State. During the month of May, almost three out of five colleges and universities witnessed some protest. About one out of four schools (more than 600) canceled some classes; one out of five (more than 500) closed for a day or longer. Over 10,000 draft cards or pledges of resistance were turned in to the Justice Department. Over the weekend of May 19-21, many people gathered in Princeton, New Jersey, for the founding conference of the Union for National Draft Opposition.

There was also a notable backlash among Americans who still supported the war. On May 8, a number of New York City construction workers were provoked by students lowering the American flag at City Hall to half-mast in memory of those killed at Kent State. They raised the flag to full staff and started beating the students. On May 20, urged on by President Nixon, Building and Construction Trades Council President Peter Brennan led 150,000 marchers through Manhattan to demonstrate support for the President's invasion of Cambodia. It was, by far, the largest demonstration in support of the war.

As the summer of 1970 ended, the University of Wisconsin's (Army) Mathematics Research Center at Madison was destroyed by a bomb. The bomb went off in the middle of the night, but a researcher was killed,

Carrying flags and signs proclaiming their support for President Nixon, construction workers jammed the City Hall area in New York City. Their rally came in response to the many other demonstrations around the country opposing the U.S. invasion of Cambodia.

Ellsberg dedicated himself in 1970 to exposing the Vietnam war as a cynical conspiracy for which he says he, and all Americans, must share the responsibility.

A CASE OF CONVERSION

Dan Ellsberg was a talented schoolboy poet and pianist, then a brilliant scholar at Harvard and at Cambridge. He also became an enthusiastic skier and scuba diver and even had a fling at skydiving. Following a family tradition of military service, he spent three years as a Marine lieutenant. His great frustration was that his service came at a time when there were no wars.

Afterward he moved to the Rand Corporation's "think tank," and in 1964 to the Pentagon as one of McNamara's Whiz Kids. Assigned to the Vietnam problem, Ellsberg considered himself a "cold war Democrat," and his straightforward notion of patriotic service was to "improve our position" against the communists. In 1965, Ellsberg volunteered for Vietnam and, as a civilian pacification adviser, found the action he had missed as a Marine:

he came under fire near the DMZ. He also saw at firsthand how the American was brutalizing Indochina, particularly its long-suffering civilians.

Back at Rand, he delved into the Vietnam papers, to which he still had access. He began to view the war as not merely wrong but criminal. As chief criminals he saw the succession of U.S. Presidents beginning with Truman. Each of them, he thought, had enlarged the war not through miscalculation or even in the hope of victory—but cynically, to avoid political risk and judgement as "the President who lost Saigon." He quit Rand, went to MIT as a senior researcher and became an eloquent antiwar writer and speaker.

Ellsberg has expressed his belief that "simple protest...is obviously inadequate" to make up for the guilt he shares.

Life Magazine, 1970.

and four other people were injured. A group calling itself The New Year's Gang took credit for the bombing and warned that, unless certain demands were met, there would be more bombings. The FBI launched a nationwide manhunt for four youthful suspects.

The Wisconsin bombing was the first movement action to cause a death. A sense of despair set in over the movement's failure to stop the war and its own drift into violence. The Nixon administration attacked the media for its protest coverage and criticism of the government's handling of the war. Editors and broadcasters cut back sharply on both.

This did not stop the students. During the 1970-71 academic year, there were serious protests on more than 460 campuses. On April 24, 1971, nearly a million people gathered in the nation's capital for the biggest demonstration in American history.

Peace Comes to Vietnam and America

In April 1972, the Nixon administration renewed its bombing of North Vietnam, provoking demonstrations at almost 700 colleges across the land. This was to be the last significant outpouring of student opposition to the war. Draft calls were steadily going down, and more troops were being withdrawn from Vietnam.

The Presidential candidacy of Senator George McGovern served as a lightning rod for many movement groups. However, all their hopes for a quick settlement of the war and new, reform-minded administration were dashed by the Nixon landslide in November.

"Try to cool it a bit, fellows. You don't want to give the impression this country is divided, do you?"

The peace negotiations in Paris dragged on through the year and were interrupted by South Vietnamese objections, North Vietnamese withdrawal, and a massive U.S. bombing campaign over Christmas. The talks resumed in January and led to an agreement. In April, the U.S. government acknowledged that the last American Prisoners of War had been sent home.

The issue of the war tore America into angry factions. At some level these factions reflected long-standing regional, religious, racial, and political differences that run deep in American society. The war also divided father and son and turned brother against brother.

Ironically, those who battled each other over the merits of the war were in some ways more like each other than they were like the great many who may have shared their opinions but who felt it was not their business to question the government. Most activists, hawk and dove, were moralistic people with a deeply felt sense of personal responsibility.

Moreover, at least in the early years, advocates on both sides felt that they represented America's best traditions and interests, that they were the true patriots. For example, advocates on both sides believed that America should stand up against repression and support popular self-determination in Vietnam. Where they differed, of course, was in the interpretation of that principle. Those who supported the war saw North Vietnam and the communists as the oppressors. In their view, self-determination for the South required elimination of that threat by any means necessary. Those who opposed the war saw the U.S. and its sponsored military regime in the South as the oppressors. In their view, we had no right to intervene in another country's civil war and certainly not to impose our politicians and form of government on them.

As the war dragged on the debate became more heated and the possibility of reconciliation more remote. Each group came to define the other as part of the problem. The passion that fueled this struggle took on cultural contrasts that went well beyond Vietnam. For many Americans the real war was over America. Vietnam became the symbolic touchstone by which Americans decided what their country had come to be and what it should have become. That is why, in the end, Americans will long argue about Vietnam. The quarrel over Vietnam is to regain a sense of what is good for America.

The passage of time has brought a healing to some of these wounds. While many continue to press their views with the same intensity as before, others have come to a deeper understanding of that complex era. Many can now acknowledge common concerns with those who were once on the other side of the barricades.

Vietnam veteran Philip Caputo said recently, "I would like one day to put my arms around this Elizabeth McAlister or Philip Berrigan and even Tom Hayden, for that matter, and literally say that we—all of us—went through something together."

Anti-war activists Tom Hayden and Jane Fonda said recently, "Whether we opposed the war in good conscience, or served in combat from our sense of duty, we all paid our dues, risking, in the words of America's founders, our lives, our fortunes, and our sacred honor. It is time we said this to each other."

The network of Vietnam veterans, activists, teachers and scholars who created this curriculum over four long years of work have gone beyond such accommodation to one of mutual respect, based on a respect for moral commitment, personal responsibility, and truth.

Conclusion: Assessing the Movement

One of the ironies of the peace movement is that, generally speaking, its critics have been more impressed with it than its participants have. Many hawks have denounced the movement for giving encouragement to the enemy while subverting public commitment at home. The most extreme among them have proposed that such people were guilty of treason and should have been dealt with accordingly.

In contrast, many participants in the movement came to despair that their efforts had no effect. Not only did American military intervention expand despite the largest demonstrations of opposition in U.S. history, but the war effort persisted four long years after a majority of the American public had turned against it.

It is difficult to assess what effects the antiwar movement might have had on the attitudes of the communists in Vietnam. We do know that part of the Vietminh strategy in the First Indochina War was to wear away at public support in France for the war. Eventual success in that struggle recommended a similar strategy in the Second Indochina War.

There is some evidence that North Vietnamese leaders were cheered by the growth of the antiwar move-

War is not healthy for children and other living things

ment in the U.S. There also is evidence that they were critical of hippie-type radicals because, in their view, they alienated mainstream Americans. In the end, however, it is safe to say that the communists knew that it was their revolution to win or lose, that they could not count on domestic debates in the U.S. to accomplish their purpose for them. At a 1991 U.S.-Vietnam conference of scholars, NLF General Tran Van Trah, Commander of the TET offensive, remarked: "Some say that American forces were defeated by the anti-war movements in America, not on the battlefield. Victory on the battlefield will influence all political and diplomatic decisions. So there is no basis for saying the anti-war movement in America defeated the American war effort."

It also is difficult to assess the impact of war protest on U.S. public opinion. Most Americans were offended by protest, especially early in the war. In fact, several polls in March 1966 confirmed that three of five Americans felt that citizens did not even have a "right" to demonstrate against the war in Vietnam. Many saw the protesters as communists or "draft dodgers." By 1970, President Nixon found hippie-looking protesters to be such a perfect foil for his law and order speeches that he would arrange, with the help of local police, for them to be there.

On the other hand, it might be said that, while most Americans rejected the messenger, they did get the message. It was usually antiwar research that exposed official lies and educated the public about U.S. policy in

Vietnam. These facts and opinions found their way into underground and mainstream newspapers, campus teach-ins, the speeches of antiwar politicians, church sermons, TV and radio talk shows, and other forums.

The accomplishments of the draft resistance movement also must be acknowledged here. Despite the risks, some 570,000 young men committed draft violations that could have resulted in prison sentences of up to five years. Of these almost 210,000 were reported to the Justice Department for possible prosecution, including about 110,000 who burned their draft cards.

Only about 10,000 cases were ultimately brought to trial. Of these 8,750 were convicted, 5,500 of whom were given probation with suspended sentences. A total of 3,250 were imprisoned, roughly half for seven-month to two-year sentences.

Those tried, convicted and sentenced were disproportionately from the ranks of activists who had openly challenged the system. Columbia psychologist Willard Gaylen interviewed several in 1968 and was surprised to find them, not dogmatic and militant radicals, but gentle, compassionate and deeply moral young men. Some were subjected to beatings, rape, and solitary confinement while in prison. Some never recovered.

Needless to say, most people did not approve of draft resisters. Perhaps no issue split the generations more than this one. Even among youth, support for resisters was confined largely to the campuses. A 1968-69 poll found 72 percent of non-college youth but only 44 percent of college youth asserting that "resisting the draft is basically wrong." In 1971, Harris found that 57 percent of college students had "respect" for draft resisters. Support was still higher among students at the larger and more selective institutions.

In retrospect, it cannot be said that the draft resistance movement succeeded in its goal of clogging up the induction system and, thus, stopping the war. However, individual acts of courage touched the consciences of many Americans and compelled critical attention to the morality of the war.

There also is evidence that the movement made a strong impression on Presidents Johnson and Nixon. In 1968, when a group of Pentagon computer operators were urging Johnson to bomb Hanoi and Haiphong, the President retorted: "I have one more problem for your computer. Will you feed into it how long it will take 500,000 angry Americans to climb the White House wall out there and lynch their President if he does something like that."

When Johnson finally decided he would wind down the war and would not seek re-election, he explained to the public:

> It is true that a house divided against itself is a house that cannot stand. There is division in the American house now. And, believing as I do, I have concluded that I should not permit the presidency to become involved in the particular divisions that are developing in this political year. I shall not seek, and I will not accept the nomination of my party for another term as your president.

In his television interview with David Frost in 1981, President Nixon admitted that he and his National Security Advisor, Henry Kissinger, were driven to distraction by the antiwar protests of the late 1960s and early 1970s. Nixon recalled that Kissinger flew into a rage when someone leaked the news of the secret U.S. bombing raids over Cambodia: "Henry said (of the leaders), 'I will destroy them.'" Nixon defended his schemes to harass dissenters through burglaries, wiretaps, mail openings, and the use of the IRS as within the legitimate power of the Presidency. "Call it paranoia," Nixon said, "but paranoia for peace isn't bad."

It was, however, this "paranoia" that drove Nixon to establish a special investigative unit within the White House which he called the "plumbers." The plumbers became part of a far-reaching plan of spying, wiretapping and burglaries designed to get the edge on political opponents. On June 17, 1972, five of them were caught in the sixth-floor offices of the Democratic National Committee at the Watergate office building in Washington, D.C. Subsequent investigation showed that the break-in and effort to cover it up reached all the way up to the President himself. The national security scandal ultimately destroyed the Nixon presidency. Richard M. Nixon resigned his office on August 8, 1974; he was the second President to be driven from office by the movement to end the war.

Discussion Questions

1. Since World War II, fear of communism has had a major influence on U.S. foreign policy. In your view, is communism a united world-wide movement? Is it spreading? Is it a threat to U.S. interests? If so, what, if anything, should the U.S. government do about this? What can be done about it? Discuss.

2. The peace movement was made up of many different organizations and individuals. Was this a strength or weakness of the movement? Explain.

3. How do you explain the fact that polls showed opposition to the war to be strongest among women, people over the age of 65, blacks and those with less education and income?

4. How do you feel about the surveillance and harassment of war protesters by federal agencies and local police? What is the justification for such actions? What are the risks to constitutional rights? Public trust in government? U.S. standing in the world?

5. How would you define patriotism? How would you define nationalism? Is there a difference between love of country and hatred or fear of other countries?

6. Consider the philosophical statement "My country right or wrong. When right, to keep it right. When wrong, to set it right." What does this statement say about patriotism? The responsibilities of citizenship?

7. Do you think there should be any legal restrictions on the display and use of the American flag? Why? How should or could they be enforced?

8. Do you think U.S. citizens have a right to protest against government policies with which they disagree? Do they have a responsibility?

9. Why do you think so many Americans disapproved of antiwar protests? Was there anything protesters could have said or done to get a more sympathetic reception?

10. What do you think of the statement that those who protested the war, especially those who went to prison for their beliefs, were the true patriots?

11. How did the movement against the war influence popular culture in the United States? Discuss music, movies, dress, art, etc.

12. Do you think the U.S. protest movement had any effect on the commitment and tactics of the enemy? Explain.

13. What is conscientious objection to war? What are the principles upon which it is based? Should eligibility for a conscientious objector classification be expanded? Should it be further restricted?

14. Some said the movement should restrict itself to opposing the war. Others said the movement should seek a fundamental reform of American society. What are the arguments in favor of each position? Which do you find most persuasive?

GIs ALSO PROTEST THE WAR

The first effort to organize opposition to the war within the military was launched in 1967 with the publication of *Vietnam GI,* a newspaper featuring uncensored news of the war from GIs just back from Vietnam or involved in acts of resistance. Edited by Vietnam veteran Jeff Sharlet, the paper was widely circulated and well received.

Andy Stapp, a Fort Sill, Oklahoma recruit, was another leader in the GI movement. Arrested for distributing antiwar literature, Stapp decided to organize a union within the military. He founded the American Serviceman's Union (ASU) which he led after returning to civilian life. The ASU's newspaper, *The Bond,* achieved worldwide circulation. The union mobilized 10,000 dedicated workers, but failed to become a force within the military.

The civilian antiwar movement tried to reach GIs by setting up counseling centers and coffeehouses near military bases. In 1971 the Pacific Counseling Service had 11 offices, six on the West Coast and five near U.S. bases in the Pacific. The first coffeehouse was set up at Ft. Jackson in 1967. Eventually, there was a network of storefront coffee-houses and bookstores at most bases in all branches of the service.

The early coffeehouses featured a free-thinking atmosphere to provide an alternative to GIs in basic training. Organizers hoped the coffeehouses would become centers of resistance, but the project failed because recruits were isolated from other GIs, restricted to base and supervised around the clock.

Efforts to hold meetings of dissidents on the base usually were suppressed by military officials. In October 1969, Military Policemen raided a secret meeting at Ft. Lewis, arresting 35 GI activists. Although formal charges were not brought, almost all the organizers were transferred, discharged, arrested on other charges or sent to Vietnam.

There also were efforts to organize sick call strikes. Although soldiers cannot legally strike, military regulations do guarantee them the right to go on sick call. However, since organizing efforts had to become public early, officers had ample time to cancel sick call privileges. A strike at Ft. Knox early in the war failed, but at Ft. Lewis, later in the war, some 30 percent of the soldiers at the base stuck together and had some impact.

The movement also had a little success in getting GIs off the base to participate in civilian-led antiwar demonstrations. Usually the military was able to block these efforts by placing the entire base on restriction whenever there were

demonstrations in the area. However, 1,000 Marines marched in a 1969 Oceanside, California rally.

Because of the serious penalties for overt organizing, many dissidents chose to publish and distribute newspapers. GI papers could be found everywhere, with such mastheads as *Fatigue Press, Attitude Check, All Hands Abandon Ship, Left Face,* and *Star Spangled Bummer.*

The papers printed everything from local gripes to antibrass, antiwar, and antiracist news and views. Although illegal, the papers found their way into barracks, bathrooms and lounge areas. One Marine organizer commented, "Guys ask if the paper is 'underground'. If we reply 'yes,' they take it. Guys identify with a rebellion if not with the revolution."

Reflecting the growing opposition to the war in the U.S., rebellions within the military increased rapidly from 1968 to 1970. In 1968, there were 68 incidents of combat refusal in Vietnam; in 1969, entire units refused orders; and in 1970, there were 35 separate combat refusals in the Air Cavalry Division alone.

Stateside desertion and AWOL rose steadily throughout the war. In 1966, the desertion rate was 14.7 per thousand; in 1968, it was 26.2 per thousand; and by 1970, 52.3 per thousand. At the height of the war, one GI went AWOL every three minutes. From January 1967 to January 1972, 354,112 GIs left their posts without permission. At the signing of the 1973 peace accords, 98,324 were still missing.

The most publicized demonstrations of GI opposition took place in the 1971 Winter Soldier Investigation, when GIs gave testimony about war atrocities, and the 1971 Moratorium, when more than 1,000 GIs threw away their medals in a dramatic gesture of protest against the war.

This action was organized by Vietnam Veterans Against the War (VVAW), a nation-wide organization that provided the structure needed to give dissident GIs a voice in the national debate. Many who helped launch VVAW later helped organize Vietnam Veterans of America (VVA). There are scattered chapters of VVAW still operating today. VVA has grown into a national organization, headquartered in Washington, with almost 30,000 members in affiliated chapters all over the country. In 1987, VVA received recognition by the federal government as an official national veterans organization, alongside the American Legion and Veterans of Foreign Wars. The Founders of VVA later organized the Vietnam Veterans of America Foundation (VVAF). In 1990, VVAF assumed operation of the Indochina Project to conduct relief programs in Vietnam and to promote reconciliation between the U.S. and its former enemy.

Death March

Not the numbers   but the sound—
murmurs in the single-file crowds
flickering windy candles,
not the place   but the names
marked on placards hung
from living necks—
to be tolled to the cameras
for a visual kaddish,
not the hour   but the clear darkness
through which mourners   like monks
in 14th-century habits   passed the shrine—
the great doomed Capitol
Taj Mahal
sepulchre of the dead Prince: Justice.

Each of us one of the silent dead
returned to march through the white city
past white TV lamps holding white candles
past the White House in our white bones,
a parade of resurrected soldiers—
bearers of ghost guns and phantom armor
decked with blood medals and chevrons of flesh
garlanded with the black hungers
of our enemies—
camouflaged as war protesters
bearing our constitutional
wounds.

—Charles Fishman

Chapter 8

Howard Elterman and Jerold M. Starr

HOW THE WAR WAS REPORTED

Walter Cronkite, popular anchor man for CBS News, on tour in Vietnam.

Introduction

Have you ever thought about how the stories in your morning paper come to be the news? There are countless numbers of happenings, both planned and unexpected, in the world every day. Yet only a few of them become published or broadcast as news events. What determines those outcomes?

First, in order to become a news event, a happening must be recorded. Then it must be promoted to the media as "newsworthy." Finally, it must be chosen and assembled by reporters and editors for public distribution.

In every newsroom there is someone, often the Managing Editor, who decides which of the many stories that arrive on his desk each day will be seen by the public. On the larger city dailies, the "gatekeeper" may see ten times more words and seven times more stories than the reader sees.

The evaluation and selection of what's news involves several criteria. The main features looked for in any item, especially for television news, are timeliness, brevity, nearness, size, unusualness, drama, visual attractiveness, and importance.

Obviously, gatekeepers ignore any old or long term, distant, small, dull, and visually boring events, especially those involving unimportant people. This still leaves many choices because most events fall somewhere in between. Moreover, there is one other criterion that should be considered because of the crucial role played by the news media in the U.S. political process: citizen education.

In the U.S. today citizens depend on the news media to inform them about their government's policies. In turn, citizens are expected to advise their political representatives. To perform that vital function, the press, in the words of Supreme Court Justice Potter Stewart, must provide "organized expert scrutiny of government [and] publish what it knows and..seek to learn what it can." Throughout the Vietnam War, however, many contended that the press did not always seek to learn as much as it could, nor publish all that it knew.

The Living Room War: Fact or Fiction?

Those who supported the war, called "hawks," were especially critical of television coverage of the war. They accused the networks of shocking the public and undermining support for the war by showing too much violence by U.S. and South Vietnamese troops. Also, Vice President Spiro Agnew frequently attacked network news programs for their alleged bias against Nixon administration policies. Millions of Americans echoed agreement with these charges. What is the truth? Were the media controlled by liberal critics of the White House and the war?

During the Vietnam War, Case Western Reserve University conducted a survey of local news anchormen in the top 140 television markets serving 95 percent of American TV households. Over half described their political orientation as "neutral." There were almost as many "strict conservatives" (21%) as there were "liberals" (27%). Regardless of their personal views, more than 70 percent said they could not insert their personal opinions into the news; that the station management had authority over the views expressed in all broadcasts.

There is no evidence that establishment critics are in executive positions in the media either. A 1986 survey of 104 television executives, producers and writers by the conservative American Enterprise Institute found them to be 99 percent white, 98 percent male, and 63 percent earning more than $200,000 a year. Some four of five were opposed to public ownership of corporations and two of three favored relaxing government regulation of business.

Such findings should not be surprising. Television, after all, *is* big business. The networks make their profit by selling time to sponsors to promote their products. Seeking to reach audiences of up to 100 million consumers, the nation's 100 largest corporate advertisers account for over 80 percent of the $10 billion in revenue collected by the major networks each year. In 1970, a bad year for the economy generally, the television industry made a net profit of $424 million.

Since the bottom line is audience size, stations generally avoid programs that tend to divide the audience. During the Vietnam War a congressional subcommittee report on the Fairness Doctrine found that more than a fourth of the 3,000 stations surveyed said they *never* broadcast any programs on important controversial subjects and almost all the rest said they did so only "sometimes."

In the U.S., commercial television is primarily an entertainment medium. Despite Federal Communication Commission requirements for informational broadcasting, the network gives news only 5 percent of its prime-time schedule; the average station features news for barely 10 percent of its 18-hour programing day.

A typical half-hour network news broadcast features 22 minutes of news. The time devoted to each story is 75 to 90 seconds. These constraints moved even Walter Cronkite, perhaps the most popular television newscaster ever, to protest, "It has become impossible to cover the news with the half-hour show. We have a responsibility that we simply cannot discharge." Edward Fouhy, former CBS bureau manager in Saigon and senior producer of the CBS Evening News during the Vietnam War, states, "Television news is a medium capable of transmitting small slices of truth. It is not capable, even if the people running it had the will, of changing the course of history." Industry insiders candidly admit they provide essentially a "headline service."

Well, what about those "small slices" and "headlines?" Were they biased against administration policy and the war? Not according to Michael Arlen, contributing television editor to the *New Yorker*. As he recalls:

Television very rarely showed us anything of a horrific or bloody...nature on the nightly news. In fact, television dutifully passed on the body counts—a distant, alienating kind of announcement—but almost never showed us death, which might have been more meaningful.

Fouhy concurs. According to him, of the 4,000 filmed reports on the network news programs during the war, only about 10 percent were "bang bang" stories, that is, stories that featured images of combat.

As for political bias, a study by Edward Epstein found that, "up until 1968, television coverage was controlled to a large extent by the American Military, and it generally reflected a controlled American initiative that seemed to be winning the countryside and decimating the Vietcong." One reason for this is that the media division of the Pentagon produced several hundred news features promoting the war effort that were shown by stations all over the country. Arlen recalls, that "for most of this undeclared war, almost nothing resembling a flunking grade was given to our military by television news." Two systematic studies of television war coverage concluded that it was politically balanced or, if anything, slightly in favor of President Nixon. In perhaps the most comprehensive analysis of this issue, Daniel Hallin concludes that television, "neither showed the 'literal horror of war' nor did it play a leading role in the collapse of support. It presented a highly idealized picture of the conflict in the early years, and shifted toward a more critical view only after public unhappiness and elite divisions over the war were well advanced."

Whether or not there was any bias in content, there is strong evidence that the actual influence of television news has been very overrated. Studies by the U.S. Surgeon General's Committee in 1969 and 1974 examined the viewing habits of national samples of 6,000 adults. Both studies found that, over a two week sample period, more than half of the adults did not watch a single evening network news program. Only about one of fifty watched TV news every night. In contrast, 90 percent said they had read yesterday's newspaper.

Moreover, many of those who reported watching television news were not paying close attention at the time. In both the 1969 and 1974 studies, videotapes of a subsample of TV viewers in their own homes revealed that almost three of five were involved in other activities and did not give their full attention to a single network news program. Only about one of seven gave their full attention to more than four news programs.

Perhaps the television industry is partly responsible for the inflated image of its public influence. After all,

that is the basis for charging such high fees for commercial time. Perhaps many of those involved in politics have had such a low regard for common sense that they could believe that millions could be easily manipulated by 75 to 90 second news "headlines" on something so monumental as the rightness of their government's policy on war and peace. However, John Mueller, Professor of Political Science at Rochester University, has found that simply not credible:

> Whatever impact television had, it was not enough to reduce support for the war until casualty levels had surpassed those of the earlier war [Korea]...the assumption that people will know how they feel about [war] only if they see it regularly pictured on their television screens is essentially naive and patronizing.

In the 1940s and 1950s, people listened to radio broadcasts, read newspapers and watched the movie newsreels to learn about developments in World War II and the Korean War. Despite its visual impact and popular access, television is just another communications medium. Its power to mold public opinion has been vastly overrated. Newspapers remained the primary source of information for most Americans throughout the Vietnam War. Of course, newspapers also were criticized severely.

The Controversy Over Press Coverage

Hawks charged the press with giving the impression the U.S. was losing a war that, in their view, it was winning. Moreover, they claimed, the press made too much of U.S. troop atrocities and South Vietnamese government corruption and too little of Vietcong atrocities and North Vietnamese government totalitarianism. Such alleged distortions often were blamed on inexperienced, lazy, but ambitious reporters eager to please editors with a liberal bias.

Some conservative critics have gone so far as to blame the press for subverting public support and causing the U.S. defeat in Vietnam. Maxwell Taylor, former Chairman of the Joint Chiefs of Staff and U.S Ambassador to South Vietnam, has charged: "In Vietnam there was the feeling on the part of some of the press that their task was to destroy the American command and to work against what was being done." Keyes Beach, Pulitzer Prize-winning Far East correspondent for the Chicago *Daily News*, agrees with Taylor: "...the media helped lose the war...because of the way the war was reported...."

In contrast, those who opposed the war, called "doves," criticized press coverage for repeating the administration's version of the war, while neglecting or burying in the back pages facts and opinions that contradicted this version. Doves charged further that when they organized demonstrations to publicize these facts and opinions, they either were ignored or were pictured as criminals and traitors, disrupting order and provoking arrests. The news photographers' alleged preference for the most bizarre and militant elements in any demonstration especially frustrated the many serious, middle class critics of the war seeking to recruit allies for their movement. We will consider media coverage of the peace movement in the conclusion to this Chapter.

Defenders of the press have conceded that its performance was sometimes flawed, but have blamed this on the complexities of covering a war on the other side of the globe, frequent lies by U.S. and South Vietnamese government and military officials, and censorship of field reporters by conservative editors and publishers.

According to Phillip Knightley, writer for the Sunday *Times* of London, in the early days of the war, "none of [the] correspondents...were against American involvement in Vietnam and they wanted the United States to win." In his view, the so-called "press mess"

Phillip Knightley, English journalist

started when correspondents began to criticize the way in which the war was being fought and the corruption of the Diem government. Diem reacted with censorship and intimidation. Associated Press (AP) writers Malcolm Browne and Peter Arnett were beaten and falsely charged with attacking the Saigon secret police.

After large scale U.S. intervention in the war, the U.S. Military Assistance Command in Vietnam (MACV) began daily press briefings. In time the "misinformation and lack of verification" of the briefings became so notorious that they were dubbed the "five o'clock follies" by the newsmen. According to David Halberstam, Pulitzer Prize-winning reporter for *The New York Times* in Vietnam 1962-63:

These reports from Vietnamese officers, never substantiated or witnessed by American officers, would be passed on, and would thereupon come out as 'American sources said'. Each day, then, there would be a positive story coming out of the briefing...negating or effectively neutralizing the story that Peter Arnett or Horst Faas would be doing that day.

Morley Safer, who opened the Saigon Bureau for CBS News in 1965, concurs with Halberstam: "the Saigon version of events was almost always at variance with what actually happened in the field, witnessed by a correspondent or described by an officer or civilian representative who gave you unfiltered information." Safer comments on one aspect of coverage: "Prior to the commitment of new American units, enemy troop strength would rise; when it was necessary to demonstrate success in Washington, enemy troop strength would dramatically fall."

Reporters who turned to U.S. military sources for the truth were similarly led astray. Mike McCusker, combat correspondent with the First Marine Division in South Vietnam, admits:

My job essentially was to cover things up from the press, to be the PR [public relations] man and come off with the Marine Corps looking like a shining knight on a white horse. If anything was coming up that would embarrass the Marine Corps, we were to take reporters someplace else and make sure they didn't know about it.

Nevertheless, critical stories did manage to get out. When they did, Saigon and Washington would conspire to counter them with more favorable reports. According to Knightley, pressure on U.S. publishers and editors by Washington resulted in "a stream of famous names—Joseph Alsop, Marguerite Higgins, Kenneth Crawford—[who] went to Vietnam and duly decided that the war was going well and that Diem was democracy's white hope." Halberstam also witnessed this manipulation of press coverage. He recalls, "the Department of Defense was constantly flying in reporters from hometown papers because they were more malleable than the resident correspondents...."

Throughout the war, the White House labored to control press coverage. In 1967, a report by the Freedom of Information Committee of the American Society of Newspaper Editors charged that President Johnson "tended to manage the news to suit his own purposes rather than to inform the public." During a 1976 national symposium, press secretaries from three administrations admitted they had been guilty of lying to White House reporters because they themselves had been given false information by White House staff.

Sometimes the veil of secrecy was pulled so tight that not even the military itself knew the truth of what was happening. General Douglas Kinnard, who planned the logistics for the American-orchestrated drive into Cambodia, states that he had difficulty getting aerial photographs of the border region. When the photos did arrive, he learned that the land was pock-marked with B-52 craters from secret raids that had been going on for two years. Kinnard says, "We weren't aware of it officially and, indeed, I wasn't aware of it at all."

Well, there you have it. How is one to sort out the truth from all these charges and counter-charges? One excellent way would be to conduct a systematic examination of what the White House said about its policies in Vietnam and what the press reported. Was the White House presentation accurate? Was it reported accurately by the press or was it distorted? If the White House presentation was not accurate, did the press correct for this and give the public a fuller and more truthful view of what was going on in Vietnam?

To investigate this question we will look at national press coverage of eight major issues or events in Vietnam, from U.S. policy before the Geneva Agreement of 1954 to the fall of Saigon in 1975. As examples of the national press we will use the nation's leading mass circulation news publications—*The New York Times*, *U.S. News and World Report*, *Time*, and *Newsweek*.

As a control for whether the failings of national press coverage of the war were due solely to the obstacles presented by Washington and Saigon or, perhaps, also

(left-right) David Halberstam of *The New York Times*, Malcolm Browne of AP and Neil Sheehan of UPI in Vietnam, November 1963

Joseph Alsop receives a briefing from two high ranking Marine officers. He and other influential journalists who supported U.S. policy in Vietnam received VIP treatment during visits there.

"...CENSORSHIP BY MACV IS UNDERSTAND-ABLE—TELLING THE TRUTH WOULD BE SELF-INCRIMINATION."

to its own failings and biases, we will compare its coverage to three examples of the alternative (to the mainstream) press—*The New Republic*, the *Guardian*, and a British weekly called the *New Statesman*.

Throughout this Chapter we will be guided essentially by the questions—did these publications accurately report the White House version of events in Vietnam and did they inform the public about findings that contradicted the White House version?

Let us begin in the spring of 1954. Imagine that on a sunny April morning you happened to glance at your newspaper while eating breakfast. See below what you would have read.

U.S. Policy Before 1954 Geneva Accords

Dulles left the impression that the United States military intervention in Indochina was neither imminent nor under active consideration at present.
The New York Times, April 21, 1954

United States leaders are said to be beginning to face up to the need for massive and effective United States military intervention to save Indochina and the whole of south Asia from communist domination.
The New York Times, April 23, 1954.

As these quotes from *The New York Times* illustrate, a reader of the national press in the spring of 1954 would have been confused about the prospects for U.S. military intervention in Indochina. By 1954, the United States was paying for almost 80 percent of the cost of France's war against the Vietminh. Despite this aid, French forces faced defeat at the battle of Dienbienphu.

The French people, long weary of the war, began to clamor for a settlement. The government consented to including such discussions in the agenda of the forthcoming international conference at Geneva. The Eisenhower administration held an emergency meeting to consider U.S. intervention in the conflict. Air strikes, ground troops, and even the use of tactical nuclear weapons all were considered and finally rejected because of objections by Democratic Party leaders and the United Kingdom.

The Eisenhower administration viewed any settlement that conceded communist control over any part of Indochina as a "disaster." It urged the French not to "sell out" western interests at Geneva. It asserted that military victory was the only guarantee of diplomatic success and assured France of continued military aid.

After the battle of Dienbienphu ended with a Vietminh victory, the U.S. reviewed its stand on military intervention. Eisenhower decided not to participate in nor sign the Geneva agreement and began to mobilize U.S. and allied forces in Southeast Asia.

What did the national press report about this policy? In the five weeks before the Geneva Conference, *The New York Times* published twelve stories on page one that did, indeed, suggest that war seemed imminent. Headlines like these announced such reports:

GROWING CONCERN OVER POSSIBLE U.S. INVOLVEMENT

WIDER CONFLICT STUDIED: CHANCE OF DIRECT INTERVENTION DISCUSSED

U.S. WEIGHS FIGHT IN INDO-CHINA, IF NECESSARY. HIGH AIDE SAYS TROOPS MAY BE SENT IF FRENCH WITHDRAW

During the same period, on the other hand, eight articles on page one of *The New York Times* presented an entirely different view of possible U.S. intervention.

As one headline put it, "DULLES SAYS U.S. IS UNLIKELY TO PUT MEN IN INDOCHINA." This story reported that Defense Secretary Charles Wilson and Secretary of State John Foster Dulles had left the distinct impression that no intervention by the United States "was in sight" or even "under active consideration at present."

If news coverage of Washington's plans for intervention was confusing, reporting of the American position at the Geneva peace talks was deceptive. Although the United States had rejected all efforts at negotiating a settlement of the war, readers of the national press were told just the opposite. Eleven front-page stories in the *Times* and additional articles in *Time, Newsweek,* and *U.S. News and World Report* reported that it was the communists who refused to compromise. As Secretary of State Dulles repeatedly said, peace prospects would improve if the communists were less "aggressive in

French soldiers at Dienbienphu run for cover as communist artillery pounds their positions.

April 19, 1954. U.S. personnel, still operating in a support capacity in Vietnam, observe developments and await further orders.

spirit." Vice President Nixon was quoted as saying the U.S. only desired an "honorable peace."

In contrast, during the same five-week period, the alternative press reported that the United States had no intention of negotiating an end to the war at Geneva. The *New Statesman* observed that the United States viewed a Geneva conference "with something less than relish," and hoped it would fail. *The New Republic* observed that to Dulles and the Joint Chiefs of Staff, "a negotiated peace in Indochina would be quite simply a communist victory," and the *Guardian* reported that the U.S. feared negotiations and intended to torpedo the conference.

In conclusion, during the five weeks leading up to the Geneva Conference, the national press did not present a consistently accurate analysis of administration policy. On several occasions they simply reported the statements of U.S. leaders that they did not intend to send troops, without mentioning other indications that government officials really were considering military intervention at the time. The national press also falsely stated that, unlike the communists, the United States sought a negotiated settlement at Geneva. In contrast, the alternative press consistently reported that Washington had serious reservations about a negotiated settlement at Geneva.

This was a significant period in U.S. Vietnam policy. As the French negotiated their withdrawal from the region, the United States could have followed suit, or it could have deepened its involvement. It chose the latter course. The consequence was twenty more years of war. Would the American people have supported such a policy if they had been fully informed?

Senator Richard Russell warned the Eisenhower administration that sending U.S. troops to help the French in Indochina would be "the greatest mistake this country has ever made."

Discussion Questions

1. What was U.S. policy in Indochina in the five weeks before the Geneva Conference?
2. How did government leaders present this policy to the press?
3. How did the national press report U.S. policy during this period?
4. How did the alternative press report U.S. policy during this same period?

1954 The Joint Chiefs that decided against intervention in Vietnam. (from left) General Nathan Twining, Admiral Arthur Radford, Generals Matthew Ridgway, Lemuel Shepherd, and Admiral Robert Carney.

Secretary of State Dulles (right) shown here with French ambassador to the U.S., Henri Bonnet, and former President Antoine Pinay.

U.S. Policy Toward 1956 Vietnam Elections

In the case of nations now divided against their will, we shall continue to seek to achieve unity through free elections, supervised by the United Nations to ensure that they are conducted fairly.

Statement read by U.S. representative at the signing of the Geneva Agreement, July 21, 1954

I would favor genuinely free elections under conditions where there would be an opportunity for the electorate to be adequately informed as to what the issues are. At the present time in a country which is politically immature...we would doubt whether...the result...would really reflect the will of the people....The United States should not stand passively by and see the extension of communism by any means into Southeast Asia.

Secretary of State John Dulles, Press Conference, April 11, 1954

The Geneva Accords established two temporary zones in Vietnam. They were separated at the 17th parallel by a demilitarized zone. The two zones were to be reunited under one government to be elected by all the people by secret ballot in July 1956. Consultation between representatives of the two zones was to begin a year earlier, July 1955.

In the judgement of U.S. officials, "the Accords were a disaster" and actions would have to be taken for preventing communist expansion in Vietnam. As early as March 1954, American officials feared that free elections would result in a communist victory at the polls. On July 7, 1954, Secretary of State Dulles told his Under Secretary, Bedell Smith, that elections in Vietnam would mean unification under Ho Chi Minh. After the Geneva Conference, American intelligence reports concluded that South Vietnam would be unlikely to defeat the communists in a country-wide election. On August 20, 1954, the National Security Council in Washington defined the major objectives in Indochina as maintaining "a friendly non-communist South Vietnam" and preventing "a communist victory through all-Vietnam elections."

From 1954 through 1956, the U.S. provided more than one-half billion dollars to establish South Vietnam as an independent, non-communist state. South Vietnamese Premier, Ngo Dinh Diem, refused to consult with the North in July 1955; nor would he permit nationwide elections in July 1956. The Eisenhower administration supported these decisions. Since the U.S. and South Vietnam had refused to sign the Geneva Accords, they argued that they were not legally committed to carrying them out. Others disagreed, pointing out that the U.S. had formally pledged not to disturb implementation of the agreement. In any event, the rejection of elections clearly meant that "reunification could be achieved in the foreseeable future only by resort to force." In 1957, the International Control Commission concluded that both North Vietnam and South Vietnam had violated the Geneva Accords.

The U.S. decision to back Diem's rejection of elections soon led to the renewal of armed conflict in the country. Nevertheless, this critical decision was almost ignored by the national press. For example, we surveyed papers from May 15 to August 15, in both 1955 and 1956 and found that *The New York Times* published on its front page only *one* article that pointed out that the United States was trying "to evade and sabotage the elections." And during these same six months over two years, the *Times, Newsweek,* and *U.S. News and World Report* published a total of only 13 articles reporting American opposition to elections in Vietnam. Most of these stories were very short and almost all featured Washington's justification for its policy; elections could not be held until the North stopped intimidating and coercing its citizens.

Readers of the alternative press were given even less coverage of the U.S. decision not to permit all Vietnamese elections. During the same six-month period in 1955-56, there were only three stories about this policy in these journals, all of which pointed out that the United States was strongly opposed to holding elections in Vietnam.

In the summers of 1955 and 1956, the government was not talking very much about its opposition to the scheduled 1956 election in Vietnam. And the press did little to bring this to public attention. In defense of the press, there was little to recommend this protracted non-happening in a small, distant country as a news event. Moreover, Vietnam did not appear to be a foreign policy crisis confronting the U.S. at the time. Thus, less coverage was given to Vietnam than to other areas and issues. In retrospect, perhaps none were as important as what was happening and not happening in Vietnam. *The Pentagon Papers* report that U.S. policy played "a direct role in the breakdown of [the] Geneva settlement," and that breakdown led to the second Indochina war.

Discussion Questions

1. What was U.S. policy toward the holding of unification elections in Vietnam?
2. What did Washington say about its policy regarding elections?
3. How did the national press and the alternative press report on American policy toward elections in Vietnam?
4. Why was coverage so slight?
5. Do you think there are current American foreign policies not covered very well by the national press? What might some of these be and why might they not make the news? How can concerned citizens find out about them?

U.S. Involvement in the Overthrow of Ngo Dinh Diem

We are launched on a course from which there is no respectable turning back; the overthrow of the Diem government. There is no turning back in part because U.S. prestige is already publicly committed to this end in large measure and will become more so as facts leak out.

Henry Cabot Lodge, U.S. Ambassador to South Vietnam in a classified message to Washington, August 20, 1963

Now the overthrow...of the Diem regime was a purely Vietnamese affair. We never gave any advice. We had nothing whatever to do with it.

Henry Cabot Lodge, June 30, 1964

President Diem was overthrown on November 1, 1963, with the direct complicity of Washington. "The nine-year drama of the Diem era was over and a new drama had begun in South Vietnam." So wrote *The New York Times* reporter, Malcolm Browne, on November 6, 1963.

The United States had played a major role in ending the drama of Diem and would suffer grievously in the tragedy soon to unfold. According to *The Pentagon Papers,* President Kennedy knew and approved of plans for the military coup d'état that overthrew Ngo Dinh Diem in 1963. "...Beginning in August...we variously authorized, sanctioned and encouraged the Vietnamese generals and offered full support for a successor government...the United States must accept its full share of responsibility."

The coup revealed the weakness of South Vietnam's position in its war against the communist guerrillas. The overthrow of the Diem government was a major turning point for the United States in Vietnam. Convinced that South Vietnam must remain anti-communist, the United States "assumed" significant responsibility for the new regime, heightening "our commitment" and deepening "our involvement."

In early November 1963, the Kennedy administration denied complicity in Diem's overthrow. For example, *Time,* in its November 8 issue, quoted State Department Press Officer Richard Phillips, "I can categorically state that the United States government was not involved in anything." And *The New York Times,* in its November 2 issue, reported, Congressional sources said today that administration officials had told them the military revolt in South Vietnam had come as a complete surprise to the United States."

Nevertheless, both the national and alternative press rejected the administration's official version of events. They asserted that Washington had been involved in the military coup more than it cared to admit. *The New York*

Lieutenant Colonel Lucien Conein (rear), a CIA agent who served as a liaison with the generals who conspired to overthrow Diem. With him are (from left) Generals Le Van Kim, Ton That Dinh, Tran Van Don, Nguyen Van Vy, and Mai Huu Xuan.

Times reported that Washington's cutback in aid and open hostility to Diem were signals to the opposition that it would tolerate an overthrow. The *Times* also reported that reliable Saigon sources believed some of the plotting generals privately saw some key American officials before the coup.

Newsweek observed that Washington was vulnerable to criticism that it had either supported or at least condoned "a military revolt against an established government in Southeast Asia." *U.S. News and World Report* wrote that "many officials in Saigon feel the United States invited army intervention against Diem when it...absolved the military forces of any complicity in the raids by [Diem's] special forces on Buddhist temples." And in the words of *Time,* "there could be no question that the United States, in policies and...pressures it brought to bear had effectively encouraged the overthrow of the Diem regime."

The alternative press also challenged the government's denial of involvement in the coup against Diem. *The New Republic* reported that the "military push" in South Vietnam had received Presidential encouragement. The *New Statesman* wrote that "American assistance was obvious enough to underline [Red China's] propaganda attack that this was an American-inspired coup." The *Guardian* wrote that the coup came as no surprise to Washington. In its view, American Ambassador to South Vietnam, Henry Cabot Lodge, had plotted the coup over several months, including cutting off aid for the South Vietnamese government's special security forces.

Discussion Questions

1. Did press accounts of the overthrow of South Vietnamese President Diem differ from those of the government? How?
2. Why didn't the Kennedy administration publicly admit its complicity in the overthrow of Diem?
3. In 1963, which version of Diem's overthrow do you think the American people believed: the version told by our government or the version reported in the press?
4. If the government denied complicity in overthrowing a foreign government today and the press reported that the United States was involved in that event, whom would you believe?

The Gulf of Tonkin Incident—1964

This new act of aggression aimed directly at our own forces, again brings home to all of us in the United States the importance of the struggle for peace and security in Southeast Asia.

President Lyndon Johnson
August 4, 1964

Having the *Maddox* and the *Joy* there, in view of what the South Vietnamese boats were up to, constituted an act of collective aggression on our part.

Senator Wayne Morse, Oregon
August 2, 1964

It all started in a charged atmosphere of melodrama. Suddenly, on the evening of August 4, 1964, at 11:36 p.m., the President appeared on television. He told the nation that, for the first time since the Korean War, the United States would launch a military offensive on communist soil. At that very moment, American planes were about to bomb gunboat bases in North Vietnam. These raids, the President said, were in reprisal for torpedo-boat attacks against American destroyers twelve hours earlier in the Gulf of Tonkin off the coast of North Vietnam.

Three days later, on August 7, 1964, the Johnson administration received a sweeping resolution from Congress which authorized it "to repel any armed attack against the forces of the United States and to prevent further aggression."

What President Johnson failed to tell the American people on that August night was that the Tonkin Gulf incident followed six months of clandestine military attacks by U.S.-sponsored forces in South Vietnam against North Vietnam. On the night before the alleged attack on the *Maddox,* South Vietnamese patrol forces had launched a midnight attack, including an amphibious commando raid, on Hon Me and Hon Nieu Islands off the coast of North Vietnam. At the time, the *Maddox* was operating within the 12 mile territorial limit claimed by North Vietnam and recognized by the

United States. The *Maddox* fired first and sustained no damage.

The second reported attack on the *Maddox* and the *Turner Joy* almost certainly never took place. Apparently, an inexperienced sonarman, alarmed by the first engagement, interpreted his own ship's sounds as those of hostile torpedoes. Captain John Herrick, Commander of the Tonkin Gulf patrol, had signaled the Pentagon that there were "no actual sightings by *Maddox...*" James Stockdale, a Navy carrier pilot circling above, said that, because it was so dark below, he had very good vision. Stockdale says, "the wake [of an attacking boat] would have been luminous. The ricochet would have been sparkling, the gunfire would have been red and bright." Stockdale searched in vain for any signs of North Vietnamese attack boats. When he heard the next day that retaliation had been ordered, Stockdale reflected:

> Well, I sat there on the edge of the bed realizing that I was one of the few people in the world who were going to launch a war under false pretenses. And so sure enough the next day we did. I led this big horde of airplanes over there and we blew the oil tanks clear off the map.

Commenting on the incident some months later, President Johnson remarked with a grin, "For all I know, our Navy was shooting at whales out there." It was, however, just the kind of incident that Johnson needed to rally congressional support for a resolution his staff and he actually had prepared many months before, a resolution they considered the equivalent of a declaration of war. Thus, the evidence seems strong that the first attack was provoked by the U.S. In an historic meeting in 1995 former Secretary of Defense McNamara asked Vietnamese General Giap about the "so-called second attack" that led to the Tonkin Gulf Resolution: "Did it occur?" Giap replied, "On the fourth of August, there was absolutely nothing.

The Tonkin Gulf incident was a major turning point for American involvement in Vietnam. *The Pentagon Papers* concludes: "After Tonkin Gulf the policy objective of gradual disengagement from Vietnam was no longer relevant....The issue for the future would no longer be withdrawals, but what additional United States forces would be required to stem the tide—and how fast they would have to be thrown into the breach."

How did the national press report this critical event? Unfortunately, it gave extensive coverage to the inaccurate version of events promoted by the government. Repeatedly in 1964 readers of *The New York Times* and the three leading news weeklies read of two "unprovoked attacks" by the communists on American destroyers lawfully patrolling in international waters. For example, in the week following the first Tonkin Gulf encounter, the *Times* published fifteen stories on its front page alone, all presenting the administration's account of what happened. The headline on August 3 told of the initial communist attack: RED PT BOATS FIRE AT US DESTROYERS ON VIETNAM DUTY.

The story that followed was based on information provided by military sources. Two days later, a *Times* headline told of the second attack: US PLANES ATTACK NORTH VIETNAM BASES; PRESIDENT

Captain John Herrick

Photograph taken from the U.S.S Maddox of a North Vietnamese PT boat in the Tonkin Gulf.

ORDERS LIMITED RETALIATION AFTER COMMUNIST PT BOATS RENEW RAIDS. Once again, the Defense Department provided the details for the ensuing story. The *Times* announced that North Vietnam PT boats had made a "deliberate attack" on two American destroyers patrolling international waters in the Tonkin Gulf. The attack was made at 10:30 a.m. Washington time by an "undetermined number of North Vietnamese PT boats."

Time, in its August 14, 1964 issue, headlined across its front cover: THE US STAND IN ASIA. The weekly reported that on August 2, the *Maddox* was forced to fire her guns at the communist attackers who kept closing in on her. Then on August 4, *Time* dramatically described the second attack, an event which eye witnesses claimed never occurred: "The night glowed eerily with the nightmarish glare of air-dropped flares and boat searchlights. For three hours the small [boats] attacked in pass after pass. Ten [communist] torpedoes sizzled through the waters....Gunfire and gun smells and shots stung the air...." *Newsweek* and *U.S. News and World Report* published similar stories. It was important and dramatic news. However, it was not true.

The alternative press provided a sharp contrast to the government and national press accounts of the Gulf of Tonkin incident. In August 1964, both the *Guardian* and the *New Statesman* questioned the government's version of events. As a result, their readers learned important information ignored by the national press.

The *Guardian* published five major articles on this subject. The radical weekly wondered if the August 2 "skirmish" had been provoked by the United States, and if the August 4 incident had even taken place. It observed that the first incident occurred near two North Vietnamese islands that had been shelled 48 hours earlier. It also noted that the *Maddox* had been within the 12-mile territorial limit claimed by North Vietnam. Perhaps, the *Guardian* proposed, the communists believed the U.S. destroyer was connected to the earlier raids against its territory.

As for the second attack, the *Guardian* wrote that this alleged encounter took place in the middle of a pitch-black, stormy night and, according to the Pentagon, at no point did the two United States destroyers identify the opposing craft. Also, the *Guardian* asked, if the two United States destroyers were under continuous torpedo attack for three hours, why were there no casualties?

The *New Statesman* also challenged the administration's version of events at Tonkin Gulf. One of its reporters wrote that "the incidents in Vietnam do not seem quite as simple as the initial headlines indicated....There is...little trust in official accounts about Vietnam...and a climate of intrigue...fogs the entire episode." Both the *New Statesman* and especially the *Guardian* gave extensive coverage to information provided by Senator Wayne Morse, the leading congressional critic of U.S. policy. They also provided accounts by communist as well as noncommunist spokespersons, accounts which proved to be more accurate than that offered by the Johnson administration.

The U.S government's account of events in the Tonkin Gulf contained "the fatal taint of deception." The national press only reported the White House version. It did not point out inconsistencies in this account, nor present other perspectives. In contrast, news coverage was much more accurate in the alternative press.

In reflecting on national press coverage of this critical incident, Edwin E. Moise has proposed that it followed two rules: (1) the press should support our boys—support and praise the actions of the U.S. Military; and (2) never accuse any United States Government spokesman of making an incorrect statement, even if you notice that he has done so.

Public opinion polls taken after the Tonkin Gulf incident revealed widespread support for President Johnson's handling of the crisis. Would the public opinion polls have been different had the government or the national press told the American people the complete story?

Discussion Questions

1. What were the circumstances surrounding the alleged attacks in the Gulf of Tonkin?

2 How did the Johnson administration present the events?

3. Were there differences in coverage of the Tonkin Gulf incident by the national press and the alternative press? What were they?

4. If, in 1964, you had read about the Tonkin Gulf incident in *The New York Times* and in the radical *Guardian,* which version, if any, would you have believed? Would you have been confused? If a majority of Americans had read about the Tonkin Gulf crisis in the alternative press, do you think they would have supported their government's policy?

U.S. Policy
Toward Negotiations

As revealed in *The Pentagon Papers* and in the writings of important diplomats, foreign leaders, and reporters, the only settlement of the war the United States was willing to accept for years required the withdrawal of North Vietnamese troops from the South and the end of what it called North Vietnamese aggression. Given that concession, the U.S. said it would halt its bombing and begin to discuss communist participation in the government of South Vietnam. From the point of view of the communists, however, this amounted to surrender.

During this period Washington was unwilling to even discuss the future political composition of the government of Saigon because it saw the leaders of South Vietnam as too weak politically to compete with the communists for popular support. Throughout 1964-67, decision makers in Washington preferred to continue military pressure on North Vietnam rather than open peaceful negotiations. For example, in late 1964 and early 1965, Washington rejected efforts by U Thant, Secretary General of the UN, to initiate peace talks between the United States and North Vietnam.

In December 1966, efforts by Polish officials to encourage talks between the two sides collapsed when the U.S. initiated bombing of Vietnam. There is some question as to whether Hanoi would have been willing to compromise in either of these proposed negotiations. What is clear, however, is that it was actions by the Johnson administration that scuttled the peace efforts. Nevertheless, during this period, the Johnson administration publicly presented a position of compromise, claiming that it was only the communists who refused to negotiate. While the communists certainly had demands of their own, it also is quite clear that the Johnson administration had not given up on its dream of military victory and was not ready to sit down at the bargaining table. This story, however, was not featured in the national press.

Discussion Questions

1. Why was the United States opposed to peace negotiations during this period? Do you agree with this position? Explain.
2. How was this topic covered in the national press?

3. Suppose the public had been informed by the media about the Johnson administration's reluctance to negotiate a peaceful settlement of the war in 1965-66. What do you think might have happened, if anything?
4. Do you see any similarity between press coverage of this topic and of U.S. support for Diem's refusal to permit the nationwide unification elections in 1956? Explain.

Television Coverage
of the Tet Offensive

A major turning point in the Vietnam War took place in late January and early February 1968. At that time, Hanoi sent 84,000 troops into Saigon, Hue, and a dozen other cities in the south. A 19-man team of communist guerrillas penetrated the U.S. Embassy compound in Saigon. However, North Vietnam did not achieve its military objectives in the Tet offensive. Local citizens in the south did not join in an uprising against the Saigon

During Tet, the Great Seal of the United States was blasted off the wall of the U.S. Embassy.

General Nguyen Ngoc Loan executes a VC suspect during the Tet offensive. The photo by AP photographer Eddie Adams shocked the world and earned a Pulitzer Prize in 1969.

government. Observers agree that the Vietcong suffered devastating losses in the struggle. U.S. troops cleared out Hue within three weeks and, by the following week, the pressure eased on Khe Sahn.

At the same time, the Tet offensive has been seen by many observers as "a smashing psychological victory for the enemy...." and "a brilliant political victory for them here in the United States." In the words of Secretary of State Rusk, "it became very clear after the Tet offensive that many people at the grassroots...finally came to the conclusion that if we could not tell them when this war was going to end...that we might as well chuck it."

Widely respected CBS anchorman, Walter Cronkite, told his viewers, "It seems now more certain than ever that the bloody experience of Vietnam is to end in a stalemate." The only rational way out, he suggested, is to negotiate, not as victors but as honorable men who did the best they could. Within weeks of Tet, President Johnson rejected General Westmoreland's request for 206,000 additional troops and replaced Westmoreland as U.S. Commander in Vietnam with General Creighton Abrams. Eugene McCarthy and Robert Kennedy en-

tered the Democratic presidential race as peace candidates, and Johnson announced he would not run for re-election.

Many hawks blamed the press for misrepresenting a great American victory as a defeat. The news media was accused of engaging in disaster-type reporting by emphasizing the boldness of the enemy's surprise attack while ignoring its military defeat. Hawks also complained about the images of violence, like the famous photo of the summary execution of a V.C. suspect by the Saigon Chief of Police.

Certainly coverage of Tet was different. Because the offensive was unexpected and took place in Saigon where reporters and camera crews were stationed, the American military was unable to control press movements. Correspondents rushed unedited photo stories back to the U.S. and "network producers in control rooms in New York had neither the time nor the opportunity to shield American viewers from the grisly close-ups of wounded Americans, body bags, and death." Peter Braestrup concludes: "Tet's peculiar circumstances—surprise, melodrama unprecedented in the war, White House ambiguity—impacted to a rare degree on the peculiar habits, susceptibilities, manpower limitations, and technological constraints of newspapers, news magazines, wire services, and TV news."

Some doves suggested that the Tet offensive changed public opinion so dramatically, not because of biased press coverage, but ironically, because it contradicted the many years of uncritical press reports of overly optimistic predictions by U.S. leaders. In the months leading up to Tet, the Johnson administration repeatedly assured the people that we were nearing a victory in the war, that there was "light at the end of the tunnel." In December 1967, General Westmoreland sounded this theme in a well-publicized address. The boldness of the Tet offensive contradicted the image of the enemy as exhausted and soon-to-be-defeated.

According to Noam Chomsky, news coverage was biased, but in favor of the Johnson administration; it "accept[ed] uncritically the framework of government propaganda" rather than risk appearing to undermine the war effort through reportage that was critical of the government. Seen in this context, the Tet offensive was especially shocking to the American people.

According to Epstein, after Tet, network news reports adopted the government's new presentation of the war as winding down. Vietnamization was said to be a military success. American troops were said to be withdrawing while the government was negotiating a settlement. Yet the war would continue for four more years, more than 20,000 American soldiers would die, and the air war over parts of Indochina actually would escalate.

Discussion Questions

1. Why was news coverage of the Tet offensive so controversial?
2. What did hawks say about news coverage and the public impact of the Tet offensive? What did doves say?
3. What impact, if any, do you think television coverage of the Tet offensive war might have had on public opinion? Do you think that television coverage could have had a greater impact on the American people than newspaper coverage? Explain.

During Tet, the worst fighting was concentrated in the Cholon district on the edge of Saigon. This aerial photo shows the devastation.

Civilians fleeing from their homes to escape the devastation of Tet.

I saw a person die like this. One day we had already gone to the holes, but there were some people who had been someplace else and didn't learn in time that the planes were coming to bomb . . .
—Artist: a sixteen-year-old Laotian youth

In my village we raised rice to earn our livelihoods, as we had always done. But this prosperity was destroyed by the dreadful craters made by the bombs from the airplanes. Not only this, but there were many kinds of poison. . . the paper that would blow in the wind, and if anyone picked it up they would suffer like the person in this picture . . .
—Artist: a twenty-eight-year-old Laotian man

The U.S. Bombs Laos and Cambodia

In early 1969, according to documents made public years later, the Nixon administration concluded that the United States would have to maintain its military presence in Vietnam. In order to guarantee the continuation of anti-communist regimes in South Vietnam and in the neighboring countries of Cambodia and Laos, the U.S. would have to make progress in the war.

One obstacle to this plan was the widespread public opposition to the war. The moral opposition of peace activists had been joined by the pragmatic opposition of millions more to force the Johnson administration to initiate negotiations with the communists the previous spring. Such dissent had to be minimized if Nixon's policy objectives were to have any hope of success. At the same time there now was important opposition to the war from within the establishment itself, from policymakers like Clark Clifford and from businessmen who feared the economic costs of a protracted war.

Thus, beginning in 1969, President Nixon began a slow withdrawal of American ground troops. He publicly claimed the war was "winding down" and we were getting out of Vietnam. At the same time, however, Nixon secretly began a massive escalation of the air war in Laos and Cambodia, while continuing the bombing in South Vietnam.

From 1969 to 1971, the Nixon administration dropped more than three million tons of bombs in Indochina, an average of six million pounds per day or 4,000 pounds per minute. This was more than 300,000 tons greater than the total number of bombs dropped by the Johnson administration in its last three years in office.

By September 1972, the Nixon administration had dropped almost four million tons of bombs. During the period from 1969 to 1971, characterized by the White House as the "winding down" of the war, 15,000 American soldiers were killed and 110,000 wounded. By 1972, according to conservative Senate estimates, the population of seven million Cambodians had suffered more than one-half million killed and three million made into refugees.

In Laos, by 1971, 50,000 people had been killed, 125,000 wounded, and 500,000 made into refugees. We don't know how many of these casualties and refugees were directly caused by the massive bombing campaign, but the number must be significant. The bombing of Cambodia and Laos from 1969 to 1971 was kept secret within the military and hidden from Congress. It was not reported by the press until Seymour Hersh's book on the subject was published later. The American public remained in the dark.

Seymour Hersh

Peace Agreement and the Fall of Saigon

In October 1972, the United States and North Vietnam finally agreed to a settlement of the war. In November the U.S. tried to renegotiate this agreement because of opposition from its ally, the government of South Vietnam. North Vietnam and the U.S. disagreed over the date to reopen the negotiations. The United States responded with the most massive bombing campaign in the history of human warfare. Over the period December 18-30, 1972, U.S. planes dropped more than 100,000 bombs on two major cities in North Vietnam. The communists returned to the bargaining table and on January 23, 1973, the Paris Peace Agreement was signed.

The Nixon administration claimed that the bombing moved Hanoi to concede terms more favorable to the United States and South Vietnam. However, even the national press acknowledged that the final terms were virtually the same as those in the original October 1972 agreement. The most critical provision allowed North Vietnamese forces to remain in place in South Vietnam.

The Accords set the stage for the release of American POW's and withdrawal of all remaining U.S. forces in Vietnam. No sooner had this operation been completed than both North and South Vietnam violated the treaty. The Thieu regime refused to recognize the provisional revolutionary government as a "parallel and equal party" to itself. Thus, there was no move to establish a National Council to hold a nationwide election. The Nixon administration hoped that continued military aid, especially air power, would stalemate communist forces in the south. The communists continued to press their attack and finally emerged victorious, seizing Saigon on April 30, 1975. They also took control of Cambodia and Laos a few weeks earlier. The United States watched helplessly as its twenty years of sacrifice in Vietnam came to nought.

Discussion Questions

1. How did the Nixon administration present the treaty to end the war?
2. How did the national and alternative press report the treaty?

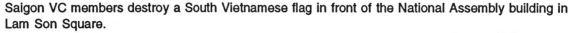

Saigon VC members destroy a South Vietnamese flag in front of the National Assembly building in Lam Son Square.

Conclusion

A number of outstanding American journalists established their reputations with excellent reporting of the Vietnam War. Such names as Peter Arnett, Malcolm Browne, David Halberstam, Seymour Hersh, David Kraslow, Stuart Loory, Charles Mohr, Harrison Salisbury, Neil Sheehan, and Sidney Schanberg come to mind immediately.

Nevertheless, as we have seen, the performance of the national press throughout the years of U.S. involvement often left much to be desired. It did an excellent job of publicizing what Washington and Saigon had to say about events, but it too seldom challenged such statements. In contrast, the alternative press more often went beyond the official line to give the public a more complete and accurate representation of events.

Since the national press had many more news gathering resources at its disposal, how can we account for its relatively poor showing in Vietnam? Any understanding of this apparent contradiction must start with the recognition that the national press is, first of all, a very big business.

There are over 1,500 daily papers published in the U.S., but only a few, like *The New York Times,* dominate the market. Seventy percent of all newspapers have circulations of less than 25,000 each and total less than 20 percent of the national circulation. In contrast, eight percent of all newspapers have over one-half of all circulation.

At the top of this industry are ten chains which earn over half of all newspaper revenue in the country. In the fifty largest cities, the main newspaper and one of the three television network affiliates is owned by the same parent company. One chain alone, Gannett, publishes 82 daily newspapers, operates seven television stations and 13 radio stations in 35 states, two U.S. territories and Canada.

Newspapers and news magazines are subsidized primarily by the advertising space they sell. Over 60 percent of the average paper is ads, and the biggest clients are the department stores and supermarket chains.

The fact that the national press is such a big business has several implications for its coverage of events. First, newspapers, magazines, and TV and radio stations are under pressure to market a commercial product on a daily or, at least, weekly basis. The routine production of so much news relies heavily on items from news sources generally considered "credible" and "newsworthy." Many studies have demonstrated that this leads to giving routine press coverage to high government officials, major corporate figures, and certain glamorous personalities.

People in the government know this and have their staff get close to journalists and give them lots of self-serving press releases. Not wanting to get "scooped" by the competition, newsmen stay close to politicians and accept their press releases. Just to make sure, politicians occasionally call news conferences to make important announcements. Reporters who too often ignore or criticize the press releases may find their names missing from the list of guests invited to the conferences. Newsmen agree that the fear of losing sources does inhibit criticism.

Because they were partisan and not elected nor officially appointed, war critics generally were low in the news establishment's "hierarchy of credibility." As a consequence, protestors felt forced to organize large demonstrations in order to draw attention to their views. In the early years of the war, such events attracted media coverage because they were large, unusual, dramatic, and offered lots of photo opportunities.

Since these were the features that made such events newsworthy, they were the ones emphasized in media accounts. One TV reporter told sociologist Herbert Gans, "at anti-war demonstrations we shot the Vietcong supporters and the Nazis because they were interesting, and also because they are what sells. You always go after the extremes...." CBS executive Stanhope Gould explains, "You wanted to get what Fred Friendly [then President of CBS News] used to call 'fire in the belly'; an emotional event with emotional people."

As a consequence, coverage of anti-war demonstrations mostly resembled crime stories. The emphasis was on the disruption of public order, police and organizer estimates of crowd size, and a listing of any scuffles, damage and arrests. Little or no attention was given to the analyses presented in the speeches themselves.

Years later these remain the principal images through which that period is now viewed. Worse yet, these images so contradicted the trivial, self-satisfied and orderly world of everyday television that they

225

"I WAS ONLY SUGGESTIN' THAT WE 'VIETNAMIZE' OUR NEWS MEDIA

provoked much shock and anger among ordinary citizens. After network coverage of the demonstrations and "police riot" at the 1968 Democratic National Convention in Chicago, there was a fierce public backlash. Millions supported the police and charged the media with paying too much attention to the demonstrators. Revelation that actual scenes of the clashes constituted only minutes of a week-long broadcast (less than one percent of total coverage) did not appease the media's critics.

President Nixon took advantage of the situation by pressuring the media to downplay public dissent. From 1968 to 1971, newspaper coverage of serious college protests fell from 40 percent to 10 percent of campuses. In 1971, CBS refused "to broadcast film that it already shot for the Winter Soldier Investigation, in which antiwar Vietnam veterans said they had committed [or witnessed] atrocities." In 1972, NBC gave strict orders that there would be no coverage of the Nixon "counter-inauguration unless demonstrators actually disrupted official ceremonies."

Nixon also dispatched Vice President Agnew to attack the networks for their alleged liberal bias against administration policies. The attacks had a powerful silencing effect. In 1972, CBS-TV News anchor Walter Cronkite observed, "I think the industry as a whole has been intimidated." Eight years later CBS Evening News producer Ray Bonn was even more vehement: "I date the decline of the serious documen-

Nixon used Vice President Spiro Agnew to intimidate network news producers from criticizing his Vietnam policies.

tary, of tough, controversial television from that time, from that administration, and from that man."

In most cases media management itself decided it would rather switch than fight. Self-censorship, already well established, became more common. In 1965, the *New York Times* censored news of a major U.S. offensive move in Vietnam because they were concerned it might provoke Russia or China to intervene. In 1966, Fred Friendly, president of CBS News, resigned because CBS top executives overrode his decision to televise live the Senate Foreign Relations Committee hearings on the war. In 1967, CBS, NBC and ABC colluded to censor live or special coverage of the October Peace March on the Pentagon.

In 1969, the "Vietnam War Moratorium," the nation's largest demonstration against the war to date, was denied coverage by all three networks. However, six months later, at the request of the White House, all three networks and the Public Broadcasting Service carried live some part of the "Honor America Day" demonstration supporting administration policy in Vietnam. Before 1969 was over, even the mildly irreverent satire of the popular Smothers Brothers had offended executive "taste" and was cancelled by CBS.

The brothers took the network to court and won a $776,000 settlement in 1973. The evidence revealed a pervasive history of network censorship, including an entire song by folk singing legend Pete Seeger which described his view of Vietnam: "Waist Deep in the Big Muddy." Two years later David Rabe's award-winning drama *Sticks and Bones*, which depicted the callous reception of a Vietnam veteran by his family, also met with censorship after being scheduled for telecast.

There were other incidents. In 1970, ABC Sports blacked out a half-time performance of the State University of New York at Buffalo band because its act, "Give Peace a Chance," was seen as critical of the war in Vietnam, racism and pollution. The network said it didn't want to be used for a political statement. However, later in the season it carried live half-time coverage of an Army–Navy game show promoting the prisoner-of-war issue. In 1971 an organization of business executives could not even buy time on television to argue against the Nixon Administration's policy in Vietnam. The case went all the way to the Supreme Court where Nixon appointee Warren Burger found in favor of the "journalistic discretion" of the media moguls to refuse such ads.

Such actions as above clearly reflect the conservative tradition within media management. Since 1932, the nation's newspapers have endorsed the Democratic presidential candidate over the Republican candidate only once—in 1964, when Lyndon Johnson received 55 percent of the endorsements and 61 percent of the popular vote. From 1968 to 1976, the press endorsed the Republican over the Democratic candidate for President by a margin of more than 7-1.

In 1967, the Boston *Globe* analyzed the editorial positions on the war of 39 of the nation's biggest papers. Four called for an all-out win policy and 16 stood behind the Johnson Administration policy without reservation. The other 19 supported the U.S. commitment, but favored deescalation and increased peace efforts. None criticized the commitment or called for an immediate withdrawal of U.S. troops.

That same year, the Associated Press (AP) surveyed American newspaper editors attending a conference on freedom of information. While many charged President Johnson with managing the news, 79 of 103 voiced "generally enthusiastic support" for the administration's policies in Vietnam. Sometimes this support motivated outright censorship. One example was the reluctance of newspapers to report evidence of the My Lai massacre (see Chapter 6). AP correspondent Peter Arnett informs us about another example:

...I filed a story from the Seril rubber plantation [in 1970] about U.S. troops looting a ton of jewelry and radios, and putting stores to the torch. The AP pulled my story—and my pictures—fearing that distribution of such material might further inflame the campuses.

In the main, Arnett conceded the "conservative AP tolerated our dispatches and our pictures," although "it didn't necessarily like them." Still, it would be hard to argue with Phillip Knightley who states that "the fashionable story of the sixties, the one that got the cover treatment, the one that earned the correspondent the approbation of his editor, was the Washington line."

During the Nixon years, additional pressure was applied to the media through government subpoenas to reporters to disclose sources to whom they had promised confidentiality. Although reporters objected that such disclosures would frighten off potential whistle blowers acting in the public interest, many ultimately submitted to the government rather than go to jail.

An even more sinister threat to democratic citizenship was presented by government manipulation of the press through plants and cover stories. Just after the war, a Senate Intelligence Committee report estimated that 900 foreign journalists, or CIA agents posing as journalists, helped the CIA plant propaganda in the world press. Much of this found its way back to the American media.

In 1989, the U.S. Army issued its own 389-page study of media coverage of the Vietnam War. Written by historian William Hammond of the Army Center of Military History, the study concluded that rising U.S. casualties in Vietnam and the lack of a winning strategy—not news media coverage—led to the erosion of American public support for the war.

The Army study characterized television coverage as "most often banal and stylized." In the final analysis, "what alienated the American public, in both the Korean and Vietnam wars, was not news coverage but casualties. Public support for each war dropped inexorably by 15 percentage points whenever total casualties increased by a factor of 10."

Today the nation faces foreign policy perils in other parts of the world. Some have the potential to become another Vietnam. And again we must ask: is the government being truthful about events, and is the press seeking to learn, and publishing what it knows?

In October 1986, *The Washington Post* reported that on August 14, 1986, President Reagan approved a plan by John Poindexter, his national security advisor, to leak "disinformation" to the press that the Libyan dictator, Moamar Gadhafi, was about to mount another terrorist campaign and that the United States might have to bomb him again.

The strategy was to make Gadhafi think that there was a high degree of internal opposition to him within Libya, that his key aides were disloyal, that the U.S. was about to move against him militarily. The goal was to provoke Gadhafi into new terrorist attacks that would justify renewed air strikes.

President Reagan denied trying to deceive the press, but the evidence showed otherwise. Moreover, it was recalled that this kind of thing had been going on for some time. For example, in 1981 there were several stories claiming that a Libyan "hit squad" was out to kill the President.

Columnist Jack Anderson, citing unnamed intelligence sources, led in promoting the scare, publishing

Peter Arnett of the Associated Press covered the entire war, arriving before the first American combat units and staying to observe North Vietnamese tanks roll down the streets of Saigon.

photos of six of the alleged hit men. Anderson later conceded that the story and photos were false "plants." In the process, the media did expose this hoax. However the terrorist image of Libya certainly lingered beyond the retraction. It is revealing to note that the Senate Intelligence Committee decided that the deception campaign against Libya stayed within the letter and spirit of rules against planting false stories in the U.S. media.

In October 1987, Congress' General Accounting Office (GAO) reported that an office within the State Department, created in 1983, had for years been arranging news media interviews for leaders of Nicaragua's Contra rebels and generating opinion articles opposing Nicaragua's Sandinista government for placement in major media outlets.

The GAO concluded that reports of Sandinista atrocities "were misleading as to their origin and reasonably constituted 'propaganda' within the common understanding of that term," thus violating a legal ban on use of federal money for propaganda not specifically authorized by congress.

As 1990 drew to a close, up to 300,000 U.S. troops were stationed in Saudi Arabia to oppose Iraq's occupation of Kuwait. Members of Congress and the general public seemed confused and concerned about President Bush's policy in the Persian Gulf. What was our national interest there? How could we best defend it?

Once again the press was confronted with obstacles to its public information mission. *The New York Times* complained about "the strict rules imposed by the military on reporters." CBS News correspondent Charles Kuralt attacked Bush administration censorship, claiming that "American reporters were able to send out more real news from the presumed enemy camp...than they were from the American camps in Saudi Arabia."

The *New Yorker* magazine found news columnists themselves guilty of "the drum beat of warrior writing"—of cheerleading for U.S. forces rather than questioning the need for war. News commentator Marvin Kalb felt moved to observe that "there is a certain whiff of jingoism on the airwaves and in print, that there is not enough detached critical skepticism."

Once the war started, the American-led military command in Saudi Arabia put into effect press restrictions under which journalists had to be assembled in groups in order to be given access to military sources. Some reporters had to wait weeks for their turn to go on escorted field trips. Reporters seeking approval to visit troops on their own sometimes never even got a response to their request from military authorities.

The military tried to control coverage further by granting preference to local over national press reporters. Debbie Nathan explained that the Pentagon apparently tried to promote more "Hi-Mom" reporting "aimed at boosting pro-war sentiment at home" by subsidizing the travel expenses and providing priority access to military briefings to about 450 reporters from local media. The military called them "hometowners."

As a consequence of these policies, as *Washington Post* service reporters Nicholas Hurrock and Storer H. Rowley revealed, "most of the news [was] being covered at any one time by about 100 journalists accompanying military units around the country, meaning that the other 700 or so reporters photographers, and television technicians [were] under-employed. They [were] either waiting for pool assignments with the armed forces or processing reports from those who [had] them."

All reporters finally allowed to go into the field were accompanied by military information officers who monitored and even interrupted interviews. Finally, the reporters' stories were subjected to scrutiny by military censors before being distributed. Phil Pruitt, national editor for the Gannett News Service, acknowledged these restrictions, but pointed out that "journalists haven't challenged the restrictions by doing things like trying to get away from the escorts. If someone would do that the issue would come up."

Certainly many reporters complained about the severe restrictions on their ability to inform the U.S. public about a war in which their country was engaged. And some reporters managed to resist military indoctrination and dig up stories that raised serious questions about government policy. However, for the most part, the media were complicit with the censorship.

Writing for the United Press Syndicate (UPS), Richard Reeves stated: "I'm amazed that the (*New York*) *Times* and other newspapers are putting the bylines of their own people over censored stories. I'm appalled

that network television has given itself over to the military broadcasting something that looks like news but is actually government dispatches and the muddled musings of correspondents standing in the middle of no place where they have been assigned and ordered to stay by men with guns. And, even with all of that, there is not even enough controlled news to go around, so the same bits of 'military cleared' film and numbers are repeated endlessly."

One story that escaped the censors but still was ignored by the national media was broken on January 6, 1991, by *St. Petersburg* (FL) *Times* reporter Jean Heller. She found that commercial satellite photos of Saudi Arabia on September 11, 1990 and of Kuwait on September 13, 1990 failed to support President Bush's claims that there were as many as 250,000 Iraqi troops and 1,500 tanks in Kuwait. Examining the photos, Dr. Peter Zimmerman, former member of the U.S. Arms Control and Disarmament Agency under President Reagan, concluded, "there is no infrastructure to support large numbers of (military) people" and no concentrations of people visible in the photographs.

As for views on the war, a hawkish bias prevailed there as well. Fairness and Accuracy in Reporting (FAIR) surveyed 2,885 minutes of war coverage by the three major networks and found that only 29 minutes (about 1%) dealt with popular opposition to U.S. policy. In short, media coverage of the Persian Gulf War was even more restricted by and biased in favor of official U.S. military policy than in Vietnam.

Clearly, informing the public is a complex task, fraught with pressures and obstacles. However, just as clearly, the quality of public opinion needed to guide political representatives in our democratic union depends on the quality of reports provided by the nation's press.

Discussion Questions

1. What do you think of the charge that the "liberal press" contributed to the failure of the U.S. to win the war in Vietnam?
2. What did Americans discover about their government from stories published during the Vietnam War? Do such revelations strengthen or damage a democratic government?
3. At the height of our involvement, there were about 120 million TV sets in the United States. What impact,

if any, did TV have on the attitudes of the American public toward the war? Can you name other issues where TV coverage had a clear impact on public opinion?

4. Was there a period of the Vietnam War (1946-1975) during which the majority of the media were generally approving of U.S. policies? If so, what would account for this? At what point(s) did this begin to change? What accounted for the change?

5. How would you characterize the relationship between the media and the government for the following three administrations: Kennedy, Johnson, and Nixon? How would you compare the relationship that exists between the media and the current administration with that of the earlier mentioned administrations? If there are any differences between now and earlier, what would account for these differences?

6. Identify some world events that have occurred recently in which there was a good deal of media coverage, especially television. How, if at all, has this coverage altered people's attitudes toward the event? Has television become even more influential as a medium as compared to ten years ago?

7. What responsibilities do reporters have to provide news of important events to the American public? What if it concerns a state of war between the U.S. and another country? Does the press have a right to enter a war zone declared off limits in order to get at "the truth" of the situation?

8. During the Vietnam War, a number of alternative presses sprang up, e.g., *The Berkeley Barb* and *Liberation News*. What function(s) did they serve reporting the Vietnam War? Was their coverage just propaganda or could it be called journalism? Do we need such publications today?

9. If you were a young correspondent on your first assignment to an area such as Central America, what lessons, if any, would you take from the media's Vietnam War experience? Explain.

NEWSPEAK ON THE PERSIAN GULF WAR

The Danish paper *Politiken* examined the British Press and discovered an English language that had gone to war.

The Allies have:
    Army, navy and air force
    Guidelines for journalists
    Briefings to the press

The Allies:
    Eliminate
    Neutralize
    Hold on
    Conduct precision bombings

The Allied soldiers are:
    Professional
    Cautious
    Full of courage
    Loyal
    Brave

The Allied missiles:
    Do extensive damage

George Bush is:
    Resolute
    Balanced

The Iraqis have:
    A war machine
    Censorship
    Propaganda

The Iraqis:
    Kill
    Kill
    Bury themselves in holes
    Fire wildly at anything

The Iraqi soldiers are:
    Brainwashed
    Cowardly
    Cannon fodder
    Blindly obeying
    Fanatic

The Iraqi missiles:
    Cause civilian casualties

Saddam Hussein is:
    Intractable
    Mad

How would the American press compare to the above?

WOMEN'S PERSPECTIVES
ON THE VIETNAM WAR

Introduction

American and Vietnamese women came from very different worlds to share the dangers and hardships of war. American women went to Vietnam for many reasons. Many saved lives and healed the wounded. Others provided humanitarian relief for the victims. Still others performed vital roles for government, military, business and the press.

Women on the American home front also were affected by the war. Both during and since the war, women tried to stop the war, cared for the returned wounded, adopted orphans, and helped refugees adapt to a new culture. Some have had to carry on as single parents. Many still mourn the death of loved ones. Others still seek to learn the fate of those missing in action. Many have partners whose periods of great stress make family relations difficult.

In large part, American and other western women in Vietnam confronted conventional prejudice about women's roles. Confident in their skills and in search of challenge, they overcame such barriers to become important parts of the Vietnam War story.

In contrast, many more Vietnamese women were forced by circumstance into new roles. To be sure, a great many took roles that were similar to those of their western counterparts: nurses, social workers, journalists, entertainers, and office workers. However, many others, driven by fear, hate and idealism, picked up the gun and became full-fledged combatants in the war. Certainly, the burden of caring for the casualties of the war was especially great for the women of Vietnam.

Regardless of their particular role, all women in Vietnam were exposed to the death and disablement of the war. These are the women's stories—stories of bravery and suffering, of victories and defeats, of small pleasures and terrible pain—and these are their personal perspectives on their war experiences in Vietnam.

ARMED FORCES

Americans

In 1965, Maj. Kathleen Wilkes and SFC Betty Adams became the first U.S. Women's Army Corps (WAC) members to serve as Military Advisors to the newly formed Women's Corps of the Army of the Republic of (South) Vietnam (ARVN). For some time military women's requests for transfer to Vietnam were denied. Many claimed that they were arbitrarily being denied the opportunity to serve. One WAC lieutenant complained, "What kind of delicate creatures do the brass think we are? There's a war going on in Vietnam, but you have to be a civilian to get assigned there. Women are fighting in the jungles with the Vietcong. Yet we aren't allowed to dirty our dainty hands." Because he valued their clerical skills, Gen. William Westmoreland requested that women be assigned to his headquarters staff.

Service in Vietnam was requisite for special training opportunities and accelerated promotion within the military. According to Gen. Jeanne Holm, former Director of Women in the Air Force (WAF), there were hundreds of jobs in Vietnam that women could have filled to relieve the men for combat. Yet women in the Army were not assigned to Southeast Asia (SEA) duty unless they were specifically requested in writing. Holm concluded that three factors combined to restrict the number of military women serving in SEA: (1) a stereotypical attitude toward servicewomen; (2) the desire to keep women from the harsh realities of the combat area; and (3) the belief of many commanders that it was easier to deal only with men.

The women who did serve in Vietnam proved they were capable of functioning under hostile fire. During the 1968 Tet Offensive, Capt. Vera Jones wrote the Women Marines director: "I sit here calmly typing this letter and yet can get up, walk to a window, and watch the helicopters make machine gun and rocket strikes in the area of the golf course which is about three blocks away."

Most of the 1,300 women volunteers were officers who served in support roles in Saigon and at the larger bases. The majority had jobs in personnel, administration and communications. A few worked in intelligence, photography and film production, data processing, supply, and air traffic control.

Staff Sgt. Betty Reid spoke for many of the office staff when she wrote, "This has been one of the most challenging assignments in my entire Army career and I've never worked as hard in all my life. [It has been] one of those jobs where I have left an office with a feeling of self-satisfaction and accomplishment and a feeling that I have been taxed to the extent of my capabilities."

As Operations Officer for the 600th Photographic Squadron, Maj. Norma Archer gave the daily briefing for air strikes. She was the first woman in history to perform this important task. Doris Allen was in intelligence operations for three years, gathering information about enemy attacks and new weapons. Her name appeared on captured enemy documents as someone to be "eliminated." Karen Johnson was the Command Information Officer at Long Binh. For two years she oversaw the production and distribution of military newspapers, and magazines, including *Stars and Stripes*.

In 1967, M/Sgt. Barbara Dulinsky became the first female Marine in history to be ordered to a combat zone. Her tour began with a security lecture on skills needed to stay alive in Vietnam such as recognizing booby traps and checking cabs for inside handles. Thirty-six women Marines served with the Military Assistance Command, Vietnam in Saigon between 1967 and 1973.

Lt. Col. Eleanor Jeanne McCallum commented: "Life at Tan Son Nhut for the most part is routine....We do, however, have our moments of excitement in the form of sporadic rocket attacks. These happen just often enough to keep the blood circulating and the adrenalin glands alive....There's a lot of satisfaction in knowing we are sharing the duty here with our male counterparts and these fellows appreciate this fact."

Vietnamese

Vietnamese women have fought to rid their country of foreign invaders since the Trung sisters led the resistance to the Chinese in 43 A.D. A million Vietnamese women actively fought against the French. Many of these women later assumed leadership in the military struggle against the Americans, performing both administrative and fighting duties.

Ha Que formed the first women's guerrilla unit against the French and went on to become President of the important Women's Union. Nguyen Thi Ngia cut off her tongue so that she couldn't betray her friends when tortured by the French. Vo Thi Sau joined a secret guerrilla unit at the age of fourteen and killed thirteen French soldiers with one grenade. Caught by the French, she was tortured and became the youngest woman ever to face a firing squad.

The South Vietnamese government did not conscript women into the armed forces. However, by 1968 more than 7,700 women had volunteered for staff and clerical positions in the army and police force. Police women checked the documents of female travelers to intercept weapons or medical supplies being smuggled to communist fighters. Madame Nhu (see Political Activists) formed female defense brigades to train women in the use of arms and the martial arts. Women also joined the Civilian Defense Corps to protect their villages, standing guard during the day to relieve the men.

Duong Thi Kim Thanh was an airborne nurse and the first woman parachutist. Carrying an M-16 rifle in one hand and gifts for the troops in the other, she regularly accompanied her Brigadier General husband to visit troops. She was killed with her husband when their helicopter crashed. Another South Vietnamese combatant, called the "Tiger Lady" of the Mekong Delta, commanded a battalion of troops against guerrilla units.

There were a great many women fighters in the communist People's Liberation Armed Forces (PLAF) organized by the National Liberation Front (NLF). All PLAF members were volunteers. Women constituted one-third to one-half of the main-force troops and 40 percent of PLAFs regimental commanders. Generally, the women did not go into direct battle with American forces. They did, however, attack major enemy concentrations and battle with ARVN troops. When not in combat, the women helped in harvesting, medical training, and building projects.

PLAFs regional fighting units had an even higher percentage of women. These full-time fighters operated only in the region where they lived. Another group, militia women, made up local self-defense units which fought when their area was attacked. These women also kept the villages fortified with trenches, traps and spikes.

Nguyen Thi Dinh joined the anti-French resistance at the age of seventeen in 1937. She was from a poor family and was taught to read by her revolutionary comrades. She and her husband were arrested by the French in 1940. Her husband was tortured to death, but she escaped in 1943 and re-joined the fighters.

After the 1954 Geneva Accords, Dinh remained in the south and became part of the underground resistance. In 1960, she led the "Ben Tre Uprising" against Diem's officials, triggering general insurrection throughout the South. Her strategies, which combined

"An Angry People Demand Justice"

both military and political actions, became the model used in other provinces. As Deputy Commander-in-Chief of PLAF, General Dinh organized women in many villages and hamlets. In 1964, she was elected to the ruling Presidium of the Central Committee of the NLF.

Ut Tich was a fourteen-year-old servant when she persuaded guerrilla forces to take her in. She became a local commander and organized a group of women fighters. Ut Tich earned a reputation as an amazing fighter before being killed in combat in 1970. Throughout Vietnam, women's work teams took her name and used her deeds as inspiration.

A number of all-female platoons, specializing in reconnaissance, communications, commando operations, and nursing, operated in Vietnam's coastal plains. In the Cu Chi region, Tran Thi Gung was known as the bold, imaginative and ruthless commander of the all-female C3 company. The company trained with a detachment of F-100 Special Forces in small unit infantry fighting, use of side arms and rifles, hand-grenade throwing, wiring and detonation of mines, and assassination. Women were among the special forces that penetrated the American base at Cu Chi in February 1969, destroyed all of the CH-47 Chinook helicopters, and killed thirty-eight Americans.

The life of a guerrilla fighter was very hard. Hundreds of miles of underground tunnels provided convenient escape from pursuing troops and bomb strikes. However, the tunnels were hot and the air stale. There were frequent water shortages, making bathing difficult. Clothing didn't dry completely. Sometimes fighters had to stay underground for days, listening to the enemy talking directly above them. Some guerrillas were killed by bombs before they could escape.

Women played an active role in supplying guerrilla forces. They also helped dig tunnels, set booby traps, carry supplies, evacuate wounded, and bury the dead. Le Ly Hayslip recalled that, as a young child, she was encouraged by cadre leaders to steal first-aid kits and grenades from ARVN soldiers. If threatened with capture, she was supposed to hide in the tunnels or, if necessary, to commit suicide. A death that came after torture was not considered heroic.

Huyn Thi An was twenty-two when she was captured in Saigon when a bomb she was making exploded. She was beaten until she talked. In prison, An refused to be interviewed by journalist Oriana Fallaci.

Instead, she said, "There's no need for the world to know about me....All you care about is having a story for your paper....All I want is to get out of here and fight again."

At age fifteen, Vo Thi Mo joined guerrilla forces in the tunnels. She hated Americans for bombing and destroying her family's home and lands. She recalled, "The first time I killed an American, I felt enthusiasm and more hatred....The Americans considered the Vietnamese animals; they wanted to exterminate us all and destroy everything we had."

Mo acted as scout for regular troops in her region. She also organized peasant women working on U.S. bases into a spy ring to learn about American operations against guerrilla forces. Mo led a group of snipers who attacked GIs outside the 25th Infantry base. She served as deputy platoon leader of the C3 unit when they attacked the main ARVN headquarters at Thai My. The entire platoon received the highest class of the Victory Medal for this operation.

In North Vietnam, women played important roles in the war effort. They formed agricultural cooperatives and worked in and ran factories, offices and schools. Women worked on repair crews restoring roads after bombing attacks. Young women without children supported the troops as supply carriers and were praised for their "feet of brass and shoulders of iron." One woman, Mother Suot, ferried troops and ammunition across a river near her home for many years until she was killed by a bomb at age sixty.

North Vietnamese women downed hundreds of U.S. planes with anti-aircraft weapons and shelled warships from positions in fishing hamlets. All women were trained in hand-to-hand combat and served as the core of the village self-defense teams. Women in the (North) Vietnam People's Army (VNPA) constituted about 20 percent of the soldiers who carried a forty pound pack for three months down the Ho Chi Minh Trail to fight in the south. They risked being killed by U.S. bombs or dying of jungle fever. VNPA women served in highly skilled positions, such as nurses, bomb defusers and liaison workers. Nguyen Van Sam married one of the women in his unit. He described his wife, "She's sweet, and full of dignity, and she's virtuous and brave in battle and I love her because she loves her country. And because, like me, she's had so little out of life."

Not long after the fall of Saigon, Vietnam faced

invasion from Cambodia by the forces of Pol Pot. In 1979, China attacked Vietnam with a force of 600,000. Beaten back, the Chinese withdrew after three weeks. Again, women in the local defense forces fought bravely to defend the villages, killing and capturing many enemy soldiers.

Discussion Question

Vietnamese women participated actively in combat. American women did not. Why do you think that was? How do you feel about that?

MEDICAL WORKERS

Americans and Other Westerners

Several French nurses won the "Croix de Guerre" honor in Vietnam. Mlle. Genevieve de Galard-Terraube was called "the Angel of Dienbienphu." In 1954, she toured the U.S. and received the U.S. Medal of Freedom from President Eisenhower.

Even before the 1954 defeat of the French at Dienbienphu, American nurses were in Vietnam training Vietnamese nurses and working in immunization and school health programs. Most were military nurses on assignment to the U.S. Agency for International Development (USAID) to help in Vietnamese provincial hospitals.

During the late 1950s, Dr. Patricia Smith visited Montagnard villages to treat patients whose illnesses were complicated by malnourishment, intestinal parasites and malaria. Later, Smith built the Minh Quy Hospital where she worked until 1975. Also during the 1950s, Dr. Eleanor Ardel Vietti was sent by the Christian Missionary Alliance to work in a leprosarium about eight miles from the city of Ban Me Thout. One early evening in 1962, a group of Vietnamese in black pajamas ordered Vietti and two men into a pickup truck. Today, she is listed as "presumed dead" on the POW/MIA list.

Roughly 7,500 American women served one year tours of duty as nurses in Vietnam and in the 5th Field Hospital in Thailand. Thousands of additional nurses were stationed in Japan, Okinawa, Guam, and the Philippines to care for the evacuated casualties. They are counted as Vietnam veterans; however, the hundreds of thousands of stateside nurses and women in military hospitals are not. However, they too have had to treat those wounded in the Vietnam War. Also not counted are the great many civilian nurses and therapists paid by the U.S. government or by charitable organizations to care for U.S. Vietnam veterans in civilian hospitals.

In addition to the Americans, there were Australian, English, Canadian, Japanese, New Zealander, and Chinese nurses volunteering in Vietnam. The Swiss group, Terre des Hommes, maintained a 220-bed hospital for children. The Germans had a hospital in Da Nang and a hospital ship, Helgoland, that served in the Delta and, later, Da Nang Harbor.

As American involvement in Vietnam increased, so did the demand for nurses. Nurses joining specifically to help in Vietnam usually chose the Army. The Navy and Air force required 18 month waiting periods and special training before requests for Vietnam were honored. The majority of Army nurses were in their early twenties. Most had less than six months' service prior to going to Vietnam.

Lt. Col. Ruth Sidisin (U.S. Air Force nurse, retired) reflected, "...the heroines of all the nurses over there were the Army nurses....I was always so struck by them—those young, young faces and ancient eyes...they were eyes that had looked into hell. Not that the Air Force and Navy nurses didn't work hard—but you know, the Army nurses just never got a break. And they were young gals. So young."

Each nurse had a different experience, depending on the year of service, assignment and location. Bernadette McKay was among the first American nurses to go to Vietnam. She was quite an attraction since the Vietnamese had never seen women do things like drive automobiles. All nurses in Vietnam faced demanding conditions. The grounds around the nurses' house were surrounded by a barbed wire fence with armed guards on 24 hour patrol. Temperatures ranged up to 114 degrees Fahrenheit and the humidity kept everything damp. Cold water showers were normal. For those who had them, an electric blanket and a light in the closet helped reduce the mildew and dry the sheets. Rats and snakes were everywhere.

Nurses regularly worked 12-hour shifts six days a week. When there were massive casualties they worked until everyone was cared for, eating sandwiches between operations to keep up their strength. Capt.

Saralee Blum McGoran thinks back, "There were times when it never let up, when I felt like a robot."

The mines and high velocity bullets caused multiple wounds and traumatic amputations. Sidisin reflects, "...not even working with earthquake victims or in the emergency room of a big hospital could equal what I saw in a single day in Vietnam. There was a whole variety of just plain trauma. There were belly wounds, amputations, head injuries, burns." Health care was complicated further by "infections and complications...we'd never even heard about—and diseases they told us people hardly ever got any more. Dengue fever. Malaria. Hepatitis. Bubonic plague."

Helicopters delivered the casualties from the battlefield to the nearest hospital facility. Soldiers who formerly would have died now required treatment. Some were torn up by shrapnel or land mines. Others had been hit by napalm and phosphorous weapons that fell short of their targets. Such burns would smolder for days.

There were so few doctors, the nurses had to perform triage. There were three categories: "expectants," "immediates," and "walking wounded." The "immediates" were prepared for surgery and the "walking wounded" were treated next. The "expectants" were moved to a special area, cleaned up and made comfortable. They could not be saved; many knew they were dying. All the nurses could do was to hold a hand, talk to them, and assure them they were not alone. This was especially painful because the average U.S. soldier was so young (nineteen years old as compared to twenty-six in WWII). The doctors were so busy that nurses often were the ones to look inside the body bags to determine the cause of death.

The success rate of these nurses was unparalleled in the history of warfare. Of those casualties who could be treated, almost all survived. However, many nurses still remember the deaths. Many don't want to think about the continued suffering of those they saved despite shattered spines and severed limbs. The incidence of paraplegia for veterans of Vietnam is 1,000 percent higher than for veterans of WWII and 50 percent higher than for the Korean War. Lt. Col. Edith Knox, chief nurse at the 67th Evacuation Hospital in Qui Nhon, recalls, "...one of the most difficult things for me was when I'd be making rounds and a young man would say to me, 'Colonel, how do I write and tell my wife I don't have a leg anymore?' How do you answer a youngster like that?"

On their days off many nurses would treat civilians in the villages or orphanages. Sometimes the German hospital ship Helgoland transferred civilian patients to the U.S. ship anchored in Da Nang harbor. Most of the patients in the Navy's People-to-People program had congenital or disease-produced defects that required corrective surgery.

American nurses also gave medical care to enemy POWs. Many found it difficult to treat those who had killed and wounded U.S. GIs. However, the only nurse killed by hostile fire, Sharon Lane, is remembered by her colleagues as one who never complained about caring for enemy soldiers.

According to military accounts, nurses were not officially involved in combat. Yet, they saw plenty of it. As early as 1964, three Navy nurses received the Purple Heart after their hotel in Saigon was bombed. Hospitals were hit by mortars. McGoran recalled one time she assisted in surgery with shells smashing around her and the doctor while the attending anesthetist and corpsmen dived for cover. Mary Dickinson remembers a direct rocket hit on her ward at Pleiku. They had to get everyone out of the ward before the fire got to the oxygen tanks.

Hospitals near heavy action often were under Red Alerts. The staff had to wear flak jackets and helmets. During attacks, patients were shoved under their beds and blankets and mattresses thrown over them for protection. When the power went out, the staff did mouth-to-mouth or mouth-to-trach breathing for the patients on respirators or with chest tubes. Not all lived to see the electricity restored.

Pre-Op

A doorgunner, lay on a litter,
        Rigid, immobile,
In the shock–ice,
        Of fear and pain,
Into twilight sleep,
        Falling,
Never to see the care in her smile,
        Or hear the sanity in her jokes,
Falling,
        Never to feel the touch,
That wiped Asian dust from his
        forehead.

—Kathie Swazuk

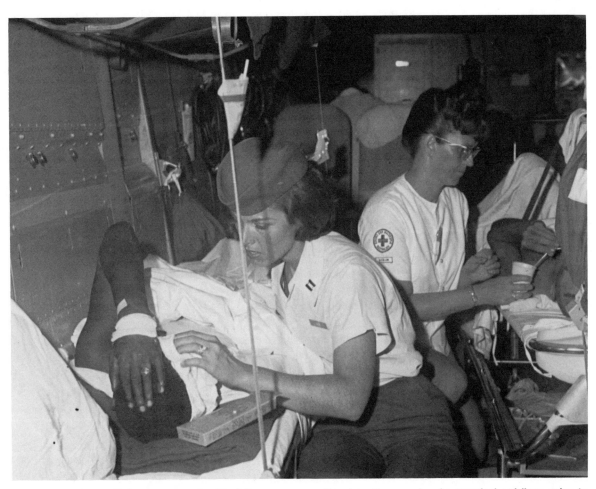

U.S. Air Force flight nurse and a Red Cross nurse attend to the needs of wounded soldiers prior to their aeromedical evacuation from Tan Son Nhut Air Base.

Sometimes enemy troops broke through the perimeters of bases and got into the hospital compounds. At Cu Chi, a wardmaster, two corpsmen and six patients were killed and a nurse wounded. One nurse is still tormented by the memory of the armed VC she was forced to kill when he crept into the nurses' quarters as they slept.

Seriously wounded GIs were airlifted out of Vietnam to hospitals in the Far East or the United States. Aerovac nurses were assigned to bases in Asia for two years. The planes transported eighty patients, including forty on stretchers. Aerovac nurses trained for six weeks to treat the special medical problems related to flying. The rate at which an IV flowed changed with altitude changes. Burn patients needed extra liquids. Comatose and respirator dependent patients needed special care. The flights often lasted as long as sixteen

hours. Nurses had to be ready to handle all emergencies and complications. The nurse in charge could order changes in the flight plan should a patient's medical needs demand it. They also served meals and beverages to the patients. Many patients hadn't seen American women since before going to Vietnam and wanted to talk. Corinne Smith remembers, "We did everything a stewardess did plus our nursing duties."

After 1968, some Air Force nurses even helped to evacuate wounded GIs from enemy territory. For flights into unsecured areas the nurses wore side arms and were trained in the use of the M-16 rifle. The nurses had to act quickly to keep the wounded on the ground from being killed or captured. Patricia Rumpza recalls, "The pilot would keep the engine running while we loaded casualties. He'd even take off with the doors still open. Sometimes as we took off the VC would be running toward the plane and we'd have to use weapons to keep them out."

Naval nurses served in Saigon, Da Nang or on ships. More than half served on either the USS Repose or the USS Sanctuary. Each ship provided full hospital facilities for 800 patients. They were similar in operation to other military hospitals, with patients arriving straight from the battlefields via small boats and helicopters.

American civilian nurses and doctors were housed in modern apartments, but their working stations were overcrowded and filthy. It was not uncommon for three people to share a single cot or to have rats running over the doctors' and nurses' feet as they worked. The nurses had to beg supplies from the military and recycle military disposals. Pat Walsh said she got smile-wrinkle lines from smiling at supply sergeants. Betty Stahl recalls one time when their hospital was hit at about two in the morning. The staff was driven to the hospital and worked more than twenty-four hours straight without water or x-ray equipment.

Most civilian patients were women and children brought in by members of their families. Often there was no hope for some of the patients. Mothers stood holding children who had already died. Triage procedures were used to save as many as possible. Walsh remembers a prayer that she would say to herself for the women she put aside for last care, "Here she comes, God. Let her in."

Coming home was as hard for these women as for the men. Friends and family members didn't want to hear about their experiences. Although most nurses remained in the profession, many did not speak about having served in Vietnam.

Veterans' organizations and the Veterans' Administration refused to recognize women Vietnam veterans. At first, women were denied assistance for Post-Traumatic-Stress-Disorder (PTSD) and excluded from the Agent Orange screening programs. Some nurses organized politically to get the help they needed. Lynda Van Devanter became the National Women's Director of the Vietnam Veterans of American, testifying at congressional hearings on behalf of the women. Eventually, the women were offered the recognition and medical services they deserved.

Vietnamese

The medical facilities and training of the Vietnamese medical staffs were not equal to those of the Americans. However, they helped to make up for that with dedication, hard work, and resourcefulness. Fighters for the VNPA and PLAF were first treated in the field, often by village women who were trained for this purpose through the Women's Association. Lesser-trained physician's assistants and nurses served in forward aid stations near battlefields. Those needing additional care were carried away in hammocks for treatment. Often it would take several hours or days to reach the regimental or district medical facilities.

In tunnels, caves, and camouflaged bunkers the communists maintained large hospitals with trained medical and surgical staffs. The Americans didn't know there was a large hospital in a cave in Marble Mountain overlooking the military base at Da Nang. About half of the staff of these hidden hospitals were women dedicated to their work and cause. One of the nurses told reporter Elizabeth Pond, "We are part of the revolution, and there is no stopping the revolution." Hospitals in the tunnels sometimes were destroyed by bombs, but they were quickly rebuilt. Nguyen Thi Tham, a pharmacist, worked in the tunnels alongside her husband who was a doctor. She was severely wounded by a bomb and received the "American-Killer Heroine" medal.

Equipment and medicines were either improvised from discarded metal, purchased on the "black market" or stolen. Medicines were often in short supply and spoiled quickly because of poor storage facilities. Nurses used herbal remedies, such as honey, for antiseptics. In the tunnels they hung parachute nylon on the

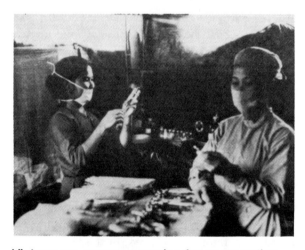

Vietnamese nurses preparing for an operation inside a hospital in one of the many tunnels

North Vietnam's Nguyen Thi Tham won many medals during the war.

walls to keep away earth and infection. They had to perform amputations without anesthetics. Many patients passed out from pain. X-ray equipment was only available in the safest locations, but, even there electricity was irregular.

Medical staff were given modern weapons and trained to be guerrilla fighters. Among the last to evacuate an area, they often were called upon to defend themselves or delay the advance of the enemy. When the fighting was intense, the medical staff became mobile and performed operations by flashlight in small boats or remote locations. They worked long hours treating wounds. Malaria also was a problem. Mosquito nets, anti-malaria drugs and insect repellents often were unavailable. There was no preventative treatment for some strains of malaria.

Le Thi Dau opened a small infirmary in the village of Bao Binh. As a nurse, Dau taught basic hygiene and baby care to the local women. She recalled that those women whose husbands were in the guerrilla "main forces" suffered from chronic depression and great stress. She did not have medicines to give them, but she listened sympathetically and offered comfort. Dau's

work was part of the communists' strategy to win the support of the villagers.

Dr. Duong Quynh Hoa was the pediatrician for the children of Saigon's political leaders. She also was one of the sixteen founders of the NLF. For want of medicines, she watched her only child, a son, die in the jungle of encephalitis. In 1960, Dr. Hoa was arrested and questioned by the Saigon police, but released. After the 1968 Tet Offensive, she helped smuggle NLF members out of Saigon. She then performed medical services at the NLF base in Tay Ninh. After the war, she was called a "Heroine of the Revolution" and named Deputy Minister of Health. Today she has a practice in Ho Chi-Minh City, but has given up her party affiliation.

Discussion Questions

1. Compare and contrast the conditions of work and sense of mission of American and Vietnamese medical workers.
2. Many of the American nurses who served felt that, while the war was a horrible experience, they did not regret their decision to go to Vietnam. How would you explain this apparent contradiction?

SOCIAL WORKERS

Americans and Other Westerners

During its ten years in Vietnam, more than a thousand women served with the Red Cross. About 600 served in the Supplemental Recreation Activities Overseas (SRAO) program. Others worked in the Service to Military Hospital program or as Field Directors taking care of emergencies for active duty personnel. Three Red Cross women died in Vietnam in non-combat situations.

The Red Cross recruited college graduates between twenty-one and twenty-four years of age, especially for the SRAO Program. These "Doughnut Dollies" lived on the bases, but traveled out to the remote firebases to conduct recreation programs, spending an hour with each unit. Jeanne Christie

Judy Jacobs (left) and Becky Fey were two of the Red Cross "Doughnut Dollies" who brought a touch of home to South Vietnam.

recalls, "When we were out in the field the men loved anything we did...some of them would flock to you and talk as fast as they could; others couldn't say a thing. But all of them would stare. They knew every movement we made."

The Doughnut Dollies served about 200 people a day, from high school dropouts to West Point graduates. The women did what they could to take the soldiers' minds off the war and to improve morale. Terre Deegan-Young explains, "I came home each day physically, emotionally and creatively drained; but it was worth it. You knew you were so appreciated. Nothing in my life will ever compare to that year."

The Red Cross also had recreation clubs on the larger bases. The clubs featured volleyball equipment, pool tables, books and other recreational facilities. There the women listened sympathetically to soldiers, some of

whom they came to know well. Women employed with the USO and the Army Special Services ran similar clubs.

The Red Cross women were not trained to deal with the wounded, but they often were called upon to do so. Penni Evans recalls being asked to take things to a wounded friend in the hospital on many occasions. Kammy McCleary Mallory described Vietnam as a "schizophrenic situation." She remembers visiting a group of Marines located just outside of Da Nang and hearing a week later that they had been wiped out. Sometimes the Red Cross women had to fly in copters carrying body bags. Sometimes their copters were fired upon.

Joan Maiman described her work in the hospital at Long Binh as everything from writing letters for injured soldiers to "rudimentary counseling." Becky Pietz found working in the Vietnam hospital quite different from stateside experience. Many of the patients were so seriously ill they could hardly talk. She resigned early because she couldn't cope with the dead and burned bodies.

The women spent much of their off-duty time with various military units attending parties, providing female companionship to young men far from home. It was appreciated. Penni Evans says that years later she met a vet who gave her a big bear hug. He said, "My God, Thank you! I didn't know how to thank you over there....You were fantastic!"

Like the nurses, many Red Cross workers came home and took jobs, but didn't talk much about their Vietnam experiences. Cindy Randolph explained, "What I didn't understand then was that, in Vietnam, you didn't deal with or process feelings....Anything that happened in Vietnam wasn't real. You just got through it. You just survived it." According to researcher Maggy Salvatore, one-third of the nurses and Red Cross women who served in Vietnam suffer from symptoms of PTSD, including depression, survival guilt, sleep disorders, substance abuse, and suicidal tendencies. Unlike the military nurses, Red Cross volunteers have not been entitled to any government benefits for medical and psychological care. However, several Vet Centers have offered PTSD counseling to Red Cross workers.

In all, sixty-eight U.S. voluntary agencies, missions, foundations and other non-profit agencies provided assistance to North or South Vietnam. Volunteers from other nations also worked in Vietnam.

The Christian Missionary Alliance first came to Vietnam in 1911. Its goal was to help the Vietnamese

> I saw at least five mothers give up their babies (something I never want to see again), each mother had tears in her eyes. What is it like to give up a child? What would make a mother do it?...So many people in Vietnam are suffering so greatly from the war, they have NOTHING to give their children except the hope for something better even if that means they will never see them again.
>
> Gloria Johnson, Social Worker
> Wisconsin Friendship Committee with Vietnam

establish a church. Those who went to Vietnam learned the language and planned to stay for most of their working careers. Many were killed in the war, including Eleanor Vietti, Ruth Wilting, Ruth Thompson and Carolyn Griswold. Betty Olson was taken captive and died in the jungle of malnutrition and disease.

Carolyn Paine Miller went to Vietnam in 1961 with her husband to translate the New Testament into the Bru language for the Wycliffe Bible Translators. Her book, *Captured*, tells the story of the eight months in 1975 they, along with eleven other civilians from four countries, were prisoners of the communists.

Sisters from various Catholic orders throughout the world went to Vietnam long before WWII. Sister Mary Thomas and her co-workers were held in a Japanese prisoner-of-war camp during WWII. After her convalescence from TB and lung surgery, she returned alone to Vietnam. At Song Be she established a school and clinic for Montagnards and developed a handicraft shop where bamboo furniture and Montagnard artifacts were sold. Although she suffered from chronic heart disease, she would not leave.

Sister Mary Lawrence came from New Zealand to work with Sister Thomas. In April 1973, Sister Thomas died, her heart finally gave out and Sister Lawrence took charge. In the fall of 1974, the North Vietnamese mounted an offensive to take Phuoc Long. The Montagnards went to the mission's clinic for refuge and a helicopter evacuation was mounted. Sister Lawrence and two other sisters remained to care for the Montagnards. In a few days, they too found it necessary to flee into the jungle. On the sixth day they were taken captive and marched through the jungle to a prison camp. They were interrogated and forced to write their life histories. After seven weeks, they were released.

Sister Lawrence continued to help refugees until ordered back to New Zealand. Concerned about the fate of Vietnamese sisters left behind in Saigon, she returned to Saigon on one of the last planes. With the airport closed, they were evacuated from the roof of the American Embassy to a ship with 4,500 refugees. Two weeks after the fall of Saigon, the sisters finally reached New Zealand.

Mennonite and Quaker volunteers were respected by all for their neutrality. During their occupation of Hue, the VNPA rounded up all foreigners except the Mennonites. Marjorie Nelson worked at the Quaker rehabilitation center at Quang Ngai. During the battle of Hue, she stayed with Sandy Johnson, an English teacher with the International Voluntary Services. The women were taken captive, but released unharmed after two months.

A neutral position didn't always guarantee release. The Germans kept a neutral position in giving medical treatment at their facilities in Da Nang. Three women and two men from West Germany employed by the Aid Service of Malta were led by a farmer into a PLAF trap. The surviving nurse, Monika Schwinn, co-authored the story of their capture and four years of imprisonment in *We Came To Help*.

Families in North America, Europe and Australia came forth to adopt Vietnamese orphans. Women from these countries collected food, clothing and medicine to donate to adoption agencies caring for the children.

Women journalists wrote articles in popular magazines about the children, inspiring some women to volunteer to go to Vietnam to care for the orphans.

During April 1975, large numbers of adopted orphans were air lifted in chartered planes out of Vietnam and taken to new homes. Many women escorted and cared for the children during these long thirty-one hour flights. It was the escorts' responsibility to feed, change, comfort and administer medicine to the children.

On April 4, 1975, forty-seven civilian women died in the crash of a C-5A transport plane during operation Baby Lift. Among the crew of the C-5A were three Air Force nurses, including Lt. Regina Aune who was badly injured. In 1976, Aune received the Cheney Award for bravery from the U.S. Air Force. Despite broken bones in her back, leg and foot, Aune directed the rescue operation and even carried children to safety until she collapsed and lost consciousness. For years, Aune was called to testify in law suits. Aune found testifying difficult because "they never let you finish grieving, and you need to do a lot of grieving when you've been involved in something like this."

Another heroine was Marine Staff Sergeant Ermelinda Salazar. Salazar was nominated by the Veterans of Foreign Wars Auxiliary for the 1970 Unsung Heroine Award in recognition of her assistance to children in the St. Vincent De Paul Orphanage, Saigon. The Republic of Vietnam also awarded her the Vietnamese Service Medal for her work with the orphans.

Vietnamese women gather remains from their destroyed homes. Ten million Vietnamese were made refugees by the war.

...I don't think I've ever taken life as lightly as I did then....I've
never really talked about the painful part of Vietnam to anyone.
Mostly because I don't want to think about it myself."

Pat Johnson

Vietnamese

Throughout the twentieth century, a terrible history of colonialism and wars destroyed much of the fabric of Vietnamese society. The Vietnamese were forced back upon their individual families for help. The communists gained a following by rebuilding voluntary communities out of isolated individuals and families.

The Communist Party emphasized equal participation in the community. Ho Chi Minh pointed out that women made up half of society; if women were not free, the society would not be free. Women were encouraged to undertake all types of tasks and were given rewards, including positions of political power, for their efforts.

The Women's Union was formed in 1929 to advocate the rights of women. Since the French declared all unions illegal, members of the Women's Union worked on a one-to-one basis in secret. They taught hygiene and literacy and supported women's demands for equality with men and for better health care facilities. Tran Thi Hoang of Quang Tri Province gave classes for women on improving production, hygiene, literacy, preventive medicine, and organizational skills. Because of her dedication, her husband, working in Hanoi, did not see her for three years.

Volunteerism was much less well established in the non-communist South. Also, opportunities for public service were less available to women. The (South) Vietnamese Ministry of Social Welfare employed some women administrators who oversaw the provision of food, water, immunizations, housing, and sanitation facilities to refugees, including widows and orphans of the war. Some orphanages had adequate food and water, others did not. Generally, their staffs were dedicated but too small.

Discussion Questions

1. The social work profession is much more established in the United States than in Vietnam. What differences in the social structures and cultures of the two societies would explain this?

2. Long before the Second Indochina War, women social workers from the West were working in Vietnam. Who were they and why do you think they traveled so far from home?

JOURNALISTS

Americans and Other Westerners

In WWII and Korea, American women correspondents like Helen Musgrove, Dickey Chapelle, and Marguerite Higgins braved hardships and wired stories to the homefront. In Vietnam, Musgrove, Chapelle and Higgins went out on patrols with the troops. Musgrove was more than fifty years old, but she still slogged through the rice paddies and flew on combat missions. The GIs gave her so many patches for her collection that she had her name legally changed to Patches in 1969. Chapelle, who was particularly fond of the Marines, was on patrol with them when she was killed in 1965. By 1965, Higgins already had made ten trips to Vietnam. In her book, *Our Vietnam Nightmare*, Higgins advocated that the U.S. make a full-scale war effort. She later died of a rare parasitic disease and was buried in Arlington National Cemetery.

Although official records of those issued press credentials have been lost, more than seventy-five female correspondents are known to have worked in Vietnam, representing such major publishers as *The Christian Science Monitor* (Elizabeth Pond), *Newsweek* (Beverly Deepe), and *The New York Times* (Gloria Emerson). Other women relied on their own resources to realize their ambitions to report on the war. When *Look* refused to let Jurate Kazickas go to Vietnam, she got letters of reference from the North American Newspaper Alliance and used TV quiz show winnings to buy a one-way

Women Civilian Casualties of the Vietnam War

Evelyn Anderson
Dickey Chapelle
Hanna E. Crews
Carolyn Griswold
Marguerite Higgins
Marie-Luise Kerber
Virginia E. Kirsch
Hindrika Kortmann
Betrice Kosin

Mrs. Horst Gunter Kranick
Janie Makel
Betty Olson
Lucinda Richter
Barbara A. Robbins
Philippa Schuyler
Ruth Thompson
Eleanor Ardel Vietti, M.D.
Ruth Wilthing

Actual rubbings from the Vietnam Veterans Memorial of the names of the eight women nurses who died in the war.

SHARON A LANE
ELIZABETH A JONES
ANNIE RUTH GRAHAM
HEDWIG D ORLOWSKI
PAMELA D DONOVAN
ELEANOR G ALEXANDER
CAROL A E DRAZBA
MARY T KLINKER

IN MEMORY OF
THOSE WHO LOST THEIR
LIVES ON 4 APRIL 1975
WHEN A DISABLED C-5A
CRASHED ON LANDING AT
GO VAP, VIETNAM DURING
"OPERATION BABYLIFT."

SAIGON MISSION ASSN.
DEDICATED 20 MAY 1989

Barbara E. Adams
Clara Bayot
Michael Bell
Nora Bell
Arlete Bertwell
Helen Blackburn
Brigit Blanc
Ann Bottorff
Celeste Brown
Dolly Bui
Tina Bui
Vivienne Clark
Wanita Creel
Mary Ann Crouch
Dorothy Curtis

Twila Donelson
Helen Drye
Rohn Drye
Marylin Eichen
Elizabeth Fuginio
Ruthanne Gasper
Beverly Herbert
Penelope Hindman
Vera S. Hollibaugh
Dorothy Howard
Barbara Kavulia
Barbara Maier
Lee Makk
Rebecca Martin
Martha Middlebrook

Katherine Moore
Marta Moschin
Margaret Moses
Marion Polgrean
Jane Poulton
Joan K. Pray
Sayonna K. Randall
Anne Reynolds
Marjorie Snow
Laurie Stark
Barbara Stout
Sister Ursula
Doris Jean Watkins
Sharon Wesley

Photo Journalist Dickey Chapelle on one of her frequent patrols with the U.S. Marines

cover the Second Indochina war.

Other French women journalists included Christine Spengler and Francoise Demulder who photographed the war during its final years. Demulder was still present to photograph the fall of Saigon in 1975. Madeline Riffaud covered the war from the perspective of the North Vietnamese for *L'Humanite,* the official paper of the French Communist Party.

Catherine Leroy was considered one of the best free-lance photographers in South Vietnam. *Life* published six pages of her photographs of the Battle of Hill 881. Leroy was hit with twenty pieces of shrapnel while on a mission with the Marines near the Demilitarized Zone (DMZ). She was still trying to get the film out of her damaged camera as she was being loaded into the evacuation helicopter. Leroy chose to stay in Vietnam when she recovered, walking with a limp because the wound to her foot would not heal.

Michaele Ray went on patrols with U.S. GIs and was the first woman to stay overnight on the USS Coral Sea. While driving alone over back roads, she was captured by the PLAF and held for three weeks. The Vietnamese told her she was their guest. She insisted on helping the women plant rice seedlings. She hid with her escorts underground as the earth shook during B-52 attacks. One of the soldiers told her, "We are poor, but proud. Very proud, too, to have a journalist share our life."

Ray came to identify with the PLAF. She found the

ticket to Saigon. Susan Sheehan and Linda Grant Martin accompanied their journalist husbands to Vietnam and wrote their own stories.

Oriana Fallaci's book on the war, *Nothing and So Be It,* became a best seller in Italy and was later translated into English. She reflects, "You know, when I reread the notebooks I have written my diary in, I am filled with astonishment...the writing in them does not belong to me—close-set, neat, careful. Even where I talk about the most appalling, incredible things. Where did I find the strength to bear that load of suffering, horror, and discomfort on my own? Day after day, week after week, without pause, without taking a breath? Sometimes I wonder if I wasn't mad, just like everyone else in this war."

Brigitte Friang spent twenty-six months covering the French war in Indochina for a Paris weekly and the magazine, *Indochine Sud-Est Asiatique.* Friang concluded that the answer to France's crumbling fortunes in Vietnam was immediate intervention by U.S. forces. In the mid-1960s she returned with French television to

Did I truly think I could, with the camera around my neck, help end the need for the carbine on my shoulder? Did I think I could make plain how warring really was, how quickly the cutting edge of fear excised every human virtue, leaving only the need to live?...And why were Americans...here? They had brought all their expertise and dedication and raw nerve from the security of their home towns to the ultimate insecurity of guerrilla warfare as far from home as it was possible to go. Was that the American idea of global leadership? I knew it was at least one American's idea—mine.

—Dickie Chapelle, Correspondent

Vietnamese soldiers in fine shape and excellent morale. In spite of the bombings, they carried on the struggle with good humor. Although she never came to identify with communism, Ray decided that, had she been Vietnamese, she would have been a fierce nationalist and fought with the PLAF.

Two other women journalists wrote books about being captured. Australian Kate Webb paid her own way to Vietnam and took one of the lowest jobs at UPI. She worked her way up to head of the bureau in Cambodia. She was captured and interrogated by the communists. She said that she was doing her job as a journalist, seeking to find the truth. The guards released Kate and her companions and told her, "Tell the truth about us." A little later, while carrying a white flag, Webb and her colleagues came across Cambodian troops. The officer recognized her and exclaimed, "You're supposed to be dead!" A woman's body had been found along the highway the day she was captured. They assumed it was Webb. Her book, *On the Other Side*, begins with a copy of *The New York Times* article reporting her death!

Elizabeth Pond of *The Christian Science Monitor* was captured along with two of her colleagues. For five and one-half weeks they were taken into homes and introduced to villagers as friends. They were allowed to interview the people. With their soldier escorts they hid from American helicopter patrols who shot at any moving bodies as if they all were the enemy.

Francis Fitzgerald's *Fire in the Lake* won the Pulitzer Prize for Literature. It demonstrated in detail that the political differences between America and Vietnam were embedded deeply in the cultures and histories of the two countries.

The New York Times correspondent Gloria Emmerson left Vietnam, but found the war experience did not leave her. She quit her job to join the peace movement. Emerson traveled around the U.S. to assess the impact of the war on the American people. She shared her observations of the common people of both nations in her book, *Winners and Losers*. In a 1985 interview with *Newsweek*, Emerson looked back on the war and reflected on U.S. policy:

"...Before we went to Vietnam, the country had not done us any harm at all—all of which is forgotten. I'm sorry that the United States, which rebuilt Germany and Japan with such swiftness, sees fit to prevent powdered milk from getting to malnourished Vietnamese chil-

Philippa Schuyler went to Vietnam to play a piano concert for soldiers in a Saigon hospital. She stayed to report on the war for the *Union Leader.* She was killed in a helicopter crash during the Tet Offensive.

dren. Do you know what I'd do? I'd chain all of the politicians to that haunting Vietnam memorial and have them read—slowly—every name aloud. Then the war would end for me."

Martha Gellhorn also wrote about the victims. She appealed to American women to help the wounded children in Vietnam in her *Ladies Home Journal* article, "Suffer the Little Children." In 1966, she wrote in the *Manchester Guardian*:

"We are not maniacs and monsters; but our planes range the sky all day and all night and our artillery is lavish and we have much more deadly stuff to kill with. The people are there on the ground, sometimes destroyed by accident, sometimes because Vietcong are reported to be among them. This is indeed a new kind of war, as the indoctrination lecture stated, and we had better find a new way to fight it. Hearts and minds, after all, live in bodies."

Vietnamese

Voice of Vietnam Radio Station employed several women who broadcast in English to American troops. The GIs called these women "Hanoi Hanna." Trinh Thi Ngo read news, including reports of anti-war actions in America, and played Vietnamese and American music. Thu Huon broadcast three hours daily. She explained to a reporter, "I take great interest in speaking to these men who are fighting my people. They did not ask to come here. They were sent to fight an aggressive war against a people who are struggling for liberty and independence."

Radio Hanoi also had special programs that explained issues in health care and extolled the contributions of women to Vietnam. Magazines and newspapers featured stories about women in combat that were discussed during women's meetings and reading groups.

Children's books were written about heroines and contained woodcuts of women with strong arms and shoulders engaged in combat or production. The daily newspapers also carried stories about the deeds of women. Several poems from the diary of a 16-year-old woman who was killed were printed in the newspaper. One of Dang Thi Ha's poems said, "From a child, I have been dreaming of becoming a fighter against U.S. aggression and a defender of the land...."

Discussion Question

Did the western women journalists who covered Vietnam agree or disagree on the politics of the war? Discuss. Do you think their political opinions biased their reports? Was it possible to be unbiased?

ENTERTAINERS

Americans and Other Westerners

The USO hired many entertainers from the U.S., Thailand and Japan to combat soldiers' boredom, loneliness and depression. Bob Hope took beauty queens with him to perform for the troops.

Martha Raye, comedian, singer, veteran of WWII USO tours, and honorary Colonel in the Green Berets, went to Vietnam every year. She spent more than two years entertaining GIs all over South Vietnam. Raye experienced many combat actions and was wounded twice. She said she felt privileged to be in Vietnam especially to help cheer up wounded soldiers. Army nurse Cheryl Nicol commented, "I never saw anyone light up the faces and spirits of patients and staff like she did. My good thoughts of Nam always include her and her willingness to give so much to us all." Raye, in turn, admired the military and civilian women she met in Vietnam: "I think it is important that [the American public] know women did their share, more than their share if that's possible. Our country owes them profound thanks."

Chris Noel became the first woman since WWII to broadcast for Armed Forces Radio. "A Date with Chris" brought music, interviews and conversation to the GIs. "The Pride of Armed Forces Radio," Noel delighted the troops by wearing a mini skirt while visiting with GIs in the field or hospitals. She came

On her fifth trip to Vietnam, Martha Raye performed "Hello Dolly."

Chris Noel interviews Nancy Sinatra.

under enemy fire many times and once went down with a helicopter when the hydraulic system failed. The communists knew her value as a morale booster and placed a $10,000 price on her head.

Back in the U.S., Noel suffered flashbacks, nightmares and illnesses later diagnosed as PTSD. Her career suffered, but she continued to help GIs. She founded the southern California chapter of the Vietnam Veterans Association and spoke out about veterans' medical needs, including treatment for Agent Orange exposure. In her book, *A Matter of Survival*, Noel described her personal story as similar to that of her veteran brothers and sisters, that is a "struggle in redirecting our lives."

Vietnamese

The communists also had entertainers. Women constituted the majority of the National Liberation Song and Dance Ensemble. In performing the traditional Vietnamese dances and songs, the women stressed the oneness of Vietnamese culture and the need for their nation to be free from outside control. New songs and dramas were written to promote socialism and nationalism and to recognize acts of heroism.

In the combat zones, entertainers performed in caves and underground theater chambers. Dang Thi Lanh, a dancer, recalled that during the Cedar Falls operation she spent fifteen days underground eating only rice and salt. Lanh also had her first child in the tunnels. A doctor arrived just in time. After several days she was taken to a nearby village where the local mothers' association cared for her. When her daughter was six months old, Lanh returned to entertain and work for the NLF. She did not see her daughter again until after the war.

Lonely soldiers also sought entertainment from

prostitutes. The communists forbade prostitution, calling it the economic exploitation of women. Men and women were strictly monitored to ensure that they concentrated only on working for the goals of the revolution.

It was quite a different story in South Vietnam, however. At the height of the U.S. troop presence, there were an estimated 200,000 prostitutes. Some women went onto the military posts to solicit soldiers. Shacks close to the base served as cheap houses of prostitution. The better houses were run by madams who had husbands in high places and hired police to protect their women from physical abuse and arrest. The government required that prostitutes buy work permits. However, there was little effort to monitor and control health conditions. In 1975, the Vietnamese estimated that there were nearly three million cases of venereal disease, almost all as a direct result of prostitution.

Discussion Questions

1. People seek entertainment to be amused, distracted, instructed and/or inspired. What kind of entertainment did U.S. GIs get? How about communist soldiers? How do you explain this?

2. The communists viewed prostitutes as victims of economic exploitation. Why might a woman become a prostitute? Do you consider them all victims? Explain.

POLITICAL ACTIVISTS

American

Although women of all ages were well represented in all groups protesting against the war, some deserve special mention. Dagmar Wilson, an illustrator of children's books, joined with three neighbors to found Women's Strike for Peace (WSP), originally to protest atmospheric testing of nuclear weapons. Later they turned to opposition to the war in Vietnam. These middle-class, suburban housewives dressed neatly when they protested against the use of napalm in 1966. Nevertheless, the newspaper reported that four San Jose "housewife terrorists" were arrested and found guilty of trying to block shipments of napalm.

Founded during World War I, The Women's International League for Peace and Freedom (WILPF) actively opposed the Vietnam War. While some members were professionals, many described themselves as mothers and housewives from nations all over the world. They pressured their governments to help end the war. The American members participated in all of the major peace rallies. In February 1965, 350 WILPF and WSP women marched outside the White House carrying posters saying "Mothers in 33 states want Peace in Vietnam." Parallel marches were held in Philadelphia, New York, Indianapolis, St. Louis, Chicago, Minneapolis, Seattle, and San Francisco. Those in Washington remained to lobby Congress.

During 1971, WILPF staged dramatic "every Tuesday" demonstrations at the White House. In one demonstration they delivered 8,000 postcards to President Nixon asking him to withdraw U.S. troops from Vietnam. WILPF chapters also organized local projects. The San Francisco branch started a Saturday protest vigil that lasted six years.

Kay Camp, President of the American WILPF, lead two delegations to Vietnam in January 1971. Delegates reported on the conditions of the civilian population and inspected the prisons. They took letters to American POWs. They signed peace agreements with the women of North Vietnam and South Vietnam. Camp reported: "Our common struggle could yet make Vietnam the turning point in human history, when the world realizes at last the utter horror and futility of war and oppression."

Raised as a Quaker, Joan Baez was committed to pacifism. She protested war in her music and reached millions of fans. Baez visited Hanoi in December 1972 and later told of her fears during U.S. B-52 bombing raids and her anguish upon seeing the death and destruction the raids left in their wake. In the late 1970s, she continued to protest the abuse of human rights, this time under the government of the Socialist Republic of Vietnam. Baez called upon President Carter to have the Seventh Fleet help the Boat People escape from Vietnam. These actions provoked unpleasant exchanges with many of her former allies in the peace movement.

Some of the women opposed to the Vietnam war had long histories of peace activism. As a member of Congress, Jeannette Rankin had voted against U.S. entry into both WWI and WWII. At the age of ninety, Rankin was giving speeches calling for the unconditional and immediate withdrawal of all U.S. forces from

Southeast Asia.

Women in Congress were divided on the war. Senator Margaret Chase Smith strongly supported President Nixon's policies in Indochina. On the other hand, Representatives Patsy Mink and Bella Abzug met with Madame Nguyen Thi Bihn, Vietnam's chief negotiator at the Paris Peace Conference, and tried to represent her concerns to President Nixon. Both Abzug and Rep. Elizabeth Holtzman were elected to Congress with support from peace activists. When the war ended, they called for complete amnesty for all draft resisters.

Analyzing the protest movement, Nancy Zaroulis and Gerald Sullivan concluded its success came from the determination of individuals to work day after day despite little support. Some had personally experienced other wars, like Elizabeth Fletcher, a WWI nurse, and Helma Waldeck, a survivor from a WWII concentration camp. Still others, like Peg Mullen, were the mothers and wives of soldiers who were killed or missing in action. C.D.B. Bryan's book, *Friendly Fire*, tells the story of Mullen's search for an explanation of how her son was killed in Vietnam. For years Mullen helped other mothers learn the truth about the war and the fate of their sons through her speeches and writings and contacts with government and military officials.

Louise Bruyn, a Quaker, walked alone from Boston to Washington, D.C., a distance of 450 miles, as a personal plea to Congress to end the war. Bruyn talked to people along the route, encouraging them to take their own actions for peace. Throughout the country others followed Bruyn's lead by walking to their state capitals.

Vietnamese

Although women in Vietnam traditionally were excluded from government, several took leadership roles. Madame Nhu, a deputy in the National Assembly, was better known as the sister-in-law and official hostess for President Diem. She was notorious for her outspoken contempt for anyone who criticized her family's regime, including the Buddhists and communists. Morley Safer described her, "as cruel and implacable a woman as I have ever talked to." American journalist Marguerite Higgins defended Madame Nhu as a survivor, suggesting that her poor understanding of Americans and the English language were partly responsible for the harsh impression she gave the press.

Miami WILPF Demonstration – Jeanette Rankin Brigade
Jenette Rankin is in center wearing glasses.

Bella Abzug presents a copy of her book to Madame Binh during an interview in Paris.

Madame Nhu declared herself a reformer. Her pro-family bill outlawed concubinage, prostitution, adultery, and contraceptives and granted divorce only with government permission. Higgins wrote of Madame Nhu that her "zeal was commendable, her timing terrible. A country in crisis can ill afford to have century-old social customs (and abuses) assaulted head-on by such controversial reforms."

Madame Nhu's press secretary and confidant, Madame Dai, was a leader in her own right. Educated in France, she became the first woman trial lawyer in Vietnam. Dai started the Vietnam Women's Movement, an organization of French speaking women, for the purpose of influencing public policy to oppose communism. She was elected to the National Assembly of the Republic of Vietnam and served ten years as a Deputy.

The oppressive Diem government provoked protests by Buddhists. Self-immolations by nuns and priests shook the governments of Diem and, later, Thieu. Reverend Mother Thich Nhu Hue explained, "Death by burning is a valuable weapon against them because,

arousing pity and horror, it forces the guilty to think....It should be an act consciously chosen by adults who have an understanding of life."

Madame Ngo Ba Thanh earned a law degree from Columbia University and went on to found the "Third Force" Women's Committee to Defend the Right to Live. She was imprisoned for her efforts to reform the government of the South. She went on hunger strikes and refused an offer to be released in return for leaving the country. Today, Ba chairs the committee in the

I am not mad and I am not unhappy. Life is beautiful and I wish I could have loved it to the end. But it is right for me to offer it for our country and our faith. May the responsibility for this act fall on the wicked men who rule Vietnam.

Note left by Huyn Thi Mai, a school teacher, when she took her life.

National Assembly which is rewriting the laws that govern economic policy.

When President Thieu blocked all opposition in the 1971 presidential election, female high school and college students joined in the protests, marching with demonstrators, setting fires to American libraries and fire bombing the jeeps of American GIs. Mrs. Kieu Mong Thu, a Deputy in the legislature, explained that to oppose the war and Thieu, it was necessary to attack the Americans who protected and supported Thieu. Twenty-three year old Vo Thi Bach Tuyet said they attacked Americans so they would see that the rulers of the South were not "good" just because they were not communists.

Madame Binh rose from poverty to become one of the highest officials in the Vietnamese government. Forced to support her five brothers and sisters, Binh became a tutor and studied for a regular teaching position. She became an activist in patriotic women's and students' organizations, was arrested by the French and imprisoned for four years.

Binh married after her release, but her husband soon was forced to flee to the countryside. She stayed in the city to organize peaceful demonstrations against the Diem government. In 1957, Binh too was forced to flee to the countryside to avoid arrest. In time, she became Vice President of the Union of Women for the Liberation of South Vietnam and Foreign Minister of the Provisional Revolutionary Government. Binh headed the NLF delegation to the Paris negotiations to end the war. After the war, she was appointed Minister of Education. Today, Binh heads the Vietnam Union of Peace, Solidarity and Friendship. Recently she told an American delegation, "The moment is favorable now to develop friendship with the U.S. We need to overcome the bad happenings and work for peace."

Women in Vietnam today occupy important positions throughout the nation. The powerful Vietnam Women's Union has trained and sponsored many leaders, such as Madame Bui Thi Cam who served as a member of parliament and delegate to a Moscow peace conference. Many women are members of the National Assembly, the Viet Bac. Many more are representatives of regional People's Councils, heads of local communes, and managers of co-ops.

Discussion Questions

1. These portraits of Vietnamese activists reveal many

different political groupings. Describe them. With whom do you agree? With whom do you disagree? Why?

2. Most of the women in the U.S. peace movement came from socially advantaged backgrounds. Why do you think they actively protested the war? What did they stand to gain or lose from their actions?

SURVIVORS AND CARE GIVERS

Americans

Twenty-year-old Maya Ying Lin, a Chinese-American student, won the design competition for the Vietnam Veterans Memorial. Visitors looking at the wall's more than 58,000 names see their own images reflected in the polished black granite. The Vietnam Veterans Memorial is now the most popular monument in our nation's capital. Every day people from all over the country place poems, letters, flowers, and medals at

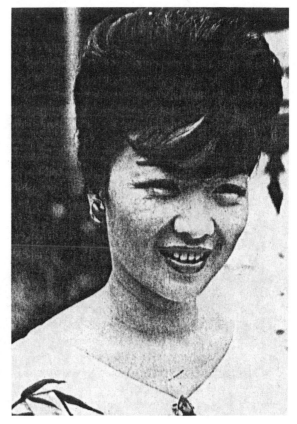

Madam Nhu

255

"the wall."

Four times a year Eleanor Wimbish places a letter to her son, William, beneath panel number thirty-two. It has helped her to cope with the pain of his death. She explains, "As I see Bill's name, with all the others, it helps me to know I am not alone in my pain....When I touch his name, my pain momentarily increases, yet it decreases....On this black wall, there is much pain, yet there is much love."

Helen Shine's three sons went to Vietnam, but only one returned alive. One son, Tony, was declared dead after being listed as MIA for many years. She describes how her continuing uncertainty makes grieving difficult: "Tony was declared missing. I know Jon is with the Lord and he's fine, but with Tony, you don't know. And it's worse. A lot of times I've felt real despair....It's terrible for the young wives. As our daughter-in-law says, she's neither wife nor widow. We'll never be sure. It's hard on parents, but it's harder on wives." There are 2,300 families who have not been able to bury the bodies of their missing-in-action sons.

Some two million men returned from the war, but more than a third have been plagued by various symptoms of PTSD. Counselors agree that many wives and lovers of PTSD victims face four common problems:

1. Veterans tend to read personal insults into women's statements and behaviors;
2. Veterans are reluctant or unable to share at a deep emotional level;
3. Veterans are jealous of any attention their wives give to family members, friends, and work associates;
4. Veterans tend to withdraw from family problems of illness, injury, or death.

As a consequence, the women must cope with verbal abuse, physical threats, property destruction, and financial uncertainty. Many veterans' centers offer special programs for the wives and children of veterans with PTSD.

Chris Noel, Donna Long, and Judi Southerland marched in a 1985 parade in honor of their husbands who died after returning from Vietnam.

Women mourn loved ones at mass funeral following the destruction of the imperial capital of Hue.

Vietnamese

Vietnamese women faced great dangers and hardships throughout the war. Many were raped by Korean and American soldiers. Many victims fought back by joining protest movements or guerrilla forces. A well-publicized rape of a mother and daughter in Saigon in 1970 sparked the organization of the Women's Committee to Defend the Right to Live. Whether conception occurred by consent or rape, thousands of Vietnamese women were left to care alone for the offspring of U.S. GIs. In all, there were 131,000 widows and 300,000 orphans in Vietnam after the war. Up to 15,000 of the orphans were offspring of U.S. GIs.

Women suspected of political activity were treated as harshly as men. Large numbers of women were imprisoned in the South during the war. American Friends Service Committee medical worker Claudia Krich said that most of the prisoners she treated told a similar story: "I was walking though the rice paddy one night, and I was arrested and accused of being VC. So they tortured me." Many political prisoners were held for years without trial. Electrical shock was used often. Many women suffered permanent damage, ranging from loss of muscle control to seizures and headaches.

The war made traditional life impossible for many women. The communists called love, marriage, and childbirth the "three postponements." Many lost their husbands and lovers and were never to have a normal family life. Others were poisoned by chemical defoliants and suffered miscarriages, embryo deaths, and genetically deformed children.

Many more Vietnamese than Americans were deprived of the opportunity to give their loved ones a proper burial. If guerrilla fighters were killed near their homes, their bodies were taken to their villages. However, corpses generally were buried quickly after battle with no effort made to notify the families. In many villages of the North, only about half of the soldiers

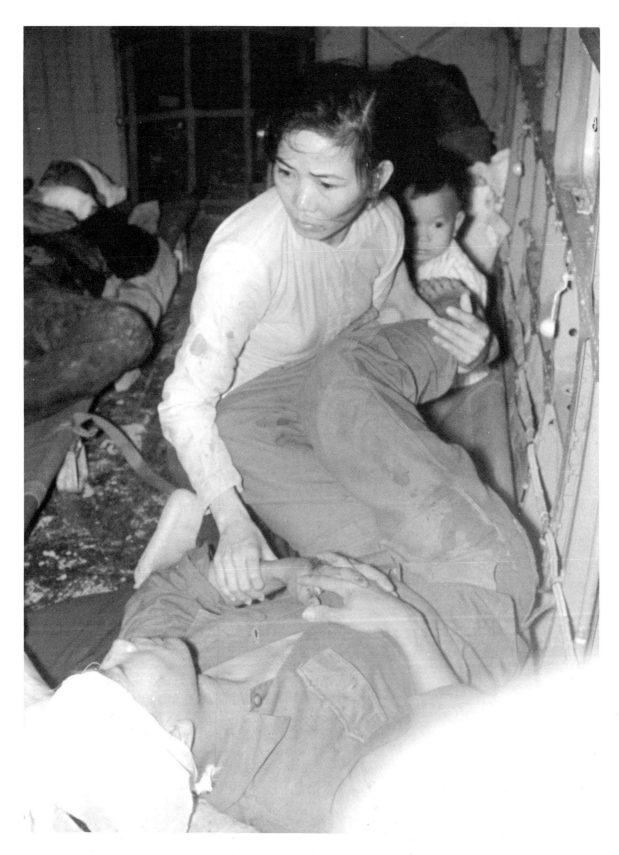

Vietnamese wife comforts her wounded soldier/husband.

returned from the war. Some 300,000 Vietnamese soldiers are listed as missing-in-action. Denial of information about the time of death and the opportunity for a proper burial were especially distressing for people who practiced ancestral worship.

Finally, the loss of so many men in battle made an especially heavy burden on women to keep families together and care for children, the aged, the wounded, and the diseased. The Vietnamese have a saying, "Women are the greatest victims of the war, but they are also its greatest heroes

Discussion Question

Why might Vietnamese mothers have given a child up for adoption? Many Vietnamese criticized this practice, especially when the adopting parents were western. Why? What do you think of Americans who have adopted Vietnamese orphans?

CONCLUSION

American women who served in Vietnam suffered death, wounds, imprisonment and depression. They also earned Bronze Stars, Purple Hearts, and the Pulitzer Prize. Maureen Walsh, a former Navy nurse, says, "I don't feel any regrets; I feel like I've pulled myself up. I've gone through school, I'm doing what I want to do, and I'm using the experiences probably with a deeper understanding than I ever would have, had I not gone over there."

Rear Admiral Frances Shea Buckley also speaks for many in saying, "I never saw anything like the suffering, and I hope I or no one else ever has to see it again." Military nurse Diane Evans goes even further: "Wars are wrong. I can't justify any war."

The accomplishments of Vietnamese women have been well publicized and memorialized. Until recently this has not been true for American women. In 1984, Evans founded the Vietnam Women's Memorial Project, Inc. as a "legacy of hope and healing." The project will construct a memorial to honor women veterans at the Vietnam Veterans Memorial in Washington, D.C. After six years, approval was granted by Congress, the National Capital Memorial Commission and the Commission of Fine Arts. On Veterans Day—November 11, 1990—the winning designs were announced. In 1993, the memorial was opened to the public.

Today these women ask: will the next generation acknowledge the abilities of women or fall back on the stereotype of women as weak? Will the next generation use its knowledge to inflict pain and suffering or work to improve the human condition?

With the belief that truth leads to better decisions, these women tell their stories—stories of suffering and courage, creativity and commitment, pride, sorrow and hope. They were ordinary women who performed ex-

> The veterans in the audience stood up first, and then everybody stood up and applauded. It's not that I had been waiting for someone to say thank you, but nobody ever had.
>
> —Shelley Saywell

traordinary deeds. They become heroines when succeeding generations learn of their accomplishments and from their experiences.

General Discussion Questions

1. The Vietnamese have a saying: "Women are the greatest victims of the war, but they are also the greatest heroes." Discuss.

2. What is your definition of a hero or heroine? Which, if any, of the women that you read about would you consider a heroine? Explain.

3. American military policies concerning the role of women have changed since Vietnam. What arguments can you make for and against the following two statements:

    a. Women should be allowed to qualify for and serve in combat.

    b. It should be official policy that women in the military be deployed so as to make the maximum number of men available for combat.

    4. Historically, wars have provided opportunities for the advancement of women. Such gains often are lost after the war. Why? What do you think about this?

THE "VIETNAM VET"

The "Vietnam Vet"
people instantly conjure
their own picture
in their mind

Is it ever of a woman?
Huddled...somewhere...
alone
sleeping
trying desperately to shut out the world
that shut her out
or
that disappeared
as she reached out to trust it

Is it ever
that vision?
that woman?

—Norma J. Griffits

Chapter 10

Fred Wilcox and Jerold M. Starr

THE WOUNDS OF WAR
AND THE PROCESS OF HEALING

A FAMILY STILL GRIEVES
P.F.C. PETER RUZILA, JR.
KILLED IN VIET NAM
NOV. 1, 1965

Americans Killed and Wounded

Carved into the polished black granite wall of the Vietnam Veterans Memorial are the names of 58,135 Americans officially acknowledged as killed in the Vietnam War. If you have never lost a friend or family member, it would be hard to appreciate how many relationships are destroyed by one death. A 1969 Gallup Poll found that 55 percent of Americans personally knew someone who had been killed or wounded in Vietnam. An estimated 43 million Americans living today have direct links with a serviceman or woman who died in Vietnam.

According to Executive Director John Holman, Friends of the Vietnam Veterans Memorial (FVVM) receives 1,000 requests a month for its volunteers to make rubbings of names on the wall. In 1990, FVVM solicited corporate donations to buy computer hardware and programs to set up a free locator service. Now 200 volunteers are able to quickly sort through 20,000 names and addresses to put the children of deceased veterans in touch with their fathers' comrades. Holman explains: "They promised their buddies to get in touch with their families. They haven't done it; it's too difficult."

Tony Cordero speaks for the children: "The average age of those who died in Vietnam was nineteen or twenty. Some had children who never knew their dads." Tony himself was only four years old when, on Father's Day in 1965, his father, Air Force Major William Cordero, disappeared when his B-57 crashed in a dense jungle. He prayed for his father nightly until 1969 when the crash site was discovered and his father's remains were buried in Arlington National Cemetery. Tony says, "The loss of a parent is always ingrained in a child's heart. You cannot run away from those emotions."

In May 1989, on the 20th anniversary of his father's funeral, Tony became motivated to reach out to others. He called his state Veterans Affairs Department who referred him to FVVM.

Wanda Ruffin, FVVM project coordinator whose husband James, a Navy aviator, was killed off the coast of Vietnam, agreed to help. She put him in touch with her daughter, Wende, and observed that "they shared experiences that no one else was able to comprehend." Now, Tony's goal is "to develop a network of friendship with sons and daughters" of GIs killed in Vietnam "in all areas of the country, regardless of their ethnic background or religion...."

Many survivors have accepted their loss as necessary, even honorable. In contrast to World War II, however, the grief of many other survivors has been aggravated by the thought that the cause was not just and the sacrifice futile.

A father despairs that, although many years have passed, his wife still wears black and his house "will never see light again." Since his son was killed "there's no parties, there's no weddings, there is no nothing." Looking into space, the man recalls painfully, "Every time I turn around, even if I go into another room, I see something...the picture, the gun. We used to hunt together. Fishing, he was with me like a little puppy dog. He wouldn't get away from me at all. Anything I needed, I had from him: 'Hey Sam.' 'Yes, Dad.' Boom. It's mine. Now, what happens? So many things I remember. If he would be sick, that would be another story. Not this way. This was a slaughterhouse way."

A retired lawyer laments to Myra MacPherson, "Here's the horror of it. We lost our *only child* there, a Marine, in 1968....I *counseled* my son to go. I'll bear the burden of that for the rest of my life. I feel I killed him. When parents lose a son in war, they're supposed to be silent and lick their wounds. It's time parents became radicalized. You clutch your teenage son to your bosom, and don't let your government send him to Central America or the Middle East. They'll lie to you in the name of national interest."

It also is impossible to measure all the costs to the 304,704 men who were wounded in Vietnam, 153,329 of whom required hospital care. The jungles and rice paddies of Vietnam were seeded with booby traps and mines that ripped legs away at the knee, shattered spines and amputated arms. Ground troops on both sides carried automatic weapons designed to lay down "walls of fire."

Ironically, while the technology for killing and maiming had been perfected, so too had the ability to save lives. Helicopter evacuation teams rushed wounded men to MASH units where medical teams stemmed the bleeding and labored to patch a shattered young body back together.

Rick Eilert, a combat Marine in Vietnam, describes the excruciating pain patients suffer when their wounds are cleaned and the dressing changed:

"The doctor began to pull the bandages from the area around his tailbone. I saw Smitty grasp the frame of the side of his rack. He held on so that his knuckles turned white....He didn't groan or scream. He just closed his eyes and buried his head in the mattress....The doctor took tweezers and began pulling foot after foot of packing out of the wound, it, too dripping pus and blood....I saw perspiration dripping from Smitty's brow, down to the mattress and the floor....Awaiting the second half of the process, Smitty rolled on his side to face me and said, 'The damn enlistment posters never said nothing about pain. It sounds naive, but I never thought that getting wounded involved so much agony'."

During the year he spent recovering from his own wounds, Eilert was surrounded by blind, burned, crippled, but still innocent young men.

SANDERS IN THE MILWAUKEE JOURNAL

"What shall I put down as the reason for dying?"

Veterans at the opening of Vietnam Veterans' Memorial in Washington, D.C., 1982

Eilert looked on sympathetically as they refused in vain to accept the obvious permanence of their injuries:

"Al really believed that he would see again. His naive understanding of anatomy and body functions was not his alone. Almost all of the horribly wounded and deformed patients believed that they would fully recover, at least in the early stages of their hospitalization. Al believed that his injuries would heal—like all the wounds portrayed on TV and in the movies...the wounded in the movies were never portrayed as crippled or maimed for life....It seemed that everything like this I'd ever seen was a sham. The actors knew that their portrayals were just acting. Now all this pain and terror was real, and forever. Just think of it...forever."

Lynda Van Devanter served as an army nurse in the operating room of a MASH unit. In her best selling memoir, Van Devanter describes being haunted by the lingering horror of the victims her unit tried to save. While having dinner in an Air Force Officers Club one night, she glanced about the room and saw:

"...the young bleeder we had lost a few nights earlier....Then, when his face was gone, I began seeing all of them—the double and triple amputees, boys with brain injuries, belly wounds, and missing genitals. I could see the morgue and hundreds of bodies strewn haphazardly....There were others who were not old enough to shave who had their faces burned off. There were married fathers who were blinded and would never see their children. Or who were paralyzed and would never be able to throw a ball, run along trails, or even lift a pencil...."

Some 6,655 Americans lost limbs in Vietnam. They are compensated according to the degree of their disablement. A veteran who has lost both legs above the knees receives $1,661 a month. One with both legs off below the knee gets $1,506, one with one leg off above the knee gets $506, and one with one leg off below the knee only $311 a month.

There are more than 33,000 soldiers paralyzed as a result of injuries sustained in Vietnam. Most have

V. A. Hospital

In memory of John Makstutis

Yesterday I didn't know this place.
Today I wished you were dead.

The hallways are hollow drum logs.
This is the white history of death:
TV, cigarettes, magazines,
all the stupid charities
cluttered on a table.

I am the stranger here.
I have never seen a man alive with his face cut off
as clean as steel below his eyes.
In the name of Christ, how do you live?
Is it the gray spiders clinging
to your eyes that keep you alive?

My own guilt clings to your eyes.
In a dream, I hear the echoes of women
pounding these halls to love you.

From the outside I bring nothing of use.

—Anthony Petrosky

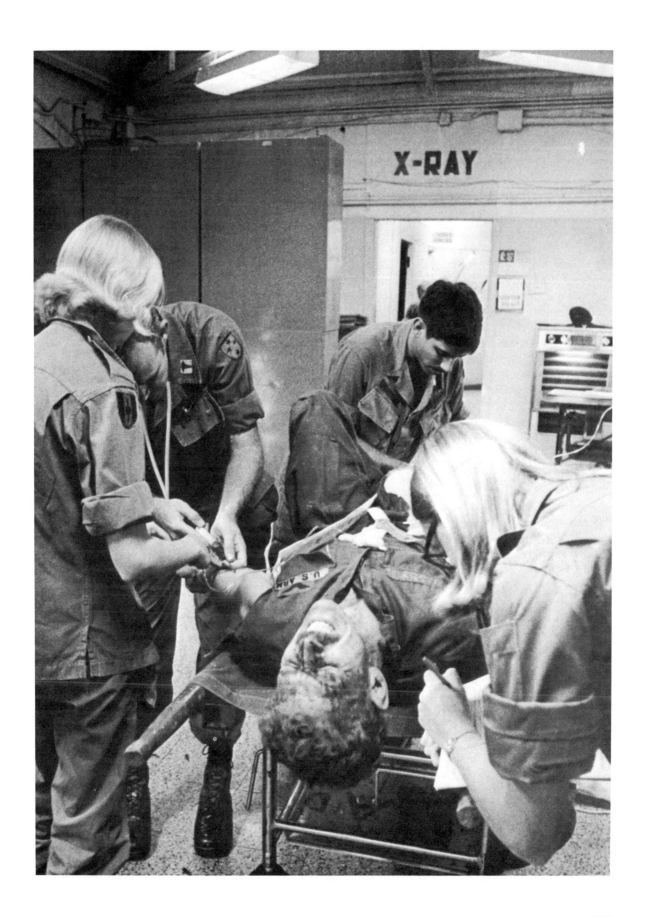

endured prolonged hospitalization involving multiple operations and long-term intensive care. They will spend most of their lives in and out of V.A. hospitals.

Vietnamese Killed and Wounded

By war's end, about 1.5 million Vietnamese had been killed—185,000 South Vietnamese soldiers, 924,000 North Vietnamese and Vietcong and 415,000 civilians. An estimated 600,000 died from U.S. bombing raids. About four million Vietnamese were wounded. Over a decade later there still are 360,000 disabled war victims compensated by the government for being unable to work, 140,000 of whom are totally disabled.

In North Vietnam, the government has established camps for those permanently injured in wars against the French and Americans. Many are invalids "brought from villages, battlefields, and prisons in the south during or since the war." Canadian Anthropologist Kathleen Gough was taken on a tour of these camps. In one room she found:

"...men suffering from head and neck wounds, all of them mute. An older man lies rigid; only his lips move....Across from him is a younger man whose tongue and throat were damaged in the recent war. He, too, cannot sit up; he writhed, apparently in agony. Beyond him lies a boy, perhaps in his teens, whose tongue was cut out during torture by the Saigon forces. He lies quite still with staring eyes; I do not think that he is conscious."

You would have to multiply Vietnam's casualty rates by at least five to make them proportional to a nation the size of the U.S. Comparatively speaking, the Vietnamese death toll was about two hundred times that of the U.S. Still other casualties were the ten million people displaced from their homes. Perhaps the most poignant of them were the 131,000 war widows and 300,000 orphans, forced to fend for themselves in the urban slums and ravaged rural areas of the south.

It is estimated that up to 15,000 of the orphans are Amerasians—children of Vietnamese and American parentage. Most were abandoned when U.S. troops pulled out of Vietnam. To date, approximately 4,000 have resettled in the U.S. However, the vast majority are condemned to unhappy lives, rejected by "pure" Vietnamese, trapped in poverty, in some cases abandoned by their mothers as well. It is no wonder these

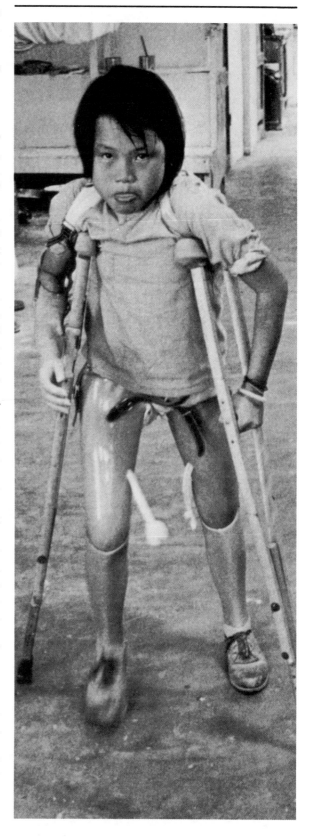

"con lai" (half breed) also are referred to as *bui doi*—"dust of life."

Americans are fortunate not to have had to fight a war on their own soil in this century. They have been spared the scenes of death and destruction described above. Nevertheless, hundreds of thousands of U.S. soldiers who served in Vietnam have returned with their own very serious wounds of war.

POW / MIA

In Vietnam, 766 U.S. soldiers were captured and interned as prisoners of war. This is a small fraction of the 1.2 million with combat experience. For these few, however, the war was filled with unique terrors. Some were incarcerated as many as eight long years. One camp, nicknamed the Hanoi Hilton, was run by a sadistic man referred to by the POWs as "the weasel."

Some of the men were put in leg irons. Others had broken limbs that were not set. Some lost one-third of their weight. Others were put in solitary confinement and forbidden to speak with anyone on pain of physical punishment. Describing the horrors of his own captivity, former POW Rick Springman writes:

"We were somewhere in the southern tip of Laos. The guards told us we'd have to build our own camp and our own cages...the cages...were living hell. Two-foot-long viper snakes crawled all over. They were known as 'two-step snakes.' They got you and you took two steps and died. If you saw somebody get hit by a viper, the only way to save him would be to take a machete and chop the arm or leg off the guy before a minute had passed. I was sitting on a log one day and a viper came out under my legs. I froze, but it kept going for some reason and left me alone. We got a lot of boiled rat to eat. Not the body, which we'd eaten before, but rat skulls. Eyeballs, jawbones, brains. It was stringy, mushy and putrid, but we ate it. The rice we got came from a 20-year-old French cache. It was green and moldy with worms and black pus in it. At first I tried to pick the bugs out of it but that was impossible. So I just ate the bugs too and hoped it was protein or something...."

The fact that Vietcong and North Vietnamese POWs experienced similar abuse should in no way diminish the outrage of civilized people. Unfortunately, such abuse is common to prisoners of war. A total of 114, or 15 percent of U.S. POWs died while in captivity. This rate is much lower than for Korea (38%) and slightly higher than for World War II (11%). It should be noted, however, that the rates for World War II varied greatly by theater. The POWs held by the Japanese faced especially cruel treatment—forced labor, a starvation diet and no medical care. Some 10,000 of the 25,000 held (40%) died in captivity.

Geoffrey Norman's new book, *Bouncing Back,* provides an encouraging footnote to this story. According to Norman, the POWs devised ingenious ways, including a "tap code," to communicate with each other on everything from poetry to existentialist philosophy. In his conclusion, Norman cites a 15-year study by Robert Mitchell which found that the POWs "were in surprisingly good health....More remarkably, the POWs generally showed an increase in their IQ scores. The classes that they had held and the games of concentration that they had played had paid off....There were no long-term psychiatric problems...the experience, grim as it had been, had not ruined these men."

According to the Paris treaty, all American POWs were to be returned to the U.S. after the war. Some 590 POWs were handed over to U.S. officials in 1973. Nevertheless, a bitter controversy persists today about whether the governments of Vietnam, Cambodia and Laos are still holding American soldiers captive.

The cause of POW/MIAs was launched in the late 1960s by a conservative student organization, the Victory in Vietnam Association, (VIVA). Incorporated in California in 1967, VIVA set up fifty chapters across the country in an effort to organize the "silent majority" to support the war.

After the Kent State and Jackson State killings in 1970, public sentiment ran so heavily against the war that VIVA decided to change its name to Voices in Vital America and to focus on the POW/MIA issue. Conservative Congressman Bob Dornan, then a local TV talk show host, introduced VIVA leaders to POW wives seeking to dramatize their cause.

Shortly thereafter the POW/MIA bracelet program was announced at a "Salute to the Armed Forces" dinner dance, featuring Ronald Reagan as keynote speaker. Bob Hope and Martha Raye were made honorary co-chairs of the bracelet program and Mrs. H. Ross Perot accepted the first bracelet.

More than 842 of the 1,814 families of American servicemen agreed to allow their husband's or son's name to be used on the bracelet. More than 35 percent of the U.S. Congress agreed to be named to VIVA's

National Advisory Board. Bracelet sales soared to 5,000 a day and VIVA's revenue increased from $30,000 in 1969 to more than $7 million in 1973.

Within weeks of the launching of the bracelet program, the National League of Families of American Prisoners and Missing in Southeast Asia was incorporated in our nation's capital. From the beginning, they were actively supported by the White House. Columnist Mary McGrory explains: "When he was elected to 'end the war and win a peace' in 1968, [President] Nixon was desperate for an alibi to keep the war going. He could not admit we had lost or abandoned our Saigon allies. He and Kissinger hit upon the notion of using the prisoners and the missing as a reason for fighting on. The families were organized, invited to the White House, visited regularly by Kissinger." Award winning Vietnam correspondent, Neil Sheehan, adds: "Some of the public seemed to be under the impression that the President was prosecuting the war solely to free the POWs..."

The League grew to 3,700 family members and was recognized by the U.S. Government and that of other nations as the official organization representing the POW/MIA families and missing men. The goal of the League has been "to obtain the return of all American prisoners, the fullest possible accounting for the missing and the repatriation of all recoverable remains." When about 50 POW wives saw Nixon's advocacy of the POW cause as a ploy to justify continuation of the war, they picketed the White House for the withdrawal of U.S. troops from Vietnam. Formally, the League always has opposed linkage of the POW/MIA issue to the political relationship between the U.S. and Vietnam.

The U.S. did not raise the issue of MIAs until 1976, some three years after implementation of the Paris peace treaty. Forty-seven American remains were returned during the Carter administration. In 1982, resolution of the POW/MIA issue was established as a high priority of the U.S. Government. This was followed by a commensurate increase in personnel and resources in the Defense Intelligence Agency, the Joint Casualty Resolution Center and the Central Identification Laboratory.

As of 1994, there were 2,231 Americans still unaccounted for in Southeast Asia, including 1,641 in Vietnam. About half of those actually were listed as Killed in Action—Body Not Recovered (KIA/BNR). Those deaths were witnessed by comrades who were unable to retrieve the bodies. More than 400 others were lost over the sea, and their remains probably never

A fellow POW talks with several others in detention in Hanoi.

will be recovered, according to U.S. officials. Even if one counts all of the above as still MIA, however, U.S. MIAs amount to fewer than three percent of U.S. combat deaths in Vietnam, as compared to 20 percent for World War II and 15 percent for Korea.

Moreover, the U.S. MIA count is tiny when compared to that of Vietnam which claims more than 300,000 soldiers still missing. The thousands who were targets of U.S. bombing raids left no remains at all. As for the others, it was common for northern soldiers to be buried hurriedly in a shallow dirt grave marked only by a few stones.

The ancestor worship of the Vietnamese requires that the remains of the dead be properly buried and venerated. Nearly 1,000 northern Vietnamese families apply to the Government each month for the chance to travel south to search for missing relatives. Unfortunately, the Vietnamese usually lack the dental records and modern technology needed for proper identification. Still they try—like Me Thi Ha, a poor retired army cook, widowed during the war: "Even if I could not find him I would like to try. I am not a religious woman, but I do know I would feel relief in my dreams if I know where my husband was buried."

In this context, it must be explained why the U.S. MIAs have remained such an issue. In past wars, MIA cases were reviewed routinely. If, after one year, no new information was turned up, the classification was changed to "presumptive finding of death." Tens of thousands of such reviews were conducted and no person presumed dead ever returned alive. This includes the Korean War where as recently as January

1996 the U.S. Pentagon still was trying to recover the remains from North Korea of as many as 3,500 U.S. servicemen.

Once a "presumptive finding of death" is made, family members are able to have a sense of closure regarding their missing family member. Also, they receive more money in compensation from the federal government. Nevertheless, from 1974–76 VIVA and the National League of Families lobbied successfully for legislation to halt the automatic revew process, claiming North Vietnam, Laos and Cambodia had not given a reasonable accounting of the remaining men. Many MIA families also filed suit to halt the process.

The suspended process left many American families, like those in Vietnam, with no sense of closure on their loss.

Take the case of Florence Carter, mother of Vernon Carter Jr. of Gainesville, Florida. In 1965, a telegram told her Vernon had been killed. It listed a time and place, and expressed official condolences. Carter's body came home in a sealed casket.

In January 1986, Carter's army buddy, Albert French, found the family after a search of twenty years. French, a Pittsburgh publisher, said, "I wanted to tell them that Vernon lived with dignity and that he died with dignity. I wanted to tell them that I think about him every day."

When he finally made contact with the family, however, French was stunned by Mrs. Carter's first question. "Is he really dead?" she asked. Because she had not actually seen his remains, her husband and she lived for 20 years with the hope it all had been a mistake. In fact, Mr. Carter was "really bothered" that

"Vernon might have been an MIA," said Mrs. Carter. French reflected, "For 20 years she lived with the hope that he'd get out of a cab one day. I didn't expect that."

Or take the case of Ensign James Charles whose plane crashed in Laos in 1968. Twenty-five years later, searchers found a medal from his church that had been given to him by his girlfriend. The Defense Department finally declared him dead. His brother acknowledged, "When they found that medal, it made us realize that he'd probably perished in the crash." His mother commented, "We've been betwixt and between for 25 years..."

Attempts to recover the remains of U.S. soldiers are confronted with numerous obstacles. Like Ensign Charles, most MIAs were pilots who were forced to crash or eject, often in the face of hostile fire. Many could have been lost at sea or in the dense jungle where organic matter decays quickly. At best, current investigations require very sophisticated scientific methods to identify remains.

The government of Vietnam has steadfastly denied holding any POWs. From 1975 through March 1990, there were 1,362 live sightings reported in Indochina. Of these, 1,248 have been resolved; 928 pertain to people who have since left Indochina and 328 have been proven to be fabrications. This left 114 sightings still unresolved.

The issue has been kept alive for many years by a great many conservative groups who have solicited contributions and lobbied Congress. Many of these groups have charged the U.S. also with having abandoned up to 25,000 U.S. GIs in Nazi POW camps to the Soviets after World War II and up to 8,000 U.S. POWs

The empty living quarters of American POWs in the Hanoi Hilton.

to the North Koreans after that war. Their allegations have been represented by Republican Senator Jesse Helms who, in 1990, issued a minority staff report of the Senate Foreign Relations Committee that claimed that "the U.S. government made a decision to abandon [several hundred] U.S. citizens still in custody of the Socialist Republic of Vietnam, Laos and Cambodia at the conclusion of U.S. involvement..."

The picture has been muddied further by occasional documents and photos promoted as proof of such claims. Always, however, experts have been able to demonstrate their inauthenticity.

In 1987, U.S. Secretary of State George Schultz dismissed as "fiction" and "rumor" any talk of an administration cover-up, stating, "We have created a large, sophisticated and top-priority intelligence effort as well as a full-scale diplomatic campaign to resolve the MIA issue." The League has criticized these other groups for "undermining the seriousness of the live prisoner issue" with their "misguided activism, fraudulent fundraising or political exploitation."

On April 21, 1991, Gen. John W. Vessey, Jr., on behalf of President Bush, issued a joint statement with Vietnamese Foreign Minister Nguyen Co Thach announcing the establishment of a temporary office in Hanoi to resolve cases of American soldiers who were listed as missing in action or taken prisoner during the Vietnam War. Vessey and Thach both "reaffirmed their governments' desires to normalize relations and agreed on the importance of continuing discussions to resolve differences between them."

In 1992, the U.S. established a Joint Task Force—Full Accounting, commanded by an Army major general with hundreds of employees at a cost of a hundred million dollars a year. In the first year, with the active cooperation of the Vietnamese, forty-eight remains were recovered. That comes to about $1.7 million per remain, a large sum, considering that the total U.S. contribution to Vietnam for prosthetic devices, assistance to displaced and orphaned children and disaster relief is only $2.75 million.

By April 1992, the total number of Americans MIA still being investigated had been reduced from 2,400 or so to a mere 244 "discrepancy cases." In January 1993, a report of the Senate Select Committee on POW/MIA Affairs concluded that there were "no grounds for encouragement" that any of the 244 men were alive.

At the end of 1993, searchers along the Vietnam-Laos border found wreckage and human remains from an American helicopter, shot down in 1990 with five men aboard. In 1994, there were five major search operations during which 100 Americans were allowed to roam through 15 of Vietnam's 53 provinces. Near the end of 1994, the last POW/MIA, Col. Charles Shelton, was declared dead. His son, John, commented, "It was for our own sanity, for our own futures. It's hung over us for so long."

After four years of studying Vietnamese documents and interviewing officials, Pentagon consultant Theodore Schweitzer concluded that Hanoi did not hold back prisoners in 1973, when the U.S. pulled out of the war.

On February 3, 1994, President Clinton announced the lifting of the U.S. trade embargo on Vietnam. This action had been preceded by a vote of Congress in which a large majority supported such action by the President.

The White House ceremony, attended by Congressional leaders and veterans who supported the President's actions, began a new era in U.S.-Vietnam relations.

In his speech the President spoke of the progress made on the MIA/POW issue and how he was "absolutely convinced" that lifting the embargo "offers the best way to resolve the fate of those who remain missing," and that the decision "will help to ensure the fullest possible accounting."

President Clinton's prediction has held true. In May 1995, the Vietnamese government turned over to a visiting U.S. presidential delegation more than 200 pages of analysis, maps and information from eyewitnesses. The Administration acknowledged that this was "new information" recently gathered and assembled by the Vietnamese. James Wold, deputy assistant secretary of defense for POW/MIA issues commented: "The level of cooperation has been very sustained. We are getting results."

Agent Orange Victims

Between 1962 and 1971 the U.S. conducted a defoliation program in Vietnam called Operation Ranch Hand. Twin-engine planes, trucks, river boats, even backpacks sprayed more than 19 million gallons of defoliants over about 4.5 million acres of South Vietnam. The objective of the program was to destroy the plant life that provided ambush cover and food supplies for the enemy. Herbicides also were used to clear the areas around the perimeters of American base camps, landing zones, waterways, and communication lines.

The effects were devastating. Today in Vietnam one sees waste-high scrub brush for hundreds of miles where once there were lush triple-canopy jungles. In some regions it may be several decades before natural vegetation reappears. Returning to their homeland after an earlier evacuation, the people of Bin Hoa were "terrified" to see that "not a blade of grass survived...the trunks of toppled coconut trees protruded along the edges of ditches, leafless bamboo stems stood pointing up at the sky....There were no barking dogs, no bird songs, not even the familiar chirping of insects. The soil was dead."

The most widely used herbicide in Vietnam was called Agent Orange after the color-coded stripe that wound around its 55-gallon steel drum container. Between 1965 and 1970, the U.S. military sprayed nearly twelve million gallons of Agent Orange in Vietnam. Dioxin, a contaminant produced as a by-product of making Agent Orange, is one of the most toxic substances known. U.S. troops in Vietnam operating in sprayed areas may have breathed it, inhaled it from burning brush, drunk or bathed in contaminated water or eaten contaminated food.

Most soldiers who served in Vietnam knew little or nothing about Agent Orange. One of them, Paul Ruetershan, found he had cancer in 1976. Friends called the clean-living Ruetershan a health nut. As he pondered the source of his fatal illness, he began to suspect it might be linked to the herbicides to which he had been exposed in Vietnam.

Ruetershan researched Agent Orange and became convinced that it was the cause of his disease. Before the end of 1977, he and his sister, Jane Dziedzic, formed Agent Orange Victims International. Ruetershan launched the campaign by filing a personal damage claim against the government.

Soon after, Ruetershan met Maude DeVictor, a Veterans Administration (V.A.) counselor in Chicago. DeVictor's own study of Agent Orange documented at least one hundred cases of possible dioxin poisoning. She shared her evidence with Ron DeYoung, a veteran's counselor at a Chicago college. They took the story to a Chicago CBS outlet, where news anchorman Bill Kurtis made an hour-long documentary called "Agent Orange, the Deadly Fog." Broadcast on March 23, 1978, it brought forth a flood of claims from veterans all over the country.

On December 14, 1978, at the age of twenty-eight, Paul Ruetershan died. On March 19, 1979, Vietnam veteran Michael Ryan and his wife Maureen, parents of a severely deformed child, joined nineteen other couples in an unprecedented class-action suit against the Dow Chemical Company and six other manufacturers of herbicides used in Vietnam. They asked that all Vietnam veterans and their families be certified as plaintiffs.

They wanted Agent Orange off the market, information provided about its dangers, a declaration from the companies that they had a responsibility to protect public health and safety, and a fund set up by the companies to award damages to victims.

Faced with the possibility of enormous damages, Dow filed suit against the U.S. government. The company claimed it informed the government about the dangers of dioxin in 1962 and tried to convince the government to use a safer herbicide. That suit was disallowed. However, the government did respond. In December 1979, the U.S. Congress directed the V.A. to study veterans exposed to Agent Orange. Submitted in 1981, the study was rejected as invalid by scientists in Congress' Office of Technology Assessment. Nevertheless, in November, Congress authorized the V.A. to provide medical care to any veteran they find may have been exposed to a toxic substance present in a herbicide.

Late in 1982, the original study proposal was turned over to the Center for Disease Control in Atlanta. In August 1984, the study, based on families in the area, was released. It found no evidence that Vietnam veterans had a greater risk than other men of fathering babies with major birth defects.

Congress directed the V.A. to conduct further studies

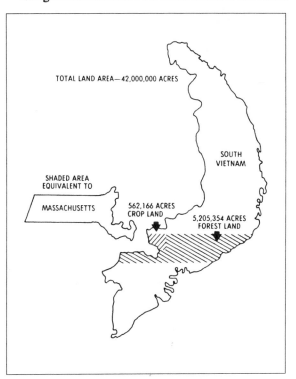

Estimated Equivalent
Area Treated with herbicides
in South Vietnam

271

"Crop dusting" Vietnam-style. Three U.S. UC 123 Providers spray defoliants over a jungle-covered area in South Vietnam.

Before and After: An unsprayed mangrove forest 60 miles from Saigon and the remains of another mangrove forest five years after spraying

as well as to establish a policy regarding claims. In August 1985, the V.A. issued a regulation recognizing only chloracne, a skin disease, as being connected to dioxin exposure. To qualify for help, a veteran had to prove the disease was evident within three months of his departure from Vietnam.

In November 1985, the Air Force released the third of three controversial studies of Ranch Hand personnel involved in the spraying missions in Vietnam. The report did not find any statistically significant differences in mortality between Ranch Hand crew members and non-exposed groups.

Despite the lack of conclusive evidence, the suit against the chemical companies was successful. The companies refused to concede any connection between the dioxin in their products and any illnesses or birth defects suffered by veterans and their children. Nevertheless, on May 7, 1984, they agreed to a pretrial settlement of $180 million to be set up in a fund to be administered later by the V.A. Monsanto Chemical explained that, regardless of the scientific evidence, the case had become a "rallying point" for everyone sympathetic to the "cause" of justice for Vietnam veterans. They chose to settle rather than contest an expensive suit in the full glare of "negative media attention" at the risk of "damage to Monsanto's reputation as a concerned, sensitive, socially responsible company."

Many veterans and their supporters reacted angrily to the settlement. For veterans who testified in New Jersey, "money was not the real issue. The issue was and remains concern for their children and families and the status of their health." The settlement was appealed.

By 1989, accumulation of interest had swelled the fund to $240 million and all appeals had been exhausted. Attorneys' fees and payments to Australian and New Zealand veterans reduced the fund to $222 million. Some $52 million was put into the Agent Orange Class Assistance Program for agencies that serve Vietnam veterans and their families. The balance of $170 million was shared by about 30,000 veterans and 18,000 survivor families considered eligible for the benefits; an average of less than $6,000 per veteran. Veterans' claims against the U.S. government still are being pursued.

What is at issue here? The evidence of the adverse health effects of dioxin on laboratory animals (like mice) includes cancer, skin disease, birth defects in offspring, suppression of the immune system functioning, and liver disorders. When Dr. Wilbur McNulty fed minute doses of dioxin to rhesus monkeys, he watched as they grew very quiet, lost their appetite, began losing weight, became thinner and weaker, and finally "just laid down and died."

Today there are many Vietnam veterans who suffer from skin rashes, numbness of limbs, kidney and liver dysfunctions, and various forms of cancer. There also are many vets who have fathered children with severe birth defects.

Proving scientifically that these diseases were caused specifically by exposure to the toxic herbicides used in Vietnam is another matter, however. There are many factors to consider here. One is that it is unethical to experiment with human beings; but animal tests are not a perfect model for human effects. Different species can react differently. Establishing the link between smoking and lung cancer with mice took daily doses of large quantities of the toxic substance over many years.

Another controversy concerns the adequacy of military records to identify veterans exposed to Agent Orange. In 1987, the Reagan administration canceled a $43 million Federal health study claiming it was scientifically impossible to establish the levels of exposure for individual veterans.

On August 9, 1990, after fourteen months of investigation, a House committee concluded that military records were adequate for such purpose and the Reagan administration had "obstructed" the study to escape billions of dollars in compensation claims. The American Legion and Vietnam Veterans of America filed separate lawsuits in Federal District Court against two Federal health agencies and the Department of Veterans Affairs for failing to complete the study.

Still another complicating factor is that many

Michael Jordan (left), 8, born with club hands, radial digits and missing fingers, and missing bones in his arms and wrists. His brother, Chad, 10, was born with similar defects. Their father served with the 1st Air Cav Division in Vietnam from 1968 to 1969.

Americans have been exposed to dioxin right here at home. Various agencies have sprayed dioxin over almost five million acres of U.S. forest, rangelands and rice plantations to kill harmful plants and weeds. Some of the residue has seeped into the water and food of populated areas like New York's Love Canal and Missouri's Times Beach, forcing evacuation. Thousands of studies of farm and industrial workers in the U.S. have found evidence of higher rates of nerve disorder and of severe birth defects in their children. Thus, even if researchers could establish exposure to dioxin in Vietnam, they also would have to control for exposure here at home in assessing the cause of a veteran's illness.

While scientists debate the finer points of research design, Vietnam veterans have come forth with their own very dramatic testimony. Jerry Strait served with the 101st Airborne Division in the heavily sprayed A Shau Valley. His daughter, Lori, was born with one hemisphere of her brain missing. Strait remembers walking through areas where "the trees are leafless, rotting, and from a distance appear petrified. The ground is littered with decaying jungle birds; on the surface of a slow moving stream, clusters of dead fish shimmer like giant buttons."

Strait now recalls giving less thought than he should have to the cysts that spread across his body, clinging to his back, legs, and arms like leeches; or to the headaches, dizziness, rashes, and stomach cramps that he and others in his platoon attributed to the heat.

Jim Wares, an Australian veteran, whose son was born with missing fingers and only a partial thumb on one hand, recalls spraying, but assumed it was to kill mosquitoes. Following the birth of his son, Wares began hearing stories of other Australian veterans whose children were born with deformed feet, cleft palates, missing limbs, holes in their hearts, partial brains, and skin rashes.

Spokespersons for the war-time manufacturers of Agent Orange dismiss such accounts as "anecdotal." Until more scientific studies are done, say the chemical companies, Vietnam veterans cannot demonstrate scientifically that their deformed offspring can be traced to Agent Orange exposure. The federal judge who heard pre-trial testimony in the Agent Orange lawsuit also was not convinced that there is sufficient proof to demonstrate a causal link between Vietnam veterans' exposure to Agent Orange and birth defects.

Since the trial, numerous studies have documented significantly higher rates of certain pathologies among Vietnam veterans than among comparison groups of Vietnam era veterans and non-veterans. A May 1990 review of the evidence persuaded V.A. Secretary Ed-

ward Derwinski to approve compensation for Vietnam veterans who suffer from non-Hodgkins lymphoma and soft-tissue-sarcomas. The latter disease affects about 1,100 veterans who will be eligible for compensation at a total cost of $8 million per year.

Soon after, Rep. Lane Evans (Democrat-IL), co-chair of Vietnam-era Veterans in Congress, introduced legislation, co-sponsored by 160 House members, to compensate veterans or their survivors for the above diseases plus melanoma and basal cell carcinoma. Evans stated: "The fight over methodology has gone on long enough. Veterans who suffer from problems because of exposure need help now. We must take action now to fulfill the promise our country has made."

A landmark 1994 study reconfirmed an association between Agent Orange, chloraine and three types of cancer: soft-tissue sarcoma, non-Hodgkins lymphoma and Hodgkins disease. With so much money at stake, however, it is safe to assume that challenges to scientific evidence in support of legal claims will continue. However, scientists working for the New Jersey Agent Orange Commission recently have developed a method that could fill an important gap in the evidence. The method involves testing blood samples to determine levels of dioxin in Vietnam veterans and a control group of men who did not serve in Vietnam.

Preliminary research indicates excessive levels of dioxin in blood samples from veterans who served in heavily sprayed regions of Vietnam. The Commission will be studying several specific groups, including infantry troops, river boat crews and women veterans. With this measure they might be able to better estimate the link between dioxin in the body and various forms of disease in humans. However, for most veterans there would still be the question of where their exposure to dioxin occurred.

It should go without saying that diseases possibly related to dioxin exposure are a major problem for the Vietnamese people also. Veterans recently returned from tours of Vietnam have described their visit to Ho Chi Minh City's Tu Dzu Hospital where jars of horribly deformed fetuses are stored. In Hanoi, senior officials in the Ministry of Health show slides of children with twisted faces and limbs.

This problem has been studied scientifically with very interesting results. Dr. Ton That Tung of Hanoi University and his colleagues have compared 836 Vietnamese soldiers, who fought in southern Vietnam where the spraying was done, to 236 soldiers who never served in the south. They found that the exposed group had a miscarriage/premature birth rate of 15.3 percent compared to 10.4 percent among those not exposed.

Moreover, 3.6 percent of all children fathered by the exposed group suffered congenital birth defects, compared with none in the non-exposed group.

Scientists returning from Vietnam report a serious "persistence of dioxin in the environment and the people." Of great scientific significance is the finding that levels of dioxin in adipose tissue and breast milk were "elevated" among people "potentially exposed in the south" where the spraying was done and even "lower" than in industrial countries among people in the north, never exposed to herbicide spraying. Dr. Arnold Schecter and others feel that this makes Vietnam the obvious site for the most rigorously controlled study of dioxin's relationship to disease in humans. The findings would not only serve the cause of Vietnam veterans, but the health education needs of all people.

Psychological Wounds

Most Vietnam veterans have achieved a successful re-adjustment to civilian life. Some 64 percent of Vietnam veterans used the G.I. Bill to further their education, as compared to 55 percent for World War II and 43 percent for Korea. Today, the Vietnam vet is as likely to have gone to college as men who did not serve. Their unemployment rate is no higher than the national average and they have a higher median income than their peers. Eight of ten are married, and almost that many are homeowners. Many veterans also have distinguished themselves in public service to the nation for which they fought. Today, Vietnam veterans serve in Congress and state legislatures, teach in schools and universities, and practice medicine and law.

There is a darker side, however. A 1988 study found that over the course of their lifetime, 31 percent of males and 27 percent of females who served in Vietnam will have suffered from various forms of "post-traumatic stress disorder" (PTSD). Estimates of Vietnam Veterans currently afflicted with PTSD vary between 500,000 and 800,000. Those who saw combat were much more likely to develop symptoms of PTSD. A poll of Vietnam veterans found that 77 percent saw fellow soldiers killed or wounded and 43 percent had themselves killed someone. According to a recent study, veterans in heavy combat were nine times more likely to have the disorder than those who served elsewhere. Vets in light or no combat were two to three times more likely to have the disorder than vets elsewhere.

The symptoms of PTSD are many: panic and para-

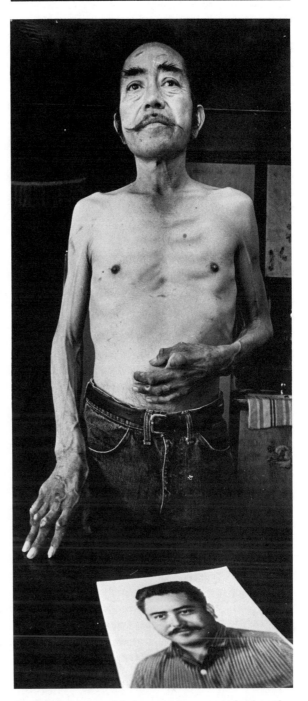

Daniel Salmon, a Vietnam veteran, worked on the construction of airstrips in defoliated jungle areas. Several years after his return to the U.S. he developed severe pancreatic problems, numbness and pains in his hands and legs, sores, headaches and weight loss. He could no longer work and after a series of amputations he died.

noia, chronic anxiety, nightmares or flashbacks to traumatic events, survivor guilt, depression, and emotional numbness. Many have trouble sleeping, some turn to drugs or alcohol for escape. A wife recalls one of her husband's frightening flashbacks:

"Oh Lord. He came home in July and the fair was in August. This was the first August after he came back, in 1967. At the end of the Hamburg Fair, at eleven o'clock at night, they lit up the fireworks....I was knocked down in the parking lot, thrown between two cars, and another woman got totally knocked to the ground. Gary tried to barricade her. I thought, Oh, my God, I'm going out with a crazy man, not realizing at the time that Vietnam was flashing back at him. He thought we were getting hit with mortars and he was trying to protect us."

Certainly, survivors of other wars have suffered from similar symptoms. In the past it might have been labeled shell-shock or battle fatigue. In his brilliant short story, "Soldier's Home," Ernest Hemingway introduces Krebs, a young shell-shocked veteran of World War I. Krebs idles away his days sitting on his front porch, passively watching ordinary people go about their everyday lives. He no longer talks about the war experiences that have made him unfit for such society. Hemingway explains, "At first Krebs...did not want to talk about the war at all. Later he felt the need to talk but no one wanted to hear about it. His town had heard too many atrocity stories to be thrilled by actualities. Krebs found that to be listened to at all he had to lie, and after he had done this twice he, too, had a reaction against the war and against talking about it."

Readers of Erich Maria Remarque's *All Quiet on the Western Front* easily can imagine why Krebs is no longer interested in looking for work or girls or church and why he lies awake at night to stave off the nightmares.

Audie Murphy, the most decorated American soldier in World War II, became a movie star and hero to millions. However, Murphy never recovered from his war experiences. An alcoholic who slept with a loaded German Walther automatic pistol under his pillow, Murphy was once asked how combat soldiers managed to survive a war. "I don't think they ever really do," Murphy replied.

The physical casualty rates for former U.S. wars and Vietnam are very similar. For various reasons, however, the rate of psychological impairment suffered by veterans of Vietnam is almost twice that of the other wars. This is due to the peculiar nature of the war itself.

Vietnam was not a conventional war in which uniformed troops battled over strategic territory. Progress was not measured in terms of how much land was gained or people "liberated" from the enemy. Ferocious battles were fought over what seemed to infantrymen like meaningless objectives. Many were killed or wounded for territory that was abandoned soon after, like the infamous Hamburger Hill. Summing up his frustration, one combat soldier demanded: "What am I doing here? We don't take any land. We don't give it back. We just mutilate bodies. What...are we doing here?"

Instead, progress in the war was measured by kill ratios and body counts with no provision for certifying identities. U.S. soldiers were disillusioned to discover that many of the people they were sent to save regarded them as the enemy, and that any of them at any time could bring sudden death. Many learned to shoot first and ask questions later. Lifton writes: "To a degree unparalleled in our earlier wars, combat in Vietnam involved the killing of women, children, and the elderly: some of whom were armed fighters, some of whom were killed inadvertently, and some of whom were killed in retaliation for deaths caused by their countrymen."

In therapy sessions Vietnam veterans go over and over the terrible anguish they felt in trying to distinguish civilians from combatants and their nagging guilt for inadvertently killing innocent people.

The system of twelve- and thirteen-month individual tours of duty further compounded the readjustment problems of veterans. New men, lacking combat experience, usually were shunned as unreliable. If they survived, they earned respect, but the composition of combat units was constantly changing. While attachments were made, the war was a lonely experience for many. Everyone kept complaints to themselves, denied their stress, and counted down the days until they could go home.

To make matters worse, soldiers were sent straight home without any opportunity to reflect on and integrate their war experiences. One day a soldier might be setting up a night ambush or burying a friend. Two or three days later he might be standing on a street corner back home trying to figure out how to fit back into "the world."

The most remarkable thing about PTSD is that it is a *delayed* stress reaction. Its symptoms do not erupt until six months and, sometimes, many years after returning home. Thus, many combat veterans were literally ticking time bombs of emotional stress waiting to go off.

The rising public opposition to the war contributed to lower enlistment rates, increasing reliance on the draft, lower morale among the troops, a deterioration of military discipline, racial tensions, and drug abuse.

Desertions doubled from 47,000 in 1967 to 89,000 in 1971. By 1971, 177 of every 1,000 American soldiers were listed as "absent without leave." By 1973, when the U.S. withdrew all combat forces in Vietnam, there were a total of about 1.5 million AWOLs and almost 600,000 less-than-honorable discharges.

The rate of desertion was higher in Vietnam than in Korea or World War II. However, only 24 soldiers were convicted of desertion under combat conditions. Remarkably, 20,000 fled after they had completed one or more full Vietnam tours and were no longer in physical danger. Many of these men can be assumed to have been suffering from PTSD.

Of course, the large majority of veterans came home with honorable discharges. And, according to a 1980 Harris Poll, more than three in four felt they received a "very friendly" reception from families and close friends upon their return from service. Vietnam veteran recognition days or weeks were held at different times over 1974-1985 under the Administrations of Presidents Nixon, Ford, Carter and Reagan. The dedication ceremony for the Vietnam Veteran Memorial in Washington in 1982 itself drew a crowd of 150,000.

None of this could change the facts that the war was especially brutal and a defeat for the U.S. The public was tired of the war and largely indifferent to the needs of veterans. According to a 1980 Harris Poll, less than half of Vietnam veterans felt that they got friendly receptions upon their return, as compared to three-fourths of veterans of earlier wars. In a 1979 national poll, 64 percent of the public agreed: "Returning Vietnam veterans were treated worse than veterans of earlier wars."

Rejection cut across political lines. Many in the peace movement recruited and supported anti-war veterans. However, after the news of war crimes became common, many others rejected veterans as "baby killers."

The Sound of Guns

1

The sparrow hawk drops to the cornfield
and in the same motion rises.
December's cold tightens around me,
a spider's web frozen white against the glass.

All day the sky is bleak with the coming snow,
the hours seem to pause like the bird
caught in an uplift of wind.
Out back the hay lies in rolls
the cows huddled together near the water troughs.

The highway runs past the brown fields
all the way west to Omaha, and just keeps going.
At the university in town
tight-lipped men tell me the war in Vietnam is over,
that my poems should deal with other things:
earth, fire, water, air.

Returning veterans probably found the rejection of older veterans more painful. The American Legion and Veterans of Foreign Wars included many World War II vets who fought in "the big one" and looked upon Vietnam vets as "losers" and "cry babies." Their spokespersons, prominent among whom was then Senator Dan Quayle, routinely argued against special benefits for Vietnam vets. Ron Kovic wrote about being spit on while protesting the war at the 1972 Republican National Convention and it became a metaphor for the feelings of abuse shared by many Vietnam vets. Very few actually had such an experience, but many felt like they had.

Even when they were accepted back, however, Vietnam veterans found that people did not want to hear about the war and had no understanding of the personal demons veterans had to battle. In the view of psychologist Edward Tick, this rejection contributed to a peculiar malady afflicting many vets. Tick calls it "Vietnam grief," a psychic suffering that is not shared by others and, thus, prolonged and unrelieved. Tick explains: "People can not grieve in a vacuum. In all religions and societies, mourners are supported by a grieving community. But the victims of Vietnam are left alone, unsupported by the American community at large in their grief. They are like the ancient Azazel, the scapegoat, that had the sins of its community tied around its neck and was then shooed out into the desert to die."

It must be acknowledged that U.S. veterans are not alone in their emotional suffering. Despite being able to celebrate victory, countless Vietnamese combatants also are haunted by images of death and destruction. For example, former Vietcong soldier, Ta Cong Tao, recalls: "We had many heavy losses. Six close friends of mine were killed. I look back and it is very painful....Sometimes at night I have bad dreams, dreams where I see my friends die—I see the sprayed

2
A friend told me once
that ours was a generation of love;
and I know he meant that this was a generation
that took too much, that turned from one death
to another.

I don't know what it is that's kept me going.
At nineteen I stood at night and watched
an airfield mortared. A plane that was to take
me home, burning; men running out of the flames.

Seven winters have slipped away,
the war still follows me.
Never in anything have I found
a way to throw off the dead.

—Gerald McCarthy

bomb, the shrapnel from the aircraft..." Another Vietnamese who has since immigrated to the U.S. complains that he finds it hard to sleep at night and "the roar of a helicopter can still leave me in tears."

One way of coping with stress in Vietnam was to take drugs. It must be acknowledged that drug use was common among youth not in Vietnam. More than half of all college students tried marijuana. In Vietnam, however, the drugs were stronger, cheaper and more available. By 1970, GIs could buy 96 percent pure heroin (compared to 3-10% back home) in a multidose vial for a mere two dollars. According to a 1971 survey, a shocking 29 percent of U.S. Army personnel in Vietnam used heroin or opium. More than half of them became addicted. A 1990 National Vietnam Veterans Readjustment Study found that 75 percent of men with PTSD developed problems with alcohol abuse and drug dependency.

The 1971 Harris Poll shows 26 percent of veterans using drugs after their return home, 325,000 of them heroin. In the first five years after their return, Vietnam veterans suffered a significantly higher rate (69%) of accidental poisonings, mostly drug overdoses, than U.S. soldiers assigned to other countries. Drug related deaths were especially high among those drafted and those whose jobs were in tactical or combat operations.

V.A. centers across the country have employed Vietnam veterans trained in counseling to work with PTSD victims. More radical therapies have been pioneered for those not cured by the standard approaches. In 1990, the William Joiner Center at the University of Massachusetts in Boston launched Operation Full Circle by taking twelve veterans back to the former battlefields of Vietnam. One of the vets reflected: "I'm hurting because I lost some good friends there. But I'm walking away. It's a release. Everything in my chest comes out. No more pain...."

In the state of Washington about 200 veterans have gone through a program that includes a cathartic helicopter flight into a simulated landing zone. Some are overcome by horrible flashbacks, but doctors and nurses express hope that the shock and grief stirred up by the experience will help the veterans move toward recovery. Others come away from the ride with a sense of triumph and hope. One said: "I was scared to death until I got on there. But I can do it now—I faced it."

In summer 1990, several Vietnam veterans were invited by 400 Oglala Sioux Indians to take part in the traditional ceremonies for returning warriors. The Sioux believe that pipe rituals, honoring dances, and vision quests mend the spirit of a warrior traumatized by battle. The tribe exalts him in public and welcomes him back into the life of the community. The rituals offered these Vietnam vets solace and a new sense of self-respect. After smoking the sacred pipe of the Oglala Sioux, Floyd Kitchen enjoyed one of his first nights of restful sleep after years of nightmares.

Other veterans have come to terms with their experience through Buddhist meditation. Near the end of 1989, Vietnamese monk Thich Nhat Hanh led a group of American vets and Vietnamese people through a traditional meditation schedule, including verse recitation and meditative walks. For Michael Stevens, the hours of silent meditation with the Vietnamese Buddhists dissolved his mistrust of the "enemy." He realized his own need to be absolved for the bombing raids he coordinated in Tay Ninh province when he was 22. Stevens asked for and received forgiveness from Sister Cao Ngoc Phuong, who had spent much of the 1960s trying to halt the very raids he had coordinated. "At last the Vietnamese in my heart/Is smiling," says a poem Stevens wrote at the end of the retreat.

Even the many who came back with no personal problems encountered obstacles to their readjustment.

"I RUSHED DOWN TO WELCOME YOU BACK!"

The average age of American soldiers in Vietnam was 19 years, as compared to 26 years for World War II. Most had no work experience or wife to welcome them home. To make matters worse, veterans came home to a troubled economy. For the first five years after the end of the war, Vietnam veterans averaged over 6.0 percent unemployment, about a third higher than the 4.5 percent for veterans after World War II. Unemployment for Vietnam veterans during the recession of the early 1980s averaged more than 8 percent. The rate for black vets was almost three times as high.

Some have responded to the above dilemmas— PTSD, drug addiction, unemployment and the rest—by committing suicide or turning to crime. All studies show the suicide rate for Vietnam veterans to be much higher than for non-veterans. One study finds that Vietnam-era veterans have a 65 percent higher rate of suicide than those who avoided the war. Another study finds that Vietnam-era veterans accounted for 15 percent of the patients, but 30 percent of the patient suicides in V.A. hospitals. Still another reveals that for the first five years after separation, Vietnam veterans had a suicide rate 72 percent higher than U.S. veterans assigned to other countries.

Finally, many were driven to crime. According to a 1979 Presidential Review Memorandum, approximately 29,000 Vietnam veterans were in state and federal prisons, 37,500 on parole, 250,000 under probation supervision, and 87,000 awaiting trial. This total of more than 400,000 in some trouble with the law is only a minority of the total who served. However, 20 percent (other estimates go as high as 24 %) is a very high rate of criminality when compared to other men in their age group.

Certainly, GIs were drawn disproportionately from the bottom ranks of society where limited economic opportunity and police and judicial discrimination contributed to criminal records. For some, however, the resort to crime was a new turn in life, prompted by the difficulties of fitting back into society after the war. Author Robert Mason shares his story:

"The car broke down and the bills began to pile up. For the time I had spent writing, I got four rejections. What did the desperate man do? I can tell you that I was arrested in January 1981, charged with smuggling marijuana into the country. In August 1981, I was found guilty of possession and sentenced to five years in a minimum security prison. No one is more shocked than I."

For others, criminal acts can be traced to the emotional scars from the war. Psychologists Hendin and Haas state: "Our work supports the observation of others that antisocial, criminal acts that are not the result of preexisting criminality are one of the major deviations through which traumatic stress may be manifested."

Describing the effects of the Vietnam War on one veteran who later turned to crime and was sentenced to two-to-six years for bank robbery, the authors wrote: "Warren's stress disorder appeared to be centered on the overwhelming fear he had managed to repress in combat, and that he had subsequently expressed in his nightmares and reliving experiences....He was absorbed with the death of friends in combat, Vietnamese civilians, enemy soldiers, and his own sense of having died...."

Thankfully, the 1970s stereotype of the Vietnam veteran as a drug-crazed, psychotic killer seems to be gone. A more realistic and usually positive image has rightfully taken its place. However, like all stereotypes, that one contained some truth. About 20 percent of white Vietnam veterans and 40 percent of black veterans are currently classified as "stressed" —more than eighteen years after the last American troops were withdrawn from Vietnam. An estimated 35 percent of the nation's homeless population are Vietnam Veterans. Between 150-250 thousand vets are homeless on any given night and at least twice that many at some time during the year. In 70-90 percent of these cases, psychiatric illness and drug abuse preceded the situation. It is an ugly truth, but one for which our nation needs to accept responsibility. Many veterans are still fighting the war and desperately need our help.

Other legal and psychological casualties of the war include the 3,200 young men imprisoned because they refused to participate in the war. Many were subjected to beatings, forcible rape, and solitary confinement. There also were about 100,000 youth who chose exile in Canada and elsewhere. By the time the war ended, between 750,000 and two million young Americans were in some form of legal jeopardy because of their resistance to the war.

Economic Costs

Vietnam was the second most expensive war in American history. The government estimates direct military expenditures at $168 billion. Other costs such as payments to other countries providing military support, interest on debts incurred by the government to subsidize the war, and payments for veterans' benefits have ballooned this figure up to between one and two *trillion* 1996 dollars.

As with all wars, these costs will continue to grow through the years. Payments of veterans benefits can extend for at least 120 years. It takes an average of 38 years to cover half of the costs. The U.S. government still pays out $12 billion a year to veterans of World War II. In fact, the U.S. federal budget for 1996 includes about $260 billion, almost a fourth of the total, just for past wars. Veterans benefits amount to $30 billion and interest on the national debt due to military borrowing and spending accounts for the rest. The Persian Gulf War will increase these figures by hundreds of billions of dollars in the years ahead.

There presently are almost half a million active compensation cases from Vietnam. The V.A. has paid out about $150 billion to date and provides an additional $7 billion or so every year for compensation, loan guaranties, educational assistance, vocational rehabilitation, and medical services. Agent Orange-related diseases could add billions more to this total.

A less visible but no less significant cost of the war was the damage done to the U.S. economy. As the war escalated, many in the business world became concerned about its long-term effects. Louis Lundborg, Chairman of the Board of the Bank of America, gravely informed the Senate Foreign Relations Committee: "The escalation of the war in Vietnam has seriously distorted the American economy, has inflamed inflationary pressures, has drained resources that are desperately needed to overcome serious domestic problems confronting our country, and has dampened the rate of growth of profits on both a before and after-tax base."

As many leading economists explained, price inflation is basically a function of how much money is competing for how many goods. Millions of Americans were employed directly in the war effort. This helped keep employment high, but without contributing to the production of consumer goods. As more wages competed for what goods there were, prices naturally went up. As prices rose, labor began demanding higher wages.

The result was a spiral of inflation that lasted until the recession of 1982. Inflation averaged about 1.3 percent per year over 1960-65, jumped to 2.9 percent over 1966-67, 4.2 percent for 1968, 5.4 percent for 1969, and 5.9 percent for 1970. Of course, federal spending on human service programs also contributed to inflationary pressures. Such spending increased greatly under President Johnson's "war on poverty." To curb this trend, Johnson would have had to raise taxes. However, he refused to do so for fear of provoking opposition to the war.

In order to control the inflation, the Federal Reserve Bank raised interest rates on loans, making it harder for people to borrow for houses and cars. This led to a 750,000 a year decline in new housing construction and a decline in new car sales. This, in turn, led to layoffs in manufacturing and increased pressure on human services. Both the U.S. budget deficit and balance of payments deficit grew rapidly.

Few people can comprehend the magnitude of the figures we are discussing. To give you some idea, however, consider these reflections on the alternative uses to which the money spent on the war might have been put. In 1972, Lekachman suggested that, just for the annual direct cost of the war at the time, the government could have rehabilitated all urban slum housing in this country, creating many construction jobs in the process. Such an investment would have helped much to alleviate the rising problem of the homeless we face today. Two years earlier, Melman used roughly the same rate of war spending and calculated:

1. Each month of the war could have financed the complete training of over 100,000 scientists.

2. Each month of the war could have financed the annual food bill for ending hunger among 10 million Americans.

3. Each month of the war could have paid the full year's cost of state and local police in every state of the union.

4. The annual cost of the Vietnam war could have doubled the Social Security benefits paid to 20 million Americans.

Of course, no one is saying that any money not spent on the Vietnam War would have or even should have been spent on the above social programs. However, such comparisons do make the trade-offs in our overall national security even more concrete for leaders and citizens.

Social and Political Costs

For many Americans the early 1960s were a time of hope. Throughout the south blacks were challenging segregation and demanding their right to vote. Congress passed major Civil Rights and Voting Rights bills; President Johnson declared a "war on poverty"; and the apathetic 1950s seemed to be giving way to a period of social and political progress. Young, idealistic Americans were leading the way.

Thirty years later it seems clear that national pride was another casualty of Vietnam. Assessing the evidence of public opinion polls, Lipset and Schneider report that, between 1966 and 1976, every major institution in American life suffered a loss of public esteem. The biggest losses occurred during the peak years of the war, 1966-1971. This includes all fifty corporations and twenty-five industries studied.

The biggest loser was the government—no longer perceived as an instrument of progress, but rather as bloated and corrupt. The proportion of Americans with "a great deal of confidence" in the executive branch of the Federal Government plummeted from 41 percent in 1966, to 23 percent in 1971, to 11 percent in 1976. "Great confidence" in the Congress fell from 42 percent in 1966 to 9 percent in 1976; "great confidence" in the military from 62 percent in 1966 to 23 percent in 1976. Pollster Louis Harris found that, by the end of 1971, the vast majority of Americans agreed that politicians make false promises, are not elected or appointed on the basis of merit, are in politics to make money for themselves, and take graft.

Other Harris surveys have produced more evidence of this greater alienation from government leaders. For example, those agreeing that the people running the country don't really care what happens to the individual citizen almost doubled, from 26 percent in 1966 to 50 percent in 1972. Those agreeing that what they think "doesn't count any more" rose from 37 percent in 1966 to 53 percent in 1972.

Similar results have been obtained by the Institute for Survey Research (ISR) of the University of Michigan. ISR researchers found a drastic decline in the number of Americans who said they could trust the government in Washington to do what is right "always" or "most of the time"—from 76 percent in 1964, to 61 percent in 1968, to 37 percent in 1974. The proportion believing the government is getting "too powerful for the good of the country and the individual person" rose from 44 percent in 1966, to 55 percent in 1968, to 69 percent in 1976. Those agreeing that the government wastes tax money soared from 46 percent in 1958, to 61 percent in 1968, to 80 percent in 1978.

Combat Marine veteran and writer W.D. Ehrhart spoke for many when he said, "For me the legacy of the Vietnam War is that I will never, never believe my government again." Unfortunately, such sentiments did not lead to closer public scrutiny of its representatives. On the contrary, a cynical citizenry seemed to lower its standards for leaders and to withdraw its participation in electoral politics leaving a post-Vietnam legacy of low voter turnout and mediocre officials.

Loss of U.S. Prestige in the World

In January 1966, Assistant Secretary of Defense, John McNaughton, stated, "The present U.S. objective in Vietnam is to avoid humiliation...to preserve our reputation as a guarantor, and thus to preserve our effectiveness in the rest of the world." President Johnson spoke frequently of not losing face in Vietnam and President Nixon sought "peace with honor." It is very ironic, then, that staying the course in America's longest war should lead to a significant loss of U.S. standing in the world community. However, that is exactly what happened.

In 1973, George Gallup polled 341 leaders from 70 different nations concerning their perceptions of the U.S. in Vietnam. Among those polled were public officials, diplomats, bankers, corporate executives, physicians, attorneys, educators, and media executives. The findings were:

86 percent thought the U.S. had lost prestige by its involvement in Vietnam;

66 percent thought the U.S. military intervention in Vietnam had been a mistake;

55 percent did not think communism had suffered a setback in Southeast Asia as a result of the war. Only 26 percent thought it had;

59 percent thought the U.S. should help to rebuild North Vietnam. Only 24 percent were opposed.

World leaders clearly were critical of the refusal of the U.S. and its client in South Vietnam to abide by the provisions of the Geneva Agreement. Many were provoked by the resort to force, especially when it reached such colossal dimensions. And the failure of such firepower to subdue a guerrilla force in a small, backward nation further undermined U.S. prestige world wide.

Destruction of Vietnam

In addition to the massive defoliation program already discussed, the U.S. military exploded more than fifteen million tons of bombs and ground munitions in Vietnam, a country less than half the size of the state of Texas. This represented four times the total dropped by the U.S. in all theaters of war in World War II and is equivalent in destructive force to about 600 Hiroshima-type bombs. Large areas of Vietnam today are pockmarked by more than twenty million craters. Hundreds of farmers still are being killed by unexploded ordnance left behind.

According to Arthur Westing, an American scientist whose research is focused on Vietnam, the bombing destroyed many towns and cities and all five of North Vietnam's industrial centers. All 29 provincial capitals were bombed, 12 of them razed to the ground. About 96 of the 116 district capitals were bombed, 51 of them razed. And about 2,700 of the roughly 4,000 rural villages were bombed, 300 of them razed. All railway and highway bridges were destroyed. Hundreds of public buildings were left in ruins. Hundreds of water conservancy works and irrigation dikes and countless acres of farmland were destroyed.

Chomsky and Herman's assessment of the destruction includes 533 community health centers, 94 district hospitals, 28 provincial hospitals, and 24 research institutes. Vietnamese authorities claim 3,000 schools and colleges, 350 hospitals, and 1,500 village infirmaries and maternity homes.

As the bombing and ground fighting escalated, Vietnamese cities swelled with beggars, prostitutes, thieves, drug addicts, and displaced peasants. The population of Saigon alone jumped from the pre-war figure of about one million to 4.2 million, all crowded into a city French architects designed to accommodate 500,000.

When the North Vietnamese Army entered Saigon in 1975, they found millions of refugees huddled in shacks built on stilts over rivers that had become open sewers. Along the shoulders of roads and highways were hundreds of thousands of refugees in more shacks, built from cardboard, tin cans and scrap metal left behind by departing Americans. Forced to eke out a living on the black market, demoralized by years of government corruption, and traumatized by the relentless death and destruction, these refugees would somehow have to be reintegrated into Vietnamese society.

Reconstruction was burdened further by the millions of South Vietnamese, malnourished and forced to live without proper sanitation, who were suffering

A group of Vietnamese orphans being evacuated from Saigon.

from malaria, tuberculosis, leprosy, cholera, bubonic plague, poliomyelitis, venereal diseases, and psychiatric disorders.

The first order of business for the new communist government was to establish political control over the population. The bloodbath, long predicted by conservatives, did not occur. Instead, about 400,000 South Vietnamese soldiers, officers, diplomats and professionals were incarcerated in a network of about 100 "re-education camps." Most enlisted men were kept a few weeks while up to 40,000 officers and government officials stayed in camp for years. As late as 1985, more than 6,000 political prisoners were being held.

By 1988, almost all prisoners were released. In July 1988, Vietnam said it would allow 11,000 former re-education camp inmates and 40,000 of their relatives to emigrate to the United States. Former South Vietnamese Gen. Nguyen Vinh Nghi was one of those not released until 1988. In a 1989 interview, Nghi recalled: "For seven, eight hours a day we go into the forest and cut wood. Every day....We had to prepare for 15 lectures, discussions with officers and representatives of the Ministry of Defense. We talked mostly about...what was wrong with our side, what was right about communism....They were not cruel, not vindictive. I think they honestly tried to understand us."

In the last year of the war, U.S. aid to South Vietnam was $2.2 billion. It paid for an army of more than a million men, the wages of most of the 400,000 civil servants and the import of rice, gasoline, fertilizer and other commodities. When this aid ended, the economy of the South collapsed. To make matters worse, the war had turned Vietnam from a rice-exporting to a rice-importing nation.

After the war, the new government instituted a five-year plan to achieve self-sufficiency in food and to establish an industrial base. At first, it sought to reduce its dependence on the U.S.S.R. and to forge new ties to the West.

Hanoi rejected the Soviet proposal for an Asian security organization and membership in the Soviet Comecon trade system. Instead, it joined the U.S. controlled World Bank, International Monetary Fund and Asian Development Bank. It actively invited foreign investment on relatively generous terms, even agreeing to waive the almost five billion dollars in reparations pledged by President Nixon in 1973.

The U.S responded by establishing an economic embargo on trade with Vietnam. The U.S. Commerce Department imposed the most stringent controls possible on exports to Vietnam. The U.S. classified Vietnam a "Category Z" country, meaning that all U.S.

A small Vietnamese girl carrying her younger brother to safety.

exports have to be licensed by the government. These controls were stricter than those applied to the Soviet Union or Cuba. In June 1977, the U.S. Senate voted 56 to 22 to instruct U.S. representatives in international assistance organizations to vote against any aid to Indochina. In fact, the U.S. was the only one of 141 United Nations member countries to reject a resolution to establish priority economic assistance to Vietnam.

As if things weren't bad enough, the U.S. State Department also blocked private relief programs for Vietnam. For example, in 1981, the State Department rejected an application for the Mennonite Central Committee to ship 250 tons of wheat flour from Kansas to Vietnam. The U.S. also organized cancellation of a $30 million World Bank loan and stopped a $5 million World Food Program project to build dams in Vietnam to reduce flooding and help with irrigation.

In spring 1977, a severe drought caused critical food shortages. Cut off from the West, still challenged by China, and economically in crisis, Vietnam turned to the Soviet Union. In 1978, the government signed a Treaty of Friendship and Cooperation with the U.S.S.R. After that, the Soviets provided about $1 billion a year. However, most of the aid consisted of long-term, low-interest loans for military equipment. In return, Vietnam permitted the Soviets to build facilities for naval aircraft and communications and intelligence gathering.

The new government in Hanoi sought to promote

progress in the areas of health, education and welfare. Drug addiction and prostitution were all but eliminated. Although one could still see street beggars in some cities, very few were homeless.

Under the communists in the north, virtually the entire urban population and up to 80 percent of rural Vietnamese had easy access to primary health care. Attempts to introduce this system to the south were only partially successful. Money was tight. More affluent provinces established their own hospitals and funding arrangements while others went without. A black market in pharmaceuticals emerged along with a gap in the quality of health care available in the city and rural areas, and between rich and poor. As recently as 1985, only 40 percent of the people in the Mekong delta had access to a health center.

In the south, some 2,500 private schools were closed or converted to state use. By 1989, only three of five primary school children were completing fifth grade. Although international agencies credit Vietnam with a high rate of literacy, in 1989 the government acknowledged that more than 8 million adults still could not

read and write. While these are not unusual statistics for a developing country, they still represent obstacles to future prosperity.

Progress was even slower on the economic front. Vietnam's first five- year plan failed miserably. The shortfall in hoped for international assistance hurt. However, the government made matters worse with its rigid handling of the economy. It suppressed wholesalers and free market activity and over-collectivized agriculture. Leaders also were biased against professional management techniques, underestimating the complex demands of running a national economy.

In 1986, the Sixth Communist Party Congress endorsed a liberal policy of economic renovation called "doi moi." The policy has moved Vietnam a long way toward a market economy and private enterprise. The state cut its subsidies to state-owned enterprises and to prices on everything except electricity, transportation and rents. Almost 5,000 of Vietnam's 12,000 state-owned enterprises already have been privatized.

The government reformed its legal system to protect foreign investment and overhauled its taxation system.

1/29/74

'Oh, when they come to your rescue, you'll know it.'

Don Wright in the Miami News

As smuggling and corruption increased, the government devised plans to combat it.

The currency was steadily devalued until the black market was eliminated. Inflation, which soared at about 800 percent as recently as 1988, was reduced to a little over 5 percent by 1993. As a result, citizens have stopped hoarding gold and are now selling it and depositing the money in banks or making investments.

Under the new farm policy, formerly collectivized land is redistributed to individual families on long-term contracts. The families pay a tax to the state (about 13%), but are allowed to keep the rice for themselves or sell it at the best price. Less than one-third of the land in the south is still collectivized. Each province is free to determine its own modes of development and even to enter into its own trade and investment relations. Party General Secretary Nguyen Van Linh acknowledges that this "is not the old definition of equality. For the person who is more skillful and works harder to get more money—this is the correct definition of equality."

Appointed to his post in January 1988, Linh enlisted the help of Nguyen Xuan Oanh, a former economist at the International Monetary Fund and leader of the South Vietnamese government in the mid-1960s. In 1989, for the first time since the war, there was a surplus of rice. Vietnam exported a million and a half tons of rice, making it the third largest world supplier, after the U.S. and Thailand. Free markets now flourish in the major cities; and restaurants, cafes, and private shops featuring imported and domestic goods have sprung up everywhere.

In 1991 Vietnam lost Soviet aid and trade worth $800 million or 7 percent of its GNP. Well over 100,000 Vietnamese workers and students were sent back from the former communist countries of Eastern Europe. Still, Vietnam showed a GNP growth rate of 6-8 percent.

Despite such progress in national production, problems remain. The infrastructure of roads, bridges, air fields, and the like is barely developed and in disrepair. External debt totals $8.6 billion and payments are a drain on the economy. International aid loans have required cutbacks in public sector spending so health care and education have suffered. The government claims an unemployment rate of 16-20 percent, but some observers suspect it might be as much as twice that high. The per capita annual income is about $200 U.S. About sixty Vietnamese a day die of starvation and one in ten children die of gastroenteritis brought on by malnutrition. Oanh says the country is seeking "a better way" than the "too liberal" capitalist economy of

the former South Vietnam and the previously "too austere" communist economy of North Vietnam. While the long term prospects are good that Vietnam might become another "Asian tiger," the road there will be painful for many.

Obstacles to Reconcilliation

In addition to resolution of the MIA question, the other obstacle to the normalization of relations between the U.S. and Vietnam was that of Cambodia. The story of Cambodia is terrible and sad. Cambodian leader, Prince Norodom Sihanouk, was overthrown in a *coup d'état* by American-backed Lon Nol in 1970.

The war then came to Cambodia in full force. By 1975, when Lon Nol was defeated by the communist Khmer Rouge army, some two million refugees had been driven into the capital city of Phnom Penh, principally by U.S. bombing. Headed by the infamous Pol Pot, the Khmer Rouge forced virtually the entire population back to the countryside where they suffered starvation and slaughter. Between one and two million people died under Khmer Rouge tyranny.

At the same time, the Khmer Rouge launched a series of raids across the border into Vietnam. On December 25, 1978, Vietnam invaded Cambodia and drove out Pol Pot's forces. The Vietnamese installed the government of Heng Samrin, a regime both friendly to Vietnam and preferred by most Cambodians to the murderous Pol Pot. They named the country The People's Republic of Kampuchea.

At the encouragement of President Carter's National Security Advisor, Zbigniew Brzenzinski, the People's Republic of China offered exile to Pol Pot and decided to "teach Vietnam a lesson." In February 1979, the Chinese invaded Vietnam. They were driven back, losing 15,000 troops in the brief struggle. However, the invasion by their traditional enemy triggered reprisals against ethnic Chinese living in Vietnam. Several hundred thousand "Boat People" were forced to flee the country.

In 1979, the United States officially recognized the out-of-power Khmer Rouge as the legitimate government of Cambodia, still entitled to the Cambodian seat in the United Nations. At the time there were three guerrilla groups fighting the Vietnamese-installed government in Cambodia: the Khmer Rouge, and two non-communist groups.

In June 1982, under pressure from China and the

U.S., the three Cambodian guerrilla factions formed a coalition government in exile with Prince Sihanouk (former Cambodian King) as president, Khieu Samphan of the Khmer Rouge as vice president and Son Sann of the Khmer People's National Liberation Front as prime minister.

Through the decade the Khmer Rouge army received about $100 million a year from China and grew to between 30,000 and 40,000 fighters. The other two groups received about $15 million annually from the U.S. and fielded a force almost as large, but not nearly as well trained or equipped. They were contained by a Vietnamese occupation force of about 140,000 troops.

Under tremendous political and economic pressure, Vietnam finally decided to remove its forces from Cambodia. From May 1988 to September 1989, all troops were withdrawn, leaving the Hun Sen government to defend itself with an army of 60,000-100,000 men. In a short time it became apparent that U.S. assistance was passing through its clients to the Khmer Rouge which dominated the coalition and began making military gains against the government.

In January 1990, the five permanent members of the United Nations security council drafted a peace plan calling for a neutral United Nations-supervised administration to run Cambodia while elections were organized. In June 1990, Senate majority leader George Mitchell (Democrat-ME) proposed to President Bush that the U.S. open talks with the Hun Sen Government and ease restrictions on development and humanitarian aid to Cambodia.

Continued news of battlefield victories by the Khmer Rouge provoked protests by humanitarian groups and pressure by Congress on the Bush administration to reform its policy. On July 19, 1990, the administration withdrew its diplomatic recognition of the rebel coalition in the United Nations and opened up a direct dialogue with the Hun Sen government.

On September 11, 1990, the four warring Cambodian factions agreed on the formation and composition of an all-party national leadership, called the Supreme National Council, and formally committed themselves to a United Nations framework for a comprehensive peace settlement in Cambodia. All parties agreed to ask Prince Sihanouk to become chairman.

The Hun Sen government objected to the original plan for a U.N. supervised disarmament and national election because it neither condemned the past genocidal violence of the Khmer Rouge nor prevented them from playing a role in a future government. The U.S. finally was persuaded to this view.

In 1993, the elections were held and the FUNC-INPEC Party, representing the U.S. backed "non-communist resistance," won 58 seats to the CPP's 52. After an absence of almost a quarter of a century, now King Norodun Sihanouk was back in charge.

Problems remain, however. Unwilling to accept their outsider role, the Khmer Rouge have committed massacres, including an "ethnic cleansing" campaign against ethnic Vietnamese in Cambodia which forced 30,000 to flee their homes. Efforts by Sihanouk's son, FUNCINPEC leader Norodun Ranavidh, to negotiate a cease-fire with the Khmer Rouge failed. Fighting between the rebels and government forces goes on. Accused of corruption, the government is seeking to reform its military. Early in 1995, in a promising development, the U.S. State Department announced: "We do not rule out lethal assistance to the Cambodian military in the future." While Cambodia no longer remains an issue dividing the U.S. and Vietnam, peace in that troubled country remains elusive.

Healing And Reconciliation

In 1972, Phan Thi Kim Phuc was a nine-year-old screaming with pain and running in terror from her napalm-bombed South Vietnamese village. She also was the subject of one of the most famous photographs of the war. She recalls: "There was terrible heat. I was running, running, running away. I tore off my burning clothes. But the burning didn't stop."

In 1989, Ms. Phuc, a twenty-six year-old pharmacology student in Cuba, made a goodwill visit to the United States so that "Americans can meet the girl in the photo." Today she bears no ill feelings: "If I ever see those pilots who dropped the bombs on me, or any American pilots, I would say to them, 'The war is over.' The past is the past. I would ask those pilots what they can do to bring us together."

In late 1990, Nguyen Ngoc Hung, a North Vietnamese language professor and former Vietcong soldier, also toured several cities in the U.S. Meeting in Pittsburgh, Pennsylvania, with American veterans of the Vietnam war, Hung reflected: "When I see American veterans crying at the Vietnam memorial, I know the pains are still there. And I know that the pains are still there among the Vietnamese people, too. Fifteen years is a long time. But we cannot wait any longer. It is time to put the war behind us and move forward."

In recent years, many American veterans of the war have made parallel gestures of reconciliation. In 1988,

Gene Spanos and six of his buddies from the 11th Engineers went back to Vietnam to help the Vietnamese remove mines that the GIs had laid during the war. Spanos explained: "After other wars it was always the practice to go in with maps and records and pinpoint where the mine fields were and have them removed. We are all fathers now, and we see no point in the mines killing little kids who happen to stray off a path and step on them." Spanos expressed the hope that his mission was "the beginning of reconciliation between two governments who've been at odds for a long time."

That same year Fredy Champagne launched the Veterans Vietnam Restoration Project. Eighty veterans from around the country signed up to join construction teams of a dozen men each to spend two months building medical clinics in Vietnam. The first clinic was built in Vung Tau. The Vietnamese were most hospitable and invited the veterans to build a similar clinic near Hanoi. Champagne acknowledged that Vietnam does not need more medical clinics. Many now lie empty for lack of equipment and supplies. Champagne says the value of the project is "symbolic" of the veterans' desires to heal their own wounds from the war and to promote normalization of relations between the U.S. and Vietnam.

Probably the most impressive program to date is run by the Vietnam Veterans of America Foundation. The Foundation promotes a political campaign to outlaw the production, stockpiling, trade and use of land mines. In Cambodia alone, there are over 30,000 amputees who have been victims of land mines. In recent years the Foundation also has organized the production and distribution of an inexpensive prosthetic device to aid such victims as well as a children's orthotics program in Hanoi to help those disabled by polio, birth defects and land mines.

Since 1987, the U.S. State Department has demonstrated more willingness to permit such humanitarian relief for Vietnam. In September 1987, the State Department announced a decision to encourage and facilitate medical aid to Vietnam, especially prosthetic devices for amputees. In February 1989, seven plastic surgeons and two other physicians became the first U.S. doctors to work in Vietnam since the war. Sponsored by "Operation Smile" of Norfolk, Virginia, the doctors operated successfully on 101 children who suffered mouth deformities.

Cultural exchanges between the two countries also are increasing. The U.S.-Indochina Reconciliation Project and the Council on International Educational Exchange have sponsored several tours of American educators to visit with colleagues in Vietnam. The Social Science Research Council has instituted programs for American scholars to do research in Vietnam.

In May 1990, the European Parliament passed a resolution demanding that the European Community normalize diplomatic relations with Hanoi and provide development aid to Vietnam "without delay." The resolution also "regretted [that] the U.S. government maintains its hostile attitude toward Vietnam" so long after the war. It called for the U.S. administration "to adopt a more reasonable attitude."

That same month at a meeting of the Asia-Pacific Council of American Chambers of Commerce, businessmen voted to support an immediate removal of restrictions on U.S. trade and investment in Vietnam.

In 1988, Sen. John McCain (Republican-AZ), a former POW, introduced a nonbinding resolution that called on the Reagan administration to set up an interest section in another embassy in Hanoi as a precursor to diplomatic ties. The lifting of the trade embargo on Vietnam early in 1994 was a major milestone in the movement toward reconciliation.

By summer 1994, the U.S. and Vietnam announced an agreement for opening diplomatic missions in each other's capital. U.S. investment in Vietnam had soared from only a few million to $78 million. However, this still lagged far behind that of other countries, especially France, Japan and the United Kingdom.

On January 11, 1995, President Clinton extended full diplomatic relations to Vietnam. The decision was opposed by Republican Senators Dole and Helms, the American Legion, POW lobby and others. However, most prominent Vietnam veterans in Congress supported the President, who stated, "Let the future be our destination. This moment offers us the opportunity to bind up our own wounds. They have resisted time for too long"

Less than three weeks later the U.S. and Vietnam agreed to exchange diplomatic missions with the U.S. Vietnamese office to be established in the old South Vietnamese embassy, abandoned in May 1975.

By July 1995 Vietnam had joined the Association for Southeast Asian Nations in a bold move toward free trade and collective security with capitalist partners Brunei, Indonesia, Malaysia, the Philippines, Singapore and Thailand. Finally, on August 7, 1995, the American flag was raised over the new U.S. Embassy in Vietnam symbolizing the reconciliation between these two former enemies. While some conservatives in the U.S. vowed to obstruct closer relations, Vietnam appeared eager to learn how soon they could get Most-Favored Nation trade status that would allow them to export to the United States at the lowest possible tariffs and allow U.S. businesses to invest freely in Vietnam. This left only Laos as the last country involved in the Indochina War to remain excluded from U.S. economic and trade ties in the region.

As this Chapter makes clear, the wounds of war were many in Vietnam and in the U.S. Millions of lives were destroyed and the social, political, and economic losses to both countries were deep and lasting. It is little wonder that some call it "the war nobody won."

Special Insert: Persian Gulf War Costs

Despite what looked like a quick and easy victory for U.S. troops in the Gulf there have been numerous reports of psychological disorder and of toxic poisoning, including such symptoms as fatigue, painful muscles and joints, bleeding gums, skin rashes, short-term memory loss and hair loss. In May 1995 the Pentagon announced a $5 million grant program to promote research into these ailments.

During the mere six weeks of the 1991 Persian Gulf War, U.S. allied pilots flew over 100,000 missions and dropped almost 90,000 tons of bombs (as compared to 7.5 million tons in Vietnam). Most bombs had an accuracy rating of only 25 percent; 70 percent missed their targets. The much publicized laser-guided "smart bombs" constituted only 7 percent of all U.S. explosives dropped in Iraq and Kuwait and only 60 percent of them hit their targets. Intelligence sources cited by NBC News estimated more than 150,000 Iraqi soldiers killed. Civilian casualties, expected to number in the tens of thousands, still are unknown. There were 182 allied combat deaths, including 121 Americans.

In retaliation, Iraqi soldiers committed acts of sabotage against Kuwait's oil wells, petroleum gathering centers, and booster stations. The two reports printed below detail some of the terrible costs to the region of U.S. bombing and Iraqi sabotage.

Discussion Questions

1. What are the criteria for including a name on the Vietnam War Memorial? Do you agree with these criteria? If so, why; if not, what criteria would you use instead?

2. What are the characteristics of Post-traumatic Stress Disorder? Why might this be more common after the Vietnam War than after other wars the U.S. has fought?

3. What did Audie Murphy mean when he stated that he didn't think combat soldiers ever really do survive a war? What evidence can you give that this was true for many Vietnam era soldiers?

4. What factors may have contributed to the fact that the rate of psychological impairment for Vietnam vets is nearly twice that of other wars?

5. What factors do you think have contributed to the alarmingly high suicide and crime rates of Vietnam vets? What solutions would you suggest for these problems?

6. In what specific ways did the Vietnam War affect the U.S. economy? Of those impacts, which were the most serious and why?

7. The reading presents several ways in which the money spent on the Vietnam War might have been spent on different social programs at home. Would spending on such programs instead of the Vietnam War have strengthened or weakened this nation's national security?

8. What is meant by the statement that "It seems clear that national pride was another casualty of Vietnam?" Support your answer with specific examples and evidence from the polling data in the reading.

9. How important was the alleged loss of American credibility and prestige in the world community as a result of the Vietnam War? If such losses did occur, how might they be regained?

10. Describe the controversy over the number of POWs allegedly held by the government of Vietnam. Why is this such an emotional issue, and what obstacles stand in the way of resolving it?

11. Vietnam faced many physical and social problems after the war ended. What actions did the government of Vietnam take to address these problems, and how did the U.S. government respond to their efforts? Analyze possible reasons for these U.S. actions in the late 1970s.

12. Vietnam's first "Five-Year Plan" failed miserably to improve the social and economic conditions of the nation. Describe and evaluate the reasons for this failure and the subsequent steps taken to remedy these problems.

13. The exodus of Vietnamese "boat people" can be tied to Vietnam's involvement with Cambodia in the late 1970s. Describe the chronology of events leading

EXCERPTS FROM U.N. REPORT
ON NEED FOR HUMANITARIAN ASSISTANCE IN IRAQ

Nothing that we had seen or read had quite prepared us for the particular form of devastation which has now befallen the country. The recent conflict has wrought near-apocalyptic results upon the infrastructure of what had been, until January 1991, a rather highly urbanized and mechanized society. Now, most means of modern life support have been destroyed or rendered tenuous. Iraq has, for some time to come, been relegated to a pre-industrial dependency on an intensive use of energy and technology.

...

There is much less than the minimum fuel required to provide the energy needed for movement or transportation, irrigation or generators for power to pump water and sewage. For instance, emergency medical supplies can be moved to health centers only with extreme difficulty and, usually, major delay. Information regarding local needs is slow and sparse.

Most employees are simply unable to come to work. Both the authorities and the trade unions estimate that approximately 90 per-cent of industrial workers have been reduced to inactivity and will be deprived of income as of the end of March. Government departments have at present only marginal attendance.

...

Food is currently made available to the population both through Government allocations and rations, and through the market. The Ministry of Trade's monthly allocation to the population of staple food items fell from 343,000 tons...to 182,000 tons when rationing was introduced (in September 1990), and was further reduced to 135,000 tons in January 1991 (39 percent of the pre-sanctions level.)

While the mission was unable to gauge the precise quantities still held in Government warehouses, all evidence indicates that flour is now at a critically low level, and that supplies of sugar, rice, tea, vegetable oil, powdered milk and pulses (legumes) are currently at critically low levels or have been exhausted. Distribution of powdered milk, for instance, is now reserved exclusively for sick children or medical prescription.

Livestock farming has been seriously affected by sanctions because many feed products were imported. The sole laboratory producing veterinary vaccines was destroyed during the conflict, as inspected by the mission. The authorities are no longer able to support livestock farmers in the combat of disease, as all stocks of vaccine were stated to have been destroyed in the same sequence of bombardments on this center, which was an F.A.O. regional project.

Threat to Grain Harvest

The country has had a particular dependence upon foreign vegetable seeds, and mission was able to inspect destroyed seed warehouses. The relevant agricultural authorities informed the mission that all stocks of potatoes and vegetable seeds had been exhausted. Next season's planting will be jeopardized if seeds are not provided by October 1991.

This year's grain harvest in June is seriously compromised for a number of reasons, including failure of irrigation/drainage (no power for pumps, lack of spare parts); lack of pesticides and fertilizers (previously imported), and lack of fuel and spare parts for the highly mechanized and fuel-dependent harvesting machines. Should this harvest fail, or be far below average, as is very likely barring a rapid change in the situation, widespread starvation conditions become a real possibility.

The mission recommends that, in these circumstances of present severe hardship and in view of the bleak prognosis, sanctions in respect of food supplies should be immediately removed, as should those relating to the import of agricultural equipment and supplies. The urgent supply of basic commodities to safeguard vulnerable groups is strongly recommended.

...

With the destruction of power plants, oil refineries, main oil storage facilities and water related chemical plants, all electrically operated installations have ceased to function. Diesel-operated generators were reduced to operating on a minimum basis, their functioning affected by lack of fuel, lack of maintenance, lack of spare parts and nonattendance of workers.

The supply of water in Baghdad dropped to less than 10 liters per day but has now recovered to approximately 30-40 liters in about 70 percent of the area (less than 10 percent of the overall previous use).

...

As regards sanitation, the two main concerns relate to garbage disposal and sewage treatment. In both cases, rapidly rising temperatures will soon accentuate an existing crises. Heaps of garbage are spread in urban areas and collection is poor to nonexistent. The collection is hampered by lack of fuel, lack of maintenance and spare parts and lack of labor, because workers are unable to come to work. Incinerators are in general not working, for these same reasons, and for lack of electric power. Insecticides, much needed as the weather becomes more torrid, are virtually out of stock because of sanctions and a lack of chemical supplies.

New Homelessness

Iraqi rivers are heavily polluted with raw sewerage, and water levels are unusually low. All sewage treatment and pumping plants have been brought to a virtual standstill by the lack of power supply and the lack of spare parts. Pools of sewage lie in the streets and villages. Health hazards will build in weeks to come.

...

As regards the displaced and the homeless, the authorities themselves have not yet been able fully to assess the impact of the recent hostilities. They have, however, calculated that approximately 9,000 homes were destroyed or damaged beyond repair during the hostilities, of which 2,500 were in Baghdad and 1,900 were in Basra. This has created a new homelsss potential total of 72,000 persons.

Official help is now hampered by the conditions described throughout this report and, especially, a virtual halt in the production of local building materials and the impossibility to import. The input of essential materials should be permitted.

...

It will be difficult, if not impossible, to remedy these immediate humanitarian needs without dealing with the underlying need for energy on an equally urgent basis. The need for energy means, initially, emergency oil imports and the rapid patching up of a limited refining and electricity production capacity, with essential supplies from other countries. Otherwise, food that is imported cannot be preserved and distributed, water cannot be purified, sewage cannot be pumped away and cleansed, crops cannot be irrigated, medicines cannot be conveyed where they are required, needs cannot be effectively assessed. It is unmistakable that the Iraqi people may soon face a further imminent catastrophe, which could include epidemic and famine, if massive lifesupporting needs are not rapidly met. The long summer, with its often 45 or even 50 degree temperatures (113-122 degrees Fahrenheit), is only weeks away. Time is short.

The New York Times, March 23, 1991

600 OIL WELLS MAY HARM MILLIONS

The gulf war has been an environmental catastrophe that poisoned the air, land and sea and could threaten the health of millions of people, scientists and environmental specialists said. All damage estimates are preliminary...But specialists agree the impact of everything that has happened in the Persian Gulf since the air war started could be devastating. About 600 oil fires, burning up to 3 million barrels a day, are spewing toxic smoke that at times has hidden the sun, *Washington Post* correspondent Molly Moore reported after traveling by road from Kuwait City to Saudi Arabia. So thick is the smoke, she said, that military officers were reading maps by flashlight at noon. Toxic black smoke has drifted 600 miles north to Turkey, 150 miles south to the Qatar and 900 miles east across Iran.

There could be serious long-term consequences, scientists said, in the vast oil slicks that are killing gulf marine life, in water pollution from raw sewage and in the devastation of fragile desert ecology by tanks, trucks and soldiers. And unknown amounts of poisonous chemicals from bombed Iraqi factories and weapon stockpiles, and of carcinogenic uranium slivers from armor-piercing allied shells, may have been released.

Tens of thousands of unexploded Iraqi land mines could threaten humans and livestock for decades. Millions of tons of rubble from blasted buildings and many thousands of wrecked trucks, tanks and cars are expected to be dumped in the desert, according to reports.

In the worst case, several experts said, some of the oil well fires will burn for years, blackening the sky with sulfurous gases and toxic particles, and threatening crops and water supplies as far away as Pakistan.

Several groups called on the Bush administration and the United Nations to organize an environmental cleanup to contain the damage. "The Persian Gulf War may turn out to be the most environmentally destructive conflict in the history of warfare," said Christopher Flavin, vice president for research at the Worldwatch Institute. His colleague Michael Renner, a research scientist, called it "an unprecedented atmospheric disaster...an enormous unplanned experiment in the atmosphere."

Taken together, the oil spills in the Persian Gulf are among the biggest ever and apparently have wiped out Saudi Arabian shrimp beds and taken heavy tolls of birds, turtles and coral reefs. But concern over the spills pales beside anxiety over the long-term effect of the oil fires... no one has ever confronted several hundred such fires at the same time, and there are simply not enough trained people or equipment available to tackle the entire job at once, especially in such a dangerous environment. The atmosphere around some high pressure wells is "extremely flammable as well as dangerous poisonous," according to a Defense Department analysis, and mines will have to be cleared before firefighting work can begin.

"It appears that the worst case has materialized," said Brent Blackwelder, an environmental expert at Friends of the Earth. "There is immediate toxicity because the sulfur levels (in the smoke) are several times higher than safe limits. As the stuff falls out, water supplies and farmland are accumulating toxic materials. If these clouds block out sufficient amounts of sun, they could depress agricultural yields, affecting many millions of people, even if there is no impact on the Asian monsoons," which some experts fear there will be, he said. The fires are consuming 2.5 million to 3 million barrels of oil a day, experts said—twice the amount that Kuwait was producing before Iraq invaded Aug. 2. Saudi officials and American scientists have said no one really knows how much oil has been dumped into the gulf in two major spills. Organizations such as the World Conservation Monitoring Centre in London have given estimates as high as 400 million gallons, twice the size of the world's previous biggest spill in a 1979 well blowout in Mexico.

—The *Washington Post*

BOAT PEOPLE AND VIETNAMESE
REFUGEES IN THE UNITED STATES

"Refugees," "Immigrants,"
or "Boat People"?

In May 1978, ten members of the Chau family including Mai, a girl of seventeen, and Son, a boy of sixteen, crowded onto a small fishing boat. Their family ranged from a six-month-old sister to their seventy-eight-year-old grandmother. Just before the war ended, Mai had entered high school with hopes of becoming a doctor, perhaps in the States. Son, a year behind Mai, had looked toward a program in engineering, also hopefully in the U.S. He had then expected to return to Vietnam to assist his father with the family's electrical supply business. But the end of the war and the change in government altered their plans.

Under cover of darkness that evening in May of 1978, the Chaus slipped away from the Vietnamese coastal town of Vung Tau, heading across the South China Sea. Their boat carried 235 people. The boat's destination was Malaysia, which the Chaus hoped would be their gateway to a new life. The trip took eight days. After they ran out of water on the sixth day, Mrs. Chau drank her children's urine in order to nurse the infant. Exhausted, the Chaus finally landed on a crystalline beach along the eastern coast of Malaysia. The local police put the Chaus in a special camp under the Malaysian prison system.

The Chaus are among the more than a million Vietnamese citizens who have left Vietnam for United Nations camps throughout Southeast Asia. After their paper work was complete, these Vietnamese settled in western countries, predominantly in the United States, Canada, Australia and France.

Some people call the Chaus "refugees," the term used by the United Nations High Commission for Refugees.

UNHCR characterizes a refugee as a

> person who is outside the country of his nationality, or if he has no nationality, the country of his former habitual residence, because he has or had well-founded fear of persecution by reason of his race, religion, nationality or political opinion and is unable or, because of such fear, is unwilling to avail himself of the protection of the government of the country of his nationality, or, if he has no nationality, to return to the country of his former habitual residence.
>
> (Statute of the UNHCR, Chapter II, 6.B)

In contrast to UNHCR staff, Malaysian police referred to the Chaus as "Vietnamese Illegal Immigrants." Like "refugees," "illegal immigrants" is a political term; it defines people as seeking residence in a country where they do not hold citizenship. When the Boat People exodus began, host countries such as Malaysia feared that an influx of Vietnamese—many of whom were ethnic Chinese—would increase the racial tension with their own ethnic Chinese populations. These host countries agreed to harbor the Vietnamese only as long as the United Nations assumed responsibility for the expense and for resettlement in another country.

UNHCR contracted with various national Red Cross organizations and other relief groups to provide food, clothing, shelter and health care. These groups, reluctant to become involved in politics, referred to the Chaus as "Boat People," a term that acknowledged the Chaus' form of transit without assigning them a political status.

A million people leaving a country of 68 million with a newly formed government is an important political event. Like any political event, it has underlying causes and precipitating incidents. First, we will examine the causes of the Boat People exodus. Then we will look at some of the people involved. Bear in mind when we say "Boat People," we're speaking of individuals as different from each other as you are from your fellow students.

Discussion Question

Think about your own ancestors who came to this country. Which ones would you call "refugees"? Which ones "immigrants"? Which ones "boat people" in the sense of Vietnamese Boat People? If none of those expressions feels quite right, make up a term that does fit. As you scan American history, does it seem we're a nation of immigrants, of refugees, of boat people or of some other category?

Who, What, Where, When and How

When the South Vietnamese government changed hands in April 1975, there was no "blood bath" as American officials had predicted. However, leaders of the former regime were placed in "re-education camps." Estimates vary as to the numbers. A minimum estimate is more than 100,000. Many stayed for as short a period as three days; others for years.

You will meet Thu-Trung, from Jacksonville, Florida, in the next section. Thu-Trung's father, Dr. Tho, served as an officer with the Army of the Republic of Vietnam. After the change of government, Dr. Tho was held in a re-education camp for three years. He did hard physical labor, and his rations were meager. Once released, Dr. Tho had to register his whereabouts regularly with a neighborhood cadre. Life under the new government was grim; there was hardly enough rice to eat. Dr. Tho saw no future for himself or for his children under the new government.

Between 1965 and 1975, a total of 2.1 million American GIs were stationed in Vietnam. American businesses, private groups and U.S. government agencies added thousands more American civilians. All these Americans pumped billions of dollars into the economy of South Vietnam. A Vietnamese teacher who had formerly ridden a bicycle to work could afford a motorcycle. Private cars appeared in the larger cities. Radios became common. Television aerials sprouted from roof tops. During those ten years, goods that once were luxuries for Vietnamese became commonplace.

On April 30, 1975, the flow of American dollars ceased. There was no money to buy gasoline to run motorcycles and cars; there was no money to buy spare parts and radio batteries. To purchase these imported products, Vietnam had to sell goods on the world market. Once, the South had exported rice, but many

rice fields were destroyed in the war.

During the early 1970s, many South Vietnamese lived on rice imported from Louisiana. In April 1975, that flow of food ceased. There was not enough rice to feed the populace, let alone to export in exchange for gasoline and spare parts. Life became grim; for some it grew so grim they were willing to risk drowning or murder by pirates for the chance to start afresh in a strange land.

By the end of 1975, 377 Boat People had left Vietnam. By the end of 1976, the number of Boat People had risen to 5,619. The next year brought severe cold followed by drought and then by the worst typhoon season in thirty years. Vietnam's rice deficit topped 1.3 million tons. Although some countries replied to Vietnam's request for emergency food shipments, the United States government did not. Heavy fighting along the Vietnamese-Cambodian border further drained Vietnam's limited resources. By the end of 1977, 21,276 Boat People had left Vietnam.

Thu-Trung and the Nguyen family you'll meet later were ethnic Vietnamese; Mai and Son and the Chau family were "overseas Chinese"—Vietnamese of ethnic Chinese origin. In South Vietnam during the war, the Vietnamese of ethnic Chinese background made up five percent of the population. However, ethnic Chinese controlled a large share—estimated at nearly 80 percent—of the commerce. Cho Lon (literally "Big Market") was the major shopping area as well as the Chinatown of Saigon.

In 1978, large numbers of ethnic Chinese Boat People began to leave Vietnam. The pressures that led to their departure were complicated. China had been allied with Vietnam during much of the war. In 1972, the U.S. and China established relations and China drastically reduced its support to Vietnam. When fighting increased along the Vietnamese-Cambodian border in late 1977, Vietnam accused China of providing military aid to the Pol Pot regime in Cambodia. In January 1978, China issued a statement calling for the "broadest patriotic united front" among "overseas Chinese."

In March 1978, the Vietnamese government finished nationalizing businesses, most of which had been owned by ethnic Chinese. In response, disfranchised ethnic Chinese along Vietnam's northern border entered China. China accused Vietnam of persecuting these ethnic Chinese and canceled all remaining aid projects.

After abortive efforts on the part of Vietnam and the United States to normalize diplomatic relations, Vietnam entered into a friendship pact with the Soviet Union in November 1978. China, which borders both the Soviet Union and Vietnam, declared the pact a "threat to the security of Southeast Asia." By the end of 1978, the Chinese-Vietnamese alliance of the early war years had completely dissolved. That fall also brought the worst flooding in Vietnam's recent history, creating a rice shortage of 7.5 million tons. By the end of 1978, 106,489 Boat People had left Vietnam.

Following repeated attacks by Cambodia along the Vietnamese/Cambodian border, Vietnam invaded Cambodia in December 1978 and overthrew the Pol Pot regime in January. Since 1975 the Pol Pot regime had maintained diplomatic relations with only North Korea and China. The regime was genocidal. By conservative estimates, Pol Pot's cadre killed more than one million people out of a population of eight million. To punish Vietnam for its invasion of Cambodia, China then invaded Vietnam on its northern border in February 1979.

Vietnam had had a thousand-year history of political domination by China. This had resulted in a traditional antagonism of ethnic Vietnamese toward ethnic Chinese. Generally speaking, ethnic Chinese merchants profited greatly during the American war. With the Chinese invasion across Vietnam's northern border in February 1979, the Vietnamese government began to fear that the large numbers of wealthy ethnic Chinese, who had lost their businesses to nationalization and who had already been encouraged by China to form a "patriotic united front," would create a threatening military and political as well as economic force.

The new government began to pressure the ethnic Chinese to leave Vietnam. Some ethnic Chinese left on government ships. Others followed on smaller, private fishing boats. Merchants like the Chau family from Cho Lon and other big-city market areas left hurriedly, taking with them their assets in gold leaf or American dollars.

Soon large numbers of ethnic Vietnamese like Thu-Trung began to escape, seeking freedom and a better life in the west. To slip by communist guards, some ethnic Vietnamese purchased papers falsified with Chinese names. Thu-Trung's father spent six months learning Cantonese so he could defend his falsified papers. Still

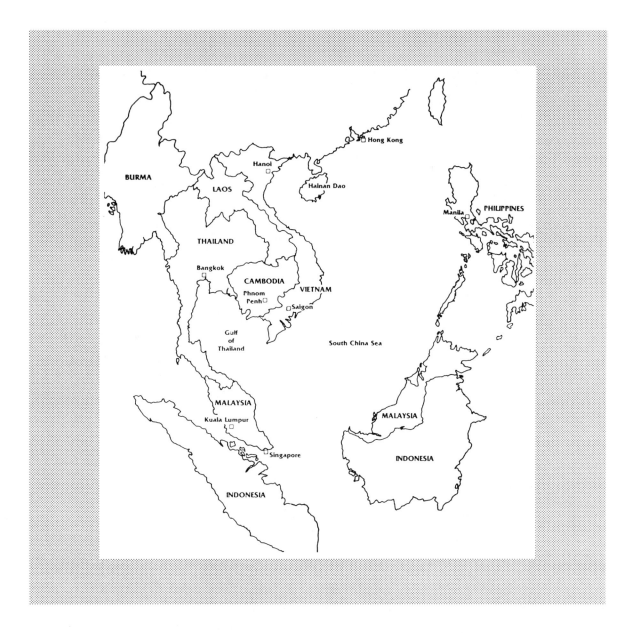

later, ethnic Vietnamese like Khen, whom we'll meet later, escaped without special papers, using only the cover of darkness. By the end of 1986, the total number of Boat People had topped 400,000, including some 24,000 in 1987.

Discussion Question

Suppose you are the commander of a city with a new revolutionary government. The struggle for power has been fierce; feelings remain intense. How will you treat people who were on the other side?

1. Will you let them (or make them) live together?
2. Will they be guarded or checked to prevent a counter-revolution?
3. Will they have rights and opportunities equal to the "winners?" Immediately?
4. What will happen to their property? What about their property if they accumulated great wealth during the old regime?
5. Will their children have the same opportunities as your children?

Boat People

After midnight they load up.
A hundred shadows move about blindly.
Something close to sleep
hides low voices drifting
toward a red horizon. Tonight's
a blue string, the moon's pull—
this boat's headed somewhere.
Lucky to have gotten past
searchlights low-crawling the sea,
like a woman shaking water
from her long dark hair.

Calm over everything, a change
of heart. Twelve times in three days
they've been lucky,
clinging to each other in gray mist.
Now Thai fishermen gaze out across
the sea as it changes color,
hands shading their eyes
like sailors do,
minds on robbery & rape.
Sunlight burns blood-orange
till nothing makes sense.
Storm warnings crackle from a radio.
Gold shines in their teeth.
The Thai fishermen turn away.
Not enough water from the trip.
The boat people cling to each other,
their faces like yellow sea grapes,
wounded by doubt & salt air.
Dusk hangs over the water.
Sea sick, they daydream Jade Mountain
a whole world away, half-drunk
on what they hunger to become.

—Yusef Komunyakaa

One Family's Escape

Question of two Boat People: "How do you know each other?"
Answer: "We were in the same boat."

Every Vietnamese Boat Person has a tale to tell. Each one feared arrest by communist cadre, each struggled against the sea, faced hunger and thirst, and perhaps fought off pirates.

The following account was written by Thu-Trung Nguyen with the help of her father, a doctor, after Thu-Trung had been in this country and studied English one year. When she wrote this piece, Thu-Trung lived in a small town outside Cincinnati, Ohio. Later, her family moved to Jacksonville, Florida, where she is in high school.

Thu-Trung uses several phrases that might need explanation:

—"Republic of Vietnam" is the pre-1975 Saigon-based South Vietnamese government, which was backed by the United States during the war.

—"jungle prison" is one of the re-education camps into which the new government placed people who had been allied with the Saigon-based South Vietnamese government.

Thu-Trung's Voyage

My name is Thu-Trung Nguyen. I was born on May 25, 1972, in Vietnam.

I left my country on January 23, 1980 with my parents, my brothers and sisters, my uncles and aunts on a small wooden boat, ten yards long, and two yards wide. My father was a physician and a major in the Vietnamese Air Force of the Republic of Vietnam. He was prisoner of the communists within three years. Because of his scientific career, he was liberated from the jungle prison. But his life was unsafe and he feared all the time after he had got out of the prison under the restricted control of the communists, so he bought a small boat. He mounted a small engine of 7 horse-power in it. And he brought my whole family to the small boat, came down along the Saigon River, watching everyone suspected around, escaping from our fatherland. We left the riverside at 6:00 PM and came to the sea at 11:00 PM. The waves were very rough. The wind blew at level 6. Night was very dark. The small boat rolled up and down on the sea. All of my brothers and sisters, my uncles and aunts, and I were sea-sick and continued vomiting. Except my mother who was holding a small kerosene lamp near the small, round and old helicopter compass so my father could see it to pilot the boat. At 6:00 AM the next day, our boat was very far from the southeast of the Vietnamese seashore. The open sea was very immense and deeply blue. The waves were very high and large. At first my father wanted to land at Indonesia, but the wind and the waves were not suitable, so he piloted the boat at 240 degrees to Malaysia. Really he did not want to land at Malaysia because we had to pass across the gulf of Thailand where there have been a lot of sea pirates.

The next night, the sky was suddenly darkened. Some dark clouds suddenly appeared in cumulus. The wind suddenly blew from all directions. The fear appeared on my father's face. Storm was coming. He used the battery to light the car beam light mounted in front top of the boat to see clearly the waves coming ahead. Suddenly, the stern was lifted off from the water surface and the boat rotated, did not run as well. My father seriously looked at the bow to find out the direction of the waves coming. The beam light worked well, but it was too tiny with the deep darkness around. We prayed. My mother collected everything floatable for the rescue purposes. We feared. A lot of things inside the boat rolled over from side to side. Even all of us also wanted to be rolled over. My father carefully and seriously avoided each rage wave coming. And when he saw stars appearing through a hole in the thick clouds in the sky, he cried: "Thanks God, we are surviving. We are still alive." Late in the second night, we saw the lighthouses of the Hon Khoai island, the far west island of Vietnam. And that means we were leaving the last part of our fatherland seashore.

The third day, we began to come into the gulf of Thailand. The sea surface was smooth. We enjoyed opening the side windows to watch fishes swimming. A lot of sharks were following our small boat. Some sharks were swimming across underneath our boat. They were enjoying our boat or they were waiting for us as their prey, I really did not know. Our boat was very small and weak to win the sea current of the gulf, so he crossed it in zigzag with the flow of the tides. It took that whole day and night to come nearby the west side of the gulf.

But unluckily, in the early morning of the fourth day, we met the sea pirates. They used weapons to rob. They disordered everything in the boat to look for gold and dollars, even the clothes we were wearing. They threw all our personal papers to the sea. They threw everything not valuable to the sea. Our parents prayed to them in the manner of the Buddhists. We feared and cried out. They cut off the rudder cable. Then they left. And we lost our last penny. But still luckily, they did not take the

compass, and the engine was still in good condition. Food, water and oil were still enough. We still cried out when the pirates left far away. But my father was very brave. He wiped off our tears. He wiped off my mother's tears. Then he said solemnly: "Forget it. Children, arrange everything in order. We continue our way." Water filled up until the half of the boat. My father repaired the cable of the rudder. We started the engine and piloted the boat southwards, along the west coast of the gulf of Thailand.

That night, we went through a float of thousands of fishing boats of Thailand. My father turned off the small kerosene lamp in the cabin. We closed all the windows of the boat. My father reduced the engine power and our boat filtered through them safely, after almost six hours of fearing of being robbed again. My father was very tired. Four nights of no sleep. He told us that we were at the sea border of Malaysia and Thailand. He anchored the boat near Kota Baru and took a sleep when my older brothers and sisters, my

uncles and aunts were watching guardians turn by turn. In the early morning of the fifth day, the 28th of January, 1980, our boat directed to Kuala Trengganu. My father looked healthy again after some hours of sleep. The happiness appeared on his face. He felt that every danger had passed. Leave the doctrine of Communism. Leave the Thai pirates. The sea was beautiful. The ranges of mountains of the West Malaysia were beautiful. The Malaysian fishing boats were fishing quietly, laboriously and lovely.

At 4:00 PM of the same day, we landed at Pulau Bidong, an island belonging to Kuala Trengganu State of West Malaysia, one border of the free world at the southeast of Asia.

Discussion Questions

1. Suppose that on your flight you can take from all your possessions only one bundle the size of a student knapsack. You will travel for an unknown time but at least for five days before reaching refuge. No one will provide for you along the way. Make a list of what you will take. Note your reason(s) for each choice. Which choices are practical? Which are emotional? Which choices are personal only for your use? Which are communal ones you'd be willing to share?

2. Make a list of six people (family members, relatives and/or friends) who will accompany you in flight. Now suppose you learn that the vehicle (boat, car, train, plane) cannot take two of the six. These two must be left behind to cope on their own. Describe how your group will make the choice. Describe the feelings of each of the two left behind, speaking in their own voices. In your own voice, characterize your feelings on leaving those two people forever.

Pirates

Thu Trung's boat was among thousands of escaping Vietnamese craft attacked by pirates from Thailand. Some Boat People families—particularly the merchants of ethnic Chinese origin—were wealthy. One such merchant beached outside the small Malaysian town of Kuala Trengganu near where Thu-Trung's family landed. The merchant knocked on the door of a local Malaysian merchant, also of Chinese origin, asking the Malaysian to hide a wooden box. The Malaysian merchant called the customs officials, who counted over one and a quarter million U.S. dollars' worth of gold leaf.

Few Boat People were that rich, but every family leaving Vietnam brought all its assets in a compact and transferrable form—gold, jewels, or "hard" (western) currency. The frail boats of unarmed escapees were easy prey for Thai pirates.

Sometimes the pirates worked singly; sometimes they worked in groups. The pirate boats, which doubled as fishing vessels, would form a circle five to ten miles in diameter. As soon as a Vietnamese boat passed between two pirate vessels, the pirates closed in. Sometimes they called out in friendly voices, offering water and ice. Then they threw their boat hooks, catching the gunwale of the Vietnamese craft. The pirates scrambled aboard. They ripped through bundles, tearing apart the collars and cuffs of clothes in search of jewels. They sliced the soles of sandals, looking for hidden gold. They raped the women, and they raped girls as young as eight and nine. They murdered.

Dr. Nguyen Duy Cung, a heart surgeon, led one of the few boats to fight the pirates successfully. While still in Saigon, Dr. Cung had taken a map and compass onto the roof of his house on clear nights. There, he studied the stars until he knew them as well as the human heart. The boat he piloted was seventy-one feet long, a little longer than a large house trailer; it carried 687 people.

Unknowingly, Cung steered his boat into a pirate ring. Another smaller refugee boat followed. Soon, an unfamiliar vessel, its sailors calling in friendly voices, approached Cung's boat. The thirsty, sweaty refugees scrambled for cakes of ice the strangers tossed to them. The Boat People grabbed anchors the friendly sailors threw onto their deck.

"Don't!" Cung shouted from the bridge. He ordered the anchor ropes cut. He spun the helm.

A second ship closed in from the other side. Cung took a new tack, then another until his boat slipped past the pirates' vessels. "But then," Cung says, his face darkening as he tells his story, "the pirates pursued the other refugee boat. I could not rescue."

Later that same evening, Cung noticed black shapes

looming over a fluorescent sea. He pushed his boat to full throttle. He could smell heavy exhaust and sense the fear spreading across the deck. The passengers wanted to surrender, but Cung refused, yelling that the pirates were angry from the earlier escape and would smash their boat and maim and kill.

"Besides," he shouted from the bridge, "the pirates are no more than fifty. We have seven hundred!" He sent the women and children into the center of the boat. He instructed the men to grab sticks and line the gunwales.

When the pirates tried to board, Cung signaled from the bridge. Yelling, the Boat People beat off the intruders. Their wooden sticks clattered against the metal blades of fishing knives.

With Cung directing from the bridge, the Vietnamese fought on, slashing and shouting and striking as the pirates' boats bobbed next to theirs. For more than an hour the Vietnamese defended their boat until the pirates abandoned the attack. Then the Vietnamese put aside their sticks and bandaged their knife wounds. One respected elder in his seventies had fallen overboard; a five-year-old girl lay dead upon the deck.

Dr. Cung and his family lived in a UNHCR-supported camp for almost a year before they were resettled in Arkansas. Several years later, they moved to southern California, where he studied for and passed the state medical licensing exams.

The pirates who attacked twenty-year-old Khen's boat were also part of a ring. Khen's boat also resisted. When the Vietnamese fought back, the pirates threw rags soaked in diesel fuel. The pirates were preparing torches when the Vietnamese hurled gasoline back at them. The pirates summoned another vessel, which sped towards the Vietnamese boat. Engines roaring, it rammed the Vietnamese craft, splitting the hull in two. Passengers screamed as they fell into the sea. They floundered, grabbing pieces of planking and empty petrol cans. The waves became glassy with the purple tint of spreading diesel fuel. The pirates fished Vietnamese from the water. Brandishing knives, they chopped off their heads and threw the heads back into the sea; the water turned blood red.

Khen was one of sixteen survivors from a boat of seventy-six. For three days, she clung to a piece of planking. Finally a Malaysian trawler picked her up and brought her into Kuala Trengganu. Khen's face was black, the skin on her cheeks cracked like a shattered windshield. Her lips and tongue were so swollen she could not speak. After Khen was admitted to a Malaysian hospital, another Vietnamese fed her by sucking milk into a straw and plugging the end with his forefinger. Then, learning over Khen, who lay motionless on her bed, he carefully pried apart her cracked lips. Slipping the straw into her mouth, he released the milk a few drops at a time.

After six months in one of the UNHCR camps, Khen left for Toronto, Canada, where she learned English. She married a Vietnamese man from a different boat and is raising their two children. Sometime after Khen's departure, the Vietnamese who had fed her left for Italy, where he now works as a plumber to support his two children.

Discussion Questions

1. Suppose you find out that pirates will attack you and your three traveling companions during your escape. What special preparations will you make? Where will you stash your valuables? How will you protect your passengers?

2. Suppose you are boat leader on a fleeing vessel, overloaded and short of water. Suppose, too, that you come upon a swamping boat of fellow escapees, who call out for you to save them. As leader of your boat, what will you do? Why? Will you involve your passengers in the decision? How will you let the people in the sinking boat know your decision?

3. Suppose your boat is about to be attacked by a single pirate vessel. As boat leader, what will you do? Will you give in or will you resist? Suppose, instead, that you unknowingly enter a circle of seven pirate boats. Will you act differently when they attack?

4. Sea water, which contains salt, increases the effects of dehydration if swallowed. It was not uncommon for Boat People out of fresh water to drink their own urine. What do you think of their choice? Is that something you can imagine doing? Might you feel differently if lost at sea? In far rarer cases, starving Boat People drank the blood and ate the flesh of a fellow passenger who had died. How do you feel about that choice?

Huy Nguyen: Brothers, Drowning Cries

1

Shaking the snow from your hair, bowl cut
like an immigrant's, you hand me your assignment—
Compare and Contrast. Though your accent stumbles
like my grandfather's, you talk of Faulkner,
The Sound and the Fury. You mention Bergson,
whom you've read in French. *Duree.* How the moment
    lasts.
Your paper opens swimming the Mekong Delta.

2
As you lift your face, the sun flashes
down wrinkles of water; blue dragonflies
dart overhead. You hear your brother call.
You go under again, down, down, till you
reach the bottom, a fistful of river clay,
mold a ball in the dark, feel your lungs struggle,
waiting to burst—

                    Where is your brother?

Against the current's thick drag, stumble
to shore, the huts of fishermen—
My brother, my brother's drowned!

Faces emerge from dark doorways,
puzzled, trotting towards you, then
all of them running to the river,
diving and searching the bottom
not for clay but flesh,

and there the man

crawls up on the beach, your brother
slumped over his shoulder, bouncing up
and down as the man runs up and down,
water belching from your brother's mouth
but no air, not air; flings
your brother to the ground, bends,
puts mouth to your brother's lips,
blows in, blows out, until your brother's
chest expands once, once, and once,
and his eyes flutter open, not yet back
in this world, not yet recognizing the blue
of the sky, that your people see as happiness,
even happier than the sun.

3

It's five years since you sailed the South China Sea
and the night Thai pirates sliced your wife's finger for
a ring, then beat you senseless. You woke to a
  merchant ship
passing in silence, as if a mirage were shouting for
  help.
Later, in that camp in Manila, loudspeakers told the
  story
of a boat broken on an island reef, and the survivors
thrashing through the waves, giving up the ghost,
and the girl who reached the shore and watched
the others, one by one, fall from starvation,
as she drank after each rain from shells on the beach.
At last only her brother remained, his eyes staring
upwards at the wind and sun, calling, calling her
  name. . . .
The camp went silent, then a baby, a woman sobbing
And you knew someone was saved to tell the story.

4

Huy,
how many ships are drifting just out of the harbor of
  history,
all waiting for a voice, like a tug boat, to pull the
  survivors
into port? (Each of them sings a skeletal song—*Who
  shall be saved?*)
At seventy, through the streets of Saigon, your mother
  hauls
bowls of soup to sell at dawn. In prison, malaria numbs
  your
brother's limbs. You wait for his death. Safe. Fat. A
  world away.

You are a man without a country, a citizen of this
    century,
and if I ask you to write this down, you do so with a
    smile
of sorrow and amusement. And where you swim each
    night, what wakes you
screaming, remains beyond your English or my
    ignorance.

— David Mura

An Island View

"I live here full of missing."
—Vietnamese Boat Person

Khen, Dr. Cung, Thu Trung and the Chau family all spent almost a year on Palau Bidong, an island in the South China Sea, before they resettled in the west. Palau Bidong had previously been uninhabited. At the height of the influx of Boat People, 43,000 people (approximately the population of Redlands, California; of Holyoke, Massachusetts; or of Ames, Iowa) lived in the camp at the foot of Bidong's volcanic cone. The island had no source of fresh water or food.

Approaching Bidong by boat, Mai and Son were struck by its beauty: the volcanic cone thrusting from a sharp blue sea, white beaches shaded by palms and peppered with the skeletal hulls of abandoned Vietnamese boats, and the camp itself. The houses were fashioned from blue plastic: solid blue plastic, striped blue plastic, checkered blue plastic, all stretched over bamboo saplings. These make-shift shelters perched on the hillside made the island look like a circus offering a thousand events.

Close up, Mai and Son felt different. Their house of blue plastic had a floor space eight feet by eight feet. That's the size of two sheets of plywood. In that space they lived with their family of ten. The walls were rice sacks, which offered little privacy from the voices and ears of 43,000 neighbors. Their diet was rice and rice and rice—adequate to survive but boring and unhealthy. Mai and Son never did become accustomed to the stench of garbage and feces.

For Boat People in 1980, there was no turning back. Ethnic Chinese had been pushed out of Vietnam; ethnic Vietnamese had left illegally. Both groups knew they would be imprisoned if they returned. Malaysia, troubled by racial discord between ethnic Malays and its own ethnic Chinese population, could not or would not accommodate the new arrivals from Vietnam into its own society.

Other Southeast Asian countries had similar concerns. Consequently, most host nations labeled the Vietnamese as "Illegal Immigrants." They agreed to hold the Vietnamese in camps under the authority of their national prison system as long as western nations would accept them for resettlement and as long as the United Nations covered all expenses.

As the Boat People exodus continued into the late 1980s, the international community came to see many Boat People as economic migrants. UNHCR started additional screening. Only those who fit the definition of "political refugee" (about 10%) were processed for resettlement. The rest were stuck in camps. In Hong Kong, families lived in "cages" 8 feet by 4 feet by 4 feet.

UNHCR worked out a repatriation program with the government of Vietnam. From June 1989 to May 1990, 2,500 Boat People were repatriated. For the first time in its history, UNHCR launched a mass information and education program to encourage people wishing to leave Vietnam to use the legal route known as the Orderly Departure Program. Some 60,000 people left Vietnam by orderly departure in 1990.

Vietnamese who left by boat gave up their nationality. When they arrived in a camp, they had no legal status. They could not marry, could not legally have children or, for that matter, die legally. But even though they no longer had nationality, the Boat People did have government. On Bidong, Dr. Cung soon became camp leader, functioning as mayor. He assumed responsibility for seven residential zones and ten administrative departments, all staffed by Boat People. The administrative departments included camp administration, health, sanitation, water, supplies (food, etc.), social welfare, internal police, labor, education, and language interpretation. As a young man, Son was required to work at least two days a week in an assigned division. If he had been skilled in a foreign language, he might have interpreted for visitors. But since Son was unskilled, he joined the laborers. Wearing shorts, flip-flops and no shirt in 100° heat, Son carried 100-pound sack after 100-pound sack of rice down the long jetty to the sweltering supply warehouse.

Mai was not required to work, but she did take a job making medical identification cards for new arrivals. Her closest friend helped inoculate the new arrivals against diphtheria, pertussis (whooping cough) and typhoid. Both young women were responsible for cooking the family's rice over small fires they built with wood taken from the mountainside. They washed what few clothes their families had in sea water.

Son and Mai lived this way for nineteen months

before resettlement. Like every other person in the camp, they suffered from the epidemic ailment that Dr. Cung called *benh lau,* the waiting disease.

By 1991, thousands of people—particularly un-skilled single men—remained in the Southeast Asian camps after six or seven years of trying to find sponsor-ship. A sponsor is a relative, American contact, church group or other organization that agrees (with assistance from U.S. government programs) to assume financial and social responsibilities for resettling a family. At best, United Nations officials needed almost a year to verify that a family of Boat People actually had a sponsor.

While waiting in the camps, most Boat People re-mained true to their former lives. On Bidong, Dr. Cung treated patients in the camp hospital before he was elected camp leader. Thu Trung went to school and played in the surf. The carpenters hammered an addi-tion to the hospital, the police patrolled the paths, the social workers cared for rape victims, the pimps plied their trade, and the robbers stole. Mothers scolded their children, the kids molded ration tins into toy boats, the earnest studied English, and the goof-offs swung be-neath the palm trees in hammocks former tenants had made from UNHCR twine.

Discussion Questions

1. Think back to a time when your days were unstruc-tured and free of commitment, perhaps a summer or a long vacation or even a week-end. Reconstruct what you had planned to do with the time. Compare how much you accomplished with what you'd planned. What do such experiences tell you about your own patterns when faced with expanses of free time?

2. Suppose that at this point in your life, you were to live in a camp like Bidong. You would sleep on a bed made of ship planks, with mosquitoes nipping your ears. You would live on rice and rice and rice. Of course you would have no computer, radio, TV, VCR, stereo, movies, musical instruments, books, paper, bicycle, motorcycle, car, ice cream, candy or pizza. There would be black market soda, but it would cost the equivalent of five dollars a can. How would you fill your free time?

3. Think back (or ahead) to a time when you didn't know where you were going to live and what you were doing next. The end of senior year might be such a time.

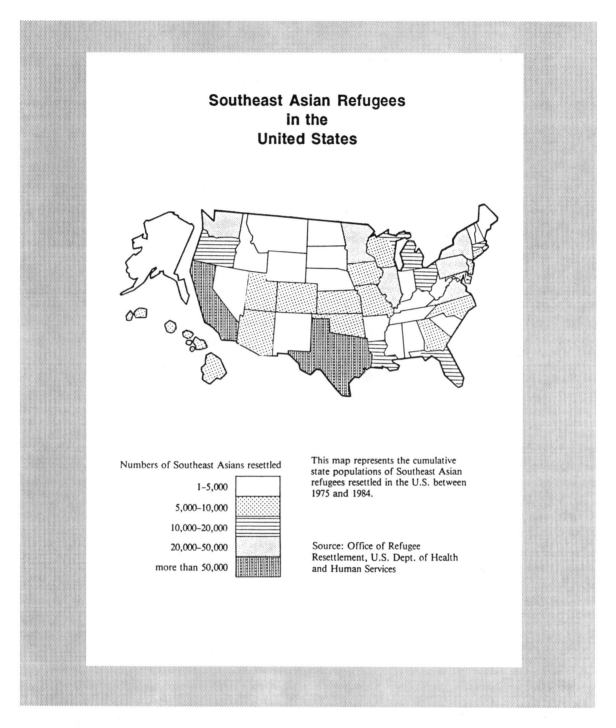

Southeast Asian Refugees in the United States

Numbers of Southeast Asians resettled

1–5,000

5,000–10,000

10,000–20,000

20,000–50,000

more than 50,000

This map represents the cumulative state populations of Southeast Asian refugees resettled in the U.S. between 1975 and 1984.

Source: Office of Refugee Resettlement, U.S. Dept. of Health and Human Services

How did you feel during that period of "not knowing"? Was it sometimes hard to keep yourself centered? If so, why? Did you sometimes feel anxious or fearful? Why?

4. Suppose you are living in a camp like the one on Bidong. All your friends have been accepted to the United States. Your life's dream, like your friends', has been to live in America. However, you do not have any contact in the United States to sponsor you. United Nations officials tell you that you MUST therefore apply for admission to Australia. You do not know a soul in Australia. Describe how you would feel. Try to do this with an image or comparison, such as "I would feel like a..." or "I would feel like the time when..."

Your Town, USA

"I'm half Vietnamese, half American. I'll never be whole in either country."
—Vietnamerican young woman

One night after the Chau family had lived on Bidong for nineteen months, they heard their names on a list read over the camp loudspeakers. The next morning they waited on the beach with 132 other Boat People. Son and Mai's grandmother, now eighty, sat on a rice sack stuffed with the family's few possessions. She held their youngest sister, now a squirming two-year-old.

At the end of the jetty stood the ship that would take their family to mainland Malaysia, where they would spend a few weeks in a special transit camp. Close friends surrounded Son and Mai, now eighteen and nineteen. Both Son and Mai knew they might never see these friends again.

Three weeks later, the Chaus ate their morning rice in the deafening squalor of the transit camp. Twenty-four hours after that, they emerged from their first airplane ride into the hullabaloo of Chicago's O'Hare airport. Grandmother balked at the escalator. The two-year-old squealed with delight when the family's bulging sack magically appeared on a conveyer belt.

Once outside the airport, there were cars and cars and cars, all whirring and whizzing; and there were roads with not one lane but eight. The signs were bigger than houses and they pulsed, red, yellow, blue. Son encountered his first snow and bitter cold. For the first time, Mai wore a coat that hung like weights from her shoulders, and she could see her own breath! All around she heard the tumbling sounds of English, which she'd studied in school for five years. However, she could not understand one word.

The Jonasons, representatives of a sponsoring church, settled the Chaus into an apartment in a Chicago suburb, where they were the only Vietnamese. The apartment was palatial compared with the blue plastic house on Bidong. There was a shower and a toilet that flushed. The Jonasons provided the Chaus with not only rice but also fruits and vegetables and even meat.

Within a few days, Son and Mai entered the local high school. Their classmates stood a head taller. Each day the American students wore a different set of clothes. Some even drove cars. When Son could catch a word, it was "football," a sport with little use for his small body. Mai, further advanced in English, blushed when she heard her new friends speak freely of what they did on dates with their boy friends. Both Son and Mai spent weeks listening to teachers talk in an unintelligible torrent. Only in math class, where they could follow the already familiar symbols, did they understand anything.

Son and Mai studied, and they studied. Every evening Rebecca Jonason came over, and the three students spread their books over the kitchen table. Patiently, with Rebecca's help, Son and Mai read each sentence over and over, trying to make sense of verbs that kept changing. They couldn't seem to discipline their tongues to curl around their front teeth for a clear "th" sound. However, by the end of the first full year, both Mai and Son were able to take the same tests as other students, even in literature and history.

At the end of two years, the Chau family moved to Orange County, California. The weather is warmer there, and a large Chinese and Vietnamese community makes them feel more at home. Mai and Son entered the local community college, where Son is studying electrical engineering and Mai, computer science. Both have made the dean's list each semester.

While Son and Mai study, the younger children watch television. They seem to have learned English instantaneously and often prefer it to Vietnamese. Their father, who works as groundskeeper for an apartment complex, can speak enough English to get along. Their mother, who tends the house, understands a little but is afraid to talk. Grandmother, growing more stooped each day, hardly speaks even in Vietnamese except when she bows before the family altar. Often she picks up the altar's yellowed photographs of her own parents in mandarin dress. Often a far-away look clouds her face.

Discussion Questions

1. Imagine that you are a Vietnamese who lived in a village outside Saigon before 1975. If you like, choose as your character someone of a different age and/or sex than yourself. Decide whether you are ethnic Chinese

The wider war in Indochina included the countries of Cambodia and Laos in addition to Vietnam. Many people in those countries also suffered terribly and many have become refugees. The pictures on pages 23, 24, 27 and 28 by Judith Canty depict Cambodian settlers in the northeast United States.

or ethnic Vietnamese. Pick a line of work for your father or yourself if you are the father. This will define your family's economic class. Now suppose you are arriving as a Boat Person in your current community. You have just left Bidong after twenty months. Characterize your first impressions upon arrival. Use as many details as possible to describe what is exciting, frustrating, terrifying, fun, angering, overwhelming, enchanting.

2. Generally speaking, the transition has been very difficult for the elderly. Imagine you are an elderly Vietnamese man or woman who has resettled in your town. Make up a life for yourself. Describe how you feel about that life and about the one you left behind in Vietnam. Write a scene narrated in the first person to illustrate these feelings.

3. We can never quantify human pain, and it is always dangerous to generalize. However, it is probably true that the transition to this country has been most difficult for Amerasian children (the offspring of American service men) and particularly for their mothers. Even though the mothers may have been legally married (most were not), they may still be viewed as prostitutes by their own people. Imagine you are an Amerasian or the mother of an Amerasian. Write a scene narrated in the first person to illustrate your feelings.

Settling In

Thuc, Hien and Nguyet are high school students who reflect three waves of Vietnamese Boat People. Their different experiences are typical of their groups. As you read their stories, try to think of which student's background is most like your own.

Full-Time Motivation

Thuc and his family of three brothers and two sisters left Vung Tau in early 1979 during the first rush of ethnic Vietnamese. Thuc was ten at the time. During the war, Thuc's father was the principal of a high school for boys in Saigon. His mother taught English and French at a girls' high school. The family lived above the pharmacy owned by Thuc's paternal grandfather. Thuc can still remember how each night he would push aside the display racks of drugs so his grandfather could drive the family's shiny new Ford into the store. His father would then close the folding outer doors and the inner iron gate.

The family fell on hard times when the war ended. The government closed the pharmacy, and Thuc's father lost his job. The family sold the car and lived on Thuc's mother's income and on savings, which Thuc's grandfather kept in gold leaf hidden in a secret panel in one of the upstairs rooms. In 1979 Thuc's grandfather bought passage for the eight family members at $2,000 U.S. per person on an illegally-leaving boat . Their boat met Thai pirates. Thuc's grandfather and parents lost the rest of their savings to the pirates.

Thuc was eleven when he arrived in the U.S. His uncle, who ran a Vietnamese restaurant and had just bought a gas station in Huntington Beach outside of Los Angeles, sponsored the family. Soon after he arrived in California, Thuc was pumping gas. As soon as his

English improved, Thuc waited on tables in the restaurant. Before long, his father found work assembling computers, and his mother took a job with a refugee resettlement agency. Soon, the family made a down payment on a new Honda.

Thuc studied hard. He'd been raised according to Confucian values, which place importance on honoring one's elders and superiors. Thuc knew the best way to repay the debt he owed his parents and grandfather was to study hard. While his American classmates were watching television and playing pick-up football, Thuc studied. He went over the sentences in his literature book word by word until he understood each paragraph. By the time he finished eighth grade, Thuc had made the honor roll. By the end of ninth grade, he was making straight A's. He practiced his violin as well and played in the school orchestra.

Everyone had spoken of the United States as the land of opportunity. Thuc assumed he would go to Berkeley to study electrical engineering. His guidance counselor thought Thuc would gain admission since he'd made straight A's all through high school and had scored high on the SAT. Thuc was bitterly disappointed not to be admitted to the freshman class in the fall of 1987 even though other students with strong records also were denied admission.

Although Asian Americans made up twenty-five percent of the entering Berkeley class, Thuc and his friends began to wonder if admissions officials were discriminating against them. To make matters worse, some of Thuc's white and black high school classmates felt the teachers had discriminated against them in favor of the Vietnamese. They accused the teachers of overlooking Vietnamese students' inadequacies and of giving them extra points for effort. The guidance counselor disagreed, pointing out that the Vietnamese were dedicated and disciplined students. Naturally their American classmates' complaints hurt the Vietnamese.

Hard-to-Get-Going Blues

According to United Nations officials, Hien is an "unaccompanied minor." He comes from the second wave of Vietnamese Boat people, who were from non-professional backgrounds. Hien didn't pay for his boat passage the way Thuc's family did. Instead, Hien jumped onto a boat at the last minute. That was in 1981, when Hien was ten. He left behind his father, a cyclo driver, and his mother, a fruit vendor. Because Hien's parents are still alive, he's not an orphan, but an "unaccompanied minor."

Since Hien didn't have any relatives in the United States, he was given a low priority for resettlement from his transit camp in Indonesia. Hien lived in the camp for five years, until he was fifteen. During that time, he was supposed to attend English language classes, but he found the classes hard and usually skipped them to run with a group of older boys. Hien's job in the camp was to monitor traffic in the outpatient clinic of the camp hospital. He made his spending money by stealing medicines from the hospital and selling them on the black market.

A Catholic Church outside San Francisco sponsored Hien and found a family with young children to take him in. Hien soon grew restless and depressed. He'd been living on his own for so many years. Now, his adoptive parents were telling him what to do. Hien pretended he didn't understand any of their English. After a couple of months of frustration in school, he played hooky, taking off for Chinatown, where he ran into some of his buddies from the camp in Indonesia. They introduced him to pot and the fast life.

Hein stayed several nights in Chinatown before he returned to his American family. Once again, he pretended not to understand their English. The school counselor arranged special tutoring for Hien in all subjects, not just English. After two years, Hien's reading, writing and mathematical skills were that of a fifth grader, though he was seventeen and in the sophomore class. He felt constantly embarrassed. At eighteen, Hien moved into a rooming house. He now shares two dingy rooms with three other young Vietnamese men. Hien and his roommates are among the fifty percent of Indochinese in California who are on welfare.

Hien has dropped out of school. He seldom speaks English. A few of his friends have joined the National United Front for the Liberation of Vietnam, a group that proposes to take Vietnam back from the communists. Hien isn't much interested in going back to Vietnam. He'll tell you he doesn't know what does interest him. He'd like to have a car that he could drive fast but, without a job, that doesn't seem a likely prospect. Mostly Hien spends his days the way he did in the transit camp in Indonesia. He hangs around, watching the world go by.

Amerasian Isolation

Nguyet's father was a white U.S. soldier named Tom, who was stationed for a year in My Tho. Tom came from Chicago. He had just turned nineteen when he met Nguyet's mother. To Tom, Vietnam was a strange and frightening place, where you could just as easily die as not. He was lonely. Nguyet's mother was young and lovely, with long flowing hair.

If Tom had another name, Nguyet's mother never knew it. He brought her fizzy soda and real chocolate from the PX, and he bought her a transistor radio. Whenever Tom visited Nguyet's mother, he turned the set to Armed Forces radio, and they listened to American rock and roll. Except for having to leave Nguyet's

mother, Tom was jubilant when his tour of duty ended. He promised to write and to send for Nguyet's mother so that she could join him in the U.S.

Nguyet was born three months after her father left for the U.S. Her mother sent letters addressed to "Tom, Chicago, USA," but she never received an answer. She supported Nguyet by selling noodle soup in the market. By the time she was seven, Nguyet was helping her mother. Some days she tended her mother's soup baskets. Other days she sold popsicles. She went to school, but that was hard because the other children looked at her blondish hair and laughed, calling her _My_!—American!

In 1987, Nguyet came to the United States with a special program for Amerasian children of U.S. soldiers. She and her mother settled in Boston, a huge and frightening city compared with My Tho. Life was hard in Boston. The Vietnamese students in Nguyet's school thought of her as American because of her blondish hair and American father, yet Nguyet didn't know any English. The American students thought of her as Vietnamese because of her facial features and language. For Nguyet, no group felt safe.

At sixteen, Nguyet is in her sophomore year of high school. She attends special education classes to help her overcome her gaps in schooling. Her mother cleans houses during the day and washes dishes in an American restaurant at night. Because Nguyet cleans houses after school, she often doesn't have time to attend the Vietnamese club set up at her school. When she arrives home at night, she's often too tired to study. The words on the page have little meaning.

Discussion Questions

1. Define what you mean by "class" in talking about strata of society. Are there classes in America? If you think so, name and describe each one you see. Which classes would Thuc, Hien and Nguyet represent in this country? In Vietnam? How easy or how hard is it to move from one class to another in the United States? If you think there aren't classes in U.S. society, defend your answer.

2. Look up Confucius and Confucianism in an encyclopedia. What are the traditional Confucian values? How do they play into the "success" of students like Thuc? What happens to the practice of these values when people are forced to leave their families as in the case of Hien and Nguyet?

Conclusion

Throughout 1989 and 1990 the Boat People remained in the world news. Southeast Asian nations, including Hong Kong, Indonesia, Malaysia, the Philippines and Thailand, no longer were willing to take responsibility for the Boat People. Malaysia pushed off an estimated 8,700 Boat People trying to land on its shores. Scores of those refugees were robbed, raped or killed by pirates after they were refused entrance.

By December 1989, there were as many as 125,000 refugees languishing in Southeast Asian detention camps, almost 50,000 in Hong Kong alone. When Hong Kong officials forced 51 men, women and children onto a plane for Hanoi in the middle of the night, there was an international outcry against "forced repatriation."

Anticipating resistance, Hong Kong officials tried to search one of its camps for weapons. Fearing they too were being rounded up for repatriation, Boat People stoned the police, jammed the locks on the camp gates and set huge bonfires at both entrances. Some 700 home-made weapons, including many knives made from metal bed slats, were found.

In September 1990, an accord was signed by Britain, Hong Kong and Vietnam. It called on UNHCR to arrange for the return of Boat People who have not volunteered to go home, but who do not object to returning. UNHCR officials said they were not certain there were such people.

The year 1993 finally brought a resolution of the war in Cambodia and easing of the Boat People crisis. About a year after implementation of the Paris Peace Accords on Cambodia, more than 275,000 refugees from the camps in Thailand had been returned to their homeland.

General Discussion Questions

1. The terms *refugee* and *illegal immigrant* imply value judgements by the person or government using them. Which group(s) of immigrants to the United States are currently considered refugees? Which are considered illegal immigrants by the U.S. government? Review the UN criteria for refugee status. According to these criteria, would you classify all of the Boat People described in this unit as refugees? Why or why not? Use specific examples.

2. Look at a map of Southeast Asia. If possible, obtain one that indicates water currents and/or prevailing winds. Trace the route of most of the Boat People from Saigon to Malaysia. Which countries did they pass on the way to Malaysia? Why didn't they go ashore in those countries? Note: Most of the refugee camps in northeastern Thailand are occupied by Cambodians. What reason(s) would prevent the Boat People from seeking help there?

3. A frequently stated argument for U.S. military intervention has been that a communist victory would result in a "bloodbath" of persecutions. Based on historical experience, was this true in Russia? China? Afghanistan? Vietnam? What were the factors that made each of these cases unique? What forms of treatment were used by the communists in Vietnam against the former elite?

4. The rigors of the journey for many Boat People provide a modern-day version of ordeals such as the westward movement in the United States, the Cherokee Trail of Tears, and the Long March in China in the 1930s. Compare the physical problems faced by the Boat People with one or more of these events. In each case, who was the "enemy"?

5. How much do you think the Boat People's decision to leave Vietnam was influenced by an idealized image of the United States? What developments in South Vietnam during the last ten years of the war encouraged such a view? Do you think refugees were more attracted by the promise of wealth or by the guarantee of freedom? Cite specific evidence from the readings.

6. Southeast Asia is a region which has historically had bitter ethnic conflicts both within and among its nation states. What connections do these ethnic conflicts have with the decisions of the Boat People to leave Vietnam? How have they affected the acceptance of the Boat People into neighboring countries as refugees?

7. Which of the people whose stories are included in the Chapter do you think demonstrated the greatest courage? Who was the best leader? Who showed the most compassion for others? Use specific quotations from the readings to support your answers.

8. Although the voyage itself was often the most dangerous for the Boat People, their time in the refugee camps was perhaps the most demoralizing. For many families who had lived comparatively well in Vietnam, the austerity of the camps was especially difficult. Many, unsure of what would happen to them, suffered from the "waiting disease." Have you ever been in a similar situation where you seemed to have no control over your circumstances or future? What did the people in the camps do to restore a sense of purpose to their lives?

9. The arrival of refugee families in the U.S. and their subsequent adjustment provides an opportunity to study how individuals react to cultural change. Which family members seemed to adjust most easily? Which have had the greatest difficulty? Social agencies are now attempting to address the mental health needs of the Boat People—problems that have emerged ten years after their arrivl ing this country. Which problems do you think would be most common?

10. The two largest groups of recent immigrants to the U.S. are Southeast Asians and Hispanics. Compare these two groups in terms of these factors:

   1. Reasons why each group came to the U.S.
   2. Adjustment problems.
   3. Attitude of the government and the general public.

In some communities, there have been conflicts between Southeast Asians and Hispanics. What do you think are the basic reasons for these conflicts? What misperceptions might each group have about the other?

Chapter 12

George C. Herring and Kevin Simons

THE VIETNAM WAR: LESSONS FROM YESTERDAY FOR TODAY

> *Shuffling down the walkway to Washington's Vietnam Veterans Memorial, a small group of high school students suddenly confronts a bewildering array of images. First, there is the wall itself—a seemingly uniform piece of glimmering black granite that silently, but inexorably, draws them further onto the grounds. Then there are the soldiers, statue soldiers whose bronze gaze extends forever toward their fallen comrades, and live, middle-aged veterans whose fading olive drab or muttered jargon betray their former status. There are the names, thousands and thousands of them, and occasionally a wreath, a note, a flag, a photograph, or some other item nestled against the base of the wall.*
>
> *Above all else, there is a powerful and pervasive sense of solemnity. Sensing the emotion and awesome grandeur of the wall, the students try to sort out their thoughts. Some merely stop and stare. A few weep. To a generation that knows the war mainly through films, there remains a strong sense of wonder mixed with confusion and curiosity. They walk away deep in thought, trying to come to terms with what they have seen and felt. Silently, each ponders the question, "What does it mean?"*

The Importance of Vietnam

The confusion and uncertainty of the students reflect a larger national uncertainty about the meaning and significance of Vietnam. Even before the last helicopter lifted off from Saigon in 1975, Americans struggled to understand and learn from the longest and most divisive war in their nation's history. Controversy raged as the war was being fought, and debate over its meaning persists today. From the Angolan crisis of 1975 to the Persian Gulf War of 1991, the shadow of Vietnam has hovered over every major foreign policy debate. The very word "Vietnam" still evokes powerful and often contradictory images as U.S. leaders seek answers to the nation's most pressing foreign policy questions.

What Americans have learned from Vietnam, to a large degree, reflects their broader political beliefs. Most have drawn the war's lessons along ideological lines. At the risk of oversimplification, we might categorize the main positions as follows: radicals see the war as immoral and view the victory of the North Vietnamese and Vietcong with enthusiasm. In general, liberals have concluded that the war was unnecessary and probably unwinnable. The most important lesson they draw is for the United States to avoid similar situations in the future. Conservatives, on the other hand, view the war as highly moral, even "noble," to quote former President Ronald Reagan. They feel that it could and should have been won. The major lesson they draw is that the next war must be fought properly so that success is assured.

The Radical View of the War

Radicals propose that the war was not a "mistake," but a logical extension of U.S. imperialism, a stubborn but futile effort to maintain U.S. control over another nation. Radicals see any interference with another nation's self-determination as unethical. Many cited this principle in criticizing both Soviet intervention in Afghanistan and U.S. intervention in Nicaragua.

In the radical view, the U.S. tried to thwart the popular will in Vietnam, first by subsidizing the French military, then by blocking the 1956 unification elections, and finally by imposing a corrupt military dictatorship on the people of South Vietnam. The U.S. was never able to establish a stable government in South Vietnam because the people's war of national liberation was too powerful. In trying, the U.S. had to resort to such cruelty that it was condemned around the world.

Radical Lessons for Today

Many radicals claim that Vietnam is the prototype for future wars of national liberation. For historian Gabriel Kolko, Vietnam confirmed the "awesome" potential of men and women to define their own futures

against overwhelming opposition. Other radicals are less certain that right will always triumph. However, they believe U.S. foreign policy must address the "roots" of social conflict around the world, especially economic exploitation and the repression of human rights. Radicals assert such a policy is both ethical and practical. They advocate a national security policy designed to eliminate the real sources of insecurity in the lives of Americans—not communism in other countries but poverty, ignorance and illness in our own country. Radicals call for a large cut-back in military spending and strong government programs to promote employment, health, education and welfare in the U.S.

In the radical view, Third World conflict is not the result of communist subversion but the legitimate expression of civil discontent. If the U.S. wants stable political allies, it should support the people's aspirations by offering various programs of social reform and relief. Radicals propose that making friends with the people of other countries is the surest route to enhancing U.S. national security.

The Liberal View of the War

For American liberals, the Vietnam War was an especially traumatic experience. Throughout the 1940s and 1950s, most liberals supported the nation's Cold War policies of containing communism, and they backed the commitment in Vietnam implied by the Tonkin Gulf Resolution of August 1964. Only when this commitment led to a protracted and inconclusive war did many liberals start a protest that eventually went beyond Vietnam to question the basic assumptions of postwar U.S. foreign policy.

Most liberals have continued to view the war critically. American intervention had been misguided from the start, the result of a dogmatic anti-communism that produced gross misperceptions on the part of major policymakers. The United States foolishly committed its power and prestige in an area of peripheral importance on behalf of a client of dubious legitimacy.

HERE IT IS FOLKS! THE **NEW** SUPER DELUXE **AMERICAN IMPERIAL!**

NOW BEFORE I MENTION THE PRICE, LET ME TELL YOU WHAT WENT INTO THE **MAKING** OF THIS AUTOMOBILE.

<u>ALUMINUM</u> FOR THE ENGINE AND TRANSMISSION FROM SURINAM, HAITI, AND JAMAICA.
<u>CHROME</u> FOR ALLOYS AND TRIM FROM TURKEY, SOUTH AFRICA AND PHILIPPINES.
<u>TUNGSTEN</u> FOR ALLOYS FROM BOLIVIA, THAILAND, SOUTH KOREA, AND BURMA.
<u>TIN</u> FOR ALLOYS FROM INDONESIA, MALAYA, BOLIVIA AND CONGO.
<u>COPPER</u> FOR THE ELECTRICAL SYSTEM FROM RHODESIA, CANADA AND CONGO.
<u>RUBBER</u> FOR TIRES FROM MALAYA AND INDONESIA.
<u>OIL</u> FOR LUBRICATION AND FUEL FROM VENEZUELA AND THE MID EAST.

AND LOTS MORE!

WE USED TO RIP-OFF LOTS OF COPPER FROM CHILE BEFORE THEY NATIONALIZED IT. LATER FOR **THEM.**

IT TAKES AMERIKAN INGENUITY AND KNOW-HOW TO ORGANIZE THIS GLOBAL RIP-OFF AND TURN IT INTO A FINE LOOKING AUTOMOBILE. SO WHEN YOU HEAR THE MELLOW SOUND OF YOUR NEW AMERICAN IMPERIAL V-8, YOU CAN FEEL A WARM SENSE OF PRIDE IN KNOWING **WHY** YOUR SON DIED IN VIETNAM.

The Invasion of Grenada

I didn't want a monument,
not even one as sober as that
vast black wall of broken lives.
I didn't want a postage stamp.
I didn't want a road beside the Delaware
River with a sign proclaiming:
"Vietnam Veterans Memorial Highway."

What I wanted was a simple recognition
of the limits of our power as a nation
to inflict our will on others.
What I wanted was an understanding
that the world is neither black-and-white
nor ours.

What I wanted
was an end to monuments.

—W.D. Ehrhart

JUST WHEN YOU THOUGHT IT WAS SAFE TO REGISTER FOR THE DRAFT AGAIN!...

VIETNAM II

STARRING
★ RONALD REAGAN AS LYNDON JOHNSON
★ EL SALVADOR AS SOUTH VIETNAM
★ WITH A SPECIAL APPEARANCE BY FIDEL CASTRO AS HO CHI MINH

Liberals have concluded that the means used were disproportionate to the ends sought, and that the United States inflicted callous and even wanton destruction on the Vietnamese people. Given the corruption of the South Vietnamese and the determination of the North Vietnamese, liberals insist an American victory was beyond reach, no matter how much power was applied.

Liberal Lessons for Today

From Lebanon in the early 1980s to Central America to the Persian Gulf, most liberals have warned that any form of intervention may lead to another Vietnam. Should the United States persist in its course in Central America, journalist Tad Szulc admonished in 1981, it would become bogged down "in an endless Vietnam-style guerrilla war" in the jungles and mountains of El Salvador and Nicaragua, a "scenario for absolute disaster."

Reading news clippings from 1964 indicating that no troops would be needed and reports from 1966 that more troops would be required, Representative Andrew Jacobs [D-Indiana] in a 1986 debate on aid to the Nicaraguan Contras implored his colleagues to remember Vietnam: "Here we go again," he warned, "Gulf of Tonkin Day....We ought to know by now that when they send the guns it does not take long before they send the sons."

This concern about the consequences of another Vietnam was evident with respect to the Persian Gulf War. Liberals were sharply divided on whether the United States should have intervened militarily in the Gulf region in the first place and, if so, in what form. Memories of Vietnam have influenced anti-interventionist feelings among many liberals. Placards at anti-war rallies carried slogans such as "Kuwait is Arabic for Vietnam." A leading cartoonist portrayed an American GI seeing a desert mirage of Asian peasants in conical-shaped hats working alongside water buffaloes in a rice field. "I feel like Alice staring into the looking glass," said Ron Kovic of *Born on the Fourth of July* fame, as U.S. troops were departing for Saudi Arabia, "seeing the same horror and nightmare about to repeat itself."

Some liberals voted for force over sanctions in the Persian Gulf. They generally advocate an interventionist foreign policy for the U.S. However, they urge a more pragmatic approach that does not exaggerate the importance of local conflicts and is addressed to the sources of local discontent. These liberals support a strategy that relies less on large scale initiatives with high volumes of fire power and more on counterinsurgency methods aimed at the leaders of revolutionary movements. Such an approach causes less indiscriminate damage, is presumably less costly, and minimizes the risks of public protest or superpower confrontation. Where such is not possible, liberals will warn against involvement—not because it is unethical but because it is impractical.

The Conservative View of the War

Conservatives have viewed Vietnam and its lessons very differently. Less influential in the last years of the war, they have found in postwar developments reason to speak out with renewed vigor on what they had always believed. They have cited Hanoi's harsh treatment of the defeated South Vietnamese, the flight of nearly a million boat people from Vietnam, and the Vietnamese invasion of Cambodia to justify the original U.S. inter-

WIELDING THE BIG STICK

LACK OF NATIONAL RESOLVE

U.S. FOREIGN POLICY

Distributed by L.A. Times Syndicate

"WELL, IT SEEMS SENATORS DODD AND TSONGAS AND A COUPLE OF OTHER CONGRESSMEN DON'T WANT ANOTHER 'VIETNAM' IN EL SALVADOR... THEY SAY THE SIGNS ARE RIGHT FOR NEGOTIATIONS."

vention in Indochina. Conservatives have claimed that Hanoi's close postwar ties with the Soviet Union has confirmed what they have insisted all along—that it was nothing more than an instrument of Moscow's larger design.

Conservatives also are certain that the war could have been won. Many of them blame the "ill-considered" strategy of gradual escalation imposed on the military by President Lyndon Johnson and Secretary of Defense Robert McNamara. If the United States had employed its air power against North Vietnam quickly, decisively, and without limit, they say, and if it had invaded the North Vietnamese sanctuaries in Laos, Cambodia, and across the demilitarized zone, the war could have been won. A very extensive public information campaign has helped to promote the belief that the nation's leaders *kept* the military from winning the war. "Sir, do we get to win this time?" the hero Rambo from the blockbuster 1985 film of the same name asked upon accepting his assignment to return to Vietnam and rescue his comrades allegedly being held captive there.

Conservatives further argue that a major cause for America's failure can be found at home. In their view, a naive and hypercritical media and a treasonous anti-war movement turned the nation against the war, forc-

ing Presidents Lyndon Johnson and Richard Nixon to curtail the effort just when victory was in sight. A spineless Congress ruthlessly slashed aid to South Vietnam in 1974, crippling the morale of an ally of twenty years and inviting North Vietnam to launch a final offensive. From this perspective, America's defeat resulted primarily from a lack of will. "Let's abandon the myths about Vietnam," one journalist has commented. "We didn't lose. We quit. For the first time in history, Americans turned tail and ran."

Conservative Lessons for Today

Conservatives also were divided on the issue of military intervention in the Persian Gulf. Some, like columnist Patrick Buchanan, expressed strong opposition to the President's policies, proposing that the potential cost of the war would be disproportionate to our nation's interest in the dispute. Other conservatives, like Senator Richard Lugar (R-Indiana), insisted that the principal mistake the United States made in Vietnam was not seeking victory. In his view, the major Vietnam lesson the United States should apply to the Persian Gulf is that the only way to wage war is "to build up overwhelming force, strike quickly with massive power, and try to get it over within days or weeks." "The quicker you do it," adds the Chairman of the Joint Chiefs of staff, General Colin Powell, "the better off you are." Former Secretary of State Henry Kissinger and others *The New York Times* labeled "hasty hawks" even proposed a pre-emptive first strike against Iraq in hopes of resolving the impasse before a Vietnam-like stalemate could develop.

Conservatives also have contended that when the nation is at war, sharp limits should be put on public debate. In invading Grenada in 1983 and Panama in 1989, the Reagan and Bush administrations gave the media no advance warning and left newspaper and television reporters at home. Media coverage in the Persian Gulf was restricted and censored by military authorities. This was a deliberate strategy based on the lessons conservatives believe they learned from Vietnam. Many conservatives joined liberals in insisting that, before committing troops to combat in the Persian Gulf, the U.S. Congress must pass a declaration of war. They did so because they felt it would ensure congressional support and provide a legal basis for curbing public opposition.

Memories of Vietnam thus continue to influence U.S. attitudes toward foreign policy. On any given issue, scarcely a position is taken without some reference to Vietnam and its lessons. The major problem, of course, is that there is no agreement among Americans on what the lessons should be. The nation is still deeply divided on the meaning and significance of the war and what should be learned from it.

Ideological Abuses of History

In proclaiming their respective lessons of Vietnam, radicals, liberals and conservatives misuse history. Conclusions on all sides have been based on superficial knowledge and faulty reasoning. All sides have manipulated history for partisan reasons, appealing more to emotion than reason.

On all sides, the lessons are based on historical "givens" that cannot be proven. The liberal argument that the war was unwinnable is as unprovable as the conservative argument that with a different strategy or in the absence of domestic dissent the United States would have won. Such questions can never be answered categorically.

The historical reasoning of all sides also is suspect. The liberal warning that each new intervention will lead to another Vietnam is less than convincing. Indeed, if that means a prolonged, inconclusive and costly war, this may be the least likely outcome, since memories of Vietnam are so fresh.

The conservative effort to ennoble U.S. intervention in Vietnam on the basis of what the Hanoi government has done since the end of the war, in Kattenburg's perception, engages "in the dubious business of judging the past from the present." Such judgments cannot help but produce wrong-headed conclusions. In the case of Vietnam, the highly emotional moral judgments made by conservatives distort both the present and the past in order to turn the tables on radical critics of U.S. intervention.

In addition, radicals, liberals and conservatives base their lessons on history that is at best debatable, at worst wrong. Radicals who see the communist victory in Vietnam as vindicating the concept of people's war conclude that similar popular uprisings will inevitably triumph elsewhere. In fact, since World War II, left-wing insurgencies have been defeated in Greece, Malaya, the Philippines, and Indonesia.

In Vietnam, the United States crushed the Vietcong insurgency in the aftermath of the Tet Offensive of 1968. The war was won not by guerrillas, but by a massive invasion of South Vietnam by North Vietnamese regular forces in 1975. The success of the communists in Vietnam was due primarily to the unique political position they enjoyed in that nation's history and to superior leadership and strategy, ingredients not easily replicated elsewhere.

The conservative argument that the unrestricted use of American power would have produced victory is equally simplistic. There is strong reason to reject the claim that the "knockout blow" from the air advocated by the Joint Chiefs of Staff would have forced Hanoi to settle on American terms. As a pre-industrial society, North Vietnam offered few strategic targets. Furthermore, the strategic bombing surveys done in Germany and Japan after World War II raised serious doubts about the ability of bombing to undermine civilian morale.

There is evidence to suggest, moreover, that the North Vietnamese were prepared to resist, no matter what the level of the bombing, even if they had to go

and Bush didn't get elected.

underground. The addition of more troops, invasion of the sanctuaries in Laos and Cambodia and ground operations in North Vietnam might have made General Westmoreland's strategy of attrition more workable, but they also would have enlarged the war at a time when the United States was already stretched thin. Each of these approaches would have greatly increased the cost of the war without resolving the central problem—the lack of popular support for the Thieu government in South Vietnam. And they might have provoked Chinese and/or Soviet intervention.

In terms of public opinion, there is no doubt that, after the Tet Offensive early in 1968, widespread and growing disillusionment with the war placed constraints on U.S. leaders. However, there is little evidence that this was caused by the actions of the antiwar movement. The movement forced Vietnam into the public consciousness, but its broader influence was limited by the division within its own ranks.

The role of the media also has been exaggerated. To be sure, reporting of the war sometimes was superficial and sensationalized, but systematic studies of news

---

Cousin

for John H. Kent, Jr., 1919-1982

I grew up staring at the picture of him:
oak leaves on his shoulders, crossed rifles
on his lapels, and down his chest so many medals
the camera lost them. He wore gold-rimmed
glasses, smiled, had jokes to tell. World War Two
exploded for me summers on the front porch
when he'd visit and talk. Wounded twice, he knew
he'd almost died. Courage rang in his voice.

Ten years from my war, thirty from his, we
hit a summer visit together; again
the stories came. He remembered names of men,
weapons, tactics, places, and I could see
his better than mine. He'd known Hemingway!
I tried hard couldn't find a thing to say.

—David Huddle

content concluded that television commentary generally reflected the position of the government or was neutral. After Tet, media reporting became more critical but so did public opinion. Media reportage probably reflected, as much as caused, the 1968 turnaround in public opinion and the growing disenchantment that followed.

Nightly exposure to violence on television may have contributed to public war-weariness, but such an assertion can never be proven. In fact, it can be argued just as plausibly that routine coverage by network television ultimately induced apathy toward the war. In sum, the media and antiwar movement appear to have had less influence on public attitudes than the growing costs of the war, especially the casualties.

Finally, even when based on accurate historical accounts, reasoning by historical analogy is, at best, a perilous exercise. History does not repeat itself. Each historical situation is at some level unique, and we cannot draw facile conclusions that because such and such happened before, the same will happen again. There is a vast difference between Vietnam, on the one hand, and the Persian Gulf, on the other. To use them analogously violates sound historical practice.

Vietnam and The Persian Gulf

umm . . .

Comparisons between Vietnam and the recent Persian Gulf War provide a good example of the limitations of reasoning by historical analogy. On the surface, there were striking similarities. In each case, the United States dispatched vast military power into the Third World to defend interests it claimed were vital against nations and leaders said to be aggressors. In each case, "lessons" from World War II—the spectre of Adolf Hitler and the so called Munich or Manchurian analogy—were used to justify the intervention. From the beginning of the Persian Gulf intervention, like in Vietnam, there were complaints about the lack of clarity in U.S. goals and mission. Was it to protect oil, jobs or international borders? Did we seek to drive Iraq out of Kuwait, destroy Iraq's army, including its alleged nuclear capability, and/or to depose Saddam Hussein as head of state?

By January 1991, demonstrations by a growing movement against the intervention recalled the anti-war

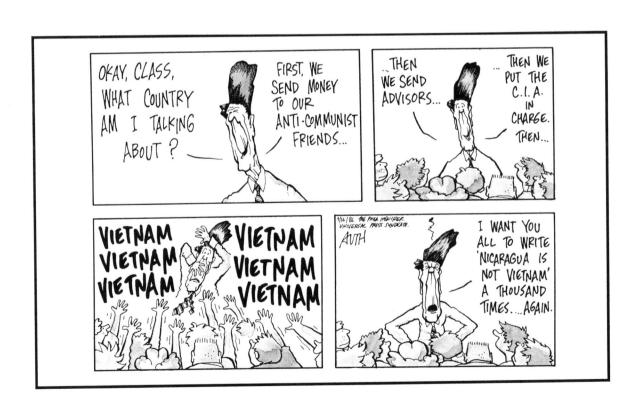

"Now this baby should get you all the way through Central America."

protests of the 1960s and 1970s. The possibility also was raised that, like in Vietnam, a long-term U.S. presence in the Middle East might stir Arab memories of earlier Western imperialism and broaden the base of opposition to the U.S. in the region.

To these authors, however, it was clear that the differences in the two situations were much greater. The American commitment in Vietnam grew slowly and incrementally over fifteen years. In the case of Lyndon Johnson, escalation was handled in such a quiet, indirect way that there were later charges of deceit and trickery. The commitment in the Persian Gulf came with dramatic speed—the largest military force since Vietnam was committed in a mere fifteen days. Of necessity it was done very much out in the open.

In terms of the way the crisis began, the Korean conflict of 1950 may be more analogous to the Persian Gulf than Vietnam, a quick, massive U.S. response to an invasion across an established border. The setting for the war in the Persian Gulf also was much different than in Vietnam. There were no jungles to hide the enemy. North Vietnam got some help from the Soviet Union and China, but Iraq had no outside support. In marked contrast to Vietnam the United States enjoyed broad international support while Iraq, like the U.S. in Vietnam, had the role of international bad guy.

Finally and perhaps most importantly, the Persian Gulf War was the first post-Cold War crisis. Unlike the Vietnam case, the great powers were in broad agreement rather than in conflict. This strengthened the U.S. position and limited Iraq's options.

On November 30, 1990, President Bush addressed

the nation and himself emphasized the differences between the impending Persian Gulf War and the war in Vietnam: "In our country, I know that there are fears about another Vietnam. Let me assure you, should military force be required, this will not be another Vietnam. This will not be a protracted, drawn-out war. The forces arrayed are different; the opposition is different; the resupply of Saddam's military will be very different; the countries united against him in the United Nations are different; the topography of Kuwait is different; and the motivation of our all-volunteer force is superb."

A short history of the war is provided in the conclusion to Chapter 3. When Iraqi forces fled in retreat, President Bush ordered a cease fire and boasted, "By God, we've kicked this Vietnam syndrome." However, he had himself emphasized the great differences in the two cases. Moreover, a *Time*-CNN national poll after the war found 75 percent of the U.S. public saying "no" to the proposition that the U.S. play the role of world policeman in the future. Victory over Iraq was sweet, but people were not accepting it as a model for U.S. foreign and military policy in the future.

To assume that the "lessons of one time and place can mechanistically be applied in another" is to be guilty of what historian William Duiker has called "cultural universalism." Any effort to correct for the strategic mistakes of Vietnam elsewhere in the world ignores the vast differences between historical situations. On the other hand, to conclude that we must reflexively abstain from any conflicts in the Third World for fear that they will lead to another Vietnam is to draw selectively on a very narrow analogy. The same can be said for any effort to replicate the strategic successes of the Persian Gulf War.

What we have so far learned from Vietnam is as likely to mislead as to enlighten us. A first "lesson" of Vietnam might therefore be to view historical lessons with a healthy dose of skepticism. One of the major reasons for U.S. intervention in Vietnam was a misreading of history—the application of hard and fast lessons from Manchuria and Munich in the 1930s to the very different circumstances of Vietnam in the 1960s. Today, once again, lessons are being drawn from the Vietnam experience to guide policy decisions in such areas as the Persian Gulf with insufficient sensitivity to the limits of historical analogies.

Learning From History

Does this mean, then, that history has nothing to teach us or, more specifically, that the Vietnam experience sheds no light on today's problems? Obviously, this is not the case. History in general and the history of American involvement in Vietnam, in particular, have much to teach us. But we must use them with discretion and caution.

To learn from a historical event, we must look beneath the surface and examine its component parts. In the case of Vietnam, in-depth analysis of how we got there and why we failed can be instructive in its own right. Such inquiry may not yield lessons that can be applied uncritically to other, seemingly similar, events. But it can suggest certain principles that can help us to make such decisions. We propose that observance of these principles could prevent a recurrence of the Vietnam experience.

Local Forces are Important

The Cold War mindset that got us into Vietnam—a set of attitudes and assumptions also used in the 1980s to justify intervention in Central America—must be viewed critically. From the early 1950s until at least the mid-1960s, we viewed the conflict in Vietnam as an integral part of our larger struggle with the Soviet Union and People's Republic of China. This assumption was based on a view of the world that was simplistic and fundamentally flawed.

Vietnamese nationalism, not international communism, was the driving force behind thirty years of war in Vietnam. Ho Chi Minh and his lieutenants were communists, to be sure, and throughout the conflict the Soviet Union and the People's Republic of China aided them. But the Vietnamese started the fight for independence from France, and the Hanoi regime fought on to achieve the age-old goal of a unified and independent Vietnam. To a considerable degree, the strength of local forces explains the origins and peculiar dynamics of the conflict in Vietnam.

U.S. preoccupation with the Cold War had profound consequences for its policy in Vietnam. By wrongly attributing the war to world communism, the United

States drastically misjudged its origins and nature. By intervening in an essentially local struggle, it placed itself at the mercy of local forces, a weak and corrupt client in South Vietnam, and a determined adversary in North Vietnam. What might have remained a local conflict with primarily local implications was elevated into a major international conflict with tragic consequences for Americans and Vietnamese. Vietnam thus suggests the centrality of local forces in international conflicts.

In today's post-Cold War world, international communism is no longer an issue. This makes attention to local forces even more imperative. Thus, it is alarming to see how little we know about the indigenous sources of conflict that fuel the ongoing crisis in the Middle East region. Local forces will necessarily vary in each situation, but the point should be clear: we ignore them at our own peril.

Many Conflicts are Local

A distorted world view also led us to exaggerate the importance of Vietnam. From the early 1950s, U.S. policy was based on the assumption that the fall of Vietnam to communism would have disastrous consequences. This assumption, in turn, was based on a model that ascribed equal importance to all areas of the world.

These assumptions were in retrospect misguided. All areas are not of equal importance and, even if they were, the defense of them would stretch the capacity even of a superpower beyond the breaking point. Great powers must therefore be selective in assessing and defending their vital interests and must not establish goals that exceed the means to attain them. A policy of global containment such as the United States attempted to implement in the 1950s and 1960s and again in the 1980s is unworkable.

The domino theory, another major justification of U.S. intervention, has been exposed by events as false. U.S. policymakers feared that the fall of Vietnam would cause the fall of all of former French Indochina, then of Southeast Asia, with repercussions extending to India and the Philippines and perhaps beyond. This did not happen. Laos and Cambodia fell, but the other nations of Southeast Asia are now politically stable, economically prosperous, and closely joined in an anti-communist alliance. The major conflict in the area since 1975 has been among communist nations, Vietnam, China,

but what about stalling for time?

and Cambodia.

The domino theory overestimated the extent to which ideology binds governments together and underestimated the extent to which nationalism keeps them apart. It also oversimplified the ease with which revolution could be exported. In Southeast Asia, Africa, and elsewhere, there has been no domino effect; and the success of revolution has depended more on internal conditions than on external influences. We should therefore be skeptical of those who use the metaphor of falling dominoes to justify intervention in various parts of the world.

The same sort of reasoning that was behind U.S. involvement in Vietnam has been behind American intervention in Central America. Indeed, what is most similar about Vietnam and Central America is the way the United States has responded to them. It would appear the height of folly to continue to operate on the basis of the same flawed assumptions that led to disaster in Vietnam. The result is not likely to be another Vietnam. Faulty reasoning cannot help but produce bad policy, however, and the lives and treasure of many people are at stake.

The Dangers of Incrementalism

Vietnam also suggests the pitfalls of incrementalism. The massive intervention of 1965 stemmed from a series of small, steadily expanding commitments over a period of nearly twenty years. From Truman's decision to provide military aid to the French in 1950 to Johnson's decision to dispatch combat troops to Vietnam in 1965, the United States enlarged its involvement step-by-step until it had invested a half-million troops and billions of dollars.

At no point did policymakers foresee the ultimate costs of the war. Each commitment seemed harmless enough, and the consequences of doing nothing appeared more ominous than those of escalation. Yet each step made getting out more difficult. In time the extent of the investment already made became its own argument for further escalation. This process makes clear the hidden dangers of small, seemingly harmless commitments.

The Limits of Power

At each stage, moreover, U.S. policymakers appear to have taken success for granted. From the first commitment to South Vietnam in 1955, expert assessments of the chances of success were pessimistic; but policymakers persuaded themselves that everything would work out. During one particularly heated debate among John F. Kennedy's top advisers, Attorney General Robert Kennedy suggested that, if the situation were as bad as reports seemed to indicate, the United States should get out of Vietnam. According to Arthur M. Schlesinger Jr., the "question hovered for a moment, then died away, a hopelessly alien thought in a field of unexplored assumptions and entrenched convictions."

Throughout its history, the United States has enjoyed an unparalleled record of accomplishment. Americans came to take success for granted, giving rise to what the English scholar, D. W. Brogan, has called "the illusion of American omnipotence," the belief that the nation could accomplish anything it set its mind to. Vietnam makes clear that the United States, like all other nations, can fail. U.S. policymakers must acknowledge this harsh reality. They would be well advised not to commit the U.S. military in unfavorable circumstances. They might well revert to the old rule of European diplomacy to support only those nations that show a capacity to stand on their own. At the very least, policymakers should leave escape hatches to be used when the costs begin to exceed the possible gains.

This is especially true because Vietnam shows the extent to which the ability of great powers to dictate positions to small, "backward" countries has drastically declined. Throughout much of the nineteenth century, the great powers used a variety of methods to dominate smaller nations. Even in the early days of the Cold War, the United States contained insurgencies in Greece and the Philippines and overthrew governments in Iran and Guatemala with relative ease and at little cost. Increasingly, however, the ability of the great powers to manipulate lesser nations has diminished.

The power of small nations has grown relative to that of the larger nations, and their leaders have learned how to use the powerful force of nationalism to resist great power encroachments. The rivalry between the superpowers, in turn, has limited their ability to determine the destinies of smaller nations. The American failure in Vietnam and the Soviet Union's failure in Afghanistan dramatically indicate the new limits of power. At the very least, as Thomas Schelling has written, Vietnam may herald the "end of an era in which we could believe that a great industrialized power is *bound* to win when

it fights a small, poor, backward country."

Know Your Enemy

As for the actual use of American power in Vietnam, the "lessons" seem less clear. While American strategy was fundamentally flawed, it is not at all certain that another approach would have produced better results. We should thus be skeptical of those who argue that a quicker and more decisive application of U.S. power would have ensured success.

Still, there is much we can learn from the way we conducted the war in Vietnam. American policymakers assumed that the gradual increase of military pressure against North Vietnam would persuade its leaders to stop supporting the insurgency in the south without provoking a war with the Soviet Union and China. If nothing else, Vietnam should make clear the difficulties of fine-tuning the use of military power in this fashion.

A fatal error was to underestimate the enemy. Americans rather casually assumed that the National Liberation Front of South Vietnam and the North Vietnamese would know better than to stand up against the most powerful nation in the world. In the Johnson White House, Bill Moyers has written, "There was a confidence—it was never bragged about, it was just there—that when the chips were really down, the other people would fold." Years later, Henry Kissinger still could confess great surprise with the discovery that his North Vietnamese counterparts were "fanatics." Since, from his standpoint, U.S. goals were reasonable, he found it hard to understand an enemy who seemed willing to risk everything to win. Kissinger and other U.S. leaders ignored the oldest rule of warfare—know your enemy.

Problems with Clients

American relations with the South Vietnamese between 1955 and 1975 suggest numerous problems that might be encountered again in dealing with client states. First, the more we committed ourselves to the South Vietnamese government, the less leverage we had to get it to take actions we considered necessary for its survival. The more deeply committed we became the less inclined we were to risk the collapse that would likely follow the withdrawal of our support.

Moreover, at least from 1965 on, the use of American power in South Vietnam was to a large degree counter-

COVERT WARS: A DEBATE

Mortin Halperin (staff member of National Security Council during the Nixon administration):

I believe that the U.S. ought not to engage in covert wars designed to interfere in the internal affairs of other countries. The constitutional grounds for this position are clear. Covert operations commit the U.S. to major foreign policy initiatives—to wage war—without public debate, without congressional debate and without giving citizens the opportunity to express their views either by petitioning the government or by voting against a president because they don't approve his policies.

Leslie Gelb (national security correspondent for *The New York Times*):

I disagree with Mort Halperin's proposition that we ought not to interfere in the internal politics of other societies. I believe that is exactly what foreign policy is. All foreign policy is the extension of one's internal policies into the internal policies of another nation.

I think the question is not, "Should you have covert operations?" The question is, "What is your policy?" If you have a policy that makes sense, it seems to me that in principle you could conduct covert operations supporting that policy....

Ralph W. McGehee (served 25 years in the CIA, including in Vietnam; author of *Deadly Deceits: My 25 Years in the CIA*):

I believe that CIA covert operations have helped destroy democracy around the world. By means of these operations, the CIA has replaced popular governments with brutal, murderous, U.S.-controlled military dictatorships that torture and kill their own citizens....The disastrous Vietnam War began as a CIA covert operation.

William Colby (CIA Director, 1973-76; author of *Honorable Men: My Life in the CIA*):

I have quite a different view. Covert action is nothing new in American life....It is true that in the 1950s, with the organization and expansion of the CIA, there was a considerable upsurge in them. Of the covert operations undertaken since then, I would say that some have been very successful and some have been disasters, some have been the wrong thing to do and some have been the wise thing to do....The Bay of Pigs was certainly a disaster. But consider our program in the Congo in the early 1960s. The question we faced in the Congo was whether that country, which had just gained its independence from Belgium, would be run by some toadies of the old

Belgian mining companies or by men aided by Che Guevara and supported by the Soviet Union. The CIA found a midpoint between those extremes—it helped Joseph Mobutu, then a nationalist member of the Congolese forces, become the third alternative. Now, I concede that the Congo—or Zaire, as it is now called—is no garden spot and that Mr. Mobutu is not the most perfect man in the world. But I think that he has considerable advantages over the alternatives.

John Stockwell (former CIA case officer in Zaire and Vietnam):

I grew up in the Congo and served there in the Marine Corps and as a CIA officer. I know the country very well, and I can say that the CIA intervention there was an unmitigated disaster. The U.S. subverted democracy in the Congo. We participated in the assassination of a prime minister who was democratically elected, Patrice Lumumba. Then we installed in power Joseph Mobutu, who is still the dictator. We have run the country into a debt of $6.2 billion—money that was spent on the multinational corporations, not on the people. In the Congo today, 25 percent of the people are starving, while Joe Mobutu has a personal fortune of about $4.5 billion. That is the result of what the CIA considers a successful covert action.

productive. The heavy artillery fire and bombing in South Vietnam wreaked enormous destruction, tearing away the economic and social fabric of the nation we were trying to assist. "It was as if we were trying to build a house with a bulldozer and wrecking crane," one U.S. official later observed.

Moreover, by assuming primary responsibility for much of the fighting, we induced a sense of dependency on the part of the people whose independence we were professing to defend. Tragically, the dependency that we unwittingly nourished persisted long after we had tired of the war. To the very end and despite overwhelming evidence to the contrary, Nguyen Van Thieu and his cohorts clung desperately to the belief that the United States would come back and rescue them. Even when a nation or government is worthy of outside support, it does them no favor to provide the support in a way that undermines the self-sufficiency that should be the object of our assistance. South Vietnam suffered the most destruction in this long and bloody war. We should ponder long and hard the morality of making a commitment to people that we may not be prepared to see through and that, in the long run, may cause them more harm than good.

War Requires Popular Support

Vietnam shows that public support for military interventions is both essential and unreliable. Wars cannot be fought in the American system without public support. Yet dissent in war is a long-established American tradition. Korea and Vietnam make clear that the longer the war and the higher American casualties, the more public support is likely to erode. Even in World War II, the "good war" against Hitler and Hirohito, General George C. Marshall saw that public support had limits.

The crucial ingredient in holding support may be success on the battlefield. Vietnam suggests that, without clear indications of success, public support will be difficult to sustain. At the same time, without public support it may be impossible to do what it takes to win. There is no easy answer to this dilemma. Certainly, leaders cannot take support for granted, as Johnson did

FEIFFER®

at the outset of the war. Nor is the secret plotting of Nixon and Kissinger a viable alternative. The only workable policy is one that can be defended in public debate. The public needs a cause it can believe in before it willingly sacrifices its young men and treasure.

The Reagan administration's Iran-Contra scandal, itself in part a product of Vietnam, underscores this vital point. White House operatives, like Lt. Col. Oliver North, who orchestrated the exchange of arms for hostages with Iran and the illegal transfer of funds to the Nicaraguan Contras, were deeply influenced by Vietnam. Their anti-communism was strengthened by America's failure there and the subsequent national reaction against global interventionism. Vietnam also left them cynical about governmental processes and constitutional limits. Thus they were determined to "win" in Nicaragua to atone for defeat in Vietnam, and they were prepared to use any means to attain that end.

The result was not what they intended. They discredited, perhaps beyond retrieval, the cause for which they fought. More important, they reinforced the very "lessons" of Vietnam they had sought to overcome. Wars fought secretly and illegally without the consent of Congress and the people are antithetical to the basic principles by which the nation is organized and threaten the integrity of its political institutions. Presidents who undertake such wars place their own administrations at risk.

The War and the Warriors

Vietnam shows what *not* to do in the raising and handling of troops. The draft policy used throughout much of the war imposed most of the burden on the lower classes. The middle and upper classes to a great degree escaped service. The obvious inequity of such a system increased class hostility. Also, by freeing the children of the elite, the draft encouraged them to be complacent about the war until the nation was deeply committed.

Today's volunteer army, a legacy of Vietnam, contains the same glaring inequities in burden sharing. Without substantial reforms, such a system could have the same negative effects on public concern and class

and racial relations as it did during the Vietnam War.

To spread the burden of fighting, the services decided early that each man should serve just twelve months in the combat zone. This arrangement did nothing to promote unit cohesion and individual and group morale.

Atrocities such as My Lai were not aberrations but a logical consequence of fighting a war of attrition where friend and foe were difficult to distinguish in a nation hostile to outside intervention. We must do everything possible to learn from and prevent a repetition of such crimes of war.

Above all, any nation that goes to war must provide for the readjustment of its fighting men to civilian life. Vietnam veterans were dumped back into an ungrateful homeland with little assistance in readjustment. This was not only callous but disgraceful and left scars that may never heal.

More generally, Vietnam demonstrates the value—indeed the necessity—of reflecting on history when making and implementing U.S. foreign policy. What is so striking now, especially with hindsight, is our abysmal ignorance of the Vietnamese. We also mistakenly rejected the relevance of the French experience in Vietnam because, it was said, the United States did not have selfish colonial goals like France and the French had not won a battle since Napoleon.

At the least, we must conclude that, rather than glibly citing familiar but misleading analogies, leaders and citizens should use history to enlighten themselves about the areas and peoples with whom they deal. The more different the history and culture of the people, the greater the need to study them in detail.

The historical perspective involves taking an issue or problem back to its beginnings to determine how we got to where we are. It is striking how infrequently this is done in internal discussions of policy problems. Unfortunately, the news media, preoccupied with daily happenings, typically ignore history and provide precious little in-depth understanding of foreign policy issues. History clarifies the context in which contemporary problems exist. To act without such perspective can be deadly.

Conclusion

Nations have long memories. Vietnam will continue to have a powerful influence on American foreign policy until some other cataclysmic event replaces it. It is therefore urgent that we study and learn from it. In doing this, we must remember that history does not yield precise, explicit answers to today's most pressing questions. Indeed, when used improperly, history is a mischievous guide. We should be wary of those who justify present-day commitments and strategies on the basis of what was done or not done in Vietnam.

On the other hand, careful analysis of how we got into Vietnam and why we failed can provide vital perspectives for today's problems. It can educate us about who we are and how we deal with other people and can offer cautionary principles, such as those cited above, that can help guide our leaders in making decisions. The past is indeed prologue, and we cannot begin to deal with today's most pressing issues without coming to terms with the longest and most divisive war the nation has fought.

Discussion Questions

1. Which films have made the deepest impressions on the "generation that knows the war mainly through films"? What images of the war do these films project?

2. What are the most commonly asked questions reflecting the mood of national uncertainty about the Vietnam experience?

3. Explain how the variety of views on the war illustrates the saying of Confucius that "you see what is behind your eyes."

4. Radicals, liberals and conservatives differed in their assessments of the legitimate ends and means employed in the war. Discuss these differences and how they influenced the way in which each group viewed the war.

5. Many liberals who originally backed the war in Vietnam changed their minds in the late 1960s. What events/circumstances led to this shift in attitude?

6. What did General Westmoreland mean when he said, "It takes the full strength of a tiger to kill a rabbit"? Discuss whether or not you believe this is a valid lesson to be drawn from the Vietnam War.

7. What were the major similarities and differences between the Persian Gulf and Vietnam? Did these differences lead to different results? Explain.

8. Evaluate the authors' statement about Vietnam that "what might have remained a local conflict with primarily local implications was elevated into a major international conflict." How does this statement relate to the "lessons" discussed at the end of the unit?

9. Was the "Domino Theory" an accurate prediction of what happened in Southeast Asia when Vietnam fell? Why or why not? Is there a more appropriate analogy?

10. What was the role of the "homefront" in the Vietnam War? What "lessons" for the future might we draw from this?

11. In the eyes of radicals, liberals and conservatives, who were the real "heroes", "villains", and "victims" of the war?

Noon

I'm digging holes for three wilted saplings—
pin oak, mulberry, flowering crab—
behind a tract house reeking freshly sawn
boards in the heat of a July afternoon.
After 22 years in dorm rooms, the Air Force,
a string of roach-filled apartments and rent
houses, I am a home owner. Transparencies
swarming from my hat, I squat on my heels
among clods of red clay and green shoots of grass
then let myself unroll. I am forty.
In ten years I will be fifty and
this yard will be shaded. Now, the heat
is excruciating. The rumble of trucks
and cars floats over across rooftops
from the throughway. It is the Delta and I
am sprawling on my back in copper-colored
dirt after filling sandbags. Through the earth
I feel the kicks of an airstrike that goes on
a klick away. Choppers are wheeling
overhead like hornets. But this
is not a poem about the war.
I'm tired of it always being the war.
This is a poem about how, if I place
my head, that stick of mulberry tree
in the shape of a Y shades my eyes from the sun.

    —Perry Oldham

REFERENCES

Ackerman, Jan. "Marine Finds War Buddy's Mom; She Finally Accepts Son's Death." *Pittsburgh Post-Gazette* (January 28, 1986).

Albert, Judith and Stewart Edward Albert. *The Sixties Papers: Documents of a Rebellious Decade.* New York, Praeger, 1984.

Ali, Muhammad. *The Greatest.* New York: Random House, 1975.

Altbach, Philip *Student Politics in America: A Historical Analysis.* New York: McGraw Hill, 1974.

Altbach, Philip and Robert S. Laufer, eds. *The New Pilgrims: Youth Protest in Transition.* New York: David McKay Co., Inc., 1972.

Anderson, H., L.P. Hanrahan, M. Jensen, et al. *Wisconsin Vietnam Veteran Mortality Study.* Madison, WI: Division of Health, 1985.

Ashmun, Lawrence R. *Resettlement of Indochinese Refugees in the United States: A Selected and Annotated Bibliography.* Dekalb: Northern Illinois University Press, 1983.

Astin, Alexander, Helen S. Astin, Alan E. Bayer, and Ann S. Bisconti. *The Power of Protest.* San Francisco: Jossey-Bass, 1975.

Baker, J. "Monitoring of Suicidal Behavior Among Patients in the VA Health Care System." *Psychiatric Annals* 14 (1984):272-75.

Baker, Walter F. "Communications." *Saturday Review* (June 1972): 72.

Ball, George W. "Top Secret: the Prophecy of the President Rejected." *The Atlantic Monthly* 230 (July 1972): 35-49.

Baritz, Loren. *Backfire.* New York: Ballantine, 1985.

Barrat, Patrice and Philip Brooks. "Amerasians: 'dust of life.'" *Refugees* 20 (August 1985): 35-36.

Baskir, Lawrence M. and William A. Strauss. *Chance and Circumstance.* New York: Alfred A. Knopf, 1978.

_____ *Reconcilliation After Vietnam: A Program of Relief for Vietnam Era Draft and Military Offenders.* Notre Dame: University of Notre Dame Press, 1977.

Bator, Victor. *Vietnam: A Diplomatic Tragedy.* New York: Oceana Publications, 1965.

Beard, Charles A. and Mary Beard. *A Basic History of the United States.* New York: Doubleday, 1972.

Becker, Howard S., ed. *Campus Power Struggle.* New Brunswick, NJ: Transaction Books, 1973.

Beitiks, Edvins. "North Vietnamese War Veterans Try to Remember but Long to Forget." *San Francisco Examiner* (August 6, 1989): A17.

Blaufarb, Douglas. *The Counter-Insurgency Era: U.S. Doctrine And Performance.* New York: Free Press, 1977.

Boettcher, Thomas D. *Vietnam: The Valor And The Sorrow.* Boston: Little, Brown, 1985.

Borton, Lady. *Sensing the Enemy: An American Woman among the Boat People of Vietnam.* New York: Dial/Doubleday, 1984.

Bowman, John, ed. *The Vietnam War: An Almanac.* New York: World Almanac Publications, 1985.

Braestrup, Peter. "The Tet Offensive—Another Press Controversy: II. In *Vietnam Reconsidered.*

_____. *Big Story: How The American Press and Television Reported and Interpreted The Crisis Of Tet 1968 In Vietnam and Washington;* 2 Vols. (ed.) *Vietnam as History.* Washington, D.C.: University Press of America, 1984. Boulder, CO: Westview Press, 1977.

Brandon, Heather. *Casualties.* New York: St. Martin's Press, 1984.

Breines, Winni. *The Great Refusal—Community and Organization in the New Left, 1962-1968.* New York: J. R. Bergin, 1982.

Brogran, D.W. "The Illusion of American Impotence." *Harpers* 205 (December 1952): 21-28.

Broughton, Jack. *Third Ridge.* Philadelphia: J.B. Lippincott, 1969.

Bryan, C.D.B. *Friendly Fire.* New York: G. P. Putnam's Sons, 1976.

Buckingham, William A. Jr. *Operation Ranch Hand: The Air Force and Herbicides in Southeast Asia, 1961-1971.* Washington, DC: Office of Air Force History, 1982.

Buttinger, Joseph. "News Forum." (August/September 1969): 459.

_____. *Vietnam: A Dragon Embattled,* Vol. I. New York: Praeger, 1967.

Cable, Larry E. *Conflict of Myths: The Development of American Counterinsurgency Doctrine and the Vietnam War.* New York: New York University Press, 1986.

Carpenter, Mackenzie. "Former Viet Cong Talks on 'Healing.'" *Pittsburgh Post-Gazette* (December 5, 1990).

Cecil, Paul Frederick. *Herbicidal Warfare: The Ranch Hand Project In Vietnam.* Westport, CT: Praeger, 1986.

Chandler, Robert W. *War Of Ideas: The U.S. Propaganda Campaign in Vietnam.* Boulder, CO: Westview, 1981.

Chomsky, Noam, and Edward Herman. *After the Cataclysm,* Volume II. Boston: South End Press, 1976.

Chung, Ly Qui, ed. *Between Two Fires: The Unheard Voices of Vietnam.* New York: Praeger, 1970.

Cohen, Mitchell and Dennis Hale, eds. *The New Stu-*

dent Left: An Anthology. Boston: Beacon, 1966.

Collison, Michelle N-K. "Black Students Have Mixed Views on Gulf War: Some Call It 'Racist,' Others Voice Support." *The Chronicle of Higher Education,* February 6, 1991:A29.

Cox, Oliver. *Crisis at Columbia.* New York: Scribner's, 1968.

Dann, Jeanne Van Buren & Jack, eds. *In The Field of Fire.* New York: Tom Doherty Associates, Inc. 1987.

Decker, Michael and James Jefferies. "Platoon—The Movie and the Law of War Training." *Marine Corps Gazette* 71,4 (April 1978):43.

"The Decline and Near Fall of the U.S. Army." *Saturday Review* LV, 47 (December, 1972): 61.

"Déjà Vu in Old Saigon: One Economist Fits All." *The New York Times* (May 13, 1989).

"'Disinformation': Ex-CIA Agents Describe World Propaganda Web." *The Pittsburgh Press* (October 5, 1986): A-19.

Donovan, Hedley. "Vietnam: The War Is Worth Winning." *Life* (February 25, 1966): 27-31.

Dougan, Clark, Stephen Weiss, and the editors of the Boston Publishing Company. *Nineteen Sixty-Eight.* Boston: Boston Publishing Co., 1983.

Doyle, Edward, Samuel Lipsman, Stephen Weiss, and the editors of the Boston Publishing Company. *Passing the Torch.* Boston: Boston Publishing Co., 1981.

Drury, Richard S. *My Secret War.* Fallbrook, CA: Aero, 1979.

Duiker, William. "The Lessons of Vietnam." *The Asia Mail* (February 1977): 203-204.

Efron, Edith *The News Travelers.* New York: Manor Books, 1971.

Ehrhart, W. D., ed. *Carrying The Darkness: American Indochina—The Poetry of the Vietnam War.* New York: Avon, 1985.

Eilert, Rick. *For Self and Country.* New York: William Morrow & Co, Inc. 1983.

Eisen, Arlene. *Women and Revolution in Viet Nam.* Atlantic Highlands, NJ: Humanities Press International, 1984.

Elshtain, Jean Bethke. *Women and War.* New York: Basic Books, Inc., 1987.

Elwood-Akers, Virginia. *Women War Correspondents in the Vietnam War, 1961-1975.* Metuchen, NJ: The Scarecrow Press, Inc. 1988.

Emerson, Gloria. *Winners and Losers.* New York: Random House, 1976.

Epstein, Edward J. *Televised War in Fact and Fiction: The Problem of Journalism.* New York: Vintage, 1978.

Erikson, Robert and Luttbeg, Norman. *American Public Opinion: It's Origins, Content, and Impact.* New York: Wiley, 1980.

Evans, Rep. Lane. "Veterans Need Help Now." *American Legion Magazine.* (September 1990): 38-39.

Everett, Arthur, Kathryn Johnson and Harry Rosenthal. *Calley.* New York: Associated Press and Dell, 1971.

Faith, William Robert. *Bob Hope: A Life in Comedy.* New York: G. P. Putnam's Sons, 1982.

Fall, Bernard. *Hell in a Very Small Place.* New York: Vintage, 1968.

Fallaci, Oriana. *Nothing and So Be It.* Garden City: Doubleday & Company, Inc., 1972.

Ferber, Michael and Staughton Lynd. *The Resistance.* Boston: Beacon Press, 1971..

Figley, C. R. ed. *Stress Disorders Among Vietnam Veterans: Theory, Research, and Treatment.* New York: Brunner/Mazel, 1978.

Fishman, Mark. *Manufacturing the News.* Austin: University of Texas Press, 1980.

Fitzgerald, Frances. *Fire in the Lake.* Boston: Little, Brown and Company, 1972.

Foster, Julian and Durwood Long, eds. *Protest! Student Activism in America.* New York: Morrow, 1970.

Freedman, Dan & Rhoads, Jacqueline. *Nurses in Vietnam: The Forgotten Veterans.* Austin: Texas Monthly Press, 1987.

Fried, John H. E., ed. *Vietnam and International Law.* Flanders, NJ: O'Hare, 1967.

Friedman, Leon, ed. *The Law of War: A Documentary History,* vol. 1. New York: Random House, 1972.

Gallucci, Robert L. *Neither Peace Nor Honor: The Politics Of American Military Policy In Vietnam.* Baltimore: Johns Hopkins University Press, 1975.

Gans, Herbert. *Deciding What's News.* New York: Pantheon, 1976.

Gardner, Hugh. *The Children of Prosperity: Thirteen Modern American Communes.* New York: St. Martins Press, 1978.

Gault, William Barry. "Some Remarks on Slaughter." *American Journal of Psychiatry* 128, 4 (October 1971).

Gelb, Leslie and Richard Betts. *The Irony of Vietnam: The System Worked.* Washington, D.C.: Brookings Institution, 1979.

"General Wanted to Continue War March." *New York Times* News Service, March 27, 1991.

Genz, Marilyn. *20,000 Men and Me.* Carpentersville,

IL: Crossroads Communications, 1987.

Gergen, Kenneth and Mary Gergen. "The Politics of Despair." *Saturday Review* (September 19, 1970): 80.

Gershen, Martin. *Destroy or Die: The True Story of My Lai.* New Rochelle, NY: Arlington House, 1971.

Gibbons, William. *The U.S. Government and the Vietnam War, II.* Princeton, N.J.: Princeton University Press, 1986.

Gibson, James William. *The Perfect War: Technowar in Vietnam.* New York: Atlantic Monthly Press, 1986.

Gitlin, Todd. *The Whole World Is Watching: Mass Media in the Making and Unmaking of the New Left.* Berkeley: University of California Press, 1980.

Goertzel, Ted. "Domestic Pressures For Abstention: Vietnam." In *Intervention or Abstention.* R. Highom, ed. Lexington: University of Kentucky Press, 1976.

Goff, Stanley and Robert Sanders with Clark Smith. *Brothers: Black Soldiers in the War.* New York: Berkeley Books, 1982.

Goldstein, Norman and The Associated Press. *John Wayne: A Tribute.* New York: Holt, 1979.

Gough, Kathleen. *Ten Times More Beautiful.* New York: Monthly Review Press, 1978.

Goulden, Joseph C. *Truth Is The First Casualty.* New York: Rand McNally, 1969.

Grant, Bruce. *The Boat People: An "Age" Investigation.* New York: Penguin Brooks, 1979.

Gravel, Mike, editor. *The Pentagon Papers,* Boston: Beacon Press, 1971.

Grinter, Lawrence E. and Peter M. Dunn, eds. *The American War In Vietnam: Lessons, Legacies, And Implications for Future Conflicts.* Westport, CT: Greenwood Press, 1987.

Halberstam, David. *The Best and the Brightest.* New York: Random House, 1972.

Hallin, Daniel C. *The "Uncensored War": The Media and Vietnam.* New York: Oxford, 1986.

Hammer, Richard. *One Morning in the War: The Tragedy at Son My.* New York: Coward-McMann, 1970.

Handler, M.S. "Neutral Vietnam Held North's Aim." *The New York Times* (July 17, 1964).

Harvey, Frank. *Air War—Vietnam.* New York: Bantam, 1967.

Hawthorne, Lesleyanne, ed. *Refugees: The Vietnamese Experience.* New York: Oxford University press, 1981.

Hayslip, Le Ly with Wurts, Jay. *When Heaven and Earth Changed Places.* New York: Plume, 1990.

Heller, Jean. "Public Doesn't Get Picture with Gulf Satellite Photos." *In These Times* (February 29,1991-March 19, 1991):7.

Helmer, John. *Bringing the War Home: The American Soldier in Vietnam and After.* New York: Free Press, 1974.

Hemingway, Ernest. *In our Time.* New York: Scribners, 1925.

Hendin, Herbert and Ann P. Haas. *Wounds of War.* New York: Basic Books, 1984.

Herr, Michael. *Dispatches.* New York: Avon, 1978.

Herring, George C. *America's Longest War: The United States And Vietnam, 1950-1975.* 2nd Ed. New York: Knopf, 1986. (Original ed. New York: Wiley, 1979).

Herrington, Stuart A. *Silence Was a Weapon: The Vietnam War In The Villages.* Novato, CA: Presidio Press, 1982.

Hersh, Seymore M. *My Lai-4: A Report of the Massacre and Its Aftermath.* New York: Random House, 1970.

Hersh, Seymour. *Cover-Up.* New York: Random House, 1972.

Holm, Jeanne. *Women in the Military.* Novato, CA: Presido Press, 1982.

Horn, A.D. (ed.) *The Wounded Generation: America After Vietnam.* N.J. Prentice-Hall, 1981.

Horowitz, Irving Louis and William H. Friedland, eds. *The Knowledge Factory: Student Power in Academic Politics in America.* Carbondale and Edwardsville, Illinois: Southern Illinois University Press, 1972

Hurrock, Nicholas and Storer H. Rowley. "TV's Need Magnified the Trivial." *Washington Post* Service, January 25, 1991.

Jacobs, Harold, ed. *Weatherman.* New York: Ramparts Press, 1970.

Jacobs, Paul and Saul Landau. *The New Radicals: A Report with Documents.* New York: Vintage, 1966.

Johnstone, Diana. "European Parliment and Changing Vietnam Policy." *In These Times* (July 7-14, 1990.): 11.

Joseph, Paul. *Cracks In The Empire.* Boston: South End Press, 1981.

Karnow, Stanley. *Vietnam: A History.* New York: The Viking Press, 1983.

Kattenburg, Paul M. "Reflections on Vietnam: Of Revisionism and Lessons Yet To Be Learned." *Parameters XIV* (Autumn 1984.)

Kelman, Herbert and Lee H. Lawrence. "American Responses to the Trial of Lieutenant William L. Calley." *Psychology Today* (June 1972) : 48-81.

Kinnard, Douglas. *The War Managers.* Hanover, NH: University Press Of New England, 1977.

Kolko, Gabriel. *Anatomy of a War: Vietnam, the United States, and Modern Historical Experience*. New York: Pantheon, 1985.

Komer, Robert W. *Bureaucracy At War: U.S. Performance In The Vietnam Conflict*. Boulder, CO: Westview Press, 1985.

Krepinevich, Andrew F. *The Army and Vietnam*. Baltimore: Johns Hopkins University Press, 1986.

Lacoutrure, Jean. *Ho Chi Minh: A Political Biography*. New York: Random House, 1968.

Lake, Anthony. *The Vietnam Legacy: The War, American Society and the Future of American Foreign Policy*. New York: New York University Press, 1976.

Larsen, Wendy Wilder & Tran Thi Nga. *Shallow Graves*. New York: Perennial Library, 1986.

Lefever, Ernest. "CBS and National Defense, 1972-73." *Journal of Communication* (Autumn 1975).

"The Legality of U.S. Participation in the Defense of Viet-Nam." *U.S. Department of State Bulletin* (March 28, 1966).

Lekachman, Robert. "The Cost in National Treasure: $400,000,000,000 Plus." *Saturday Review* Magazine (December 1972): 44-49.

Lens, Sidney. "How It All 'Really' Began." *The Progressive* (June 1973).

Levy, Charles J. *Spoils of War*. Boston: Houghton-Mifflin, 1974.

Lewis, Paul. "U.N.'s 'Big 5' Offering Resolution to End War." *New York Times* News Service, March 27, 1991

Lewy, Guenter. *America in Vietnam*. New York: Oxford, 1978.

Life Magazine (December 5, 1969).

Lifton, Robert J. "Beyond Atrocity." *Saturday Review Magazine* (March 27, 1971).

—————. *Home from the War*. New York: Simon & Schuster, 1973.

Lipsman, Samuel, Edward Doyle, and the editors of the Boston Publishing Company. *Fighting for Time*. Boston: Boston Publishing Co., 1983.

Livingston, Gordon. "Letter to the Editor." *Saturday Review* (September 20, 1969).

Lloyd, Norman, Maynard Parker and Russell Watson. "The Killings at Song My." *Newsweek* 74, 23 (December 8, 1969).

Lomperis, Timothy J. *Vietnam: The War Everyone Lost—and Won: America's Intervention in Vietnam's Twin Struggles*. Baton Rouge: LSV Press, 1984.

MacPherson, Myra. *Long Time Passing: Vietnam and the Haunted Generation*. New York: New American Library, 1985.

Maitland, Terrence, Stephen Weiss, and the editors of the Boston Publishing Company. *Raising the Stakes*. Boston: Boston Publishing Co., 1982.

Mandelbaum, Michael. "Vietnam: The Television War." *Daedalus III* (Fall 1982): 157-168.

Mangold, Tom and Penycate, John. *The Tunnels of Cu Chi*. New York: Berkeley Books, 1986.

Marshall, Kathryn. *In the Combat Zone*. New York: Penguin Books, 1987.

Matsakis, Aphrodite. *Vietnam Wives*. Kensington, MD: Woodbine House, 1988.

Maurer, Harry. Strange Ground Americans in *Vietnam 1945-1975: An Oral History*. New York: Henry Holt and Company, 1989.

May, Ernest R. *"Lessons" of the Past: The Use and Misuse of History in American Foreign Policy*. New York: Oxford University Press, 1975.

McAlister, John T. *Vietnam: The Origins of Revolution*. New York: Doubleday, 1971.

McKay, Bernadette A. "Civilian Assignment." *American Journal of Nursing* (February 1968): 336-338.

McLear, Michael. *The Ten Thousand Day War—Vietnam: 1945-1975*. New York: Saint Martin's, 1981.

McVicker, Sara, J. "Invisible Veterans: the Women Who Served in Vietnam." *Journal of Psychosocial Nursing* (October 1985): 12-19.

Melman, Seymour. *Pentagon Capitalism*. New York: McGraw-Hill, 1970.

Melville, Keith. *Communes in the Counterculture*. New York: Morrow, 1972.

Miller, Carolyn Paine. *Captured!* Chappaqua, NY: Christian Herald Books, 1977.

Mueller, John. In *A Guide to Vietnam: A Television History*. Boston: WGBH Education Foundation, 1983.

—————. *War, Presidents and Public Opinion*. Lanham, MD: University Press of America, 1985.

Nathan, Debbie. "Just the Good News Please." *The Progressive,* February 1991: 25-27.

Nguyen Thi Thu-Lam. *Fallen Leaves: Memoirs of a Vietnamese Woman from 1940 to 1975*. New Haven: Council on Southeast Asia Studies Yale Center for International and Area Studies, 1989.

Nguyen Tien Hung and Jerold L. Schecter. *The Palace File*. New York: Harper and Row, 1986.

Nixon, Richard M. *No More Vietnams*. New York: Arbor House, 1985.

Noel, Chris. *Matter of Survival*. Boston: Branden

Publishing Company, 1987.

Norman, Geoffrey. *Bouncing Back: How a Heroic Band of POWs Survived Vietnam.* Boston: Houghton Mifflin Company, 1990.

O'Brien, James. *A History of the New Left, 1960-1968.* Boston: New England Free Press, 1968.

Oberdorfer, Don. *Tet!* Garden City, NY: Doubleday, 1971.

Palmer, Bruce Jr. *The 25-Year War: America's Military Role In Vietnam.* Lexington: University of Kentucky Press, 1984.

Palmer, Dave Richard. *Summons Of The Trumpet: A History Of The Vietnam War From A Military Man's Viewpoint.* San Rafael, CA: Presidio Press, 1978.

Palmer, Laura. *Shrapnel in the Heart.* New York: Vintage Books, 1988.

Patti, Archimedes L.A. *Why Vietnam? Prelude to America's Albatross.* Berkeley: University of California Press, 1980.

Perkus, Cathy, ed. *COINTELPRO: The FBI's Secret War on Political Freedom.* Intro. by Noam Chomsky. New York: Monad Press, 1975.

Peterson, Richard E. and J.A. Bilorusky. *May 1970: The Campus Aftermath of Cambodia and Kent State.* New York: Carnegie Commission on Higher Education, 1970.

Pike, Douglas. *PAVN: People's Army of Vietnam.* Novato, CA: Presidio Press, 1985.

Pisor, Robert. *The End of the Line: The Seige of Khe Sanh.* New York: Norton, 1982.

Podhoretz, Norman. *Why Were We In Vietnam?* New York: Touchstone, 1983.

Pollner, Murray. *No Victory Parades: The Return of the Vietnam Veteran.* New York: Holt, Rinehart and Winston, 1971.

"Postservice Mortality Among Vietnam Veterans." *Journal of the American Medical Association* (February 13, 1987): 257.

Powers, Thomas. *The War At Home: Vietnam and the American People, 1964-68.* New York: Grossman Publishers, 1973.

Race, Jeffrey. *War Comes to Long An: Revolutionary Conflict in a Vietnamese Province.* Berkeley: University of California Press, 1971.

Ray, Michele. *The Two Shores of Hell.* New York: David McKay Company, Inc., 1986.

Riddell, Tom. "The $676 Billion Quagmire." *Progressive* (October 1973).

Robinson, J. P. "The Audience for National TV News Programs." *Public Opinion Quarterly* 35 (1971): 403-405.

Rogers, Barbara & Nickolaus, Janet. "Vietnam Nurses." *Journal of Psychosocial Nursing* (Winter 1985): 11-15.

Roszak, Theodore. *The Making of a Counterculture: Reflections on the Technocratic Society and its Youthful Opposition.* Garden City, NJ: Doubleday Anchor, 1969.

Russo, Frank. "A Study of Bias in TV Coverage of the Vietnam War: 1969 and 1970." *Public Opinion Quarterly* 35, 4 (1971): 539-543.

Sack, John. *Lieutenant Calley, His Own Story.* New York: Viking, 1971.

Safer, Morley. *Flashbacks: On Returning to Vietnam.* New York: Random House, 1990.

Sale, Kirkpatrick. *SDS* New York: Random House, 1973.

Salisbury, Harrison E. (ed.) *Vietnam Reconsidered: Lessons from a War.* New York: Harper & Row, 1984.

Santoli, Al. "We Never Knew Our Fathers." *Parade Magazine* (May 27, 1990): 21

Saywell, Shelley. *Women In War.* New York: Penguin Books, 1985.

Schell, Jonathan. *The Military Half: An Account of Destruction in Quang Ngai and Quang Tin.* New York: Knopf, 1968.

Schlesinger, Arthur, Jr. *Robert Kennedy and His Times.* New York: Ballantine Books, 1979.

_____ *The Bitter Heritage.* Boston: Houghton Mifflin, 1966.

Schlight, John, ed. *The Second Indochina War Symposium: Papers and Commentary.* Washington, DC: GPO, 1986.

Schultz, George. "The Meaning of Vietnam." *Department of State Bulletin* 85 (June 1985): 13-16.

Schwinn, Monica & Diehl, Bernhard. *We Came To Help.* New York: Harcourt, Brace and Jovanovich, Inc., 1976.

Scranton, William, Chair. *The Report of the President's Commission on Campus Unrest.* New York: Avon, 1971.

Sharp, U.S. Grant. *Strategy for Defeat: Vietnam in Retrospect.* Novato, CA: Presidio Press, 1978.

Shepard, Barclay M., et al. *Proportionate Mortality Study Of Army And Marine Corps Veterans Of The Vietnam War.* Office of Environmental Epidemiology, Veterans' Administration. Washington, D.C., 1987.

Shepherd, Donald and Robert Saltzer with Dave Grayson. *Duke: The Life and Times of John Wayne.* Garden City, NJ: Doubleday, 1985.

"600 Oil Wells Burning May Harm Millions." Press News Services, March 3, 1991.

Skolnick, Jermore H. (Director). *The Politics of Pro-*

test: *A Task Force Report Submitted to the National Commission on the Causes and Prevention of Violence.* New York: Simon and Schuster, 1969.

Spector, Ronald H. *Advice and Support: The Early Years of the United States Army In Vietnam 1941-1960.* Washington, DC: Center of Military History, 1983.

Spragens, John, Jr., and Joel Charny. *Obstacles To Recovery In Vietnam and Kampuchea.* Boston: Oxfam, Inc., 1980.

Sricharatchanya, Paisal. "Fighting a Phantom Army." *Far Eastern Economic Review* 138, 47 (November 19, 1987): 30.

St. Cartmail, Keith. *Exodus Indochina.* New York: Heinemann, 1983.

Stanton, Shelby L. *The Rise and Fall of an American Army: U.S. Ground Forces in Vietnam, 1965-1973.* Novato, CA: Presidio Press, 1985.

Stremlow, Mary V. *A History of the Women Marines, 1946-1977.* Washington, DC: U.S. Government Printing Office, 1986.

Strick, Lisa. "The Child I Couldn't Forget." *Good Housekeeping.* (May 1988): 157, 2399-241.

Summers, Harry G. Jr. *On Strategy: A Critical Analysis of the Vietnam War.* Novato, CA: Presidio Press, 1982.

Szulc, Tad. "El Salvadore is Spanish for Vietnam." *Penthouse* 15 (September 1983.)

Taylor, Maxwell D. *Swords and Ploughshares.* New York: Norton, 1972.

Taylor, Telford. *Nuremburg and Vietnam: An American Tragedy.* Chicago: Quadrangle Books, 1970.

Tepper, Elliot L., ed. *Southeast Asian Exodus: From Tradition to Resettlement: Understanding Refugees from Laos, Kampuchea and Vietnam in Canada.* Canadian Studies Association, 1980.

Terry, Wallace. *Bloods: An Oral History of the Vietnam War by Black Veterans.* New York: Random House, 1984.

Thayer, Thomas C. *War Without Fronts: The American Experience in Vietnam.* Boulder, CO: Westview, 1985.

Thies, Wallace J. *When Governments Collide: Coercion and Diplomacy in the Vietnam Conflict, 1964-1968.* Berkeley: University of California Press, 1980.

Thompson, James Clay. *Rolling Thunder: Understanding Policy and Program Failure.* Chapel Hill: University of North Carolina Press, 1980.

Thompson, W. Scott and Donald D. Frizzel. *The Lessons of Vietnam.* New York: Crane, Russack & Co., 1977.

Tick, Edward. "Vietnam Grief: Psychotherapeutic and Psychohistorical Implications." *The Psychotherapy Patient* 2:1, Fall, 1985.

Townsend, Peter. *The Girl in the White Ship: A True Story of Escape, Faith & Survival.* New York: Holt, Rinehart & Winston, 1981.

Trullinger, James Walker Jr. *Village at War: An Account of Revolution in Vietnam.* New York: Longman, 1980.

Tuchman, Gaye. *Making News.* New York: The Free Press, 1978.

Tuchman, Barbara W. *The March of Folly.* New York: Knopf, 1984.

Turley, G. H. Colonel. *The Easter Offensive: Vietnam, 1972.* Novato, CA: Presidio Press, 1985.

Turley, William S. *The Second Indochina War: A Short Political and Military History 1954-1975.* Boulder, CO: Westview Press, 1986.

Useem, Michael. *Conscription, Protest and Social Conflict: The Life and Death of a Draft Resistance Movement.* New York: John Wiley, 1973.

Van Devanter, Lynda and Morgan, Christopher. *Home Before Morning.* New York: Warner Books, Inc., 1983.

"Vietnam Vets Find Peace in Healing Ceremonies: Rituals Help End the War Within." *Utne Reader,* March/April 1991: 324-36.

Walker, Keith. *A Piece of my Heart.* New York: Ballentine Books, 1985.

Walzer, Michael. *Just and Unjust Wars: A Moral Argument, With Historical Illustrations.* New York: Basic Books, 1977.

Webb, Kate. *On The Other Side.* New York: Quadrangle Books, 1972.

Weinberger, Caspar W. "The Uses of Military Power." *Defense* (January 1985): 2-8.

Westby, David. *The Clouded Vision: The Student Movement in the United States in the 1960's.* Lewisburg, PA: Bucknell University Press, 1976.

Westing, Arthur H. *The Environmental Aftermath of Warfare in Vietnam.* London: Taylor & Francis, 1982.

Westmoreland, William C. *A Soldier Reports.* Garden City, NY: Doubleday, 1976.

Wilcox, Fred A. *Waiting For An Army To Die: The Tragedy of Agent Orange.* New York: Random House, Inc., 1983.

Wilson, George C. "A Separate Peace: Vietnam Veterans Go Back to Find a Way to End the War Still Raging Within." *The Washington Post.* National Weekly Edition (April 2-8, 1990): 10-11.

Zielenziger, Michael. "Copter Flights Help Veterans Confront Past." *The Philadelphia Inquirer* (September 9, 1989): 7B.

GRAPHIC CREDITS

Chapter 1

Page 3—Al Cardwell reprinted from Steven Cohen (ed). *A Guide to Vietnam: A Television History*. New York: Random House, 1983; Alfred A. Knopf, Inc.

Page 4—Herbert Krohn. *New York Quarterly*

Page 7—*The Tale of Kieu*. Translated and annotated by Huynh Sanh Thong, Illustration by Ho Dac Ngoc. New Haven: Yale University Press, 1983.

Page 9, 13—Collection of D. Seylan

Pages 12, 17, 23, 24—Wide World Photos, Inc.

Page 15—(top) Terry Cannon. *Vietnam: A Thousand Years of Struggle*. New York: Peoples Press, 1969

Page 15—(bottom) Indochina Curriculum Group

Page 16—Black Star

Page 19—Bill Mauldin. *Chicago Sun Times*, 1972

Page 21—Michigan State University Archives and Historical Collection

Page 26—Steve Hassett. "Christmas" *Demilitarized Zones*, Jan Barry and W.D. Ehrhart (eds). East River Anthology, 1976

Page 27—*The Nam*, Marvel Comics Group, 1986

Chapter 2

Pages 29, 40, 45, 46, 48, 49, 53, 55—Wide World Photos, Inc.

Page 32—Archimedes Patti Collection

Page 34—Bettman Archive

Page 36—USIA

Page 37—Jan Barry. "In the Footsteps of Genghis Khan" *Winning Hearts and Minds: War Poems by Vietnam Veterans*, Jan Barry, Basil T. Paquet and Larry Rottmann (eds.)

Page 42—Cecil Stoughton, Lyndon Johnson Library

Page 56—Douglas Marlette, *The Charlotte Observer*

Chapter 3

Page 57—Smithsonian Institution

Page 61—Official seal of the United Nations

Pages 62, 66, 67, 69, 73 (bottom)—Wide World Photos, Inc.

Page 63—Frank Scherschel. *Life* Magazine, 1954 Time, Inc.

Page 64—National Archives

Page 65—Ron Carter. "Vietnam Dream" *Four Quarters*, Spring 1976, La Salle University

Page 71—Richard M. Mishler. "Ceremony" *The Beloit Poetry Journal*, v. 31, #4, Summer 1981

Page 73 (top)—Pictorial Parade

Page 74—Jules Feiffer. Universal Press Syndicate

Page 82—Douglas Marlette, *The Atlanta Constitution*

Chapter 4

Page 89—Associated Press

Page 90— *The Wilson Quarterly*, Summer 1983. Copyright ©1983 Woodrow Wilson International Center for Scholars

Page 92—*Saturday Review*, December 1972. Vol. LV, No. 47, p. 67

Page 96—Lawrence M. Baskir and William A. Strauss. *Chance and Circumstance: The Draft, the War, and the Vietnam Generation*. N.Y.: Alfred A. Knopf, Inc., 1978

Page 98—Mark Jury. *The Vietnam Photo Book*. New York: Random House, 1986.

Pages 100, 101, 102—Liberation News Service

Page 103—Horace Coleman. "OK Corral East Brothers in the Nam" *Carrying the Darkness: American Indochina—The Poetry of the Vietnam War*. New York: Avon Books, 1985

Page 105—W.D. Ehrhart. "Guerrilla War" *To Those Who Have Gone Home Tired: New & Selected Poems*, W.D. Erhart; New York: Thunder's Mouth Press, 1984.

Chapter 5

Page 119, 122, 123, 130, 138, 140—Wide World Photos, Inc.

Page 121—*A Guide to Vietnam: A Television History*, 1983. WGBH.

Page 124, 141—Tony Auth. Copyright ©1975 *Philadelphia Inquirer*, Universal Press Syndicate. All rights reserved

Page 125—"The Handbook for U.S. Forces in Vietnam"

Page 127—Ted Richards, 1972

Page 129—Frank A. Cross, Jr. "Gliding Baskets" *Free Fire Zone*, Basil T. Paquer and Larry Rottmann (eds.) 1st Casualty Press, 1973

Page 131—Bryan Alex Floyd. "Corporal Charles Chungtu, U.S.M.C." *In The Long War Dead*, Bryan Alex Floyd (ed.). The Permanent Press,1983

Page 133—Marc Riboud

Page 139—Vietnam Veterans Against the War

Chapter 6

Pages 145. 157—U.S. Army Photos

Pages 148, 149, 152, 156, 158—Ronald Haeberle. *Life* Magazine, ©1969 Time, Inc.

Page 150—Tony Auth. © 1975 Philadelphia Inquirer. Universal Press Syndicate. All rights reserved

Page 152(top)—Dick Lourie. "For All My Brothers and Sisters." *Arima*, Dick Lourie (ed.). Hanging Loose Press, 1979

Page 153—©1970 by SANGA MUSIC Inc. All rights reserved

Page 161—United Press. International Photo

Page 163—St. George, Saigon, December 16, 1969

Pages 164, 165—"American Response to the Trial of Lt. William L. Calley" *Psychology Today* Magazine, June 1972.

Page 166—©1971 *Newsweek*, Inc. All rights reserved

Page 172—Steve Bentley. "Reflections on a Visit to the Soviet Union." Maine *VVA Quarterly* 1990, Vol 2, No. 2

Chapter 7

Page 175—Bernie Boston. Washington *Evening Star*

Page 176—"Popular Support for Vietnam War and Two Presidents," Alfred A. Knopf, Inc. and the Woodrow Wilson

International Center for Scholars

Page 179—Courtesy of Benedict J. Fernandez

Pages 181, 185, 187, 188, 190, 192 (top), 193—Wide World Photos, Inc.

Page 182—Lisa Law. *Flashing on the Sixties.* Chronicle

Page 192(bottom)—Copyright ©1970 (and 1972) Jules Feiffer. Universal Press Syndicate. All rights reserved

Page 194—*Life* Magazine, 1970

Page 195—Alan Dunn; © 1967, *The New Yorker* Magazine, Inc.

Page 200—Mark Jury. *The Vietnam Photo Book.* New York: Random House, Inc. New York, 1986

Page 202—Charles Fishman"Death March" *Mortal Companions.* Pleasure Dome Press, 1971

Chapter 8

Page 203—Copyright © Jutka Rona

Pages 208, 226—St. George

Page 211—Eastfoto

Page 212—U.S. State Department

Page 216—(left) U.S. Navy, (right) Defense Department

Page 222—Fred Branfman. *Voices From the Plain of Jars.* New York: Harper & Row, 1972

Page 223—Simon and Shuster

Chapter 9

Page 233—Carol Titus, Public Relations Coordinator, Aultman Hospital

Page 235—*The People of Vietnam Will Triumph*, The People's Republic of China, 1967

Page 236—Norma J. Griffiths. The "Vietnam Vet." *Visions of War, Dreams of Peace,* Lynda VanDevanter and Joan Furey, Warner Books, New York, 1991.

Page 238—Kathie Swazuk. "Pre-Op." *Visions of War, Dreams of Peace,* Lynda VanDevanter and Joan Furey, Warner Books, New York, 1991.

Page 239—National Archives

Pages 240, 241—Tom Mangold and John Penycate. *The Tunnels of Cu Chi*

Page 242—American Red Cross

Page 244—Dickie Chapelle. © 1962 National Geographic Society. November 1962, p. 735

Page 246—Donna Long

Page 247—Caz Page, Wexford, PA

Page 248—Dickie Chapelle. © 1962 National Geographic Society. November 1962, p. 723

Page 249—*The Union Leader,* Manchester, NH

Page 250—National Archives

Page 251, 256—Chris Noel. *Matter of Survival.* Braden Publishing Company, Boston, 1987

Page 253—Women's International League for Peace and Freedom, Philadelphia

Page 254—Clergy and Laity Concerned Papers, Swarthmore College Peace Collection

Page 255—Wide World Photos, Inc.

Page 257—National Archives

Page 258—Dickie Chapelle © 1962 *National Geographic* Society, Novembver 1962, p. 29.

Chapter 10

Pages 261, 263, 272—Wendy Watriss

Page 264—Anthony Petrosky "V.A. Hospital" *Jurgi Petraskas,* Louisiana State University Press, Copyright ©1983

Pages 265, 266—Mark Jury. *The Vietnam Photo Book.* New York: Random House, 1987

Pages 267, 268, 270, 282, 283—Wide World Photos, Inc.

Page 276—Gerald McCarthy. "The Sounds of Guns." *War Story,* Gerald McCarthy (ed.). New York: The Crossing Press. 1977

Page 278—Tony Oliphant. *The Philadelphia Inquirer,* July 16, 1986

Page 284—Don Wright. *The Miami News,* January 29, 1984

Chapter 11

Page 299—Yusef Komunyakaa. "Boat People" *MSS*

Page 305—David A. Mura. "Huy Nguyen: Brothers, Drowning Cries." *Breaking Silence: An Anthology of Contemporary Asian-American Poets.* The Greenfield Review Press, 1983

Pages 308, 313, 314, 317, 318—Judith Canty

Page 316—Office of Publishing and Promotion Services for Migration and Refugee Services, United States Catholic Conference

Chapter 12

Page 323—Vietnam Veterans Against the War and the Indochina Curriculum Group

Page 324—W.D. Ehrhart. "The Invasion of Grenada" *To Those Who Have Gone Home   Tired: New & Selected Poems.* W.D. Ehrhart (ed.). New York: Thunder's Mouth Press

Page 325—Douglas Marlette. The *Atlanta Constitution*

Page 326—Don Hesse. Copyright © St. Louis *Globe Democrat.*

Page 327—Gary Brookins. The Richmond *Times Dispatch.* North America Syndicate, Inc.

Page 329—David Huddle. "Cousins." *The Little Review*

Page 330—Tony Auth. Copyright ©1986. *Philadelphia Inquirer.* Universal Press Syndicate. All rights reserved

Page 331—Carol K. Simpson. 1985. *Mill Hunk Herald,* 1987

Page 338—Copyright© 1971 Jules Feiffer. Universal Press Syndicate. All rights reserved

Page 341—Perry Oldham. "Noon." *Carrying the Darkness: American Indochina—The Poetry of the Vietnam War,* W.D. Ehrhart (ed.). New York: Avon Books, 1985

INDEX

Those who couldn't agree on the war do agree on...

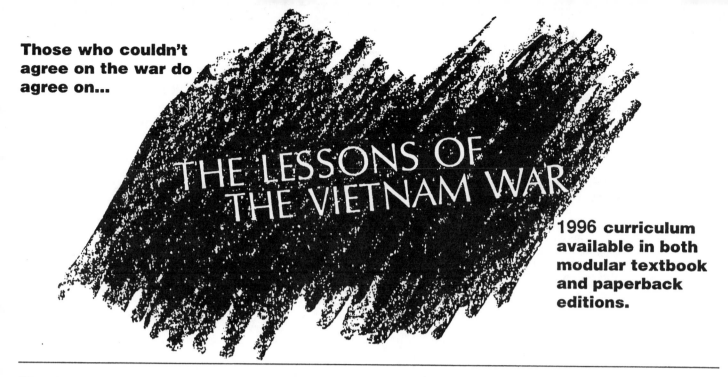

THE LESSONS OF THE VIETNAM WAR

1996 curriculum available in both modular textbook and paperback editions.

The Lessons of the Vietnam War:

- Covers all facets of the War from a diversity of perspectives

- Teaches students how to think critically about conflict resolution in international relations

- Teaches students how to reason ethically about moral choices

- Sensitizes students to cultural differences

- Written, reviewed and classroom tested by a nationwide network of Vietnam War scholars, teachers and veterans

- Over 200 illustrations

- Discussion questions in all units

Units included in curriculum:

Unit 1
Introduction to Vietnam: Land, History and Culture

Unit 2
America at War in Vietnam: Decisions and Consequences

Unit 3
Was the Vietnam War Legal?

Unit 4
Who Fought for the U.S.

Unit 5
How the U.S. Fought the War

Unit 6
When War Becomes a Crime: The Case of My Lai

Unit 7
Taking Sides: The War at Home

Unit 8
How the War Was Reported

Unit 9
Women's Perspectives on the Vietnam War

Unit 10
The Wounds of War and the Process of Healing

Unit 11
Boat People and Vietnamese Refugees in the U.S.

Unit 12
The Vietnam War: Lessons from Yesterday for Today

"...a widely praised academic curriculum on Vietnam."
Time Magazine

"Today, teaching about the Vietnam War is taking a step forward with the introduction of... the first comprehensive curriculum...The Lessons of the Vietnam War."
The Washington Post

Senator John F. Kerry
"As a Vietnam Veteran and United States Senator I believe this textbook will provide an essential educational resource for the next generation of Americans."

General John H. Johns, National Defense University
"A balanced, dispassionate assessment of the very emotional controversial events that occurred."

Donald H. Bragaw, President, National Council for the Social Studies
"A fine contribution... based on the war as it was lived and experienced, reflecting the pride, the horror and, indeed, the shame that many felt about this episode in our history."

Thomas Lickona, author, *Educating for Character*
"The most comprehensive Vietnam War curriculum ... meticulously developed ... representing a wide range of views on the war."

Peter Frost, Professor, Williams College
"This is more than the core of a good high school course. It is first-rate stuff and it qualifies for college-level study."

Mary Stout, President, Vietnam Veterans of America
"We lost more than 58,000 people in Vietnam and many of them were these kids' fathers. American students deserve a solid, objective textbook explaining why we went there and what happened."

Jan Scruggs, Founder, Vietnam Veterans Memorial
"A serious and thoughtful attempt to bring an understanding of that war's history and impact to American youth."

John Jay Bonstingl, author, *Introduction to the Social Sciences*
"I wholeheartedly recommend the entire Lessons of Vietnam War program to all social science educators."

New resource now available:

Teacher Trainer Handbook:
Professional Development Workshops
140 pages
$29.95

Would you like to conduct workshops and conference sessions for honoraria, travel, career recognition and to promote our educational mission? This handbook guides you through every step–from marketing through planning and evaluation of a variety of offerings. Includes special sections on mapwork-geography exercises, teaching critical thinking, interacting with videos, interviewing Vietnam veterans, coordinating oral history projects, using literature and personal narrative, and learning about culture.

Also from CSSE

Videotape
"Teaching the Vietnam War: Classroom Strategies" 1/2" VHS, 72 minutes
$44.95

"A must for anyone planning to teach the Vietnam War, this video features experienced teachers discussing and demonstrating how they handle the most sensitive aspects of the war." **Richard Wilson, Social Studies Coordinator, Montgomery County, MD Schools**

Resource Guide
Resources for Teaching the Vietnam War: An Annotated Guide
$9.95

Edited by Ann L. Kelsey, County College of Morris Learning Resource Center. Everything a teacher needs to prepare lessons and make student assignments. Includes descriptions and ordering information for books, videos, speakers and other resources.

The Lessons of the Vietnam War, now available in four ways:

Teacher's Manual
48-page Teacher's Manual
$10.00
Projects and activities with reproducible handouts for all units/chapters.

Module Edition
12 32-page units in 3-ring binder
$29.95

Paperback Edition
12 chapters plus index
$22.95

Individual Units
$4.95 per copy
$3.00 each with order of 10 or more
List titles and quantities of particular units that you want on a separate sheet and attach it to this order form.

Name: _____

School: _____

Address: _____

City: _____ State: _____ Zip: _____

Check Enclosed ☐ Purchase Order Number: _____

Send to:
Center for Social Studies Education
3857 Willow Avenue
Pittsburgh, PA 15234
Phone: 412-341-1967
FAX: 412-341-6533

	Quantity	Total
Teachers Manual $10.00		
Module Edition $29.95		
Paperback Edition $22.95		
Individual Units		
Video $44.95		
Resource Guide $9.95		
Teacher Trainer Handbook $29.95		
Subtotal		
PA residents add 7% sales tax		
Shipping and Handling (10% of Subtotal)		
Total		